Buying a property
GREECE

Contents

About the authors

Marc Dubin has lived in Greece since 1989, after visiting yearly since 1978. He is the author or part-author of numerous guidebooks on subjects as diverse as Greek back-country trekking, music and restaurants. Between 1993 and 2004 he bought, and restored, two adjacent ruins on the island of Sámos; they are now splendidly habitable, if home also to the odd gecko.

Frank Kydoniefs is a partner in the family firm of Helen Kydoniefs, which has been established in England since 1975. With a presence both in London and Athens, the firm specialises in private international law and providing legal advice to clients buying property in Greece.

Conceived and produced for Cadogan Guides by **Navigator Guides Ltd**, The Old Post Office, Swanton Novers, Melton Constable, Norfolk, NR24 2AJ
info@navigatorguides.com
www.navigatorguides.com

Cadogan Guides
Network House
1 Ariel Way
London W12 7SL
info@cadoganguides.co.uk
www.cadoganguides.com

The Globe Pequot Press
246 Goose Lane, PO Box 480, Guilford,
Connecticut 06437–0480

Copyright © Cadogan Guides 2004
"THE SUNDAY TIMES" is a registered trade mark of Times Newspapers Limited.

Maps © Cadogan Guides, drawn by Map Creation Ltd.

Cover design: Sarah Gardner
Cover photographs: © Tim Mitchell
Colour essay photographs: © Tim Mitchell and Marc Dubin
Editor: Anna Amari-Parker
Proofreader: Susannah Wight
Indexing: Isobel McLean

Printed in Italy by Legoprint

A catalogue record for this book is available from the British Library
ISBN 1-86011-124-122-X

Introduction

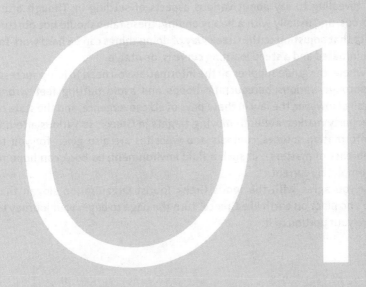

Greece is among the most alluring realms in the Mediterranean. Clean seas, a high degree of personal safety, an improbable variety of landscapes for such a small country, and still-reasonable living costs, combine to make it an increasingly popular choice for foreign home-buyers. The vivid, rough-and-ready country of the 1960s which first attracted artists, writers and the generally footloose has come of age.

The book includes a detailed survey of the most popular regions in Greece for property purchase, with an enticing photo essay to whet your appetite. This is designed to help you decide, for example, between the best amenitied (and more expensive) venues like Crete and the Ionian Islands and the more unspoilt but logistically challenging spots, such as the tinier Cyclades or the Zagorian villages of Epirus.

Because of the realities of the Greek economy, most purchasers will be looking either for a permanent retirement home or a seasonal second home, rather than to live and work in Greece, and appropriate chapters cover all the financial and legal implications of these alternatives. Projects for the restoration of older property still (just) outnumber new-builds in the ambitions of purchasers; unfortunately, Greek workmanship is not always what it could be, and pitfalls yawn for the unwary renovator. An extensive chapter, gleaned from hard-won experience, details the most desirable materials and techniques available, with a thorough glossary for making sure you can communicate your wishes to sometimes reluctant craftsmen.

Scattered throughout the book are anecdotes from seasoned expatriates who have already successfully bought property in Greece, and have something revealing to say about various aspects of settling in. Though often humorous, and usually with a happy ending, these tales should not obscure the fact that adjusting to the Greek way of doing things can be hard work for the uninitiated and a steep learning curve is inevitable.

Elsewhere, the guide supplies all the information you need to jump successfully through various bureaucratic hoops and avoid putting feet wrong culturally. However, the law in these days of EU convergence, and the state of the property market, are both moving targets in Greece, so various alternative information sources, contacts and websites are also given for you to stay abreast of matters – in such a fluid environment, no book can hope to stay completely current.

So, if you agree with the 1990s Greek Tourist Organisation slogan that 'there's no place on earth like Greece', turn the page to begin your journey to acquire your portion of it.

First Steps and Reasons for Buying

02

This book is designed and written with the express purpose of showing you how to find, purchase and if necessary either restore or new-build a property in Greece. Quite possibly, by the very act of reading this book, you may have already decided in principle to make the leap. If you're still pondering the question, the following introductory section will serve as an *aide memoire* for all the things that may have struck you favourably about Greece on holiday visits, while the end of the section brings you down to earth with a realistic assessment of Greek bureaucracy and a summary of the types of visa you might need to visit or take up residence.

Why Greece?

Perhaps no other country is burdened with such a hoary reputation to live up to as Greece. The home of the ancient gods, the cradle of democracy, the wellspring of philosophy and science, the dance of Zorba: the clichés pile to the ceiling, threatening to collapse under their own weight and obscure a clear-eyed, unsentimental appreciation of the country as it is today – Greece without columns, if you will. As Sir Patrick Leigh Fermor trenchantly observed in his classic work *Roumeli*, 'The strangers who form the deepest regard for Greece are not the ones who are bear-led; they are the solitaries whose travels lead them, through chance or poverty or curiosity, along the humble and recondite purlieus of Greek life.' During the early to mid-twentieth century, many prominent figures – including Elizabeth David, Lawrence Durrell, Lord Kinross, Henri Cartier-Bresson, Henry Miller and Dilys Powell – forsook unsatisfactory lives in northern Europe to find various, and sometimes obscure, aspects of Greece to be a balm for their senses, their chosen vocation, their very souls. After five decades of steady modernisation and urbanisation, some of the magic has inevitably fled. But more than enough remains to seduce many first-time visitors, and keep aficionados hooked for life.

Despite recent development, Greece is still largely non-industrial; the few factories tend to be restricted to just west of Athens and around Thessaloníki. This means clean sea and (outside Athens and Thessaloníki) exceptional air quality, allowing an unimpeded view of the Greek landscape. This varies from soaring limestone palisades to forested mountains embracing steep river valleys, to purple-shadowed islands silhouetted against a cobalt- and rose-coloured horizon. The man-made environment is no slouch, either: the temples of the ancients get their due, but more recent, numerous monuments include country churches with tiled or coloured domes, and traditional villages that – both in aggregate in their setting and individually in architecture – appeal to casual tourists and potential home-hunters alike. Millions of rolls of photographic film have been expended on these spectacles, but the unwary find that the famous Greek light is like no other, and capturing it successfully is a lifelong apprenticeship.

You can begin serving that apprenticeship by taking up at least part-time residence in Greece, and the more time you spend there, the more benefits you will enjoy in terms of an increased quality of life. Most evident of these benefits is the climate, certainly compared to that of northern Europe. Sufferers of Seasonal Affective Disorder (SAD) and bronchial complaints will – unless they settle in the far north of the country or in the largest towns – find themselves instantly improved, if not cured. Winter can be among the most beautiful times of the year, with snow-dusted ridges looming above evergreen citrus and olive groves. Storms there certainly are, but gloomy weather conditions rarely remain constant for more than three or four days at a time, and the Greeks have made a fine art of designing conservatories (*liakotá*) on both traditional and modern country homes to take advantage of sunny January and February days. Summer can actually prove too hot for those unaccustomed to a Mediterranean July or August – you will probably adopt the universal habit of the 3–5pm nap (*mikró ýpno*) – but the often long, lingering green springs and golden, windless autumns are a delight: life as it's meant to be.

Mediterranean climatic conditions have given birth to the much-vaunted Mediterranean diet, in its purest form rich in healthy olive oil, wild greens, onions, pulses, yoghurt and cheese, with meat, seafood and wine taken in moderation. It's no surprise that historically the Greeks, especially the islanders, have been amongst the longest-lived people in Europe. Put another way, living and dining Greek-style is good for you. What may come as a shock is that contemporary official statistics rate Greeks among the most obese people in the EU, although the traditional diet is less to blame for this than imported bad habits, such as a growing trend for junk fast food and an increasingly sedentary lifestyle. Thoroughly mortified by this ranking (especially in the run-up to hosting the 2004 Olympics), the country is now awash with gyms and rather more dubious slimming salons (relying on pills and fad diets), and increasing numbers of Lycra-clad cyclists are braving the dangerous roads.

But Greece certainly doesn't have a monopoly on Mediterranean climate and diet; what makes the country stand out from its potential rivals for your affection is the human factor. Rural Greeks especially are (in the main) forward to the point of bluntness, intensely curious about new acquaintances, and open-handed with offers of food and drink. Some of the famous hospitality no doubt serves to keep a foreigner in the dark about a locale or a family, and in his or her 'place' as subservient to the giver. But beyond all this anthropological dissection remains simple generosity, deeply inculcated over the ages. The cult of Zeus (Xenios) – the injunction to treat all wandering strangers handsomely lest they be the god in disguise – retains its adherents.

Another highly attractive aspect of the human landscape is a notable sense of personal safety. Despite being nudged up since the early 1990s by massive immigration and the emergence of sharp economic inequalities, the crime rate in Greece remains well below the European norm. Crimes against persons are still unusual enough to make the national news, while surreptitious theft (including burglary) has traditionally been regarded as a severe breach of *filótimo* (literally, 'love of honour'). Sharp practice – for example, surrounding rotten oranges by sound ones in a crate to claim an EU subsidy – is, of course, far from unknown, but in such cases the would-be Odysseus perceives that the playing field is level, and it's up to his opponent to beware.

In no other arena does safety extend further than with children, who can (certainly in the countryside) be allowed to circulate in freedom without fear of kidnapping and molestation. Children are indulged (arguably to excess) and cherished, especially now that the native-born population is shrinking, with a birth rate well below replacement level. In a healthy departure from northern European norms, children are not ghettoised; from the start, they are fully integrated into Greek social life, most obviously in being habituated to late-night suppers at tavernas and, while fully expected to behave like children, they are not allowed to have veto power over the adults' nocturnal schedules.

Speaking of which, tavernas at their best serve as an informal showcase for Greek music and lyrics, the latter based in turn on a vibrant mid-20th-century tradition in poetry that resulted in two Nobel laureates (Odysseus Elytis and George Seferis). Playing and singing is still vital to the culture, and the best entertainments are arguably not the organised 'Greek nights' or the mega-venue concerts to which one buys tickets in advance, but the intimate *tragoúdhia tis paréas* – a small group of men (or women), maybe a bit tipsy, interpreting well-loved songs to the accompaniment of unamplified *bouzoúki*, guitar and accordion. This can go on well into the small hours – an edict to move mandatory closing times back from 4am to 2am was essentially booed out of the hall a few years back – because the social Greek is necessarily nocturnal.

If you crave café-posing or more organised nightlife, it's to be found in every sizeable mainland and island town. The 1990s saw massive pedestrianisation of many city centres, and walkways are now lined with a vast selection of outdoor afternoon cafés and indoor-outdoor after-dark clubs (rarely in the same district, mind you). Quite a bit of this is gay-friendly, or at least gay-neutral; there are sizeable gay scenes in Athens, Thessaloníki, Pátra and (most famously) on Mýkonos island. Some of modern Greece's most prominent artists, novelists and musicians have been gay in varying degrees of openness, though, as else-where in the Mediterranean, opportunistic (male) bisexuality is the cultural norm, and the passive role is disparaged in slang – and in law, through certain lingering civic disabilities. For example, if you identify yourself as 'homosexual', you are excused from military service with the equivalent of a dishonourable discharge, which makes it impossible to get civil service work. But such strictures are likely to be challenged in the European Court of Human Rights, and there's nothing like the level of opprobrium that prevails in, say, Cyprus.

What some charitably call exuberance or high spirits, others will label noise. Greece is undeniably a high-volume country, especially during the summer when the countryside fills up with returned emigrants from Athens and abroad. Villages reverberate to the sound of mothers with foghorn voices summoning their children, or the more aesthetic clangour of church bells. You always know when a party has won an election, or a team a football match (no more so than with Greece's surprise Euro 2004 football victory; nobody in Athens slept that night). Easter Midnight services are punctuated by dynamite explosions and, in some locations, improvised rocket barrages. On Sunday evenings in garrison towns, the flag is ceremoniously lowered and the army marching band parades down the quay. Yet juxtaposed with all this can be an all-encompassing quiet, if not to say serenity. Even in large coastal towns, during the small hours it's possible to hear nothing but the lapping of wavelets on the shore – *flísvos* – and it's easy to warm to a language and culture that has a single word for the phenomenon.

The sea has indeed profoundly shaped Greek character – it's one cliché that can survive intense scrutiny. Because of the lack of industry and the limited number of major rivers, nowhere else in the Mediterranean has such clean waters. But they can be deceptively clear – the Aegean is also tops for destructive storms that seemingly brew out of nowhere, over and above the normal annual summer Force 6–8 gale known as the *meltémi*. The Greeks themselves are avid sun- and sand-worshippers, and (*meltémi* permitting) keen sailors and amateur fishermen. Living on or near the coast, it will be almost impossible to resist the temptation to buy a boat of some sort to mess around in – many of the best, secluded swimming spots are only accessible by sea.

Last but not least, there's one 'why not' to be cited. Subject to the exceptions enumerated under 'Working and Employment' (*see* pp.205–8), you should not expect to find ample employment opportunities in Greece. Before the May 2004 accession of 10 new members from central Europe, Greece was usually fighting it out with Portugal for the dubious distinction of occupying the economic cellar of the EU by all benchmarks, particularly in the un/under-employment rate and level of salaries – the latter averaging half of what they are in Britain) (though it must be noted that the Greek cost of living is now considerably more than half that of northern Europe). Freelancers and the self-employed of all stripes can also anticipate severe difficulties in collecting amounts owing, which doesn't do wonders for your cash flow.

Buying as a Second or Retirement Home

As internal infrastructure and links with the rest of Europe steadily improve, having a second – or retirement – home in Greece is looking more and more like a sensible decision and not just a whim indulged in after one beer too many on a beach-based package holiday. Although there's much to be said in favour of renting for a year on a trial basis in a likely area, ultimately long-term rental is not financially attractive. Over a ten-year period, you could spend in rent as much as sixty to seventy-five per cent of the cost of a basic one-bedroom apartment in a purpose-built coastal development. Like England, Greece doesn't have much of a renter's culture – the desire to own some real estate is deeply ingrained at all social levels. Owing to a rural, village-based past and the frankly unpleasant summer conditions of many large Greek towns, ownership of a second, rural or semi-rural holiday home is considered entirely normal. Even people who don't have the means for a second property tend to take their summer holidays in the same resort year after year, an echo perhaps of the pastoral transhumance that once prevailed across mainland Greece. In common with most other continental Europeans, Greeks have extensive vacation periods – a month or so in August, a week or two at Easter and Christmas at a minimum – in which to take advantage of a leisure property, and also leave 'town' for the weekend at every opportunity. By the standards of Spain and Italy, prices are still eminently affordable (though creeping up steadily) – roughly on a par with France, and usually quite a bit more than Cyprus, Croatia or Turkey. But perhaps you're already smitten with Greece and money is no longer a primary factor in your decision.

Buying as an Investment

Buy-to-let property investment is still in its infancy in Greece, but has already become subject to excessive hype by unscrupulous developers (in Crete especially) and unreasonable expectations on the part of would-be buyers. Quality villa holiday companies such as *Sunvil* and *Greek Islands Club* report being bombarded by proposals from new owners in unsuitable, identikit housing projects who were rashly promised that they could recoup their investment through rents within five years or so. Put simply, it ain't gonna happen, especially if your property lies beyond easy reach of the major charter-served airports – say, an hour or two of travelling by land or sea. Moreover, you may adore your multilevel, minimalist-cubist house on Síkinos (Where?), or your three-storey stone mansion halfway up a deep canyon in the Ágrafa Mountains (again, Where?), and you might expect potential punters to feel the same at first glimpse of your web-page, but if your chosen locale fails the 'Where?' test, you do not have much of a market.

To have even a ghost of a chance of establishing successful buy-to-let premises for foreigners, your property must be in an area of instant name-recognition and be easily reachable, as described above. At present, this means Crete (close to Haniá, Iráklio, or – soon – Sitía airports), Corfu, Zákynthos, the Argo-Saronic Islands (Éyina, Póros, Ídhra, Spétses), Skiáthos, Skópelos, Rhodes, Kós, Sými, Hálki, or the inner Cyclades within reasonable distance of Athens airport and at least two of the three Attic ferry ports: Ándhros, Tínos, Sýros, Páros, Náxos, plus Mýkonos and Santoríni which have direct flights from overseas. Other islands with May–October charter access, such as Sámos, Kefalloniá and Lésvos, prove to be far less suitable because a lack of genuine competition among the charter operators serving them pushes peak-season flight costs to unacceptable levels. You cannot expect a family of four, having already paid out over £400 for a week in a self-catering two-bedroom villa or house, to then pay £700–800 for two adult fares and two half-price child fares – they will go where they can get £99 specials (Rhodes, Crete, Kós). Finally, your property should have some distinguishing characteristics – a well-restored old house with tastefully modernised kitchen and bathroom(s), and safety considerations such as banisters or anti-slip bathtub strips, will always be more appealing than one of the piled-high- and-sold-cheap villa developments, of which there is already a glut on Crete and several of the Cyclades.

If you intend to rent to Athenian weekenders who may arrive by car and/or sea, then the outlook changes: the hot areas for second homes – and trial rentals – are currently the southwest Attic coast, around Lagoníssi; Pórto Héli (on the Argolid opposite Ídhra) as well as Parálio Ástros and Náfplio further west in the same region; select parts of the Corinth Gulf coast (e.g. in or near Akráta, Náfpaktos, Galaxídhi); the Messinian peninsula of the Peloponnese, near the end of the recently completed expressway from Athens; the southwest facing coast of Évvia; and Kéa or Kýthnos islands in the Cyclades. Athens-based Greeks also like properties in the rest of the Cyclades and Crete, but seem to be put off by the remoter Dodecanese and most of the Ionians save Corfu. If you are contemplating a property in northern Greece, only the Kassándhra and Sithonía peninsulas of Halkidhikí, and perhaps the Pagasitic Gulf shore of Mount Pílio, will appeal to Thessalonians. For a full description of these areas, *see* the next chapter, **Where in Greece: Profiles of the Regions**.

Foreign owners should proceed with care when attempting to rent out properties that lie within border zones (*see* pp.72–5 for a discussion of the concept). It used to be that one of the conditions for owning such a problematic property was that it was your primary residence in Greece and not to be used for commercial purposes (i.e. buy-to-let). Take current legal advice before attempting to put such a property on the rental market.

Buying with the intention to resell within a short time-frame is probably unwise. Except for a few high-profile resorts and islands – where the amount required for a foot-on-the-ladder investment can already be off-puttingly high – property values increase slowly in Greece, at or just above the level of inflation. The resale market for second-home properties is simply too young in Greece to make any reliable predictions of steady equity growth.

Red Tape

The Administrative Organisation of Greece

Greece has a rather hierarchical, highly centralised system of governmental organisation, which is likely to endure; recent reforms by the now-out-of-office PASOK government, albeit substantial, have only nibbled at the edges of the issue. From the lowest level of authority to the highest, the levels are: the *kinótita* (village, commune); the *dhímos* (municipality); the *eparhía* (county, in the American – not British – sense); the *nomós* (province, prefecture); and national ministries in Athens – balefully abbreviated as *Athína* by those who must contend with them.

In a pre-election reform of 2002, the authority and scope of *kinótites* were curbed, and they were made subordinate to the nearest *dhímos* – apparently, there were too many corrupt and readily influenced *próedhri* (village council presidents) doing things manifestly against public interest and policy as set by the local *dhímarhos* (mayor). *Kinótites* are still, however, responsible for matters like taking your water meter reading, and the *kinótiko grafío* (community records office) is where you'll go to register formally your ownership of a village house, and where you might complain about the unmaintained public lane in front of your house sprouting weeds, and the like.

Dhími (in the plural), often with rather improbable names from remote history or mythology, now tend to be collections of up to a dozen villages or *kinótites*, often with wide geographical scope and potential responsibility for things like sewage treatment plants, local bus services, rubbish collection and the changing of burnt-out streetlamps. A large *dhímos* will have a major police station, to whose security division you will apply for residence permits (*see* p.12).

You usually won't hear much from or about your *eparhía*, though they can be more obvious on the islands, where you may find that the tax-office districts and other official functions like city planning are organised roughly or exactly along *eparhía* lines, necessitating tedious boat trips (e.g. from remote Astypálea to Kálymnos). In Greece there are 52 *nomí* (provinces), each with a *nomárhos* or governor, elected rather than appointed since 1994.

Permanent residents who are nationals of an EU member-state are eligible to vote for gubernatorial and mayoral candidates in local elections, as well as non-geographically limited Euro MPs in the Euro elections. Criminal or civil justice in the first instance, and Greek parliamentary representation, are also organised by province, except in Athens and Thessaloníki, where population density gives rise to a welter of sub-districts for allotting MPs. Provinces with an MP not of the ruling party can, unsurprisingly, expect relative neglect in the matter of disbursements for infrastructure improvements. Certain matters pertaining to national security, the customs service and the like must be referred to Athens for a final decision.

Bureaucracy

All those multiple levels of government guarantee a corresponding quantity of bureaucracy or *grafiokratía*. The mountains of red tape are a legacy of several factors: of a time when the civil service was the major (sometimes only) employer-for-life, and of lingering governmental attitudes that saw the governed as bad children trying to get one over whenever possible, or peasants getting above their station – in either case requiring strong discouragement or severe testing for attaining whatever privilege was at stake. Thankfully, matters are improving slowly, and some government offices now could even be described as efficient, if not exactly pleasant to deal with. Native Greeks suffer immensely from delays and obstructiveness as well; you are not being singled out because you're a foreigner. Always add a safety margin of twenty per cent to any time estimate you're given for completing any particular ordeal-by-paper.

Accordingly, artful dodging has always been a necessary skill for getting by in Greece – anyone high-minded enough to obey every one of the thousands of extant laws, many obsolete and never formally repealed, and to get every required chit of paper, would soon be truly tired of life. For example, some of the most worthwhile restaurants in the islands do not have the appropriate municipal permit for the size of kitchen and preparation area they possess, or for the number of chairs positioned out on the public pavement – but their regulars will not stop frequenting them, nor are the proprietors going to apply, because the municipality has made it clear that no more permits of that type for that neighbourhood will be granted. Matters trundle on for years until, or unless, a jealous rival makes a formal complaint.

Whichever side of the law you choose to stay on in Greece, stamina and cunning are *de rigueur*. It's becoming progressively harder to live in the hitherto thriving 'black economy' – estimated still to amount to a third of gainful activity – and Greece is becoming steadily more 'European', largely because the EU has forced it to do so, but it will never in a million years become a 'Switzerland-on-Aegean'.

Visas for Short-term Travel

EU nationals do not require a visa in advance to visit Greece, and embassies and consulates will not grant such. British, Irish and other EU passport holders may travel to Greece as tourists for periods of up to 90 days, provided their passports are valid for the intended period of stay. Passports of EU citizens are not stamped by the Greek border police on entry and exit, so stays in excess of 90 days are not easily detectable.

Citizens of the USA, Canada, Australia and New Zealand also do not require tourist visas for stays of up to 90 days (cumulative) within any 180-day period. However, their passports must be valid for 180 days from the date of initial entry, and they will be stamped in and out of Greece. For the other 90 days in the period, they must leave not only Greece but the entire Schengen Zone, whose members are: Austria, Belgium, Denmark, Finland, France, Germany, Greece, Iceland, Italy, Luxembourg, the Netherlands, Norway, Portugal, Spain and Sweden (but not the UK or Eire). Fines for overstaying are heavy, and penalties may include being banned from the Schengen Zone for another 180 days. Tourist-visa extensions for non-EU/EEA nationals are no longer routinely given, and cost in excess of €450 for theoretical availability.

If you are a non-EU national but a permanent resident of any of the Schengen Zone countries, you are entitled to enter any Schengen state on the same basis as EU nationals, provided you show your proof of residence in your home Schengen country along with your passport. If an EU national marries a non-EU national, then the spouse and offspring – if they are not yet resident in the EU – will be issued what's called a Schengen Visa free of charge by the nearest Greek consulate, upon presentation of proof of kinship (marriage and birth certificates).

Note that even though Iceland and Norway are not in the EU, they are part of the EEA and Schengen Zone, and therefore travel rights of their nationals to Greece are essentially as those of EU nationals.

For a list of Greek embassies and consulates, see pp.261–2.

Residence and Work Permits

Once established in Greece beyond 90 days, everyone – including, technically, EU nationals – is obliged to obtain a residence permit (*ádhia paramonís*).

In the very largest cities (Athens, Thessaloníki, Pátra), there is a *tmíma allodhapón* or aliens' department, but everywhere else you visit the *tmíma asfalías* (security division of the closest major municipal police station).

The first time you're issued with a permit, you should allow four to six weeks for all the necessary steps to be completed, the commonest delay being for a battery of required health examinations at the nearest state hospital, performed at reasonable cost. There, you will be chest-X-rayed to screen for TB, blood-tested for hepatitis B and C, HIV and a couple of other nasties, and have an 'evaluation' by a neurologist or psychiatrist (making eye contact and displaying normal spinal reflexes will get you marked down as 'sane'). Then you trot along yourself with all the assembled results to the local public health office, where a periodic (once weekly as a rule) meeting of its administrative council will vet and endorse these and issue you with a certificate of approval. You should also assemble:

- **Three or four approved passport-sized photos (any small-town photographer knows what to do).**

- **Your *A-fi-Mi* or tax registration number (*see* p.143).**

- Photocopied pages from your Greek savings passbook dating back at least a year (two or three won't hurt) to show that you're bringing money into the country.

- Documentary evidence that you're contributing to a public pension scheme somewhere in the EU. In the UK, you can obtain a 'to whom it may concern'-type letter from the Department of Works and Pensions in Longbenton, Tyneside (**t** (0191) 225 4811), detailing the amount and frequency of your Class 1 or Class 2 contributions; ring to request one, which will be sent to the address of your choice within three weeks. This must then be translated into Greek (your local lawyer or notary in Greece should be able to do this).

- A document which proves how and when you entered Greece.

- Evidence to prove that you and members of your family have medical insurance and self-sufficient funds.

Finally, bring all this paperwork – including the health certificate – to the Aliens' Department or Security Division, where your *ádhia paramonís* should be ready within three working days, and at no further expense other than a fistful of revenue stamps (*hartósima*). Permits are generally issued for terms of five years; renewals generally go much more smoothly as, in particular, you do not have to submit to the health tests again.

It's currently very difficult to get a residence permit if you are not an EU national or of Greek descent – you're put in your place with notices in many police stations to the effect that 'non-EU applications will only be considered on Wednesday from 10am to 11am'. It is somewhat easier if you're married to a Greek or other EU national, but first-time applications should ideally be done at the closest Greek consulate in your country of habitual domicile.

Except in the border areas, you do not need a residence permit to actually buy property, but you will need a tax registration number (*see* p.143). The fact of owning holiday property, however, does *not* exempt non-EU/EEA nationals from having to observe the rules for stays in the Schengen Zone as outlined above.

If you intend to take up employment or establish your own business, you should contact the nearest consulate general, well in advance of your proposed stay, to obtain specific guidelines. You will need to supply a copy of the letter offering him employment endorsed by the appropriate directorate of labour.

Greek Citizenship

Greece is one of the most difficult countries of Europe in which to be naturalised, with (in common with Germany) a strong stress on 'blood line' – *omoyéni* (overseas nationals of demonstrably Greek origin) have always had a much easier time of it. Before the 1990s, the number of foreign non-Greek males (foreign females almost automatically acquired Greek nationality upon marrying a Greek) who had been successfully naturalised could be counted on two hands, with digits to spare. New laws in 1993 made the process easier, but not by much; your chances of a positive decision are much better in the case of marriage to a Greek, with resulting Greek offspring. Be aware that one or both parents becoming naturalised could result in automatic liability of their son(s) to military service in Greece, which does not plan to abolish conscription any time soon.

In theory, any alien over the age of 18 may apply for naturalisation. First a declaration of intent, witnessed by two Greek citizens, must be made before the *dhímarhos* or *kinotárhis* of the place he or she lives. In the case of an *omoyénos* living abroad, an application must be submitted to the Greek consul in his/her country of habitual residence.

Persons without any Greek background must be resident in Greece for ten out of the previous twelve years *before* the submission of an application to be naturalised, or for five consecutive years *after* such a declaration is made. You cannot be considered for naturalisation if you have a Greek criminal record arising from a long list of offences, which include high treason, 'offending public morals', smuggling, white-slave-trading, counterfeiting and narcotics-dealing or possession. Parts of this law, which dates originally from 1955, were clearly intended to make it impossible for Communist rebels who had fled behind the Iron Curtain after the 1947–49 civil war ever to regain their citizenship.

In all cases, applications for naturalisation are forwarded to the Ministry of the Interior, which conducts an investigation of the alien concerned. In case of refusal, no reason will be given, and re-application cannot be made before a year has passed. Granting of citizenship is irrevocable unless the alien has perjured himself or herself in some respect in the application process.

Omoyéni must support their claims to Greek origin by presenting all pertinent written records (birth or baptismal certificates, marriage certificates, passports of Greek parents, etc.); photocopies must be officially translated into Greek, and certified as genuine.

Where in Greece: Profiles of the Regions

This section doesn't pretend to be a comprehensive survey of all the recognised regions of Greece, since buyer interest in Greece is very focused on the island groups and certain exceptional areas of the mainland that garner attention by virtue of their distinctive architecture and alluring scenery. Even the most avid fans of Greece will concede that there is little or no reason to buy a property in the parched, grain-growing plains of Thessaly in the centre of the country, the hard-scrabble, gaunt hills of Étolo-Akarnanía in the west, the rolling countryside of Macedonia and Thrace with their relatively harsh climate and remorselessly utilitarian housing stock, or (taking the latter theme to its extreme conclusion) the concrete-laced urban centres of Athens, Thessaloníki and the various other smaller towns of the Greek peninsula. It is certainly conceivable – and done – to buy a flat in Athens or Thessaloníki, but the majority of foreigners who do so have either married locally, or have secured long-term employment in Greece, or both. It is generally a strategy of necessity – not investment or pleasure – and such properties do not, in fact, appreciate readily in value except in proportion to any improvements made.

As well as the mainland, Greece comprises six recognised island archipelagos and two big, 'stand-alone' islands, Crete and Évvia. These are all to varying degrees popular property-buying venues with both Greeks and foreigners, though obviously anything with good international and domestic air connections or proximity to Athens attracts an extra premium. One of the delights of sampling each group is to see just how different each island can be from its neighbour – habitual generalisers are apt to come unstuck.

The Argo-Saronic Islands

These are the closest islands to Athens and among the best connected, taking their tag from the Argo-Saronic Gulf in which they lie. Most played a crucial role in the early days of the modern Greek state and offer a decent complement of traditional housing for sale. Though all have severe water shortages, most of them have retained considerable patches of pine forest; despite being plagued much of the year by 'three-islands-in-one-day' cruises full of shutter-clicking trippers, it's amazing how normal life can seem once the trippers have departed – not least in the presence of fully stocked market halls on each of the main islands. The people are of a different background from the population of Attica and most of the Peloponnese – they are descended from *Arvanítes*, or Albanian Orthodox settlers, in early medieval times. It is a fact seldom noted in conventional histories that the Idhriot and Spetsiot fleets so instrumental in the Greek War of Independence were crewed by intrepid Argo-Saronic sailors who barely spoke a word of Greek; their dialect, *Arvanítika*, still (barely) survives among the oldest generation on Salamína and Angístri islands.

The odd island out here is **Salamína** (Salamis), which had its moment of glory in 480 BC, when the Persian fleet of Xerxes was decisively defeated by a Greek coalition. Since then, it has assumed a gritty, solidly working class identity, with swimmable water only on the side away from the industrialised mainland and little that appeals to those without family ties here. **Éyina** (Aegina), the next island beyond in the gulf, has rather more going for it: close enough to Piraeus for the locals to commute to work in Athens and famous for its pistachio orchards, 'ghost' village at Paleohóra and an admirably preserved temple to the minor nymph Aphaea. The lively, characterful port town (known also as Éyina and briefly the capital of fledgling Greece) faces west, with some older houses available – though many buyers prefer newer properties in north-coast Souvála or hill hamlets such as Pahiá Ráhi. Little **Angístri**, due west of Éyina, has more pine trees and traces of Arvanitic culture, better beaches, and a large group of second-home-owners in the hillside hamlet of Metóhi, which was bought up and restored years ago (thus any properties going will be second-generation purchases).

Due south of Éyina, and separated from the Argolid Peninsula of the Peloponnese by the narrowest of straits, volcanic **Póros** is actually two islands: piney Kalávria and tiny Sferiá, joined by a slender isthmus. Póros Town almost completely occupies Sferiá, climbing its western flank with tiers of houses and serves as the major sailing centre of the Argo-Saronic Gulf – there are several hundred metres' worth of yachts moored stern-to in front of the bars, and chandlers along the improbably long waterfront.

Beyond Póros, the frequency of the conventional ferry service drops (though hydrofoils fill the gap), since there's little need of them – both Ídhra (Hydra) and Spétses bask in vehicle restriction regimes which add considerably to their charms. **Ídhra**, among the oldest, most established resorts in Greece, has also hosted foreign home-owners since the Second World War, and has a thriving artistic scene. A notably strict set of architectural protection rules, along with a lack of proper roads, means that the external profile of the amphitheatrical port, with its 18th- and 19th-century stone mansions and more modest red-tiled and wood-shuttered vernacular houses, has changed little since the last sponge fleets went into permanent dry-dock half a century ago. Real estate is predictably expensive, whether in the main town or in the satellite hamlets of Kamíni and Vlyhós. Once you're established, however, the cost of reaching the island from Athens, meals out and supplies is not exorbitant. There are also a handful of excellent, remote beaches that you can reach either by water-taxi or by walking along one of the well-preserved donkey tracks (donkeys still play a necessarily vital role on the island).

Spétses, thinly disguised by John Fowles as Phraxos, is irrevocably linked with his blockbuster 1966 novel, *The Magus*, based in part on his experiences teaching English here in the 1950s at the Anargyros College. Previously, it was even more nautically distinguished than Ídhra, being home to revolutionary war admiral Bouboulina – a formidable lady said to be so homely that she seduced her lovers at gunpoint. The maritime tradition lives on in intricate *votsalotá* or pebble mosaics adorning the courtyards of various churches (and not a few grand mansions, which make up the most desired housing stock here – as expensive as, or more so than, anything on Ídhra). It is evident, too, in the still-active boatyards (where traditional wooden *kaïkia* are built from scratch) and in the range of excellent seafood restaurants. Local tourism, of the aristocratic Greek and British expat variety, dates from the 1920s and 1930s, and that is still very much the tenor of the clientele here. Despite falling victim to severe fires in 1990, this is still one of the greenest Argo-Saronics. A ring road takes you around the island, past several excellent beaches; the island's vehicle ban does not extend to motor scooters or the occasional bus.

The Cyclades Islands

For most outsiders, the Cyclades – with their cubist, whitewashed houses heaped in tidy villages and a windmill or two as a finishing touch – are the epitome of Greece. Even in the wilds of the north mainland, or among unrelated island groups at the opposite end of the country, almost any newsagent's rack can muster a fistful of postcards with the requisite hackneyed image. For the Greeks themselves, the Cyclades occupy a not-so-dissimilar psychological niche: a repository of *ur*-folklore (not least as the original home of *nisiótika* or island folk music) and, barring Latinate touches on Sýros, Tínos and Náxos, the least foreign-influenced corner of the country. For Athenians, in particular, it's a well-loved archipelago, with a new generation of high-speed catamarans out of Piraeus, Rafína and (soon in the offing) Lávrio making even distant Santoríni comfortably feasible as a weekend break. Several members of this group are reasonably well served by air from Athens, too, though the only ones with international charter arrivals are Mýkonos and Santoríni.

With several notable exceptions, these islands are arid, rocky and treeless except in sheltered locations, with many dwellings dependent on wells and cisterns and the rocks put to good use in dry stone walling – a highly developed art in most of the Cyclades. For much of the year, the concept of 'shelter' becomes all-important as the Cyclades are buffeted by constant winds, none more notorious than the *meltémi*, a high-pressure northerly at its worst from late June through to early September. If you might be driven crazy by the sound of the wind moaning incessantly in the power and phone lines above your abode or scouring the narrow village lanes – or by being trapped here days longer than planned owing to a ban on ship movement – then these islands probably aren't for you.

Especially in the spring, and away from the main tourist centres, there's a well-developed (if low-key) local cuisine based on humble ingredients. Wild fennel fritters, *khtipití* (spicy cheese purée), wild artichokes, wild asparagus with scrambled eggs, watercress from a rare flowing stream, *fáva* (yellow lentil) purée and sundried tomato-based dishes from Santoríni, and a plate of quick-fried *marídhes* (picarel), all washed down with tawny, sherry-like wine from remote, barely economical vineyards, are likely components of a memorable Cycladic meal.

The closest island to Athens, **Kéa** (Tziá), is reached from Lávrio and inevitably has a pronounced weekender feel. It is unique among the Cyclades in having a substantial covering of native oak trees and is almost unique (neighbouring Kýthnos and Ándhros mimic it) in having an indigenous architectural style featuring tiled roofs, especially in the photogenic *hóra* (old town) of Ioulídha. There's a low-key yachting ethos at Vourkári on the same bay as Korissía port; a growing number of purpose-built, sea-view villas speckle the slopes west of Korissía, and also near Koúndouros in the far southwest of Kéa. Old houses in Ioulídha can be difficult to secure, but isolated farmsteads – for example, around Káto Meriá in the south-centre of the island – can be excellent value.

Kýthnos – also accessible from Piraeus as well as Lávrio – has two characterful inland villages in Hóra and Dhyropídha, but is probably the quietest and bleakest – if not to say dullest – of the Cyclades. Athenians with limited means have been coming here for years to buy land and erect villas but 'Thermiá' – the alias stems from some still-running thermal springs in the north – is unlikely to ever be a focus of foreigner interest.

One stop down the (shipping) line, matters change dramatically at **Sérifos**, one of the more exclusive of the 'minor' Cyclades. Although it has several inland villages, most acquisitive interest focuses on the superb *hóra*, draped over a rocky hogback, which featured extensively in *Greek Style* (*see* **Further Reading**, p.270). Bare and craggy, Sérifos is blessed with good beaches, reasonable walking opportunities and – most importantly for home owners – an unusually high water table. Adjacent **Sífnos** is more popular, cosmopolitan and expensive; Athenian and foreign second-home ownership is a well-established pattern in the inland villages of the central *kámbos*, plus the Catalan-Venetian designed *kástro* on the east coast. Numerous rural monasteries dot the island, none more photogenically than that of Khryssopiyís, cut off at the far end of a sea-washed spit on the east coast and star of many a tourist poster. Besides beaches as good as or better than that of Sérifos, there's a long-standing tradition in pottery and a lingering culinary distinction in the tavernas of Artemónas – which is also where the largest, most sumptuous houses are.

Still further south, the duo of **Mílos** and **Kímolos** were long able to forgo tourism owing to their mineral wealth. Mining is still important and sleepy Kímolos with its single, characterful *hóra* incorporating a *kástro* is unlikely ever to see more outsider traffic than it does now, but Mílos is the surprise of the western Cyclades. Like its more famous sister Santoríni, horseshoe-shaped Mílos is essentially a collapsed volcanic caldera, the deep bay in the middle marking the former 'hot spot'. The centre of real estate activity here is the island's summit, where the atmospheric villages of Pláka and Trypití shelter under the Venetian citadel and have seen foreign ownership of property for a few decades now – some of the finest sunsets in the Aegean are a bonus, though gardening isn't really possible and prices are surprisingly high. Further interest is lent by the ancient catacombs and boathouses burrowed into the soft lava downhill nearby and a healthy scattering of sheltered beaches, two of which – Paleohóri and Tría Pigádha – sport hot springs seeping up in the shallows. There is an airport, though flight seats tend to be prebooked by mining executives.

Due east lie two more architectural showcase islands – **Folégandhros** and **Síkinos** – whose ridgetop *hóras* each incorporate a *kástro* from the days when pirates were a constant menace. Such *kástra* (in the plural) had either just one entrance to a courtyard for entry to the houses, or sometimes a few restricted archways into a warren of lanes, but the almost windowless backs of the dwellings ingeniously double as the fortifications. Unsurprisingly, properties in the *kástra*, usually the oldest surviving on these islands, command premium prices, with newer, less idiosyncratic houses being built towards the village borders, as well as the occasional windmill for conversion. Both Folégandhros and Síkinos have steep-sided shorelines with limited beaches or coastal settlements – and an equally limited ferry service, helping to preserve their tranquillity (except in peak season).

Returning to the north end of the Cyclades, this time at the top of the easterly chain of islands, **Ándhros** – due east of the Attic Peninsula – like Kéa suffers from pronounced weekender syndrome, with massive Friday and Sunday evening shuffles between Rafína and the northerly port of Gávrio. This means that villas for wealthy Athenians are sprouting within easy reach of the harbour, but most of the island – well off the island-hoppers' beaten track – retains considerable character. There's a tradition of Anglophone patronage at the few beach resorts (notably Batsí), a corresponding local Anglophilia (many of the men have worked on ships), and a world-class modern art museum in the *hóra*, positioned unusually on the east coast. Ándhros is also one of the best-watered and most tree-covered of the group, its smallholdings divided by the famous *frákhtes* or artistic dry stone walling. Steniés, just north of the *hóra* and with a sea view, is probably the most attractive village, though isolated groups of rural houses, especially near Kapária and Zaganiáris, are worth enquiring after.

To the southeast, somewhat drier **Tínos**, reached from Piraeus as well, is the Lourdes of Greece, with a wonder-working shrine of the Virgin in the port town that draws huge crowds of Orthodox pilgrims on March 25 and August 15. This obscures the fact that about half the population is Catholic – a legacy of the Venetian occupation, which ended only in 1715. It also has an equally strong craft tradition, from willow-osier basketry to carved marble fanlights. Another oddity, introduced by the Venetians, are the *peristereónes*, ornate multi-storeyed dovecotes sprouting everywhere. There are a few serviceable beaches, but the pride of Tínos is its inland villages, especially around the Venetian citadel of Exóbourgo, where house restoration proceeds in arcaded Tarabádhos, Arnádhos and Dhýo Horiá; nearby Triandáros and Tripótamos have already been fairly well bought up and restored since 1982, leaving only second-generation sales, if any. In the northwest, Kardhianí, and slightly less inviting Isterniá, are also likely spots; otherwise, there is land for sale and new developments along the south coast facing Mýkonos.

Sýros to the west also has a substantial Catholic population, concentrated in the hilltop district of Áno Sýros with its vernacular dwellings overlooking the elegant, UNESCO-recognised port of Ermoúpoli, a favoured venue for Athenian weekenders since the late 1980s (with estate agents catering to them). Provincial capital of the Cyclades, with marble-paved streets and *belle époque* mansions (a few sporting painted *trompe l'œil* ceilings), it is a proper town and something of an architectural anomaly for the archipelago, complete with the Apollon Theatre – claimed to be a miniature replica of Milan's La Scala – a lively market street and the central Platía Miaoúli, focus of the weekend evening stroll. Like many of the Cyclades, Sýros is more fertile than it appears from the sea, presenting you with the unusual spectacle of grazing cattle on inland farms. Water supply problems have (mostly) been sorted by a combination of an aqueduct from a pure spring in the north and a desalination plant near the harbour. Though obviously Ermoúpoli is the main attraction for those with the financial resources, there are good beaches on the west and south coasts, with both isolated farmhouses and land suitable for new-builds available – and a well-established community of foreigners. Besides having good connections with Piraeus, and links to Rafína and Lávrio, too, there's a small airport (sporadic Athens flights only).

Directly across the straits from Tínos is arid **Mýkonos** – its harbour town the quintessential stereotype of the Cyclades, with its sculpted marshmallow churches and labyrinth of streets designed to confuse pirates. Mýkonos has seen tourism and property ownership by off-islanders for nearly as long as Ídhra. Originally outsiders only passed through *en route* to the ancient sanctuary on the nearby islet of Delos, but for some decades now Mýkonos has been a prime destination in its own right: nearly a million tourists in a good year, a significant proportion of them gay. The main attractions of Mýkonos lie in the *hóra*'s often outrageous nightlife (albeit less so since the closure of the premier transvestite-revue clubs), a garland of south-facing beaches and (in Hóra) some of the most sophisticated and expensive restaurants in the Cyclades. If you don't find a suitable, already restored house in the port town, there is an ever-increasing number of new-build villas and plots of land out in the countryside being promoted – none of which, of course, comes cheaply. An airport with good seasonal connections from several points in Greece, as well as the aforementioned international arrivals, completes the picture.

Páros, the next island south, is very nearly as popular and as expensive, with a good balance of everything people expect from the Cyclades: idyllic beaches, a maze-like capital, characterful inland villages and monasteries – though it has to be said that the island doesn't really stand out in any one category. It has also pretty well supplanted Sýros as the sea transport hub of the Cyclades, but doesn't (yet) receive direct international air service. Accordingly, property on Páros is sought after, with a large foreign community, various estate agents, and a preponderance of villa developments within sight of the sea (especially around Parikía and Naoússa ports). The appealing inland villages of Léfkes and Márpissa towards the east coast have some old houses to offer, and rural farm cottages are much sought-after. Despite access via only a shuttle boat from Poúnda on Páros, both conventional tourism and house-hunting activity – including the odd purpose-built development – spill over on to the satellite island of **Andíparos**, graced with a single, *kástro*-plan village.

Náxos, just across the straits from Páros, can be equally crowded during summer in its *hóra* and beach resorts, but the rugged interior (Mount Zás, at 1,001m elevation, is the highest point in the Cyclades) preserves a more traditional, even raw, feeling, and abundant vegetation. It's still a partly agricultural island, with a vast central *kámbos* – the Tragéa – planted with olives, a distinctive citron liqueur brewed and a variety of other produce taking advantage of a high water table. The Venetian Duchy of the Aegean, based here from the 13th to the 16th centuries, left a legacy of towers and fortified mansions across the island. You're unlikely to secure one of these jealously kept properties but older houses change hands in remoter, partly sea-view villages, such as Apíranthos, Potamiá, Komiakí, Kóronas and Moní, as well as in the picturesque *kástro* district of the *hóra*, while plots suitable for building are sold inland from the long beaches lining the southwest coast. There are estate agents and also an airport but, as on Páros, it only takes internal flights.

Easternmost of this archipelago, **Amorgós** is a long, narrow, particularly windswept island with two ports (Katápola and Eyiáli), a holdover of the days when road links between the two ends were poor (walking the length of Amorgós is still a popular activity). Spurred by its role as partial setting for Luc Besson's film *The Big Blue*, Amorgós is definitely up-and-coming, with a mixed, discerning foreign clientele, both transient and resident. Most buying activity centres on a cluster of lovely villages – Tholária, Langádha, Potamós – above Eyiáli, and in Hóra too, a stone's throw from Hozoviotíssas, the most spectacularly set monastery in the Aegean. So far, the island has been protected from being overrun by having no airport (there's insufficient flat ground), a dearth of beaches and occasionally being cut off by storms. Having said this, catamaran service has eased its isolation considerably, compared to the days when Amorgós was used as a place of internal political exile. Between Náxos and Amorgós, the beach-rich '**Back Islands**' of Dhonoússa, Skhinoússa, Koufoníssi and Iráklia are rapidly developing out of their former status as havens for true solitude-seekers, though amenities and connections are still too sporadic to make prolonged residence there really attractive.

Any hint of solitude has long since vanished from **Íos**, south of Náxos, the original party-then-flop-on-the-beach island since the 1960s and early 1970s. Figures such as Cat Stevens (in his pre-Yusuf Islam days) bought property here back then but the avant-garde and now ageing hippies have definitely moved on, despite the island's trying to reinvent itself in a more upscale mode. Local society has been so warped by its long-running clientele that there are scarcely any traditional eateries or proper shops remaining. Unless you're of an overtly bibulous, youthful and chronically sociable nature, there seems little to recommend an Íos home-hunt, though the palm-tree-tufted Hóra (and only proper village) is admittedly stunning on a visual level.

Like Mýkonos, legend-shrouded **Santoríni** (Thíra) has true international cachet – with prices to match. Touted (with some intellectual acrobatics) as the lost Atlantis, this crescent of multicoloured, striated lava and associated islets are all that remain of a much larger volcano that cataclysmically collapsed during the 17th century BC. The explosion and resulting tidal wave not only destroyed the Minoan town at the south tip of the formerly round island but severely damaged the main Minoan centres on Crete. Ongoing, low-level vulcanism means regular earthquakes (the worst recent one in 1956), which has resulted in a local architecture featuring barrel-vaulted, troglodytic dwellings. Like other volcanic terrain, Santoríni produces excellent wines (arguably the best in the Cyclades) and sweet tomatoes (used fresh or sundried), but very little else; there's only one freshwater spring on the island, in a lump of non-igneous rock beside the ruins of post-eruption Classical Thera. As on Mýkonos, the local social profile is distorted by industrial-strength tourism, particularly of the cruise-ship variety. There are more jewellery and fur shops than you'd think could possibly be supported; pricey, ambitious tavernas, especially in Ía and the main town of Firá; and a certain type of American-collegiate-trustafarian tourism depicted in the rather forgettable 1980s film *Summer Lovers*. All that said, Santoríni is unique – there's nothing remotely resembling it in the Mediterranean except one or two of the Aeolian islands off Sicily – and it is enduringly popular, with a mix of Athenian and foreign home-owners, the latter now having the option of arrival by seasonal direct international flights. Ía and surrounding villages at the northwest tip are the most upscale, though other villages like Imerovígli and Firostefáni, with views of the now-submerged caldera, are also prime targets, as are Pýrgos and Messariá in the interior of the island. Beyond Santoríni, lonely little **Anáfi** – truly end-of-the-line since ferries no longer venture beyond to Crete or Dodecanesian Astypálea – shares its architecture with Santoríni but without any airs and graces. It's possible to find a traditional house in the single, hilltop *hóra* above the little harbour, though the sale of building plots behind a necklace of four idyllic beaches commenced at a leisurely pace some time ago. There's now a rough road some way inland from these, supplementing the walk or boat ride of past years, though there's little traffic of any sort outside of high summer.

Crete

Crete is the largest Greek island (and indeed the fifth largest island in the Mediterranean). It is perhaps the one part of Greece that could – just – make a go of it as an independent country, surviving on its burgeoning tourism and agricultural enterprises. It is a place of superlatives: home to the highest Aegean mountains, with three snowcapped massifs well exceeding 2,000 metres in elevation; cradle of the earliest European civilisation (the Minoans), who left several palace complexes and a museum full of art to admire; the most populous island, with over half a million souls; and host to the longest (and usually sunniest) growing – and tourist – season in Greece, from late March to mid-November. Megalónissos (the Great Island) is the local nickname for Crete, and much more than size is meant by that. Island pride is legendary, covering the full spectrum from gargantuan hospitality to breathtaking arrogance.

Like the northern mainland, the northeast Aegean and Dodecanese, Crete is one of the newer additions to the country, being unified with Greece in 1913 after a 15-year interregnum in which it had been semi-autonomous. Before that, over three centuries of Ottoman rule – which saw nominal apostasy to Islam by many Cretans for reasons of convenience – followed on from over 400 years as a Venetian colony. These two empires are responsible for much of the built environment on the island today, especially the form and monuments of the old quarters at Iráklio, Réthymno and Haniá, the three largest cities. These, and most of the balance of the population, live along the fertile north coastal plain, which subsides relatively gently from the various mountain ranges; a divided motorway linking the main seaside towns greatly speeds transport. All of the mega-tourist resorts are on the north coast as well, taking advantage of the infrastructure and the longest beaches – though nowhere in the Aegean does the *meltémi* blow harder than here. Cross the mountains to their much sheerer slopes dropping to the south coast, however, and the permanent inhabitants, tourist facilities and high-speed roads all become dramatically scarcer – though agriculture (especially winter hothouse culture) remains conspicuous, extending even to banana plantations near Árvi.

After Corfu, Crete has the largest contingent of Brits living abroad, and it seems set to overtake its Ionian rival – spurred on by yet another locally set *Home in the Sun* English TV series and also because villas, either single or entire developments' worth of them, are the preferred strategy for housing new-comers. That said, it is possible to find old properties for restoration in the old towns of Haniá and Réthymno, as well as village houses in their hinterlands. Foreign interest is spread fairly evenly along the entire north coast, from Kastélli

Bay in the west to the environs of Sitía in the east – just so long as it has a sea-and-mountain view (not difficult to arrange), the site's a winner. The marketing of all this is uncharacteristically well-organised for Greece, with numerous estate agents in operation; prices, not surprisingly, are climbing faster than anywhere else in Greece. At the time of writing, there are two busy international airports at Haniá and Iráklio but the hitherto minor one at Sitía in the far east is being upgraded to receive charters from overseas (estimated completion date 2006). Crete's south coast has been neglected up to now, owing to its relative remoteness, but the shoreline east of Ierápetra – especially around Makrýialos where there's room for villa estates to spread out – will definitely take off once the Sitía airport refit is finished. If you need to come via Athens or Thessaloníki, the domestic air service provided by both internal airlines to Iráklio and Haniá is excellent, while there are daily sailings from Piraeus – many of them high-speed services – most of the year to this pair, as well as Réthymno, and less regularly to Áyios Nikólaos and Sitía.

The Dodecanese Islands

The most southeasterly archipelago in Greece, beyond Crete and the Cyclades, was also the last incorporated into Greece, in March 1948. Until then, these islands had undergone a turbulent history, with more than the usual number of foreign occupiers, including the crusading Knights of St John (who left castles everywhere) and the Italians, in addition to the expected Ottomans, given that Anatolia is visible from the majority of these islands. Blessed with the longest warm season in the Aegean outside of Crete and some of the most distinctive architecture, the Dodecanese are not surprisingly firm favourites among both short-term visitors and vacation-home-owners. More than in any other group, there are strong contrasts between adjacent islands – in terrain, vegetation and housing stock. On Kós and Rhodes, there are even small Turkish populations (or Muslim Hellene, as they're officially called) and also on Rhodes the shattered remnant of a Jewish community, effectively wiped out in 1944. The Turks remain by a quirk of history: tolerated by the Italians and exempt from the Treaty of Lausanne which saw most other Greek Muslims obligatorily exiled to Anatolia in 1923 in exchange for Greek Orthodox refugees.

The island's considerable distance from the mainland (only Rhodes, Kós, Léros and Pátmos have an occasional high-speed ferry service, otherwise it's up to 18 hours from Piraeus to Rhodes via up to seven intervening ports of call) and pricey domestic air fares mean that, for once, foreign owners tend to out-number Athenians in the second-home sweepstakes. Rhodes is the best served by air with two domestic airlines and numerous charters piling in; it is also the local transport hub for hydrofoils, catamarans and extremely useful peripheral air links to Kárpathos, Kós, Léros, Astypálea and Kastellórizo – which (save the last-cited) also get regular service from Athens. This remoteness – and the pressure of tourism – mean that staples are among the priciest in Greece. On the plus side, however, as a 'showcase' province the Dodecanese are often used to pilot various initiatives – such as the first fibre-optic phone system in the country and the first area to have (in theory) its real estate completely recorded on the *ethnikó ktimatolóyio*.

Given the southerly location, the availability (or otherwise) of fresh water is a pressing issue. Only Rhodes, Kós, Tílos and Kárpathos have it in any quantity; everywhere else the tanker boat from Rhodes can be seen engaged in filling municipal cisterns. These arid conditions might conceivably have saved most of the smaller islands from the steamroller of tourism – there simply isn't enough water to support the construction of mega-resorts.

Diamond-shaped **Rhodes** is one of the holiday meccas of the Mediterranean, encompassing both high life (€700-a-night luxury hotels, a casino, world-class windsurfing, some of the best exotic-cuisine restaurants in Greece) and low life (epitomised by the notorious lager-lout-dominated resort of Faliráki). Most of the tourist industry is concentrated on the leeward, Mediterranean-facing southeast coast with its extensive beaches rather than on the exposed Aegean side with its mostly rocky shore. At the very northern tip shines the star attraction: intricately fortified Rhodes Old Town, a well-preserved legacy of the Knights of St John, who had their headquarters here from 1306 to 1522. They, and the Ottomans who succeeded them, left behind a medieval precinct that has as rivals only Jerusalem and Carcassonne. In the newer town, which grew up around the walled quarter from the 18th century onwards, the Italians who displaced the Ottomans in 1912 left an ambitious, eclectic collection of Art Deco structures, many remodelled in severe Internationalist/Rationalist style during the 1930s and at the height of Fascist rule. More benignly, the Italians introduced the art of wine-making to the island, still going strong and even stretching to a perfectly palatable 'champagne' that dares not speak its name.

Like Corfu, Rhodes has a significant proportion of foreign permanent residents; about seven per cent of the 110,000 total population. They are scattered across the island, but the infrastructure impels most to live in the northern half. Ancient houses of the Old Town are an obvious possibility for restoration but they can make for rather claustrophobic living, with no view other than of adjacent rooftops and usually no garden. Additionally, the entire district within the Knights' walls is an archaeological area, with a strict protection regime in effect. All renovation plans, and the ongoing work itself, will be carefully vetted, with heavy fines and/or delays for deviations from the approved course. Halfway down the east coast, eminently scenic Líndhos, with its old sea captains' mansions arrayed around its ancient acropolis, has hosted a variable expat community since the early 1960s, though here the preservation regime has deferred slightly to the demands of mass tourism, which really set the tone of the place nowadays. Some old Líndhos veterans have sold up and gone 'around the corner' to Péfkos, buying land to erect villas. There's even a purpose-built, Cypriot-funded holiday housing estate outside Lárdhos, the next village. Further down the east coast, Yennádhi has become very popular – offering both older houses in the village centre and plots for new-build villas on its outskirts. Elsewhere on the island, the only places with much patronage by outsiders are Kritinía, Siánna and Monólithos on the southwest coast and Lahaniá village, tucked away into a well-watered ravine in the far south. Here, exquisite vernacular houses with ornate gateways are occupied mostly by Germans on long-lease-in-exchange-for-renovation agreements, rather than as outright purchases.

Nearly 70 nautical miles east of Rhodes but just a couple of nautical miles from the Turkish town of Kaş, **Kastellórizo** (aka Meyísti) is emphatically the end of Greece and the location of the Oscar-winning 1990 film *Mediterraneo*. Once a thriving trans-shipment port of well over 8,000 souls, owing to one of the best natural harbours in the area, it has come way down in the world, owing to Greco-Turkish antagonism, neglect by the Italians, and extensive Second World War destruction. Just a few hundred people live in the surviving handful of handsome three-storey houses lining the port – it's what Greeks call a *klouví* or birdcage, while the less charitable dub it the largest open ward in the country. Time was that the extensive Kastellorizan diaspora – scattered between Perth, Sydney and New York in the main – was tenaciously loyal, hanging on to bomb-blasted plots in the hope of rebuilding. But a contingent of foreign owners is slowly developing, though most of these are on the basis of 100-year leases (*andiprosopía*). That said, it is probably one of the least practical choices of island base. Regular air links with Rhodes have stablised but ferry connections remain a sore point and there are no beaches to speak of; rather than pay carriage costs of goods from already pricey Rhodes, locals do most of their shopping in Turkey, every Friday at the Kaş market.

One hundred and eighty degrees around Rhodes, going anticlockwise from Kastellórizo, **Hálki** is another barren limestone one-town islet with an exquisitely picturesque harbour – in this case built from the profits of sponge-diving. It too more or less emptied out in the first half of the past century, Italian strictures prompting massive emigration to Florida, but, unlike Kastellórizo, it has recovered through the offices of a particular type of tourism. During the late 1980s, most of the 150 or so houses of Emborió port were restored and made available to a handful of upmarket British package firms, and it is their clientele who occupy them almost non-stop from April to October – and engender the decidedly artificial social scene of the town. With a steady income guaranteed by leasing out their properties to the holiday companies, most local owners are disinclined to sell – though foreign ownership for private use does occur. A more promising venue, should it ever be provided with utilities (the archaeological authorities permitting), is the abandoned hill village of Horió, 3km west. Horió is still the province of the archeological authorities and so no development is allowed; however, owing to a slump in short-stay tourism, ruins are beginning to be sold (at ruinous prices) in Emborió.

Approximately halfway between Rhodes and Crete, long, narrow, mountainous **Kárpathos** ties with Kós as the second largest of the Dodecanese in land area. It is a decidedly introverted place, very much dominated by the ethos of returned emigrants from Canada and the USA, who make it one of the wealthiest communities in Greece. Coastal plots of land for new-builds are available and there are a few old houses being sold in the mountain villages. Between the remittance economy and well-developed beach-and-walking tourism, it's one of the most rurally neglected islands, though the anthropological-curiosity villages of Dhiafáni and Ólymbos in the north make more of a show of keeping to tradition. Should you secure a property here, sparse semi-direct ferries from Piraeus (via Crete), infrequent flights from Athens to a huge, partly military airport, and very unreliable charters from overseas will be a constant problem, forcing most to arrive via Rhodes.

By contrast **Sými** – a short sail north from Rhodes – is arguably the hot-property capital of the Dodecanese. And, little wonder, given its achingly picturesque harbour settlement, with neoclassical mansions stacked in tiers up the rocky hillside. This 'Ídhra of the Dodecanese' is also built on a foundation of sponges, but now lives from well-mannered, middlebrow tourism – and daily excursions from Rhodes that cause locals in the know to vacate the quay area between 10.30am and 4pm. They head off to the equally attractive hinterland of this still partly forested island blessed with deep, pebbly bays – a paradise for yachtsmen and (in the cooler months) walkers – and dotted with picturesque little monasteries. A clutch of excellent restaurants, and the yearly Sými Festival in August/September, are further attractions. There's a sizeable expat community from various countries. A handful of local estate agents preside over a brisk, well-established trade in properties for restoration – which don't come cheap and are inching up in price all the time. The local shipping company provides reasonable year-round links with Rhodes, making winter residence feasible as well as peaceful. However, residents and overnighters have encountered difficulty booking a one-way journey on the excursion sailings, which are really aimed at day-trippers.

A short distance southwest, tranquil (except in August) **Tílos** is the backwater of the 'major' Dodecanese. The least maritime of these islands, it was, in fact, once the bread-basket of the group; today it is depopulated and, like most of its neighbours, exists largely on seasonal tourism. A long-running hunting ban has resulted in an explosion of bird life, and plans are on the books to rehabilitate the surviving network of walking trails, some of them centuries old. Historically there were two main villages, each presided over by a castle: Megálo Horió in the west and Mikró Horió at the centre of the island. Mikró was abandoned after the Second World War and its inhabitants moved down to the port of Livádhia, now also the main tourist resort. Village property in Megálo Horió is scarce and snapped up quickly; from its tiered houses, the views over a fertile, citrus-planted *kámbos* to Éristos Bay – one of many excellent beaches – are unbeatable, albeit slightly sullied by the new constructions of those who have bought land on which to build. Livádhia appeals to few long-term residents but, again, building plots on the outskirts are the norm. Mikró Horió, as a 'decommissioned' village, lacks mains electricity, water or phone service, but this hasn't stopped a few stubborn returned islanders from restoring their homes. Should utilities ever be provided, expect a few to come on the market – while the view to the sea is more restricted than at Megálo Horió, the hillside setting is magnificent. Tílos has its own catamaran link to Rhodes but reliability has been an issue and the island remains one of the worst connected in the Dodecanese; second-home owners popping over for a week on a charter to Rhodes often spend up to four of the ostensible seven days on Rhodes – two at the outset waiting for the catamaran to sail, and two at the end of their stay, having been forced to leave Tílos early by uncooperative schedules.

Round, oak-green but largely waterless **Níssyros** is often described as volcanic, but this is severely understating the case; the entire island is, in fact, a dormant volcano. Hot springs, a deliberately unexploited geothermal potential (the locals sent the power company packing through two referenda on the issue) and periodic destructive earthquakes (the last one in 1997) emphasise the point – as do the audible gurglings in the several craters that pockmark the lifeless volcanic caldera occupying the middle of the island. Much of the population has emigrated to Astoria, New York; those who stayed benefit handsomely from the revenue generated by the pumice quarries on Yialí islet just offshore. Up on the caldera rim are two airy, photogenic villages: Nikiá, which faces Tílos, and all-but-abandoned Emborió, which faces Kós and Turkey's Knidos Peninsula. Emborió, whose population decamped to the little port of Pálli, has been a popular target for second-home hunters since the 1980s, with new owners often surprised to find steam-vent-powered saunas in the basement. The houses are extremely interesting architecturally when intact, though a pile of rubble is more the norm. Prices are inflated and renovation costs in the largely roadless village rub salt in the wound. Níkia, more of a going concern, has dwellings on a grander scale but they seldom come on the market. Mandhráki, the colourful main harbour town, also has a few properties available, along with an improbable number of tavernas and a reasonable selection of shops. There's just one good beach, on the east side of the island. The ferry service here is slightly better than that of Tílos but the main daily link is with Kós.

Kós is the second most popular tourist destination in the Dodecanese after Rhodes, of which at first glance it seems a miniature version, right down to the numerous grandiose 1920s Rationalist structures. But here the Knights' castle encloses naught but a junkyard of archaeological fragments and the Hellenistic past is more evident, exposed by a 1933 earthquake and excavated by the

Italians, notably at the hillside Asklepieon, irrevocably linked with the semi-legendary Hippocrates. Kós is also flatter and more fertile acre for acre than its provincial big brother, with good beaches fringing much of the coast. Bucket-and-spade tourism has sucked most authentic life from the handful of interior villages; the flip-side of this coin is that some are effectively abandoned, with houses for sale to outsiders – most notably at Asómatos, at the foot of forested Mount Dhíkeos. Evangelístria down the hill, and thoroughly deserted Haïhoútes further into the forest, are also possibilities. Kós receives a respectable number of charters from overseas, has internal flights provided by two airlines at present, and is an important secondary Dodecanesian ferry and hydrofoil hub, with occasional high-speed service.

Way out west from Kós and Níssyros, shaped like a butterfly on the wing towards the Cyclades (which it more closely resembles), **Astypálea** is arguably the most bohemian and least 'packaged' of these islands – indeed, as at Kastellórizo, there is no package tourism, though plenty of yachts grateful to find a good haven in a long stretch of open sea. The lack of tours is a consequence of notoriously fickle ferry links, though these have improved in recent years, and there are now eminently useful regular flights to Léros, Kós and Rhodes, as well as to Athens. Astypálea is another one-village island, the fortified Venetian *hóra* among the loveliest in the Aegean, and the venue of choice for predictably expensive second-home purchases. It's theoretically possibly to buy land for new-builds at Livádhi to the west or Maltezána, a small resort by the airport but that would be to completely miss the point. The best beaches are hard to get to overland and the hills *en route* are bare; boat trips are accordingly popular.

North across the straits from Kós, **Kálymnos** could hardly be more different: a harsh lump of limestone, arranged in three ridges divided by relatively lush valleys. Originally the main sponge-divers' island of the archipelago, this pursuit is now effectively extinct, as are the tourist enterprises on the beachy north-west coast – essentially handling the overflow from Kós – devised to replace it. So it's an interesting time in the island's history, as Kálymnos struggles to reinvent itself as a rock-climbing and hiking destination. Some people find the overweening macho ethos a bit hard to take (even the women are men, says a local saying) and nowhere is this more obvious than in the bustling main town of Póthia. This just pipped Kós Town as the second largest municipality in the Dodecanese at the 2001 census, and testosterone-fuelled, exhibitionist motorbike traffic reigns supreme. All that said, there's a growing expat community here, taking advantage of some handsome old mansions; the Kalymnians, in particular, excel at wrought-iron work. Should you want a more rural setting, there are often entire farms for sale – complete with walled citrus orchards – in the valley of Vathýs, where the greenery contrasts sharply with the bare rock overhead. Drinking water is problematic and must be purchased from a municipal pipeline as most well-bores have been invaded by the sea.

Opposite the moribund resorts of Myrtiés and Massoúri lies the satellite islet of Télendhos: home to about 35 full-time inhabitants, blissfully car-free but with a significant tourist trade – and the first stirrings of property sales. Kálymnos has a half-built airport, seemingly destined never to begin operations; transfers from Kós are effected by roll-on-roll-off (ro-ro) ferries that are timed to dovetail with flight arrivals. Ferry service, except for the lack of high-speed departures, is much the same as for Kós.

Separated from Kálymnos by the narrowest of straits, **Léros** is the sleeper of the Dodecanese, with some of the best tavernas and loveliest neoclassical houses in the archipelago offsetting distinctly average beaches and the island's unfortunate institutional reputation. A major naval air base under the Italians, who left behind the model Rationalist town of Porto Lago (today Lakkí), Léros went on to host a concentration camp under the colonels' junta and later was home to several sanitaria for mentally disabled children and Greece's incurable mentally ill. Their maltreatment was rather sensationally publicised overseas in 1989, but EU-supervised improvements have been effected, including the designation of the main hospital as the teaching facility for the nursing faculty of the University of the Aegean. All but one of the sanitoria have been closed down and the inmates 'mainstreamed' into care facilities across the island. Needless to say, most home-buying tends to take place not in and around Lakkí, but at the conjoined villages of Plátanos, Ayía Marína, Krithóni and Álinda near the centre of the island. In the hills to the west are a few rural houses and plots suitable for building; a local estate agent will help you find them. The water table is fairly high but in recent years has been contaminated by livestock manure. Léros has daily air links with Athens as well as several other Dodecanese; ferry, hydrofoil and catamaran connections to Sámos, Kós, Rhodes and Athens are adequate.

The arid islet of **Lipsí**, administered from Léros but traditionally a dependency of the monastery on Pátmos, got some rather unwanted publicity in 2002 as the place where the head of the November 17 terrorist group was finally run to ground. Since then, relative calm has returned, interrupted only by a seasonal influx of British and Italian tourists lodged in the single port town. The village itself is not especially appealing and, for many years now, a pattern has been established of off-loading land for villas on the ridges east of town – now spreading to the fields west of the ferry dock. The island has reasonable beaches and a lively after-dark social life considering its size; ferry, hydrofoil and catamaran connections are adequate.

The most northwesterly of the Dodecanese, **Pátmos** derives much of its undeniable cachet from its role as the purported setting for St John's writing of the *Book of Revelations* – and for the monastery commemorating the evangelist, visible far out to sea at the top of the most sumptuous *hóra* in the Greek islands built from the proceeds of 17th- and 18th-century shipping wealth. Not surprisingly, this is where outsiders have been buying grand mansions since the 1960s; as at Líndhos on Rhodes there's very little left unrestored, so second-generation sales are the norm. Pátmos is volcanic, in a low-key way, and thus water is a critical issue – all of the *hóra*'s mansions have cavernous cisterns. Demand for property on this palpably atmospheric island exceeds supply, such that plenty of land suitable for building – some of it just inland from the many excellent beaches that spangle the coast – is being assiduously peddled. Occasionally, isolated farmhouses of considerable character, with a bit of land around them, become available in the valleys around the northerly village of Kámbos. The main port and nucleus of habitation, Skála, has its tolerable corners but is not really a focus of real estate interest. Local tavernas are good, as are ferry, catamaran and hydrofoil connections to Kós, Rhodes, Sámos and Athens, such that you don't much notice the lack of an airport (there's not enough flat ground).

The Northeast Aegean Islands

Strewn at fairly regularly intervals just off the Turkish coast, these islands have the most Anatolian feel in the Aegean (with the arguable exception of Rhodes). From the 15th and 16th centuries respectively, Límnos, Lésvos and Híos all had substantial Muslim populations, who, as on Crete, only departed after 1923 – leaving behind the odd mosque or isolated minaret, and a substantial influence on local cuisine, language and architecture. To call the northeast Aegean islands an archipelago is perhaps stretching the truth; they are only loosely joined by history – a medieval Genoese occupation and subsequent Ottoman rule being the common denominator – and equally desultorily connected by modern ferry lines. Aside from Thássos and Samothráki, administered from Macedonia and Thrace respectively, this group falls under the regime of the Ministry of the North Aegean, set up to oversee its incorporation into the 'fatherland' after being taken by Greece during the First Balkan War in 1912.

All of these islands have airports (except for Thássos and Sámothraki, which are served by airports just opposite on the north mainland), and Sámos and Lésvos airports receive seasonal direct charters from overseas. Ferry links with Athens, Thessaloníki and Kavála are reasonable, though perhaps not as good as they might be – if you fail to coincide with a high-speed craft, you're looking at a 15-hour journey from Piraeus to Lésvos; twelve hours to Sámos.

Compared to the limited choice of fishy things in the Cyclades and Sporades, seafood is king in these islands – especially on Híos, Lésvos and Límnos. Proximity to the Dardanelles Straits, with their seasonal migrations of species between the Black Sea and the Aegean, plus the nurturing river mouths of Asia Minor opposite, ensure a plentiful supply.

Sámos, the southeasternmost of this chain, and with the balmiest climate, is (aside from Thássos) the most visited and, despite catastrophic fires of recent years – including one in July 2000 which burned about one-fifth of the island's surface – about the greenest. Most famous for an ancient capital with its Hera temple (whose artefacts are the glory of the archaeological museum in the capital of Vathý), and a world-class sweet dessert wine (made after most of the must has been shipped to France to become communion wine), it's a successful all-round island that does many things well: beaches (especially in the west, and along the south coast), tavernas and atmospheric villages – but no one thing (wine aside) superbly. Outsiders – who for unknown reasons have historically included a large contingent of painters among them – overwhelmingly tend to buy old tiled, stone-built or lath-and-plaster village houses, rather than land in the countryside on which to build villas. The favourite targets are Áno Vathý, the hill village above the harbour founded in the 17th century; Ámbelos, with a spectacular balcony-like setting about halfway along the north coast; Áno (Paleó) Karlóvassi, one of the several quarters making up Karlóvassi, the island's vibrant second town in the west; and certain villages in the citrus- and olive-growing country south flank of Sámos, including Kouméïka, Neohóri and Koumaradhéï. The recently expanded airport is the busiest in this archipelago, with numerous international charter arrivals daily from May to October, several daily domestic flights to and from Athens, good service on the peripheral air link between Rhodes and Thessaloníki, and similarly varied ferry access.

Ikaría, just west of Sámos, is a world apart, despite falling nominally in the same province. It has always been a backwater, used as a place of exile for troublesome Byzantine nobles and, from the 1930s onwards, for troublesome Communists. The hospitable islanders defied orders not to interact with the Reds sent to live in their midst under house arrest; they in turn obligingly proselytised the Ikarians, who were impressed by the prisoners' idealism. The results include punitive neglect from Athens, an island with a notably high rate of emigration to that capitalist Great Satan, the USA, and a high rate of voting for the Left come election time. Physically, Ikaría is an elongated, narrow mass of schist, punctuated with hot springs and bounded on the north by – in summer anyway – some of the roughest sea the Aegean can muster, while the much calmer south flank looks out to Pátmos and Náxos. Historically, the idiosyncratic Ikarians didn't sell property to outsiders, but with a decade or so of tourism behind them, resistance to the notion is crumbling. Most of what's on offer lies between and around the north-coast port of Évdhilos and the main northwestern resort of Armenistís. Another Ikarian quirk (of many) is a strong aversion to living in densely packed villages; houses tend to have a generous swath of land and apricot orchards around them, and potential purchasers will benefit from the enhanced privacy. There's a tiny airport (domestic flights only) and reasonable ferry links on the Sámos-Cyclades-Piraeus line.

Between Sámos and Ikaría, the little islet of Foúrni has a surprisingly large port town, though any land-for-villa sales are likely to be on the slopes overlooking Kambí Bay, and for most (despite reasonable ferry links), it's a bit too out of the way and its amenities too sparse.

More or less due north of Ikaría, and across a narrow, breezy strait from Turkey's Çeşme Peninsula, **Híos** was (unlike Sámos and Ikaría) one of the main Genoese strongholds in the northeast Aegean, and their tenure from 1346 to 1566 left a superb architectural legacy, especially in the fortified mastic villages of the south. Mastic is the solidified sap of *Pistacia lentisca*, a shrub that grows across much of Aegean Greece and the Middle East, but only here producing resin of marketable quality. It was the basis of the island's prosperity for many centuries, and the mastic villages were specifically designed by the Genoese overlords to protect the mastic farmers and the precious crop against pirate raids. The centre and north of the island is more rugged countryside, covered largely in pine until the devastating fires of the 1980s. During the 19th century, Híos endured massacre as a reprisal for joining Sámos in revolt against the Ottomans, and, in 1881, a devastating earthquake; since then, livelihoods have been made in shipping, though mastic-based products – including chewing gum and toothpaste – are still prominently pitched.

The main town, largely though not completely of post-quake vintage, is eminently satisfactory for shopping and eating out but is not really a venue for property-hunting. The really baronial properties are in Kámbos, a fertile district just south of the airport covered in tangerine orchards divided by high walls. Substantial manor houses, with a *manganós* (water wheel) at the centre of extensive courtyards, in theory make superb restoration projects if you can get one. However, as some have lain in ruins since the 1881 earthquake, and nearly as many fall under the remit of the archaeological authorities, they will prove exceptionally expensive to renovate. The mastic villages or *mastihohoriá* – in particular, Mestá and Ólýmbi – have an altogether more *kasbah*-like architecture with their arcades, blind alleys and maze of streets lined by two-storey dwellings – though some find the claustrophobic ethos and lack of opportunity for gardening off-putting. In the centre of the island, beyond the celebrated Byzantine monastery of Néa Moní, the villages of Avgónyma and Anávatos are the obvious showcases, but Avgónyma has been bought up and restored, and Anávatos is in effect an archaeological site. This leaves Volissós, a collection of stone-built houses under an ancient castle (and inland from the best beaches) in the far northwest of Híos, as the main attraction for those after property. It's been so, however, since the late 1980s, and prices are now frankly reaching stratospheric levels. You may instead want to try in nearby but less frequented Sidhiroúnda or Lithí, also with sea views and quick access to the beach.

Híos has two inhabited satellite islets: Psará and Inoússes. The latter, home to some of Greece's wealthiest shipping families, is served most days by dedicated *kaïki* from Híos Town and has a fair stock of appealing neoclassical and vernacular houses, some of which are advertised for sale from time to time.

Híos has daily ferry links with Piraeus, and domestic service at its dinky airport provided by two Greek airlines but no direct flights from any English-speaking countries.

Still further north, and the third largest Greek island after Crete and Évvia, **Lésvos** remains one of the most traditional. The age-old livelihoods of olive oil production, ouzo-distilling and stock-raising remain vital here, despite the arrival of tourism since the early 1980s. Its volcanic, mountainous landscape is covered in olive groves (said to contain eleven million trees), pine, oak or grain fields, and deeply indented by the two large gulfs of Kallóni and Yéra, which seem more like lakes than arms of the sea. The sandiest and most protected beaches are on the south-facing coast, though there are also some decent ones between Sígri and Mólyvos, subject to the vagaries of the north wind. Though horse-drawn carts disappeared a decade or so ago, horses and donkeys are still disproportionately important in the local culture (particularly to get the olives out from roadless hillsides), and island festivals are famously long, musical and inebriated (though curiously local wine, poor and in limited quantity, does not feature in the tipple). Historically, Lésvos was (after Híos) the most important possession in the regional Genoese mini-empire, which endured from the mid-14th century until its defeat by the Ottomans; initially harsh rule by the sultan ensured that, before the events of 1919–23, nearly a third of the island's population was Muslim.

With over 50 inland villages built in warm-hued lava rock (not counting the more touristified coastal settlements), Lésvos has long been a popular venue for second-home-hunters, not least because the sheer number of houses boosts the chances of finding something suitable. Tourism, and property ownership by outsiders, came first to the showcase castellated village of Mólyvos in the far northwest, as far back as the 1970s; prices are now steep, if not completely out of reach, so you're better off concentrating a search in such nearby sea-view villages as Lafiónas, Skoutáros and Skalohóri to the southwest, or Petrí, Sykaminiá, Ipsilométopo or Klió to the east, at the base of 968-metre Mount Lepétymnos. There is also a pattern of purchases on the western peninsula at such spots as Eressós (inland from the resort of Skála Eressoú), sleepy Sígri at the western tip of Lésvos, and landlocked Vatoússa; the southeasterly peninsula is less popular, but Vríssa and Vassiliká are attractive possibilities. The capital of Mytilíni on the east coast, often doubling as the alias for the island, is too busy (and in places, shabby) to appeal to most, though there are some outstanding examples of 19th-century tower-mansions in the townships immediately to the south. The airport just south of Mytilíni, as on Híos, receives domestic flights from two Greek carriers, but, unlike Híos, gets plenty of overseas charter arrivals from May to October.

Límnos, northwest of Lésvos and halfway to the Greek mainland, is also volcanic but far less naturally vegetated and (in the eyes of some) rather bleak. Unlike on Lésvos, wine-making is pursued with some enthusiasm and the local vintage is among the best in the Greek islands – as are local cheese, meat and honey. Because of its position astride the entry to the Dardanelles, it has always been strategic militarily: the Ottoman surrender to the Allies was signed on a battleship anchored here in October 1918, and the Greek armed forces maintain a high-profile presence here. Most tourist facilities, and villages of appeal to house-hunters (especially weekending Greeks from Thessaloníki), are concentrated in the western leg of this H-shaped island, with the appealing little capital of Mýrina and its massive fortress as the focus. Half a dozen truly excellent beaches to either side of Mýrina have characterful villages perched on the hillside just inland, for example Kondiás and Thános, built of the same lava blocks as used on Lésvos. The airport, in the centre of the island, is served mainly from Athens and Thessaloníki, and seats can be hard to come by because of the priority given to conscripts; direct international flights from the UK are very limited. Ferries tend to call more regularly from Lávrio, Thessaloníki and Kavála than Piraeus.

Thássos, effectively a chunk of marble just offshore from the Macedonian mainland port of Kavála, has long been popular with both Thessalonians and foreign holidaymakers. Until devastating forest fires of the 1980s and 1990s, it was also one of the most piney of these islands, and still has some lovely beaches. Local architecture here is more generic-Balkan than further south, though, unusually, upper storeys of houses tend to be of stone (rather than lath-and-plaster), except in the *hayiátes* or full-length overhangs. The most popular villages for property are Theológos, in the middle of the island, where slate-roofed houses with walled gardens compensate for a lack of sea view. If you crave that, you're better off in west-facing Sotíras and Megálo Kazavíti, both of which have hosted outsiders for some time now. Kavála airport opposite gets flights from Athens on both domestic airlines, plus a few overseas charters in season – then it's a ro-ro ferry or hydrofoil transfer from the mainland to the Thassian capital of Liménas.

Dramatic **Samothráki**, the northeasternmost Greek island, has the highest Aegean mountain at its heart – 1611-metre Fengári (the ancient Saos) – and is home to the ruins of the Sanctuary of the Great Gods, one of the major pilgrimage sites of the ancient world. Rugged natural beauty – which extends to hot springs and coastal waterfalls, as well as forest – does not translate into abundant amenities, and the island sees few tourists and even fewer property-hunters, both being put off by the very short summer season this far north. The west-facing Hóra is appealing, as are south-facing Lákoma and Profítis Ilías, the latter two near the only substantial beach on Samothráki. Both local airlines provide good links between Athens and Alexandhroúpoli on the Thracian mainland, but the ferry service from there to Samothráki can be erratic out of season.

Halkidhikí

The three-pronged peninsula just southeast of Thessaloníki, Greece's second city, has some of the best beaches on the mainland on the two westerly bits –

and not a lot else. The third, easternmost extension is **Mount Áthos**, the semi-autonomous monastic republic – most definitely off-limits to property-hunters, as well as (by the terms of a millennium-old edict) all women. This leaves Sithonía and Kassándhra to the west; before 1923 and the extensive resettlement of refugees from Asia Minor, much of the land was the property of the Athonite monasteries, and unsuccessful participation in the 1821 Greek revolution had meant depopulation and destruction of what few inland villages that existed in reprisal, with very few re-establishing themselves afterwards. Halkidhikí is the only part of the northern mainland that sees any foreign buyer traffic – and, courtesy of those wonderful beaches, is also one of the few places in the country with extensive holiday apartment development. The only village with much character on **Kassándhra** is Áfytos, an ensemble of warm-toned stone houses on the east coast, though it, too, is caught up in tourism and, ironically, the beach below is perhaps the least distinguished in the region. The village of Kalándhra has a number of old traditional houses for sale, a departure from the usual norm here of beachfront apartments and villas. On quieter **Sithonía**, the only inland villages are Sykiá, tucked in the head of a valley down near the tip of this peninsula, and Parthenónas, overlooking the west coast from the base of Mount Ítamos. The latter was abandoned during the 1960s and never provided with mains electricity, but this hasn't stopped wealthy Greeks and foreigners from slowly but steadily buying and restoring its fine old houses.

The disadvantages of buying here are a very limited choice of flights into Thessaloníki (the closest airport) and a very short season – the beach areas don't get going much before late June, and pretty well wind down by the end of August.

The Sporades and Mount Pílio

Located bang in the middle of Greece, these regions – one island group, one contiguous mainland peninsula – share a thick carpet of vegetation, idyllic white, sandy beaches, turquoise seas, long-standing popularity as a destination with both Greeks and foreigners and a resolute lack of archaeological remains for those who couldn't give a toss about ancient glories. With heavy winter rainfall, water is not as much of a problem here as it is on more southerly archipelagos. The Sporades (meaning 'scattered' in Greek, the same root as our word 'sporadic') are in fact no more or less scattered than any other island group, but the name has stuck. They comprise (from west to east, beginning from the Pílio Peninsula) Skiáthos, Skópelos, Alónissos and – much more remote – Skýros. Despite their geographical centrality, they are tricky to get to, both from the rest of Greece or from overseas: only Skiáthos has an airport, which receives seasonal charters, while hydrofoils from Thessaloníki and domestic flights to

Skýros have been eliminated or cut back in recent years. The most reliable access is via the port of Vólos, which has at least daily ferries or hydrofoils as far as Alónissos, while Skýros is only reached from the little port of Kými on Évvia.

Skiáthos is the most numerically popular of these islands, with dozens of postcard-perfect beaches. But short-term tourism does not equal ample real estate opportunities; the single, heavily commercialised town is not a great draw and such second-home property as there is tends to be existing villas and land-for-building on the south-central Kalamáki Peninsula.

Neighbouring **Skópelos** is for many more appealing, with two major villages (Skópelos Town and Glóssa), plus a handful of smaller settlements. Prune plums are no longer grown commercially but many farmsteads supporting almond and olive trees remain, along with a stronger architectural homogeneity than on Skiáthos, featuring schist roofs and beaked chimneys. A 1964 earthquake created a windfall for property-hunters: the westerly village of Klíma, with sock-you-in-the-eye views, was declared unfit for continued occupation and its inhabitants moved down to the nearest bay into a purpose-built compound. Beginning in 1985, most reparable houses were snapped up by foreigners and Athenians, such that second-generation sales now prevail – beware of any remaining houses without existing electrical meters, because, as it is an offi-cially 'decommisioned' village, you may not be able to have any utilities supplied. You may have better luck in Mahalás (officially Athéato), the oldest hamlet on the island, next to Glóssa – though the number of houses is limited, and 'Athéato' means 'without a view' (it does, in fact, glimpse a patch of the sea). Glóssa and Skópelos Town itself are also possibilities, as are isolated farmsteads which occasionally come on the market.

Alónissos, marooned in a stretch of the Aegean so remote and pristine that a marine park to protect monk seals has been established nearby, is far less visited than the preceding two islands. Yet it supports a large body of outsiders with property in the old hilltop *hóra*. Ripped by the same earthquake that hit Klíma, it has, since the late 1970s, been bought up and restored by Athenians and foreigners – leaving the former owners in the purpose-built, antiseismic port of Patitíri.

Skýros has retained some of the strongest folklore in the Aegean, most notably its outrageous carnival traditions – and a dwindling number of older people in traditional everyday dress. It's another one-village island – the *hóra* is particularly striking – with contrasting halves: the north rolling and piney, the south flatter and more scrubby. Large tracts of Skýros are occupied by the Greek military, which limits the scope of plots that can be purchased to build on. This hasn't, however, stopped an appreciable expat community (mostly English and Dutch) from developing, attracted in part by the island's 'alternative' ethos (courtesy of the London-based Skyros Centre and its offshoots).

Mount Pílio (Pelion to many foreigners) is the latest overnight sensation in Greece, overdue for a discovery that has been helped along by regular admiring features in *Sunday Times* travel supplements and the provision of occasional charters to formerly military-only Vólos Airport. That said, you may still find it more convenient to fly into Skiáthos and arrange onward transport from there (seat-only capacity into Vólos is very limited at the time of writing). What you'll find on arrival is a radically different version of Greece than the cubic-Cycladic stereotype. Huge mansions, of a type generally seen only much further north in the Balkans, attest to an 18th-century renaissance fostered by limited autonomy granted by the Ottomans. Water, audible when not visible in hillside rivulets, is emphatically not a problem; the peninsula – core of the Thessalian province of Magnisía – reaches 1,421m just above the little ski resort of Agriólefkes, and winter trips from the far side of Pílio to the somewhat grim provincial capital of Vólos are often dependent on snow-ploughing. The northeasterly slopes facing the Aegean have a damp, continental climate with severe winters even below the snow line – chestnut trees and shade-loving shrubs thrive – and fantasy beaches to match the best on any of the nearby islands. The southwesterly flank, its inferior shingle beaches lapped by the Pagasitic Gulf, is milder and drier, vegetated in olive groves, pine and broom. Cobbled trails still link a number of villages, and gigantic plane trees – esteemed since ancient times – cast their shade over the exquisite, often multi-levelled central plazas, which are a distinguishing feature of Pílio communities.

Foreign ownership in the area is in its infancy but bound to grow in future years. Setting aside the multistorey lath-and-plaster mansions – more practical as museums or inns than as family residences – there are numbers of sturdily built, two-storey stone houses, the luckier of them with a garden or at least a small front courtyard. There's a preference thus far for the more temperate south-facing slopes, with houses going in such hill villages as Miliés, Áyios Yeóryios, Áyios Vlássios, Argalastí, Afétes, Láfkos and Promýrri, all of which have at least partial views of the sea. On the northeast side, try looking in the villages of Lambinoú, Zagorá, Pourí and Xouríkhti. The marketing of sea-view (if not actually seaside) apartments and villas has begun around Áfyssos, on the Pagasitic coast, and near Áyios Ioánnis, main resort of the Aegean coast. Bear in mind that amenities are limited to bakeries, bottle shops and petrol stations in even the largest villages, and for a proper shopping trip you'll be obliged to somehow cover up to 65km of road to Vólos; the former useful hydrofoil line serving coastal settlements on the south tip of Pílio has been suspended and is not likely to be reinstated.

Central Greece: Évvia and Galaxídhi

Although it's the second-largest Greek island after Crete, mountainous, narrow **Évvia**, just south of the Sporades, rarely feels like one. And while there are ro-ro ferry crossings from several points on the central mainland just opposite, the most reliable all-weather access is the road-and-rail bridge to the gritty capital, Halkídha. Thinly populated, fertile yet rugged in the interior, Évvia has long been popular as a resort and summer residence for the rest of central Greece, but is just catching on as a second-home venue with foreigners – often those spending the working week in Athens. That said, there's a long-standing British connection, especially in the forested north: the Noel-Baker estate and mines, dating from the War of Independence, and a small expat community in and around Límni, the most conspicuously attractive coastal town, with neoclassical charm attesting to a brief 19th-century heyday in shipping. The interior villages with the best combination of character and easy access are Avlonári, east of Halkídha, and Mýli at the foot of Mount Óhi in the far south, inland from Kárystos and the Marmári ferry terminal. Otherwise, the favoured strategy involves buying a plot of land facing Évvia's less protected north coast and building a villa, especially near the sandy beaches below Ayía Ánna; a few old houses are for sale in the village centre of Ayía Ánna.

Galaxídhi, on the north coast of the Gulf of Corinth, is another neoclassical port town that traced a shooting-star trajectory of shipping wealth through the 19th century, only to subside into obscurity upon the advent of steam power. (Greek fleet-owners were generally reluctant to abandon sail; it took the likes of Onassis and Nearhos after the Second World War to re-establish the country's pre-eminence in shipping.) Smaller, sleepier and more architecturally homogenous than Límni, it has an utterly different setting as well: the conspicuously bare coastal hills of Fokídha province, their earth tones emphasised by occasional purple-orange tailings from the local bauxite industry. The town, curled around two bays, is a bit hot and airless in the summer but makes a lovely winter retreat, especially with skiing on Mount Parnassós just an hour or so's drive north. It has long been popular with Athenians and foreigners living in Athens – there's a local estate agent serving them – but isn't really practical for flying visits from abroad. The quickest way there by car from Athens involves following the motorway along the Corinth Gulf's south shore, and then coinciding with the ferry from Éyio to Áyios Nikólaos, just west of Galaxídhi on the Fokídha side.

The Peloponnese and Kýthira

The Peloponnese Peninsula, joined to the rest of Greece only by a girder bridge at the Corinth Canal (and a much more spectacular, high-tech, suspension one at the Río-Andírrio Straits), is one of the most beguiling parts of the mainland. Within its boundaries lies a bit of everything associated with Greece – ancient ruins, medieval castles and fortified mansions, well-tended vineyards, hallowed, cliff-hung monasteries, Byzantine churches, long beaches – as well as a few things that ordinarily are not: some passable ski resorts, vast apple and pear orchards, subtropical vegetation in the far southwest. The Peloponnese has a suitably botanical alias: the Moriás, supposedly derived from its map outline resemblance to the leaf of a mulberry tree (*mouriá* in Greek). Historically, it was crucial to the development of the modern Greek state: many of the battles of the War of Independence were fought on the Peloponnese, several of the Greek warrior chieftains hailed from the peninsula, and the capital of the young country was briefly here, at Náfplio.

Today, the main towns are Pátra in the northwest, Trípoli near the centre, Kórinthos at the peninsula's gateway, by the eponymous canal, and Kalamáta in the far southwest. However, as with provincial capitals elsewhere on the main-land, war and earthquakes have not been at all kind to these places (and the Greeks themselves have compounded the damage with insensitive postwar building), so the focus of interest for real estate is emphatically elsewhere, espe-cially well-preserved older settlements in the southern half of the peninsula.

Despite the fact that the Peloponnese is one of the more popular parts of Greece for tourists, access to places you'd want to buy property is surprisingly tricky – the more so since the hydrofoil services down the east coast and the domestic air service to Kálamata have been suspended. Kalamáta airport does, however, continue to get seasonal charters from overseas, and the new motorway from Athens will eventually reach Kalamáta as well within 3½ hours, slicing through the heart of the peninsula via Trípoli. Indeed, it is the Athens-based weekenders with their own cars who get the most out of properties here.

Náfplio, near the head of the Argolid Gulf and capital of **Argolídha**, is the exception that proves the above-cited rule about shabby provincial centres. It is an elegant, Venetian-flavoured neoclassical town stuck in an agreeable time-warp since the nation's capital shifted to Athens in 1834 – though there's an inevitable new town fanning out from the old quarter, sheltering under not one but two massive castles. Property is, naturally, at a premium (*see* Austen Kark's memoir on the subject, listed on p.270).

The most central, and mountainous, province of the Peloponnese is **Arkadhía** (Arcadia to you, as in 'Arcadian idylls'); the easterly, and least-known portion, shelving down to the Argolid Gulf is **Kynouría**. Immediately east of the Párnon range are a cluster of villages in chestnut-shrouded valleys, which are beginning to get some attention from buyers. Prastió is the architectural showcase but hasn't much of a view; Kastánitsa is less of a piece architecturally but glimpses the gulf and clean fine-pebble beaches lie under an hour's drive away. Most popular, however, despite a somewhat airless canyon setting just inland from the sea, is Leonídhi, with its sumptuous walled mansions, though it's rather less convenient now that the hydrofoil service seems to have gone for good.

West of Trípoli lies classical Arcadia, a realm of deep river canyons and stone-built villages and monasteries clinging to their banks. The best of these are clustered near the headwaters of the Alfiós River, along its tributary the Loúsios: Dhimitsána, Zatoúna, Karýtena and Stemnítsa, which offer imposing multistorey mansions with arched ground-floor entrances, round-topped windows and top-floor balconies. Tiled roofs have a surprisingly shallow pitch considering the harsh winters, but, again, a short drive separates you from the excellent beaches on the Peloponnesian west coast.

All this acknowledged, **Messinía** – occupying the far southwestern lobe of the three-pronged mulberry leaf – has long been the target of choice for Peloponnesian property seekers: the climate is much more forgiving, the beaches just a few steps away, transport regular and major amenities to hand. At the tip of the peninsula, between the former Venetian strongholds of Methóni and Koróni, stubby bananas can just about be persuaded to ripen most years. **Koróni** town proper is a relatively homogenous 19th-century neoclassical showpiece, a sort of miniature Náfplio without the tourists; there's the odd apartment being pitched at the outskirts, but otherwise you're discreetly nudged towards land and freestanding structures in the surrounding countryside. On the other side of Kalamáta, across the Messinian Gulf at the foot of pyramidal Mount Taïyettos, the entire coast is a hive of real estate activity, with everything from beach-view studios to old stone houses, and the international airport an affordable taxi ride away. Up to the provincial border, this is known as the **'Outer' Máni**; the **'Inner' Máni**, the desert-like middle lobe of the mulberry leaf over in Lakonía province, has always been the realm of Greece's hard men. A sort of rough local equivalent to Sardinia or Sicily, it was only latterly evangelised, in the 9th century, though thereafter distinguished by Christian fervour (and reactionary politics since the War of Independence). The severe topographic and climatic conditions gave rise to elaborate blood feuds, essentially the outgrowth of competition for scarce resources; tall fortification towers formed an essential part of these vendettas, which adhered to clan lines. The tower houses are scattered, to a greater or lesser degree, in over 30 hamlets and villages, mostly in sight of the sea, all the way round the Greek Land's End of Cape Ténaro to Yíthio, the lively, partly neoclassical port of **Lakonía**.

Elsewhere in Lakonía, **Monemvasiá** – a sort of miniature Greek Gibraltar-cum-Dubrovnik – commands the approaches to the third lobe of the mulberry leaf, the otherwise little-visited Vátika peninsula. Before Yíthio arose, this intricately fortified town – divided into rock-top and lower districts – was the harbour for Byzantine Yeráki and Mýstra inland. It also exported the famous malmsey wine, a corruption of the medieval tag Malvasia. The upper quarter, save for a church or two, has crumbled away since the end of Ottoman rule, but the lower town bucked decline long enough to have been rediscovered by wealthy Athenians and foreigners since the 1970s. Cars are banned within the walls – all services are in the modern cantonment of Yéfira just west – and the surviving houses (when available for sale) are superb, but you must contend with one of the strictest preservation regimes in Greece. The continued probable lack of hydrofoil service has made it a bit of a non-starter as a weekend retreat from Athens.

Just off the Vátika peninsula, reached other from Neápoli, Yíthion or a daily flight from Athens, **Kýthira** is traditionally numbered amongst the Ionian Islands – even though the closest other one, Zákynthos, is nearly 70 nautical miles northwest – but today, curiously, it is administered from Piraeus. Like the rest of the Ionians (save Lefkádha), it avoided a period of Ottoman rule but was part of the half-century-long British protectorate, which ended in 1864. Before this, Kýthira had been a major Venetian outpost, controlling the sea lanes to Crete, and theirs is the major architectural influence, with results not unlike those on Náxos or Tínos. In modern times, the main social pattern has been mass emigration to Australia, with returned Kythiran emigrants dominating the place in summer; at other times of the year it's popular in a low-key way with trendy Athenian weekenders. In mythology, Avgó islet, just offshore, is a claimant for the title of Aphrodite's birthplace (Cyprus strenuously disputes this) but the island's decidedly unromantic topography consists of an elevated, rather cheerless plateau, slashed by ravines where springs nurture vegetation and villages. For village houses, the castellated *hóra* at the south tip and the fortified oasis village of Mylopotamos are obvious choices, but you'll have more space (and possibly a garden) around Livádhi (near Hóra) or Potamós (in the north, near one of the two ferry ports).

Zagória in Epirus

Just north of the provincial capital **Ioánnina**, close to the Albanian border, lies one of the most scenic portions of the Pindus mountain range: the Zagória district. Its 46 villages are arrayed around the limestone bulwark of Mount Gamíla and the Víkos Gorge bounding it and comprise the heart of a national park that has protected the area (to some degree) since 1975. Since the union of Epirus with Greece in 1912, it has become one of the poorest parts of the country – so it comes as a surprise to find the imposing stone-built mansions of the Zagorohória, as these villages are called, matching their surroundings perfectly, down to their limestone-tile roofs and field-stoned courtyards, accessed by deep-eaved gateways. Their multistorey interiors are equally impressive, with painted storage cupboards, functional fireplaces and well-placed windows admitting plenty of light. It's all the legacy of 18th- and 19th-century wealth engendered by the local timber and livestock trade, as well as (in common with much of Greece) remittances from abroad by the huge body of itinerant or semi-exiled able-bodied men in central Europe, who returned home only periodically to sire more heirs.

Of the 46 villages, only a handful (those closest to the national park) enjoy strict architectural protection, while the remotest villages are unlikely to appeal. The main tourist focal points of central Zagóri – Monodhéndhri and the two Pápingo villages at either end of the Víkos Gorge, and Tsepélovo just east – are almost totally devoted to providing services to the many hikers and more casual tourists who throng here much of the year, and, even assuming that property were to become available, prices are prohibitive. The best strategy involves hunting in the less obvious central villages or more peripheral ones looking towards (but not directly bordering) the national park: Kapésovo, Vítsa, Koukoúli and Kípi in the centre, and Eláti, Dhíkorfo, Dhílofo and Áno Pedhiná further southwest.

One result of the severe depopulation is very limited amenities, including miserable public transport links to Ioánnina. You pretty much have to keep a car here to survive, with access to the closest reasonable shops at Kalpáki some 20 to 35 kilometres west eased by recent road improvements (though for a really big shop you'll need to go the full distance to Ioánnina). At an average village altitude of over 1,000m, winters are for real here, and if you think you've left de-icing car windscreens behind in your former northern home, think again. Ioánnina has good domestic air connections with Athens but is unlikely ever to receive direct flights from abroad. The small expat community here, mostly English 'refugees' from the scene on Corfu (*see* below), come and go if needed via charters from busy Corfu Airport.

The Ionian Islands

These six islands off the coast of western Greece, four large and two small, are Greece at its most Italianate and least Balkan. For this, the Venetians and their four-century administration, ending only in 1797, are responsible, leaving a palpable legacy in music, the local dialect and (especially) cuisine – pasta dishes are a firm favourite in these islands, as are Italianate stews such as *bourdhéto* (white fish in a sauce of tomato, red pepper and olive oil) or *sofríto* (veal or beef stewed in white wine, garlic and vinegar). Following the turmoil of the Napoleonic Wars, the British took over in 1814, maintaining a half-century protectorate which ended only in 1864 when they ceded these islands (along with Kýthira, covered above) to the Greek kingdom as a condition of Prince George of Denmark (henceforth George I of Greece) acceding the throne. As is the way of these things, nationals of the former colonial masters Italy and Britain contribute the vast majority of both short-term tourists and second- (or main-) home-owners. Greeks are, however, more conspicuous on Lefkádha and Itháki, while Corfu's staggering 10,000 foreign residents include significant numbers of Dutch, Scandinavians, Swiss and Germans.

By a twist of geology, all these islands have a shared characteristic of dramatic cliffs – often, but not always, fringed by superb sand beaches – on their western shore facing the open Ionian Sea, while the less dramatic east coasts opposite the Greek mainland tend to have scrappier, pebbly bays. Geology in the negative sense is ever-present, with still-active faults and a still-visible aftermath of the August 1953 earthquakes which devastated most of the southerly Ionians.

The heaviest rainfall in Greece – not always obligingly falling between October and May – keeps Corfu, in particular, almost electric-green, though paradoxically, mains water can be brackish owing to overdrawing of the water table – in Kérkyra Town, drinking water has to be purchased from metered taps. Zákynthos is nearly as wet (and as green), though Kefaloniá, Itháki and Lefkádha are drier and more stereotypically Mediterranean in vegetation. Instead of the *meltémi* as in the Cyclades, these islands are cooled in summer by the rather less violent northwesterly *máïstros*.

Corfu (officially known by its ancient name, Kérkyra) is pretty much the main event and has been so since Classical times. Immortalised in literature from Shakespeare to Lear to Durrell to Henry Miller, it manages – despite the blatant commercialisation of the east and north coasts in particular – to transcend the hype. Though damaged in parts by heavy fighting in 1943–44, the exquisite, Venetian-designed Old Town, bracketed by two fortresses, does no harm at all to the island's reputation. Another attraction is a selection of excellent restaurants, both cosmopolitan and local, distributed across the island. From the slopes of Mount Pandokrátor in the north of the island, the views across to Albania remain much as they were when Edward Lear painted them in 1848–49. Though there small stands of forest and wild scrub, the fabled greenery is overwhelmingly of the cultivated variety; the Venetians paid a bounty for every olive tree planted under their tenure and it shows.

Corfu is the most popular destination for property purchase, especially among the British, who are said to number some 6,000 – an expat scene to gravitate towards or avoid, according to temperament. Despite the mass market reputation of local tourism, there is, in fact, a broad mix of property for sale – old village houses needing work, already converted historic buildings, modern apartments and villas in coastal resorts, and land for building everywhere on the island – plus a range of estate agents. The most expensive and exclusive area is the northeast coast between Nissáki and Áyios Stéfanos Sinión, nicknamed (for obvious reasons) Kensington-on-Sea. More affordable studios and apartments can be found in and around the mass market resorts of Benítses, Mesongí and Aharávi. If you accept the space constraints imposed by the Venetian architecture, you can be in the heart of the action with an apartment in Kérkyra Town. Given the dozens of hill villages, especially around 917m Mount Pandokrátor, possibilities for old fixer-upper houses are almost unlimited, but more popular venues include (in the north) Áyios Pandelímon above Aharávi; Áyios Márkos, Strinýlas and Spartýlas above Pyrgí; Perouládhes and Magouládhes in the far northwest; or (taking matters to extremes) the remote 'ghost villages' of Paleó Perithiá and Méngoulas well inland from Kassiopí. In central Corfu, more convenient to town and the airport, try in Áyii Dhéka and Gastoúri, just above Benítses; Sinarádhes just west and Áyios Matthéos further south are handier for excellent beaches. The far south of the island, flatter and thus with less chance of a sea view, is far less popular. Aside from the somewhat inflated prices of staples, shops and amenities are excellent, with frequent high-speed ferries to Igoumenítsa on the mainland, and regular air links on the two domestic airlines to Athens, should you fail to secure a seat on a direct charter.

Little, steep-sided **Paxí** (Paxos in ancient times) is clearly visible in normal conditions from the south end of Corfu, of which it was long an olive-growing dependency. Aside from olive trees, there is little else in abundance: certainly not sandy beaches (most are shingle, except on Paxí's satellite Andípaxi), ground water (despite the same high winter rainfall as Corfu) or hotels (just three, officially). Yet Paxí exerts an undeniable charm and is a firm favourite with British villa-based holidaymakers and yacht flotillas – who together crowd the place out in season – as well as a growing contingent of second-home-owners. There are coastal settlements at Gáïos, Longós and Lákka, but there are no real inland villages aside from Magaziá and Bogdhanátika. Rather, there are clusters of houses – not even constituting proper hamlets – scattered among the dense olive groves. Property-owners choose between renovating smallish but characterful olive farmsteads, usually without views, or buying land for building on sea-view headlands around Lákka and Longós in particular.

Like Évvia, **Lefkádha** (ancient Lefkas) is only technically an island: the channel between it and the Etolo-Akarnanian mainland was cut during the 7th century BC and is now spanned by a floating bridge that moves to permit the passage of shipping. It is also the only member of the Ionian group that saw a significant period of Ottoman rule – from 1479 until the Venetians succeeded in establishing themselves in 1684 for just over a century. A hulking, mountainous land mass, covered in olives and cypress and in springtime spangled with yellow broom, it is the least visited of the big Ionians. Package tourism largely confines itself to the three resorts of Nýdhri (the biggest and busiest), Vassilikí and Áyios Nikítas, though Greeks are keenly appreciative of a place that has preserved rural lifestyles and crafts in the hill villages – and which is immune from the weather and price vagaries of ferry-boats. West coast beaches here are among the best in the Ionians, but by a trick of currents and positioning seem to catch more than their fair share of drifting rubbish. Lefkádha Town, immediately across the channel from the mainland and now a major yachting centre, owing to its perfectly sheltered lagoon-harbour, made some interesting responses to the 1953 earthquakes: church belfries comprised of anti-seismic girders and houses where the stone-built ground floors have been preserved, supporting lighter, half-timbered upper stories usually sheathed in corrugated tin. That said, the town is too bustling and workaday for most, and house-hunting focuses on the hill villages in the northern half of Lefkádha, around the fertile Sfakiótes Plateau; here properties in Spanohóri, Lazaráta, Pinakohóri and Kavállos have all already undergone tasteful renovation. Karyá, at the centre of the plateau, has the most pleasant shaded square on the island; just south, Vafkerí has been a bit over-restored. Immediately south of town, above the east coast and with fine views of the straits to the mainland, Katoúna is another popular village, while, overlooking the west coast, Dhrymónas has the best-preserved pre-quake architecture. A limited number of international charters, and infrequent domestic flights from Athens, arrive at Áktio airport, 20 minutes' drive from Lefkádha Town.

'Captain Corelli's Island' is what a book riding on the reputation of Louis de Bernières' blockbuster proclaims **Kefalloniá** to be, and the island looks set to survive its association with both the book (not universally popular among native islanders) and the film (which bombed and left only a pair of eponymous cafés to mark its passing). It is, in fact, the largest of the Ionians and (at 1,628m Mount Énos) by far the highest – but it is also the driest of the bigger islands, which could become a limiting factor for development. As *Captain Corelli's Mandolin* made clear, the population is noted for a carefully nurtured eccentricity – and a far-flung diaspora from southern Africa to the Great Plains of the USA, which lends a note of cosmopolitanism.

The 1953 earthquakes hit hardest here, wrecking the elegant capital of Argostóli and all the southern villages. Only in the far north, beyond castle-guarded Ássos port, do any older traditional houses survive, in and around the ridgeline villages of Vassilikádhes, Mesovoúnia and Manganós, and these few are being snapped up and repaired by a discerning (if not to say toffee-nosed) clientele who've enjoyed holidaying at Ássos or Fiskárdho. Elsewhere on the island, buying property very much means land sufficient to build a new villa on, for example on the inclined Livathó Plain southeast of Argostóli. Houses built immediately after the earthquake – with period features such as terrazzo or artisan-tile floors, marble sinks and pantile roofs – are rare and desirable. What the tremors couldn't destroy are some of the best panoramas in the Ionians: to neighbouring Itháki and Zákynthos, or along the cliffscapes of the island's northern half. Prices are absolutely skyrocketing on Kefalloniá this season, at well over the rate for Crete and Corfu; one owner reports having more than doubled their 2001 investment of €95,000 for purchase and 2002–04 improvements of €70,000. International charter arrivals to the airport south of Argostóli are reasonably frequent (if often pricey); by contrast, domestic links from Athens are not what they could be, considering Kefalloniá's size.

Just east of Kefalloniá, separated by a narrow, almost rectangular strait, little provincial brother **Itháki** – Homeric Ithaca – is often unjustly overlooked by foreigners, though Greeks in the know have been coming here for years. Even more than the Kefallonians, Itháki natives have been modern-day Odysseuses, working on ships or in every nation of the Greek diaspora before returning here to run businesses or retire. It's a friendly, laid-back place whose two main deficits – sandy beaches and fresh water – have served to protect it from mass tourism. The main town and port, Vathý, was mostly levelled by the 1953 earthquake but, unlike on Kefalloniá, was lovingly rebuilt for the most part in vernacular style. As on Kefalloniá, the north of the island fared much better, due in part to the underlying rock strata, so inland villages such as Anoyí, Áyia

Saránda and Exoyí, plus the upmarket coastal resort of Kióni, look much like they did before 1953. Thus it's possible to find an old house, though most buyers are after sufficient land for new-builds out among the olive groves that cover much of Itháki. Access is problematic, which has kept foreigner numbers low until now; with no airport, your choices boil down to going via Kefalloniá, or – if coming via Athens – by year-round ferry from Pátra or summer-only ferry from the Etolo-Akarnanian port of Astakós.

After Corfu, **Zákynthos** was the Venetians' favourite Ionian island – '*Zante, fior di Levante*', went their jingle – and its central plain and eastern hills are the most fertile in the group. The main town was the most elegant in the archipelago after Kérkyra, but alas, as at Argostóli, it all came crashing down in that fateful week of August 1953 and was likewise rebuilt in uninspiring reinforced concrete. The island's post-quake salvation was perceived as mass tourism, which duly installed itself around the broad beaches of the south and also (more moderately) along the Vasilikós Peninsula and sandy coves of the east coast. Subsequent tensions between the islanders and some of their less discerning guests – aggravated by a long-running, occasionally violent dispute between hotel and taverna proprietors and conservationists fighting to protect endangered turtle-nesting sites on the southern beaches – mean that a warm welcome is not universally assured here. Long-term residents thus gravitate towards the northern half and interior of the island, where building plots are the norm, or to the bare handful of villages on the arid western ridge which more or less survived the earthquake: Kiloméno, Éxo Hóra and Mariés, with much-photographed pre-quake churches and a handful of old houses on offer. With well over half a million overseas tourists in a good season, a charter to the airport – second busiest in the Ionian – should be possible, though, if you're forced to go via Athens, domestic service is sparse.

Selecting a Property

04

Although Greece is not one of the larger countries in Europe – at just under 132,000 square kilometres (51,000 square miles) – Greek territory is distributed in such a way, and its travel infrastructure is still so deficient in many aspects, that it will seem much bigger as you travel around it. However, presumably you won't be journeying all over Greece; the preceding **Where in Greece: Profiles of the Regions** chapter, plus the 'Research and Information Resources' section (*see* pp.93–4), will have helped you narrow your interests down to perhaps one mainland region and a handful of islands. Once you've settled on your island or province, it's time to analyse what makes for a successful property purchase, how to find available properties, and what you can expect to pay for renovations, newly built villas or plots of land.

Travelling to Greece

With a minimum distance of 2,000 miles between Greece and most points in northern Europe, going by plane is the simplest, quickest and generally the least expensive way of arrival. Given the 3½-day travel time overland from Britain, even if you pedal-to-the-metal, driving is not a conspicuously practical option unless you have lots of furniture and other goods to transport, and freight can be surprisingly reasonable if you fill up an entire seagoing container. Travelling by rail, or rail and trans-Adriatic-ferry, is only for die-hard train spotters; Rail Europe in Britain won't even quote you a through-fare, and coach links, which have dwindled to nought, were always intended for masochists.

By Air

The bad news is that Greece has yet to attract the plethora of no-frills airlines that France, Spain and Italy do and, given the current tumultuous state of aviation, is unlikely to in the future. While Greece has nearly 40 operational airports, and nearly half of those currently tout themselves as 'international', just two – Athens and Thessaloníki – receive year-round, scheduled direct or stopping flights from Britain and Ireland. Everywhere else is served by only seasonal charters, or leisure-airline 'scheduled' services with a fare and booking structure akin to charters, typically operating from May through October.

The best fares (relatively speaking) are into Athens' 2001-inaugurated Eleftherios Venizelos Airport. The long-standing duopoly on direct flights from the UK exercised by British Airways and Olympic Airlines, the Greek state carrier, has recently been broken by easyJet (the lone exception to the lack of no-frills arrivals) and HellasJet (a subsidiary of Cyprus Airways, which in the first year or so of its operation has received consistently good marks for competitive fares, punctuality and in-flight service).

Travel industry observers have for years been foretelling the doom of troubled Olympic Airlines, consistently near the bottom of consumer polls for service, and certainly with an unenviably poor record for timekeeping on international departures. The EU has warned the Greek government that it cannot keep on illegally subsidising the airline, and has levied stiff fines for the airline's misappropriation of convergence funds, but somehow, like the bumblebee that should not be able to fly, it continues doing so. Olympic's main problem is that it's grossly overstaffed, and, faced with its formidable unions, no foreign buyer for it has thus far been found. The word is that after the 2004 tourist season, with their Athens Olympic Games, the airline as it exists will probably be allowed to go under, a new one will be reconstituted, and the surplus staff will be sacked.

If you are flying onwards from Athens to a provincial airport, at a time of year and/or to an island or mainland centre where there are no direct charters available, it's vital that you reach Eleftherios Venizelos airport from overseas well before the departure of the last flight of the day to your final destination – otherwise, you face a time-consuming and expensive shuffle into mid-town Athens and back again the next day. Arrival between 1pm and 5pm allows (from April to October at least, but sometimes not daily) a quick same-day connection to Sámos, Páros, Santoríni, Corfu, Ioánnina, Zákynthos and Lésvos, as well as Haniá and Iráklio (Crete), Rhodes, Ioánnina, Kavála, Kefalloniá, Kós, Límnos, Mýkonos, Alexandhroúpoli and Híos. Arrive at 6 to 7pm, as is typical with a midday departure from Britain, and you'll miss the onward flight to the first batch of airports cited, as well as the last hydrofoils to the Argo-Saronic Islands. For other sparsely served domestic destinations like Mílos, Skiáthos or Léros, your only option is a red-eye flight from Britain (10.30pm) which gets in at 4am, with up to half a day's additional wait for the next onward flight.

At present, the only semi-civilised morning departures from Britain are operated by British Airways (about 7.30am in summer, 8.30am in winter, five days a week from Heathrow and daily from Gatwick only in summer, at 9.45am); easyJet (daily from Gatwick at around 7am) and HellasJet (daily from Gatwick at 11am), which arrive at around 1.45pm, 2.45pm and 4.45pm respectively. Among indirect services out of Heathrow, we've had luck with Swiss via Geneva (departs at around 8.15am, arrives Athens 3.30pm) and Lufthansa via Munich (departs at around 7.30am, arrives Athens 3pm). BA and Olympic operate midday flights from Heathrow that arrive (air traffic controller whims permitting) sometime between 6.30 and 7.15pm, while easyJet's 1.40pm service out of Luton gets in at 7.30pm. Otherwise there are late afternoon or red-eye services several days a week out of Manchester on Olympic and HellasJet, and daily from Heathrow. You'll get little joy flying to Thessaloníki: Olympic flies five times a week from Gatwick, departing at about 5.30pm and touching down long after the last domestic flight has left.

For more on local air service within Greece, *see* pp.64–5.

Especially if starting travel from British regional airports, or from Ireland, you may prefer to pay a little over the odds for the convenience of a direct charter to your Greek home. With the rise in property ownership in Greece, especially on the islands, charter airlines such as Excel, Thomas Cook and TUI have been obliged – albeit grudgingly in some cases – to offer a limited number of flight-only seats. However, fares to less popular islands like Sámos or Kefalloniá (especially at peak season) compare poorly to piecing together an itinerary via Athens, with an onward domestic flight and charter departure times that are often barbaric (just before 5am, or after 10pm).

One excellent resource is **www.cheaperholidays.com** (**t** 0870 745 6800); hit the 'Flights Search' link to come up with flight-only possibilities. If you ask for results to be displayed by 'Number of nights' (not price) and leave 'Display all' in the departing airport space, this site will fetch return flights of five, six or even seven weeks' duration rather than the typical two weeks of most holidaymakers.

Useful Scheduled and Charter Airlines in the UK and Ireland

- **Aer Lingus**, UK **t** 0845 084 4444, Republic of Ireland **t** 0818 365 000, **www.aerlingus.com**. Gets you to the UK (Heathrow) for onward travel.

- **BMI**, **t** 0870 607 0555, **www.flybmi.com**. Good connections from the north of England and Scotland to Heathrow; code-share agreement with Olympic.

- **British Airways**, **t** (UK) 0870 850 9850, **t** (Republic of Ireland) 1800 626 747, **www.ba.com**. Flights from Heathrow and Gatwick to Athens. Return fares typically £120–220 depending on the season.

- **easyJet**, **t** 0870 600 0000, **www.easyJet.com**. Flights from Luton and Gatwick to Athens. One-way fares range from £40 to £160 depending on demand; no-frills in-flight service.

- **Excel Airways**, **t** 08709 98 98 98, **www.excelairways.com**. Flights-only to almost every major charter-served airport in Greece, mostly from Gatwick and Manchester but often Glasgow, Birmingham, East Midlands as well.

- **HellasJet**, **t** 0870 751 7222, **www.hellas-jet.com**. Flights from Heathrow, Gatwick and Manchester to Athens. Return fares typically £100–210 depending on season.

- **Lufthansa**, **t** 0870 8377 747, **http://cms/lufthansa.com/fly/uk**. Flights from Heathrow to Athens via Frankfurt or Munich.

- **Olympic Airlines**, **t** 0870 606 0460, **www.olympicairlines.com**. Flights from Heathrow and Manchester to Athens; also Gatwick to Thessaloníki. Return fares typically £130–220 depending on season.

- **Swiss Airlines**, **t** 0845 601 9956, **www.swiss.com**. Flights to Athens via Geneva or Zurich; note that in-flight service is now no-frills. Return fares £140–230.

- **Thomas Cook, t** 0870 750 0316, **www.thomascook.com**. Good selection of flight-only seats to Corfu, Kefalloniá, Zákynthos, Kós, Lésvos, Santoríni, Skiáthos, Sámos and Rhodes from half a dozen UK airports.

- **Thomson, t** 0870 165 0079, **www.thomson-holidays.com**. Limited flight-only deals to Corfu, Rhodes, Iráklio (Crete), Zákynthos, Kós, Sámos, Kefalloniá, Skiáthos and Kavála (for Thássos) on **TUI**, its parent company airline.

By Road and Sea

Driving to Greece is not an economical option, with two water crossings involved – the Channel and the Adriatic Sea – along the only routes that can sensibly be recommended, especially for property in the Ionian Islands. It's really only worth it as part of large family group, when the cost of two sets of ferry tickets can be justified, and it's certainly not something you'll want to be doing two or three times annually.

The fastest way from England over to the continent is the **Eurotunnel** service (t 0870 535 3535, **www.eurotunnel.com**) via the Channel Tunnel. Eurotunnel operates shuttle trains 24 hours a day for cars, motorcycles, buses and their passengers. The service, which charges per vehicle rather than per passenger (thus being more economical for families), runs continuously between Folkestone and Coquelles, near Calais, with up to four departures per hour (only one per hour midnight–6am) and takes 35mins (45mins for some night departure times). You can just turn up and buy your ticket at the tollbooths (after leaving the M20 at junction 11a), though at busy times it is advisable to book in advance. Prices depend on the time of year, time of day and length of stay; it's cheaper to travel between 10pm and 6am, while the highest fares apply for weekend departures and returns in July and August.

The traditional, alternative cross-Channel options are the **ferry** or **hovercraft** links between Dover and Calais or Boulogne (the quickest and cheapest routes), Ramsgate and Dunkerque, or Newhaven and Dieppe. Irish drivers will prefer routes bypassing Britain, direct to Roscoff or Cherbourg, or from the southwest of England to St-Malo or Caen. Ferry prices vary wildly, charging per passenger as well as per car, and company websites tend to be reticent about showing the most economical periods; you may have better luck on the phone. Even during the summer there are cheaper tickets available through specialist discount websites such as **www.cross-channel-ferry-tickets.co.uk**.

- **Brittany Ferries, t** 0870 366 5333; **www.brittanyferries.com**.
- **Condor Ferries, t** 0845 345 2000; **www.condorferries.com**.
- **Hoverspeed, t** 0870 240 8282/t 0870 460 7171; **www.hoverspeed.com**.
- **Irish Ferries, t** 0870 517 1717; **www.irishferries.com**.
- **Norfolkline, t** 0870 870 1020; **www.norfolkline.com**.

- **P&O Ferries, t** 0870 520 2020; **www.poferries.com.**
- **SeaFrance, t** 0870 571 1711; **www.seafrance.com.**
- **Stena Line, t** 0870 400 6748; **www.stenaline.com.**
- **Superfast Ferries, t** 0870 234 0870; **www.superfast.com.**
- **Transmanche Ferries, t** 0800 917 1201; **www.transmancheferries.com.**

Once on the French side, the most direct route to Italy is Calais–Reims–Geneva–Milan and then down the Adriatic coast to the Italian port of your choice. If you transit through Switzerland, you'll have to buy a motorway tax sticker and supplementary insurance. Even using the quickest French *autoroutes* and Italian *autostrade* (with their hefty tolls), the journey will involve two overnight stops, plus a third on the Adriatic ferry between Italy and Greece.

From Italy, there's a choice of five ferry routes to Greece. Ancona, Bari and Brindisi are linked most frequently with Igoumenítsa (the port of Epirus in western Greece) and/or Pátra at the northwest tip of the Peloponnese, the closest port to property in Messinía or the Máni. Most boats sail via the island of Corfu and during July and August – sometimes into June or September – at least one company calls weekly at Paxí, Kefalloniá and Zákynthos *en route* to Pátra. You may stop over at no extra charge if you get these halts specified on your ticket. Generally, ferries run all-year-round but services are reduced between December and April. Ferries also sail less regularly from Venice and Trieste to Pátra via Igoumenítsa/Corfu. Fares to Greek destinations are common-rated – from any Italian port, a sailing to Pátra costs the same as it does to Igoumenítsa or Corfu. The cheapest of all the crossings is from Brindisi to Igoumenítsa but this line does not continue to Pátra. However, you will quickly discover that the extra cost in Italian motorway tolls and fuel will offset the Brindisi or Bari route's savings over those from Ancona, Trieste or Venice. The shipping companies are well aware of this and set their prices accordingly, and many drivers reckon it's worth taking the longer sailings and sparing wear-and-tear on their vehicle (from Trieste, 32 hours to Pátra; from Venice, 28 to 34, depending on the speed of the craft; Ancona to Igoumenítsa clocks at about 15 hours; to Pátra direct 19 hours; from Brindisi, it's just 8 hours to Igoumenítsa).

Especially during the peak July–August season, it's essential to book tickets a few weeks ahead. During the winter, you can usually just turn up at the main ports (Brindisi and Ancona have the most reliable departures at that time of year) but it's still prudent to book a few days in advance. A few phone calls or Internet searches before leaving home are advisable as the range of fares is considerable (though not quite so wide as on the Channel crossings). The travel times from the same port also vary hugely – a high-speed craft will shave nearly five hours off the conventional 25-hour crossing from Venice to Igoumenítsa.

- **Agoudimos Lines; www.agoudimos-lines.com.**
- **ANEK; www.anek.gr.**
- **Blue Star; www.bluestarferries.com.**

- **Fragline; www.fragline.gr.**
- **Hellenic Mediterranean Lines; www.hml.gr.**
- **Med Link Lines; www.mll.gr.**
- **Minoan Lines; www.minoan.gr.**
- **Superfast; www.superfast.com.**
- **Ventouris; www.ventouris.gr.**
- **Viamare Travel Ltd.,t** (020) 7431 4560; **www.viamare.com**. The UK agent for most of these companies.

By Rail

There is little to recommend a rail journey from Britain (unless you are phobic about flying), especially if you end up with a home in the islands, and bearing in mind Greece's rudimentary mainland train network. As with driving, the most comfortable route is through France and Italy, followed by a ferry crossing. It's not currently possible to buy a through ticket by train from Britain to Greece; should you attempt to piece together the various sectors (London–Paris, Paris–Italy, Italy–Greece) you'll find that just a one-way fare exceeds £300. It is much cheaper to cross Europe on an InterRail pass, and, if you wish to return by land (rather than flying back one-way on easyJet or HellasJet), to purchase another InterRail pass in Greece. Until 1990, the all-overland route through former Yugoslavia was the most popular, but this remains a non-starter for the foreseeable future. A more roundabout alternative from Budapest goes via Bucharest and Sofia to Thessaloníki, from where Athens is six or seven hours further on the train.

If you're determined to do it, consult **www.seat61.com**. Named after British Rail former employee Mark Smith's favourite seat on the Eurostar, this non-commercial site is superior to any other in terms of planning a train journey from the UK to just about anywhere in Eurasia. You can't buy tickets here but all the necessary links are provided.

Travelling around Greece

Having braved the airways, sea lanes and highways to Greece, it's time to consider mobility once you're there. The country's rugged geography (*see* pp.67–8) would have made constructing a transport infrastructure an arduous task at the best of times. The 20th century, in particular, was not, for Greece, the best of times – it is said that in 1949, at the conclusion of a decade of world war and civil war, not a single bridge remained intact on the mainland, and most of the railway rolling stock was destroyed. Since then, with considerable outside assistance, the Greeks have had to reinvent the wheel – literally and figuratively.

A number of high-profile infrastructure improvement projects were planned to be completed around the 2004 Athens Olympics: the Attikí Odhós, a toll motorway around Athens' northern suburbs linking the airport area with Elefsína in western Attica; a light-rail extension to the airport from the outer-most metro station at Dhoukíssis Plakendías; an ambitious suspension bridge at the Río–Andírrio Straits, built by a French-Greek consortium; and the Via Egnatia motorway, spanning Thrace, Macedonia and Epirus from the Turkish border to Igoumenítsa.

On the mainland, as the foregoing summary of works suggests, the car is king; despite the fact that Greece is one of the few European countries not to manufacture them, they are everywhere – borne out by nightmarish parking situations in even the doziest provincial capitals. Buses largely eclipse the deficient rail system, while for getting to and between the islands, there's an often bewildering assortment of ferries, ro-ro craft, catamarans and hydrofoils. On the smaller islands, you'll at some point probably hire a scooter to help with property-hunting, while for getting about the mainland or the larger islands only a rental car really makes sense. Taxis are useful and (except in Athens' rush hour or peak tourist season) easy to find. Internal flights link Athens and Thessaloníki with most major towns, with an important peripheral hub on Rhodes and Corfu.

By Road

Buses

Greek buses are run nationwide by a single syndicate known as the **KTEL** (Kratikó Tamío Ellinikón Leoforíon); schedules are organised by and within each province, and shown on **www.ktel.org**. Services on the main intercity routes – particularly on the mainland, Crete and largest islands – are efficient and frequent. On secondary roads and on smaller islands, departures are less regular and have long gaps, but many remote villages will be connected (at least on weekdays) by a school or market bus to the provincial capital. Assuming that the village in question hasn't become too depopulated to support a service – or its inhabitants too prosperous to need one – the bus will leave at or before dawn, returning from the provincial capital between 1.30 and 3pm. On the islands there are usually buses to connect the port and main town for ferry arrivals or departures.

Long-distance buses are coloured a distinctive two-tone cream and green, typically Mercedes brand, though other high-tech, air-conditioned midnight-and-turquoise-blue models are beginning to appear. They are Germanically prompt as a rule (unlike ferries and aeroplanes), so be there in time for the scheduled departure. Even in medium-sized towns, there can be at least two scattered terminals for services in different directions, so make sure you have the right station. For major lines, such as Athens–Pátra, ticketing is computerised, with assigned seating. On smaller rural/island routes it's generally first come, first served, with tickets dispensed on the spot by a conductor (*ispráktoros*).

Driving

Greece has the highest accident rate in the European Union after Portugal, and on mainland motorways or the larger islands it's easy to see why: there's all of the recklessness and little of the skill displayed by (say) Italian or German motorists. Overtaking is erratic (passing on the right is definitely not unknown), tailgating and barging out heedlessly from side roads are preferred pastimes (plus a major cause of accidents), lane lines (especially the median divider) are considered merely advisory, turn signals seldom get used, and motorbikes hog the road or weave from side-to-side. Drink-driving is also a major problem; Sunday afternoons in rural areas are particularly bad, as revellers return from long liquid lunches, and for the same reason you should be extra vigilant when driving late at night at weekends or on national holidays. Well-publicised police campaigns are under way to combat booze at the wheel.

Matters are made worse by poor road conditions: signposting, though given in both Greek and Roman alphabets, is absent or badly placed; pavement markings are faded; asphalt can turn into a one-lane surface or a dirt track without warning on secondary routes; railway crossings are rarely guarded; and you're heavily dependent on magnifying mirrors at blind intersections in villages with narrow, steep streets. Uphill drivers insist on their right of way, as do those first to approach a one-lane bridge; flashed headlights usually mean the opposite of what they do in the UK, here signifying that the other driver insists on coming through or overtaking.

There are **express highways** between Pátra, Athens and Thessaloníki, as well as the brand-new Via Egnatia across northern Greece (being opened in stages), on which tolls are levied at each sporadically placed gate. They're nearly twice as quick as the old roads (which run more or less parallel to them) and well worth using by novices to Greek conditions. But even on these so-called motorways, there may be no proper far-right lane for slower traffic, which is expected to straddle the solid white line at the verge and allow rapid traffic to pass.

Parking is a trial in all mainland provincial capitals and many of the larger island ports. In the central areas, there is almost always some sort of control zone, and you have to have a pretty good understanding of Greek to decipher the posted regulations, assuming you can find a space. Typically there are two- or four-hour limits, with pay-and-display tickets to be purchased from staffed kiosks (*períptera*) or automatic vending machines (as opposed to the UK-style kerbside machines), but sometimes there are resident-only zones for which such tickets are not valid. The pay-and-display tickets are typically cardboard strips – you punch out or cancel the time and date of parking at the start. When in doubt, park beyond the last limitation signs and walk into the centre.

Speed limits (seldom observed) are 120km/hr on motorways; 90km/hr on standard roads (80km/hr for those towing trailers); and 50km/hr in built-up areas. Wearing a seatbelt is compulsory (you will probably be fined for non-observance at the many checkpoints), as is keeping a first-aid kit in the boot (many rental companies skimp on this), and children under the age of 10 are not allowed to sit in front. It's illegal to drive away from any kind of accident, and in serious cases you can be held at a police station for up to 24 hours for doing so. In practice, once police are informed that there was no personal injury, they rarely come out to investigate.

Driving licences issued by any European Union state are honoured but an International Driving Permit is required by all other drivers. This must be arranged before departure – easiest through your local automobile club – as the Greek motoring association ELPA no longer issues IDPs to foreign nationals.

Visitors with proof of AAA, AA or RAC membership are given free **roadside assistance** from **ELPA**, the Greek equivalent (395 Messógion Ave, Ay. Paraskeví, Athens 15343, **t** 210 606 8800), which runs breakdown services on several of the larger islands and at strategic points across the mainland. In an emergency, ring their assistance service on **t** 10400. Many car rental companies have an agreement with ELPA's equally widespread competitors, **Hellas Service** (**t** 1057), **Interamerican** (**t** 168) and **Express Service** (**t** 154); however, you will always get a faster response if you dial the local number for the province you're stranded in (ask for these in advance). For the full story on keeping your own car in Greece, *see* pp.215–20).

Taxis

Greek taxis are among the cheapest in the EU – as long as you get an honest driver who switches the meter on and doesn't use high-tech devices to doctor the reading.

Use of the meter is mandatory within city or town limits, where Tariff '1' applies, while in rural areas, or between midnight and 5am, Tariff '2' is in effect. Otherwise, throughout Greece the meter starts at €0.75, though the minimum fare is €1.50; baggage in the boot is charged at €0.30 apiece. There are surcharges of €1.20 for leaving or entering an airport, and €0.60 for leaving a harbour area. If you summon a taxi by phone on spec., there's a €1.50 charge, while a prearranged rendezvous is €2.20 extra; in either case, the meter starts running from when the driver begins heading towards you. All categories of supplementary charges must be set out on a laminated card affixed to the dashboard. For a week or so before and after Christmas and Orthodox Easter, a gratuity of about 10 per cent (*filodhórima*) is levied. Any or all of these extras will bump up the basic meter reading of about €8 per 10 rural kilometres. In heavily frequented areas, tariffs to popular destinations are posted by the taxi ranks. Taxis are allowed to carry a maximum of four people, aside from the driver.

Scooters and Motorbikes

On the smaller islands, hiring a scooter or larger motorbike on arrival is a popular move by both tourists and house-hunters alike. Small scooters with automatic transmission are known in Greek as 'little ducks' (*papákia*) after their characteristic noise, and are good transport for all but the hilliest terrain. Before riding off, make sure you check the bike's mechanical state since many are only cosmetically maintained. Bad brakes and a dodgy starter are the most common defects; typically, dealers keep the front brakes too slack, with the commendable intention of preventing you going over the handlebars. Make sure there's a kick-start as a back-up to the battery as ignition switches commonly fail. If you break down, it's your responsibility to return the machine, though better outlets often offer a free retrieval service.

Accidents among foreign and local bikers are routine occurrences, with annual fatalities edging into two figures on the busier islands. Many visitors come to grief on rutted dirt tracks, by attempting to cut corners (in all senses), or by riding two-up on an underpowered scooter simply not designed to propel such a load. Don't be tempted by this apparent economy – you won't regret getting two separate scooters, or one more powerful motorbike to share; also remember that you're likely to be charged an exorbitant sum for any repairs if you do have a wipeout. 'Underpowered scooter' includes those swarms of ultra-trendy, low-slung models with fat, small-radius tyres. They may be fine for Athens but are unstable on anything other than the smoothest, flattest island roads. If you need to visit properties at the end of a steep dirt drive, it's best to get a traditionally designed bike with large-radius, knobbly, narrow tyres (if available). Also consider bringing or buying cyclists' or motorcyclists' gloves; you'll look stupid in the summer but you'll look even more stupid with all the skin scraped off your hands when you take a spill. Hospital casualty-ward staff are wearily familiar with treating all varieties of 'road rash'; wounds, especially on the back of the hand, can take months to heal and leave huge scars. Another worthwhile and, indeed, mandatory precaution is to wear a crash helmet (*krános*); many rental outfits will offer you an ill-fitting, 'derby'-style one merely to comply with the law, and some may make you sign a waiver of liability if you refuse it.

If you do buy an island property, chances are that you or someone else in your family will purchase a scooter or small motorbike. For more on this, *see* p.219.

Car Hire

If in a group, exploring the mainland or one of the larger islands, it makes more sense to rent a car. And if your property reconnaissance is likely to take longer than three weeks, leasing a vehicle may prove more competitive, as Greece is not one of the cheapest countries in which to rent over the counter. Rates start at around €330 per week in high season (July–Aug) for the smallest, A-group vehicle from a one-off outlet or local chain, including unlimited mileage, tax and insurance. International chains' brochures (Hertz or Avis) threaten alarming rates of €470 for the same period, but no rental company expects to fetch that price (except in August). Outside peak season, at the smaller local outfits, you can often secure a car for about €35 per day, all inclusive, with even better rates for three days or more. Autorent, Budget, Payless, EuroHire, European, Kosmos, National/Alamo, Reliable, Eurodollar and Just are dependable Greek or smaller international chains with branches in many towns, and are usually considerably cheaper than Hertz, Sixt or Avis.

'Rack rates' in Greece never include 18% VAT, collision damage waiver (CDW) or personal insurance. It is recommended that you pay a few daily extra euros for 'Super Collision Damage Waiver' or 'Liability Waiver Surcharge' (or whatever the particular agency calls it), otherwise you may be hit with a minimum €300 fee even for the tiniest scratch or missing mud-flap. All agencies will want either a credit card or a large cash deposit up front; minimum age requirements vary from 21 to 23.

It is often thought that an overseas booking company can secure a better price than dealing direct with an international chain or a Greece-based entity. This is frankly an urban myth; the only UK-based company the authors have any time for is **Transhire** (**www.transhire.com**). None of these brokers has a fleet of its own, but must rely on whatever allotment – often very limited – that the affiliate in Greece decides to concede to it. Customer service also often leaves much to be desired. As long as you plan long enough in advance, even in August, you can almost always match (or better) the middlemen's price by visiting the major chains' websites and either looking for special offers, or deploying a frequent-flyer membership discount code. For North American- or other non-EU-resident house-hunters, New-York-based **www.europebycar.com** has been recommended for arranging long-term, VAT-free leases, priced in dollars, but they are unlikely to save EU nationals a great deal of money.

In terms of models, many of them may be unfamiliar to UK or North American drivers, but the more up-to-date companies tend to offer the Subaru M80 or Vivio, the Fiat Cinquecento or Seicento and the Suzuki Swift 1000 as A-group cars, and Opel (Vauxhall) Corsa 1.2, Fiat Uno/Punto, Peugeot 106, Daewoo Matiz, Hyundai Atos, Citroën Saxo, Renault Clio/Twingo, Toyota Yaris or Nissan Micra in the B-group. A load of two adults with luggage will require B-category at a minimum, in which the Atos, Yaris and Clio are the most robust models. The badly designed and underpowered Suzuki Alto 600 or 800, Fiat Panda 750 or 900 and Seat Marbella should be avoided if offered as bottom-end cars, and indeed have been phased out by the more reputable agencies.

By Rail

The Greek railway network run by **OSE** (Organismós Sidherodhrómon Elládhos), is limited to the mainland and by no means all of it. Given the mountainous

Profiles
of the Regions

1 *Harbour, Póros*
2 *Fishing nets, Ídhra*
3 *Saronic Gulf*
4 *Bougainvillaea house, Ídhra*
5 *Póros and Galatás*

Argo-Saronic Islands
<< *page 16*

These six islands southwest of Athens in the Argo-Saronic Gulf are among the most accessible in Greece, making them an especially popular choice for week-ending (or even commuting) Athenians. While other archipelagos in the open Aegean may have better beaches, the seascapes and vernacular architecture of Ídhra, Spétses, Póros and Aegina in particular ensure their steady popularity amongst house-hunters. These islands were disproportionately important during the country's early history – Ídhra and Spétses contributed their fleets, Aegina served briefly as the capital – and the patina of that brief era of glory lingers. The traditional housing stock is to a large extent n eoclassical (with substantial elaborations and variations on Ídhra and Spétses), mirroring in large part the styles of the Argolid peninsula often just an olive pit's throw across narrow straits.

4

5

Cyclades Islands
< < *page 18*

The 23 inhabited islands of the Cyclades – meaning 'the islands around (ancient Delos)' are for many visitors the quintessence of Greece. Stereotypical, dazzlingly white Cubist dwellings overlooked by a windmill in full sail, the stars of countless posters and postcards, have passed beyond cliché to become effectively a brand, celebrated in countless coffee-table books. It's instructive to remember that until the mid-1960s the windmills still ground locally produced grain, and that Cycladic ancient art and contemporary architecture earned plaudits earlier on from sculptors like Brancusi and Henry Moore. Except for Ídhra, Rhodes and Corfu, these arid, largely unproductive but beach-garlanded islands have attracted admirers for longer than any other part of the Aegean. Mýkonos, Santoríni and Páros are the big Cycladic attractions, but every island here has its unique charms and second-home-owning population.

1 *Converted windmill, Santoríni*
2 *Katelímatsa and Monastíri beaches, Anáfi*
3 *Cathedral, Fíra*
4 *Fíra*
5 *Private house, Kéa*
6 *Holiday apartments, Oía, Santoríni*

Crete
<< *page 24*

'Megalónissos' – the Great Island – is one Greek name for Crete; 'Levendómana'– breeder of heroes – is another. As the writer Saki (H. H. Munro) observed, the Cretans produce more history than they can consume locally; the islanders themselves will leave you in no doubt that they are Cretans first and Greeks second. The place attracts superlatives by the carload: the oldest civilisation in Europe, the longest and hottest summers in Greece, the most productive Aegean agriculture, the highest, most rugged Greek-island mountains, the most vital indigenous music, and the fastest-growing expat population. With a decent local infrastructure and links to the rest of Europe, Crete's popularity for both casual tourism and extended residence is easy to understand.

1 Gramvoússa
2 Lassíthi
3 Sitía
4 Grand architecture, Haniá
5 Zambelíou Street

Dodecanese Islands

<< *page 25*

The Dodecanese are the newest (1948) territorial additions to Greece. Before that, a sequence of ruler-occupiers from earliest times had left some of the most striking monuments in the Aegean, most notably the commanding castles of the Knights of Saint John. 'Dhodhekánisos' means 'twelve islands' in Greek, but there are actually seventeen currently inhabited islands in this chain, extending from Kastellórizo in the far east to Agathoníssi in the extreme north. Neighbouring islands often contrast sharply in character, for example limestone, partly forested, maritime Sými and partly volcanic, fertile, well-watered Tílos. Rhodes, Kós and Pátmos are not necessarily the most popular choices for home-hunters, who often favour less obvious, less touristed islets like Astypálea, Léros and Níssyros.

1 View of castle, Turkey, Kastellórizo
2 Forested gorge, Nanoú, Sými
3 Harbour, Lipsí
4 Windmill, Andimáhia

Northeast Aegean Islands

<< page 32

The archipelago of the northeast Aegean remains comparatively undiscovered. Tourism has made relatively few inroads, which makes it popular for both Greek and foreign second-home owners. The volcanic rock of Samothráki, Límnos and Lésvos is exploited for some of the sturdiest traditional island houses; Thássos architecture is more generic-Balkan; Híos offers unique, Genoese-influenced architecture; while Sámos displays a variety of landscapes and building styles, from lath-and-plaster in a forested montane environment to stone-built on a pebble shore. Ikaría, Foúrni and Inoússes are lonelier and will appear more attractive to seasoned Hellenophiles who don't require cutting-edge infrastructure.

1 Mólyvos after storm, Lésvos
2 Village centre, Kondiás, Límnos
3 Vineyards below Manolátes, Sámos
4 Fisherman, Híos
5 Tomatoes drying, Híos

The Sporades and Mt Pílio
<< *page 37*

The mountainous Pílio peninsula, and the Sporades islands just offshore, comprise some of the lushest, most alluring terrain in Greece. The Sporades, especially the holiday mecca of Skiáthos, have been known to foreigners for decades; Pílio is a relatively recent 'overnight sensation', though Greeks have been visiting for decades. Skópelos, Alónissos and Skýros are somewhat quieter islands with more traditional architecture than Skiáthos; beyond Alónissos extends a patch of the Aegean so unspoilt that it's become a reserve for the rare Mediterranean monk seal. Everywhere, some of the best pale-sand or fine-pebble beaches in Greece, superb yet intimate seascapes, and an assortment of interesting real estate possibilities, vie for your attention.

1 *Approaching Damoúhari, Mt Pílio*
2 *Cobbled way, Tsangarádha-Damoúhari, Mt Pílio*

Zagória in Epirus
<< *page 43*

1 Astráka Towers, Mikró Papingo, Zagória
2 Voïdhomátis springs, Víkos Gorge, Zagória

Probably nowhere else in the country do vernacular architecture and nature mirror each other as much as in Zagória, a relatively compact zone of the Píndhos mountain range in northwestern Greece. Here 46 villages are built of the same bedded limestone which soars overhead as the peaks, cliffs and pinnacles of the Gamíla range, one of the country's greatest karst formations. In this wild and severely depopulated region, bears still roam and wolves are on the increase; they and the striking landscape benefit from partial protection in one of Greece's oldest national parks, encompassing not only Gamíla but the yawning Víkos gorge, among the longest and deepest in Europe.

The Peloponnese

<< page 40

The Peloponnese (Pelopónissos) is the most scenic portion of the mainland, and the kernel from which the modern nation grew after the war of independence. It's also some of the most fertile territory in Greece, and, were it intensively farmed, the peninsula could feed the entire country. Happily it is not, so the Peloponnese remains old-fashioned, with an abundance of well-preserved historic sites from all eras, and opportunities to restore architectural-heritage properties or start anew near one of the region's beaches. Aside from the neoclassical showcase of Náfplio, the foci of foreign ownership lie in the south, where three sub-peninsulas dangle: subtropical Messenía with its beaches and citadel town of Koróni; the austere Máni region (especially the 'outer' Máni near Kalamáta), and the east coast, from the Argolid peninsula down to the 'Greek Gibraltar' of Monemvasiá.

1 Seafood restaurant, old Náfplio
   harbour, Argolís
2 House façades, Koróni
3 Harbour at sunrise, Gýthio, Laconiá
4 Beach near Diroú Caves, Máni, Laconiá
5 Orange groves near Epidauros, Argolídha

5

Ionian Islands
<< *page 44*

The Ionian islands, trailing like a yacht flotilla off the west coast of Greece in the eponymous sea, represent the country at its most Italianate and modern. A four-century-long Venetian occupation, followed closely by a British protectorate which ended only in 1864, have seen to that, and the archipelago ranks as a firm favourite amongst British holidaymakers, second-home owners and permanent expatriates. Superb beaches, a lush landscape nurtured by heavy winter rains and a lively cultural life are the main attractions. Most northerly Corfu, its little neighbour Paxí and Kefaloniá, the largest of these islands currently rank as the most popular with UK home-seekers; the not-quite-island of Lefkádha and tiny Itháki are more specialist tastes. Kýthira, easiest reached from the southern Peloponnese and administered from Piraeus, is only really Ionian by history and sentiment.

1 Harbour, Lefkáda
2 Shipwreck Bay, NW Coast, Zákynthos
3 Sundial house, Avlémonas, Kýthira

terrain and the budget constraints of the impoverished nation, Greece built its first railways only in 1881 – the last European country to do so aside from Albania. Partly because of the way Greece incorporated new territory in stages, there was never any integrated, overall plan for the rail system. Sections were built in isolation with single-line track at different gauges, usually to serve a local industry; many ceased operating or were even dug up after the Second World War. The railways of Macedonia and Thrace, in particular, were designed under the aegis of the Ottoman empire. A popular urban myth in Greece states that the line from Thessaloníki to the modern Turkish frontier meanders because the German contractor was paid by the kilometre, but in reality, the sultan – mindful of Istanbul being menaced by hostile gunboats in 1877 during the Russo-Turkish War – stipulated that the tracks should be invulnerable to naval bombardment.

With such a pedigree, it comes as little surprise that rail travel in Greece remains a minority interest. Though generally cheaper than buses, trains are almost always slower except on the recently improved line from Athens to Thessaloníki, and always fail to get you the full distance to where you're going house-hunting. Despite the theoretical availability of EU largesse for improvements, the government appears to have given up on the rail system. The mammoth tunnelling works through the Pindus Mountains between Grevená and Ioánnina for the Via Egnatia made no provision for train tracks, which would have permitted the long-mooted extension of the network from the Kalambáka railhead to the ferry terminal at Igoumenítsa. Plans for a coastal spur line between Thessaloníki and Xánthi via Kavála appear to have been abandoned.

The best places to obtain photocopied, single-sheet **schedules** for each line are the OSE offices in Athens at Sína 6, or in Thessaloníki at Aristotélous 18, or at the main train stations in these cities. The Greek rail website (**www.ose.gr**) currently displays schedule information in Greek only.

The only services remotely up to northern European standard, usually with German-made rolling stock, are the Intercity (IC) departures between Pátra, Kalamáta, Athens, Lárissa, Vólos, Kalambáka, Thessaloníki and Alexandhroúpoli. These attract stiff supplements in both first and second class; do make seat reservations, especially on the popular Athens–Thessaloníki ICs.

By Sea

There are several different varieties of vessel plying the Greek seas: ro-ro barge short-haul ferries (nicknamed *pandófles* or 'slippers' and designed to shuttle vehicles short distances); medium-sized to large ordinary ferries (operating most services); high-speed catamarans, also medium-sized to large (matching hydrofoils in speed but which usually carry cars); and hydrofoils (for passengers only). Basic fares, controlled by the Ministry of Transport and Communications with an eye towards encouraging continued residence on remote islands, are generally reasonable. However, short-haul lines with monopolies – for example, Alexandhroúpoli–Samothráki and Kými–Skýros – are invariably overpriced.

Only the largest companies produce annual schedule booklets, which may not be adhered to as the season wears on. Otherwise, the best and most current resources for checking departures are the websites **www.ferries.gr** (on which you can make bookings), **www.gtp.gr** or **www.gtpweb.com**. You can assume a reasonable frequency to the major islands from Easter until October, but some of the more obscure islands only have appreciable services from late June to early September – essentially Greece's school holiday season. In winter, they may be connected only once a week.

On the spot, the most reliable, up-to-date information is available from the local **port police** (*limenarhío*), which in Attikí maintains offices at Piraeus (**t** 21045 11310), Rafína (**t** 22940 28888), Lávrio (**t** 22920 25249) and at or near the harbours of all fair-sized islands. Smaller places may have only a **marine station** (*limenikós stathmós*), often just a single room with a VHF radio. Port police officers rarely speak much English but keep complete schedules posted and, meteorological report in hand, are the final arbiters of whether a ship will sail or not in stormy weather conditions. If you become an island home-owner, you will quickly become conversant with the Beaufort Scale and what that means in terms of shipping: at Force 6, hydrofoils stop running; at Force 7, catamarans are grounded; at Force 8, all sea traffic ceases. This assumes a northerly wind; for obscure reasons, a south wind is reckoned more dangerous, and if it's blowing, you can shave half a Beaufort number off the above limits.

Since the much-publicised wreck of the *Express Samina* at Páros in September 2000, port police have become stricter about confining craft to safe harbour in marginal weather conditions (the last thing Greece needed was another public relations disaster before the 2004 Olympics). EU rules are also more stringently enforced, stipulating the compulsory retirement of superannuated rust-buckets, of which Greece had a plentiful supply. The age limit for service on scheduled routes is currently 35 years, though this is set soon to go down to 30 years. Since the shipwreck, the worst of the remaining fleet has been withdrawn and some new, purpose-built craft have been ordered by the more forward-looking companies, rather than employing the old strategy of relying on hand-me-down Baltic Sea or Channel ferries.

Routes – especially through the Cyclades and Dodecanese – vary enormously, as does the speed of the craft. There can be stopping, 'milk-run' services and express departures to the same island, though surprisingly, there will be no difference in fare if the same type of boat is being used. However, high-speed or catamaran-type services are generally about twice as expensive as conventional ferries although you don't necessarily get halved travel time. For example, a conventional ferry from Piraeus to Sámos, stopping at Páros, Ikaría, Foúrni and both Samian ports, might take 13 hours, but a high-speed craft calling at Sýros, Páros, Náxos, Ikaría and Sámos typically takes nearly 8 hours.

The longest single journey from Piraeus is to Rhodes, potentially up to 18 hours; from Thessaloníki, travel times are much greater and a major disincentive to start from there.

Tickets for any type of craft, including hydrofoils, must be bought at designated agents in advance. Long gone are the days when you could trot over the gangplank as it was being winched up and then buy a seat at the purser's office; overloading scandals and the *Express Samina* wreck have seen to that. For shorter, daytime trips, deck class (*tríti* or *gámma thési*) is fine; there is no better seat than on the sheltered side of an open deck, watching assorted islands glide by. For overnight trips, you'll want at least a second-class cabin berth; first-class cabins can cost hardly less than a plane fare, though they may have fewer bunks, a better position in the ship and a complete bathroom.

You'll need to buy a separate ticket for a car, typically four to five times the passenger deck-class fare. Technically, written permission is required to take rental cars on ferries, though in practice few crew will quiz you on this. It's really only worth dragging a rental car from the mainland to the larger islands like Crete, Rhodes, Híos, Lésvos, Sámos, Corfu or Kefalloniá. Even in these cases, unless you're planning an extended house-hunting stay, or have negotiated an excellent long-term rate for the car elsewhere, you may find it cheaper to leave your car on the mainland and hire another on arrival.

Greek ferry food tends to be overpriced and unappetising, with the honourable exception of the overnight ferries from Piraeus to Crete. Come prepared with drinks and sandwiches at a minimum.

Hydrofoils – commonly known as *dhelfínia* or 'flying dolphins' – are about twice as fast (and at least twice as expensive) as ordinary ferries. However, they're a useful alternative to regular ferries if you are pushed for time and can conveniently fill gaps in ferry scheduling. Their main demerit (aside from frequent engine breakdowns) is that they were originally designed for cruising on placid Russian or Polish rivers and are quite literally out of their depth on the open sea. Even in moderate seas, they give a bumpy ride. Except for the Argo-Saronic lines, most hydrofoil services don't operate or are heavily reduced from October to June and are prone to arbitrary cancellation if not enough passengers turn up.

At the time of writing, hydrofoils ply only among the Argo-Saronic Islands close to Athens; between Kavála and Thássos; between Alexandhroúpoli and Samothráki; among certain of the Cyclades; and in the Dodecanese and east Aegean from Rhodes as far up as Sámos and Ikaría. The principal mainland ports are Aktí Tselépi in Piraeus, Vólos and Áyios Konstandínos, as well as Igoumenítsa, Kavála and Alexandhroúpoli.

Catamarans attempt to combine the speed of hydrofoils with the (relative) reliability and vehicle-carrying capacity of larger ferries. The fact that they are newish, sleek and purpose-built in France or Scandinavia has not prevented periodic breakdowns, as they are in near-constant motion at peak season, and thus skip necessary maintenance. Their interiors are resolutely soulless, with none of the romance of old-time ferries: ruthlessly air-conditioned, with no deck seating to take the air and the most banal Greek TV blaring at you from numerous screens – paying a few euros extra for upper class (*dhiakikriméni thési*) gets you a better view and less crowding, but does not spare you the TV. Cabins are non-existent and food facilities even more dire than on conventional ferries. Experienced Greek hands hate them, at best regarding them as a necessary, time-saving evil. Car fares are the norm for the distance travelled, though passenger tickets cost at least double that for a comparable ferry journey.

By Air

Olympic Airlines and its subsidiary **Olympic Aviation** (**www.olympic-airlines. gr**, nationwide lo-call **t** 801 1144444) at present operate the majority of Greek domestic flights. They cover a broad network of islands and larger mainland towns, though most routes are to and from Athens or Thessaloníki. Airline operation has been officially deregulated within Greece since 1993, but the only surviving private airline to successfully challenge the state-run carrier is **Aegean** (**www.aegeanair.com**, nationwide lo-call **t** 801 11 20000). Aegean has cherry-picked the high-volume, high-profit routes from Athens and Thessaloníki to Crete (Haniá and Iráklio), Santoríni, Mytilíni, Mýkonos, Rhodes, Kós, Híos, Corfu, Kavála, Ioánnina and Alexandhroúpoli. Aegean often undercuts Olympic for price and surpasses it for service.

Tickets for both airlines are most easily obtained from travel agents (their own high-street outlets are thin on the ground) or through their respective websites (you can now book on the Olympic site, but only Aegean issues e-tickets at present). Both airlines publish printed English-language schedules twice yearly (spring and autumn), but again, their websites will have the most current timings. Fares for flights to and between the islands, including the domestic airport tax, usually work out at around three to four times the cost of a ferry journey. However, on certain inter-island hauls that are poorly served by boat (Rhodes–Kastellórizo, Kós–Astypálea or Corfu–Kefalloniá being the best examples), you should consider this time well bought. Peripheral routes between Rhodes and Thessaloníki, and Corfu and Zákynthos, with all intermediate stops, are heavily subsidised until 2007 and cost less than a hydrofoil would. If you have already purchased your return ticket out of Greece, and subsequently buy a domestic flight back to Athens that connects directly with your homeward flight, bring your international ticket along to be photocopied and verified so that you don't end up paying two sets of Greek domestic taxes.

Island flights often fill at peak season and require reservations at least three to four weeks in advance. If a flight you've set your heart on is full, waiting lists exist and are worth signing on to at the airport check-in counter; there are almost always one or two no-shows or cancellations. You can change your flight, space permitting, without penalty as late as 24 hours before your original departure; after that, a €15 service charge applies. The flights themselves can be cancelled in very bad weather, as many Olympic services use small 50- or 68-seater ATR turbo-prop planes, or even smaller De Havilland 37-seaters, none of which will fly in strong winds or (depending on the destination airport) after dark. Aegean tends to use more reliable small jets, such as the BAE RJ-100.

Size restrictions also mean that the 15kg domestic baggage weight limit can be fairly strictly enforced, especially on the De Havillands; if, however, you've just arrived from overseas or purchased your ticket outside Greece, you are allowed the 20–23kg standard international limit. All services operated on the domestic network are non-smoking.

Climate

Greece's fabled resort climate is a big part of its attraction for foreigners: Mediterranean *par excellence*, with less humidity than in much of Italy, and usually without the furnace-like summer temperatures of Cyprus. But this stereotype masks a reality of quite varied climatic zones and is, in fact, limited to the coastal regions where olive groves are present. 'Moderated continental' is a more accurate tag for the weather elsewhere, with hot, muggy summers and cold winters. Harsh extremes of heat and cold and increasing winter wetness as global warming takes effect easily reduce an abandoned wattle-and-daub house with a collapsed tile roof into matchwood within a decade, especially on Sámos, Thássos or Mount Pílio. Although there are numerous microclimates (the northeast coast of the Pílio Peninsula with its temperate broad-leaf forest, for example), precipitation in general is highest in the Ionian Islands (particularly Corfu and Zákynthos) and the western mainland, where the Píndhos mountain range forces moisture-laden air from the Ionian Sea to disgorge its load as rain or snow. Except for the western Peloponnese, the rest of the country lies effectively in a 'rain shadow', though the East Aegean Islands hugging the coast of Anatolia, which generates its own weather patterns, are far wetter than the Cyclades and eastern Crete. Aside from the Píndhos ranges north of the Gulf of Corinth, a dozen other mountains exceed 2,300m, home to numerous ski resorts that are the delight of urban Greeks, though they're unlikely ever to figure in the travel plans of northern Europeans. In the foothills of these mountains, recent winters have seen dozens of villages cut off by heavy snowfalls for prolonged periods; Greece's limited number of snowploughs simply couldn't cope. Out on the islands, snow is rare with the obvious exception of lofty Crete. Every other year on average, summits over 1,000m on Kefalloniá, Sámos, Lésvos, Náxos, Híos and Samothráki get a dusting of white stuff some time between Christmas and February.

Seasons in the regions where you're most likely to end up with property are fairly predictable, though inevitably being affected by the greenhouse effect (*to thermokípio*). Spring isn't really in full swing until the blood-red corn poppies emerge some time in April, and the dates shift later the further north you go. Crete and the southernmost Dodecanese, on the other hand, are usually three weeks ahead of everywhere else. The pattern in recent years has been for unnaturally warm Aprils and cool Mays, with the last rains as late as mid-May and generally a prolonged springtime that gradually heats up. Consistent summer heat – up to 40°C in the mainland cities – and comfortable swimming don't really commence until June; shortly after, the northerly *meltémi* provides natural air-conditioning and plays havoc with boat schedules throughout most of the Aegean. Barring the odd July thunderstorm (most common on the mainland mountains), there's no further reliable rain until around September, typically a brief squall around the middle of the month which accompanies the last gasp of the *meltémi*. After this, the weather settles again for the golden, calm days of October, dubbed the 'little summer of St Demetrius' (*kalokeráki tou Ayíou Dhimitríou*) – like the North American Indian summer. Temperatures gradually diminish into mid-November, with swimming still possible at midday, especially on Crete, until the first serious storms occur some time between the end of that month and Christmas. More storms, often causing serious flooding in recent years, punctuate the calendar until the end of January, when halcyon days ensue in the Mediterranean climate zones (*alkyonídhes méres*). This is a variable period, lasting up to a month, of calm, sunny days (but cold nights) that allow midday meals outside, in legend mandated by Zeus so that the kingfishers (*alkyónes*) could mate in peace. Given the current shortage of kingfishers, this time is more reliably signalled by the blooming of the almond trees, from January to February, depending on the exact location; it's a good time to pop over to a property, prune the vines, harvest the citrus and assess (and remedy) any storm damage thus far. Once the *alkyonídhes* are over, the weather usually turns miserable and blustery again until early April.

One constant of Greek weather is the **wind directions** and what they herald. The north winds (*voriás* or *tramoundána*) are always cooling, whatever the time of year, and in winter bitterly so, though generally they scour the skies clean. A south wind (*nótios* or *óstria*) is warmer, but brings cloud and usually rain; it's also disliked for making people irritable. Winds up to 45 degrees to either side of true south, including the classical southeasterly wind (*siróko*), are capable of transporting large amounts of Libyan and Egyptian Saharan dust and depositing it, with or without rain, on hung-out laundry, garden tables, car bonnets, etc. The much rarer west wind (*zéfyros* or *ponéndis*) is gentle, warm and invariably bears fair weather. The Venetian names for the 16 recognised points of the wind-rose, given above as the aliases, have equal currency with the classical Greek ones and figure prominently as the names of bars and cafés.

The best websites for a Greek weather forecast are local ones – **http:// forecast.uoa.gr** and **www.poseidon.ncmr.gr** – run respectively by the University of Athens Physics Faculty and the National Centre for Marine Research, with English pages available. Worldwide weather sites such as Yahoo's are invariably out-of-date and/or inaccurate for Greece and should be disregarded.

Geography

Greece, with its islands, is the multitudinously frayed southeastern end of the Balkan Peninsula. The country's rugged terrain and sizeable (18%) proportion of territory as island groups has, since the time of the ancient city states, encouraged separate regional development. For such a small country, there are numerous dialects, in contrast to, say, Russia, which though far vaster, has remarkably few speech variations. As opposed to the 52 officially demarcated provinces, seven general regions are recognised: northern Greece, comprising Macedonia and Thrace; Epirus in the far northwest; central Greece and Évvia; the Peloponnese; the Ionian Islands; the Aegean Islands; and Crete. As noted, land communications were late in coming; until a few decades ago, it was easier to sail from Athens to the eastern Peloponnesian coast, or from Haniá to Crete's southern shore, than it was to go overland.

Mountains cover three-quarters of the country, most of them with a core of karstic limestone peppered with caves, sinkholes and underground rivers. The Píndhos, in particular, form a geological unity with the coastal ranges of former Yugoslavia, Crete and the Turkish Toros Mountains, also known as the Dinaric Arc. Sadly, they are increasingly being deforested; fires, usually set by arsonists, are responsible, and a Mediterranean zone forest of Aleppo, black or Calabrian pine needs more than 50 years to recover fully from a blaze.

The remaining quarter of Greece's land area, mostly in the Peloponnese, Thessaly and Macedonia, is intensely cultivated; most of the farmland occupies the beds of former lakes or alluvial drainage. Just a few perennial freshwater natural lakes survive on the mainland, more suited for irrigation, fishing and wildlife conservation than recreation. Rivers tend to be short and swift – the sea is never more than 80km distant – and most of them are dammed at some point to provide more irrigation and occasional hydropower. The only major rivers that amble along in a north European manner in their lower reaches are the Aliákmonas and Áxios in Macedonia, the Strymónas and Évros in Thrace, the Pínios in Thessaly, the Ahelóös in Étolo-Akarnanía and the Árakhthos in Epirus.

Greece is lapped by the Ionian and Aegean seas, as well as by the open Mediterranean beyond Crete and Rhodes, and the various sheltered gulfs closer in, such as that of Corinth and Évvia. The coast is famously convoluted, with numerous sheltered anchorages that are the delight of yachters. But, contrary to the tourist propaganda, beaches – whether of sand or pebbles – are the exception rather than the rule; much of the shoreline is inhospitable cliff. Behind some beaches lie extensive wetlands, which serve as important wildlife refuges, particularly for migratory birds that call in on their way between Africa and northern Europe; lagoons and marshes at Kalógria near Pátra, the Évros Delta, Mesolóngi and Korissíon on Corfu are some of the more important ones.

Last but not least, Greece is still an active subduction zone, with the African tectonic plate slowly burrowing under the European plate. This has produced numerous geological faults, frequent (often destructive) earthquakes and a significant level of geothermal activity with over 100 thermal spas scattered across both mainland and islands. The boundary of the plate-collision zone is traced by a handful of extinct (or merely dormant) volcanoes: the Méthana Peninsula; Póros; the submerged calderas of Mílos and Thíra; and Níssyros. In the northeast Aegean, Lésvos, Límnos and Aï-Strátis islands are also of volcanic origin, but that has more to do with a geological unity with northwestern Anatolia than it does with plate tectonics.

When (Not) to Go

The timing of a house-hunting visit will be determined not just by the seasonal availability of air and sea transport, but also by local holidays. Like the French, Italians and Spanish, the Greeks tend to take a significant portion of the summer off – Athenians for all of August, Thessalonians a bit earlier, from mid-July to 15 August, the feast of the Assumption and one of the major national holidays. Getting seats on transport and finding hotel vacancies at these times is pretty much a non-starter, nationwide. It is also fairly futile to pursue house-hunting queries at this time as most lawyers, notaries and estate agents, not to mention the property-owners themselves, will be at *their* second homes by the seaside, up in a hill village, or even abroad. Athens, in particular, begins to come back to life after about 22 August, but isn't really firing on all cylinders until families with school-age children return from their ancestral island and mountain villages the weekend before term-time, usually around 2–6 September.

Easter weekend, from the Thursday until the following Tuesday, also sees the country pretty much shut down and everyone closeted in family gatherings. Similarly, from Christmas to New Year, people without family commitments prefer to retire to the more reliably snowed-up ski resorts, Mount Pílio, Rhodes (for a bit of winter sun) or Crete.

Choosing a Location

The **Where in Greece: Profiles of the Regions** chapter should have given you a pretty fair idea of where foreigners (as opposed to Greeks) tend to buy property, and what the relative attractions of the various venues are. But there are further subdivisions and nuances in the process of actually choosing an island or mainland location. Where you eventually end up has everything to do with such specifics as your family and employment status, whether you are willing to keep a car in Greece, for how long at a stretch you'll be staying in your Greek property, the financial resources available to you, and your ability (and desire) to immerse yourself in the Greek language and culture.

If you are a family with children or teenagers, it would be cruel to bury them in some isolated mainland mountain village or on a sleepy island like Anáfi or Gávdhos, without distractions or recreational facilities (for example, the possibility of renting mountain bikes or scooters). We know of at least one such family successfully installed on remote Tílos, but the offspring are now in their late teens, trilingual in French, Greek and English, and actively participate in the various family businesses that have been set up. In one case, they even intend to settle during the winter in a large Greek city on their own. If you intend to be resident during term-time, be aware that there are private (and expensive) English language schools only in Athens and Thessaloníki; elsewhere, your offspring will have to be integrated into the Greek educational system (*see* pp.213–14), which often leaves something to be desired.

If you intend to carry out any sort of business activity in Greece, there will have to be a local market for what you're offering or a reasonable utilities infrastructure for telecommuting with northern Europe. The Greek telephone system has improved considerably since the mid-1990s, but there are still a few isolated mainland areas – for example, eastern Zagória in Epirus – where fixed-phone exchanges are so primitive that they can't support e-mail transmission, let alone Internet transactions.

Ease of access from overseas and cost will determine whether your geographical area is feasible for a holiday house or only really for a semi-permanent

One Man's Story

Back in the late 1950s, the late philhellene and scholar Kevin Andrews brought his wife and two young children to live in a primitive mountain village of western Ikaría lit only by oil lamps. It was then, he said, a kind of Shangri-La: the tiny steamer called in the small hours at Armenistís (now a busy tourist resort), you went bag and baggage up the hill on a donkey path as there were no roads, and you arrived before dawn at a place still mentally and physically in the previous century. At the conclusion of a two-year stay, he was properly crushed when, going to bid farewell to his supposed friends, they confessed that they'd never really trusted him and kept him at arm's length because (given his fluent Greek) they were convinced he had been sent there by higher-ups as a spy for the security police (*asfália*). In those days, nobody came to Ikaría unless they were a Communist deported there to lve under house arrest or someone whose job it was to keep tabs on these internal exiles.

A Typical Search but an Atypically Quick – and Amicable – Result

Alf Meir and Roberta Beach Jacobson are a German/American couple who decided to downshift from a hectic urban life in Germany in 1994, the year of their first visit to Greece. Initially they were smitten with the Cyclades, in particular Ándhros, but prices were already way beyond their means; 'Ándhros was full of shipowners and prices were quoted in US dollars, not drachmas!', says Roberta. Once taken, the decision to relocate to an island was unshakeable but it was by no means precipitate. 'Our move from Germany was planned over several years. We studied modern Greek in evening classes and considered a number of islands to live on. We had a bare minimum of deceptively simple needs: adequate water, trees, some paved roads, a hospital or clinic, a bus system, shops open in winter, and an airport. We researched islands from travel books and the Internet and compiled a short list of possibles. Most of the islands we visited over the next four years lacked either the water or the trees. Kárpathos wasn't even on our list, but when the Olympic Aviation Dornier 18-seater (retired from use in 2002) touched down there in May 1999, we knew almost immediately that this was the right island for us.'

In the first few days, Alf and Roberta looked at a range of properties, from brand-new to derelict, and quickly settled on a 200-year-old farmhouse in the hill village of Pylés, which has spectacular views of the sea and sunset. Just to be sure, they brought a building inspector from Germany who checked the house out (which, promisingly, had a new roof). He pronounced it a good bargain and the purchase process began with an unusual amount of trust and goodwill on all sides.

'We lived there rent-free from September 1999 until March 2000 when the last papers were signed. The sellers wouldn't take any rent from us even though we hadn't made a deposit. We could not have afforded to live in a tourist studio or hotel for so many months if we'd bought a crumbling uninhabitable dump to totally fix up. Besides, we'd brought our cat and all our other belongings with us in an old post-office truck because removal quotes were sky-high.'

Alf and Roberta had a hard time convincing friends and family that they hadn't lost their minds. 'Nobody back in Germany could understand why we'd want to relocate to a remote island with no cinema, shopping malls, street names or even house numbers.' But they have no regrets and haven't travelled further than Rhodes since 1999. They've renovated and modernised the house in stages, by themselves, as time and finances allow: first, the kitchen; next, a proper indoor bathroom to replace the traditional courtyard privy. Like many successful island transplants, they telecommute, and are both travel journalists for a number of Greek and overseas publications.

residence. In any case, popping over for the weekend, as second-home-owners in France and Spain do, is simply not an option (except in emergencies), as a glance at the map should confirm. Are you really going to travel for a return journey time of at least eight to 10 hours (not counting stopovers and changes in mode of transport in Greece), and accommodate the effects of the two-hour time difference from the UK and Ireland, just to spend 48 hours at your property? Yes, you may have snagged that brilliant last-minute £99 seat-only charter to Corfu, but if you then spend nine hours and €180 more per person, round trip, on a ferry to Igoumenítsa; a bus to Ioánnina; and then a pricey taxi to your Zagorian village because there's no onward bus that day (or in some cases, on any day), where does that leave you? You should allow an average (factoring in seasonal variations) of £250 for each return journey to almost any point in Greece from the UK. The general consensus seems to be that stays of less than a week at a time – some say two weeks – are simply not worth it, and your lifestyle needs to allow this amount of holiday time.

If you do end up on a large island, or almost anywhere on the mainland, you will almost certainly choose to keep a car, either imported from overseas or purchased locally, and may need to arrange for its storage and maintenance when you're away.

Large expat communities in Greece, whether to gravitate towards or run a mile from according to your temperament, are limited. The main Anglophone ones are in Corfu, Kefalloniá, Crete, Ídhra, Messinía in the Peloponnese, and Athens; to a lesser numerical extent, they are also found on the islands of Páros, Santoríni, Skiáthos, Skýros, Paxí, Póros, Éyina, Ándhros, Évvia and Sými. Significant foreign populations can also be found in Rhodes, Pátmos, Kárpathos, Mýkonos, Náxos, Sérifos, Sýros, Tínos, Folégandhros, Lefkádha, Sámos, Astypálea, Skópelos and Alónissos, but the range of nationalities is much broader.

Conversely, purists and total immersion freaks should not make the mistake of holing up somewhere at the ends of the Greek earth: you may become the object of consuming curiosity, not always benevolent. The gregarious Greeks, welcoming enough to short-term visitors even in the smallest village, more or less expect foreigners to keep company with their own kind. If you settle on a remote hilltop with an unobstructed view of Turkey, and ostentatiously pursue some (to the Greeks) inexplicable hobby such as bird-watching, astronomy or map-collecting, you will definitely set tongues wagging. Remember the UK plane-spotters arrested for spying a few years ago...

There is a huge practical and psychological difference between living on the mainland or a large island, and living on a small island. Large islands, such as Rhodes, Kefalloniá, Crete or Híos, tend to have an amorphous, quasi-mainland feel with urban noise, traffic congestion, a surfeit of modern construction and all other continental ills – in short, not always what the Greeks call picturesque (grafikó). For the most part, it's the little islands (nisákia), with their more homogenous architecture and more easily visible vestiges of rural culture, that star on tourist posters and immediately tug at the heartstrings. Smaller places (and this includes small villages on the larger islands and the mainland) tend to be more expensive for equivalent properties: both on settling in, when sellers correctly reckon that the intimacy of a village or island lends it exclusivity; and later on, when the limited quantity and availability of daily staples drives their prices up, or necessitates costly trips to the nearest large town with its modern supermarkets. Exclusivity is reinforced if the local archaeological service steps in with a preservation order on a particular village or island, which not only severely limits the number of new-builds allowed, but dictates what you can and cannot do in the way of renovation.

To decide between a large or small place, you'll have to form a clear picture of what you want out of your Greek home. Will you be working freelance from there several months of the year, needing access to air-lifted post (maybe even a courier franchise), art-supply or computer stores, a hi-tech phone connection? Can you not live without brown bread, avocados and pineapples, toasted sesame oil, exotic spices, western-style ground coffee, or any other dietary craving or necessity (it gets very tedious hauling large quantities of these things over in your luggage, whether from Athens or abroad)? Do you have a chronic medical condition that necessitates having a decent hospital or clinic (whether state-run or private) nearby? Do you intend to do some serious gardening, with the quantities of non-brackish water that implies? Do you want to be able to attend films or concerts in the off-season as well as in summer? Then you need to be near a large mainland town or on a large island.

Or, on the other hand, do you want to be able to walk or cycle to the beach from just about anywhere on the island? To enjoy something approaching uniformly aesthetic architecture? To know almost everyone by sight if not by name? To forgo the option of getting away when the boats are cancelled in gale-force weather because there's no airport? To have no intention of being there from October to Easter, when everything is shut as tight as the proverbial drum? To be assured of a healthily increased resale value for the property? Then by all means, go for a small, trendy island.

The *Paramethória Periohí*: Border-Zone Properties

There's one more all-important concept to bear in mind when considering which part of Greece to buy in. This is the border region (*paramethória periohí*) which applies to properties in a significant fraction of the country. This zone currently includes all of the Dodecanese, Skýros, all of the northeast Aegean islands plus Samothráki (officially part of Thrace), as well as a strip extending a specific number of kilometres inwards from the northern land frontiers with Albania, the FYROM, Bulgaria and Turkey. Crete, Santoríni, Anáfi and the Ionian Islands no longer fall within this zone but did until the early 1990s.

In the cited areas, the purchase of real estate by foreigners is still subject to various restrictions. These ostensibly arose for reasons of national security given the historically indifferent-to-bad relations that Greece has had with all of its neighbours. The limitations essentially meant that, until the early 1990s, nobody without a Greek passport or Greek ancestry could purchase properties in these areas in their own name.

Two principal dodges were concocted for getting around the law. Some people formed a Greek limited company (with or without a majority Greek share-holder) which was the official owner of the property. This was an expensive strategy: the companies had to have a minimum on-paper capital then of 10 million drachmas (equivalent to about €29,500 today); to be absolutely sure of tenure; you then had to spend more money quietly buying out any Greek share-holder at a later date. Most people, however, designated a Greek friend or acquaintance, sometimes the lawyer handling the sale, as their proxy (*andipró-sopos*), who bought the house on behalf of the foreigner in their name. All manner of codicils, promissory notes and other bits of paper of dubious value circulated to prove that the foreigner 'really' owned the house or rather the value of the house; most *andiprósopi* behaved honourably, but a significant minority did not.

When the full provisions of EU membership for Greece took effect in 1993, one of the results was that EU citizens would now have the right to own border-zone property in their own name – subject to certain conditions (*see below*). There was a subsequent move by numerous foreigners to see off their *andipró-sopi* and have new title deeds reissued in their own name or, if they were non-EU subjects, in the name of a spouse who was an EU national. Most *andiprósopi* demanded a tidy sum to be removed from the house; in some cases equal to the amount the property had appreciated since the original purchase.

The effect of article 26, Law 1892 of the Greek Parliament (enacted August 1990) was to begin to usher the system of dummy companies and *andiprósopi* out of the door. By ameliorating the restrictive provisions of Article 25, it provided an avenue for foreigners to acquire real estate without complications in the border zone. All EU nationals – Greeks included – can now acquire such property in their own name, subject to the approval of a provincial tribunal (*epitropí*) which meets approximately monthly or according to caseload. Greeks or those of Greek descent are shooed in automatically; EU foreigners can expect to be scrutinised more closely, but in practice, refusals are extremely rare.

The same, however, cannot be said for EEA nationals (Switzerland, Norway and Iceland), North Americans and Australians. They, or rather their notary and/or attorney (preferably Athens-based), must directly petition the Ministry of Defence in Athens for a special waiver of the prohibition to purchase under their own name. The appropriate division is known as the YEETHA or Yenikó Epitelío Ethnikís Amýnas (General Staff of National Defence) subdivision DIPAS or Dhiévthynsi Pliroforíon-Asfálias (Directorate of Intelligence-Security). The petition must cite Article 26 of the above-named law, state that you wish to buy the property for your own use as a residence (not as a business premises), list how much money you import into Greece annually, and state how your profession has some bearing (if any) on your fervent philhellenism. Letters of

The Twice-bought House

A young German woman – let's call her Beate – decided to buy a house on Sámos during the 1980s. In the most unwise of the various shaky strategies then available to foreigners in the frontier islands (*akrítika nisiá*), she appointed her current Greek boyfriend – a certain Lakis – as her *andiprósopos* and proceeded to invest a fair bit of money in refurbishing the cottage. The relationship with Lakis eventually went the way of most foreign female-local male liaisons in Greece, and Beate appeared from overseas one day to find the locks changed and Lakis firmly installed, ingesting controlled substances, listening to heavy metal rock at full volume and, according to the neighbours, having painted the entire inside black. At this point, many people would have reckoned it an expensive lesson and cut their losses, but Beate was made of sterner stuff. She did the rounds of local lawyers, but although Lakis was not a popular island character, nobody was willing to take on the case – the odds of success looked slim and a lingering xenophobia meant there would be a heavy stigma attached to anyone who took up the cudgel against a homeboy. Finally, one of the more distinguished Sámos solicitors – and the honorary Swedish consul – decided he liked Beate's gumption and would give it a try.

The wheels of Greek justice grind with the slowness of poured chilled treacle, but the case finally got heard several years later. Luckily for Beate, she'd had the presence of mind to carefully keep all the banking paperwork that showed she'd given Lakis the money to buy the property in his name. The judge ruled that, while she could not have the *house* back because, at the time of the original purchase, it was illegal for foreigners to own property *per se* on Sámos, she was nevertheless entitled to have the original sum of *money* back and it was to be treated as a loan with interest accrued. However, the principal would be the original purchase price in drachmas, disregarding its heavy devaluation against the German mark since then, and Beate was not entitled to compensation for any of the improvements she had carried out. Still, half a loaf was far better than originally expected and there was a certain frisson on the island as it was the first time a foreigner had bested a local in court. Wastrel Lakis, whose lifestyle had now extended to keeping a roadhouse (*koládhiko*) stocked with ladies of ill repute, was in no position to come up with the mandated sum so the court subsequently ordered him to sell the house for whatever he could to raise the funds. By now it was indeed legal for EU citizens to own property in their own name on Sámos; Beate just happened to have a German friend in place to buy the house from Lakis. The money passed from the friend to Lakis to Beate, who promptly paid off the helpful friend and resumed occupation of the house until she, in turn, sold it on in 2002.

support from local officials, the listing as references of other prominent Greek friends (who will, incidentally, be contacted), samples of published literature or artwork relating to Greece, your CV translated into Greek – are all helpful and indeed essential; laying it on with a trowel is the order here. You can expect delays of six to nine months in the granting (or not) of the waiver and probably a personal inspection of you and the prospective property by a military officer, who files a report with the DIPAS. If you haven't heard anything after six months, this is where influence (*méson*) – if you have any in Athens – must be applied. Your dossier is not disposed of one way or the other until the file is signed off by the Minister of Defence himself, or more likely by his immediate deputy.

If, as a non-EU national, you don't think you have the required stamina and confidence for such a long procedure, it's probably best to save time and angst by excluding the *paramethória periohí* from your list of possible property venues.

Choosing a Property

Narrowing choices down to the mainland region or island where you'll be living is only part of the game. The next crucial step is to zero in on a particular property. It cannot be overemphasised just how important it is to adhere to certain criteria in the selection process. It's safe to say that you'd be happier with a well-chosen house on your fifth-choice island than nightmare real estate on the island of your (sweet) dreams. Remember that, once settled, you'll be spending a good 75% of your time in and within a stone's throw of the property. The view, the neighbours (if any), the noise levels, the nearest shops and a host of other factors will be crucial to your enjoyment, or otherwise, of the place. Some of the criteria may seem obvious to the point of being patronising to the reader, but in the excitement of acquisition it is all too easy to dismiss in haste potentially irritating items that will return to haunt you at leisure.

Buying property in Greece is not – I repeat *not* – like buying a terraced house in London. Some factors apply to all kinds of property available, others pertain only to one of the three main categories: old village houses for restoration, land suitable for building, and new- or recent-builds ready for occupation. We'll consider the universal aspects at the outset.

Although the number of estate agencies is growing by leaps and bounds (*see* pp.94–5), most property is still advertised only by little white rectangular stickers with 'POLEITAI' (For Sale) written in red Gothic capital letters, by hand-painted messages on rocks, trees or sides of buildings, or by crude signs – all with a semi-legible phone number or two to contact. Alternatively, you can tap into the neighbourhood bush-telegraph by asking at your favourite *kafenío* or taverna. This implies that you've been visiting the island or region repeatedly or are even renting medium-term prior to buying; if you put the word around that you are interested in buying, and are found to be likeable and trustworthy, you'll be approached directly or indirectly with offers. Many of the best deals are initiated by word of mouth: bargains don't need much advertising, but will be passed along between parties already acquainted.

More Heirs Than Those On Your Head

Tom Stone, author of the best-selling memoir *The Summer of My Greek Taverna* and the forthcoming *Zeus: A Biography*, lived in Greece for nearly three decades, mostly in Thessaloníki, as well as in northern Pátmos where, in the early 1980s, he spotted a two-storey, four-room farmhouse with an acre of partly vegetated land. The owners were distant descendants of Byzantine royalty, whose principal Patmian residence was now a hilltop mansion overlooking the harbour, 14km away. In their heyday, the family had used the farmhouse, only 100 yards inland from the sandy bay of Kámbos, as a summer retreat. But, as everywhere in Greece, the ravages of the Great Depression and the Second World War had prompted massive emigration and the house had lain abandoned since. Now, the only family members remaining on Pátmos were two elderly spinster sisters living in musty, Faulkner-like seclusion in the mansion.

'I was told to get in touch with their brother, the family patriarch, who resided in Athens,' says Tom. 'The instant I learned his asking price – the drachma equivalent of about $6,700 back then – I was ready to close the deal. I asked my lawyer how long the process would take. It was March. My wife and I were expecting our first child in May and wanted to move in, with running water and electricity installed by the start of the summer. That wouldn't be problem, would it?

'The lawyer, his shock of white hair sweeping up and back from an almost non-existent brow, smiled at my unabashed American need to plug in and play on the spot. He took my arm, guided me to a chair and sent his secretary to get us some Greek coffee. He then explained how Greece's complicated dowry and inheritance systems made it necessary to get the signed approval of each of the property's potential heirs before the deed could be handed over to me. These included – in addition to the two sisters on Pátmos and their brother – several other brothers and sisters, not to mention their aunts and uncles, as the property was the legacy of the collective grandparents.

'"Of course," I said, beginning to feel slightly queasy.'

Privacy is paramount, but at the same time, be wary of property that is too isolated or inaccessible. Greece generally has one of the lowest burglary rates in Europe but rural properties are definitely more vulnerable – within a village, people who don't belong stick out like a sore thumb. Many village houses have bad (or no) road access, which is great for cutting down noise levels once you're established, but will just about double the cost of construction or renovation as you have materials transported in on donkey-back or in wheelbarrows over a Heath Robinson-esque system of plank catwalks.

Worst of all, if you're too far out of the municipal grid (*dhimósio skhédhio*), getting public utilities supplied can be a nightmare unless you're happy to live off a mobile phone and solar generator. The power company will charge you per pole and length of cable necessary to reach your manse and the telecoms will do

'"Of course," continued the lawyer, "some of these have died. And some have had children who are now adults with children of their own. And husbands as well who may have acquired an interest in the house as part of the dowry. And, of course, if some of these have died, then…". He spread his hands wide in a gesture of utter submission to the vagaries of Fate, Greek-style.

'"How many in total?" I squeaked.

'He shrugged. "We can't be sure."

'Several months passed. My wife and I had our baby, a daughter, and continued to live in a rented house in the same valley, from whose terrace we could longingly gaze, like Tantalus, at our beloved house which seemed to be constantly receding just out of reach.'

By November of that year, Tom's lawyer's search had turned up 22 heirs living in pockets of Hellenism as far apart as Melbourne and Milwaukee. But during the lawyer's attempt to persuade them to sign off on the sale of a tiny, dilapidated house on a remote little island that 90% of them had never even visited, several of the signatories died, requiring a search for their heirs as well.

How many relatives signed their consent? Tom isn't sure – he thinks 35, surely some sort of record for the number of heirs encumbering a successfully completed sale. Finally, more than a year and a half after he and his family had hoped to move in, Tom went to the Athens lawyer's office to complete the deal.

So the title was clear? Well, not exactly. The patriarch himself was in attendance to apologise for the fact that one of his cousins, a widow in her seventies living on Rhodes, had refused to give up her share. But Tom was assured that since she owned only a tiny percentage of the property, this would never pose a problem. Worn down by the interminable delays, Tom hastily signed the required papers and banished all thoughts of that last, recalcitrant heir from his mind. Surely she would never show up to cause a fuss?

But on the bright October day that Tom and his family finally moved into their renovated farmstead, she did. What happened then makes good reading in the second section of *The Summer of My Greek Taverna*.

the same if they have to open an exchange box (*kassétta*) specially for you – with minimum charges in either case typically exceeding €1,000. Water may come only from a traditional well or deep bore (*yeótrisi*), and, despite some recent rainy winters, dry years are more common in Greece than not. Deep bores may have to go down 100 metres or more, especially in the Cyclades, and, depending on the rock strata and depth, are either expensive or astronomically so.

Sewage, on the other hand, will be collected in a more shallow septic tank (*vóthros*) if you're out of the local urban grid. Ascertain that the *vóthros* (if any) is in good condition and large enough to accommodate the number of sinks, baths and toilets that you intend to fit on the property. Installing, enlarging, repairing or moving a *vóthros* are all expensive operations costing several thousand euros.

Learn from the applicable municipality if any new roads, especially bypass ones, are planned in your area. Find out what else is going on, or is likely to happen in the near future, around your chosen property. Assume the worst in all sight-lines that matter to you; the only foolproof view in Greece is the one from the edge of a cliff. Otherwise, like the proverbial dog and its privates, someone will build a tall villa in front of you, because they can. In much of rural Greece, two- to three-storey height limits apply, but especially if there's a slight slope to the ground, people slip in an extra lower-ground floor with the rationale that it's not a full storey, but goes only partway back into the hill.

A site plan or *topografikó* (*see* below) is required for all real estate sales; it will list – sometimes less than authoritatively – the owners of all land and structures around you. Find out where they are and what they're up to. Have they emigrated, but will return upon retirement, or are they young and living locally, with immediate plans for the place? One of your potential neighbours might be willing to sell a small plot that is useless to them but very handy for you, especially if it gives you a downhill buffer zone.

Hope for a property with just a few heirs (*klironómi*) who live in Greece (it's usually too much to ask to expect them all to be in the same province). The Greek inheritance system stipulates that all offspring (and/or their spouses) get an equal share of parental property. As the heirs to a particular property in turn die, their offspring inherit, increasing the number of heirs exponentially. Large numbers of heirs tend to drive the price up as everyone wants a respectable share of the proceeds. You, or rather your lawyer, can easily spend months or even years collecting signatures of consent or powers of attorney (*plirexousíes*) from kin in South Africa or Australia with a share in the property, or visiting the old folks' home to convince the gaga auntie to put her scrawl on the necessary paperwork (worth the effort as, when she goes, there will automatically be several more people to chase up). At the end of this period, there may be demands for more money over the initially agreed price, or (worse) a stubborn holdout who cannot be prevailed upon to sign. Meanwhile, the Greek real estate market will have been marching on, certainly in a way not to your advantage. Many theoretically desirable properties remain unsold because the heirs cannot agree to let it go or at what price. It's hard to give up on dream premises but it's best to confine yourself to the realm of the possible – generally conceded to be a maximum of six or seven heirs.

Try not to acquire anything with public easements, squatters' rights or any other ambiguity. Property that has lain idle for years, especially vacant land, tends to attract such situations. Grazing of animals or use as a bean patch, car park or even a rubbish tip can be the basis for unpredictable claims – but the favourite strategy for seizing land that doesn't belong to the protagonist is fencing, which will usually elicit a robust response from other interested parties. By customary law, if someone securely fences and uses an abandoned plot for 10 consecutive years without being challenged, it becomes theirs. Another ploy to 'eat' land is to have it included in the *topografikó* – official though it may be, the dimensions and boundaries on it are totally dependent on the say-so of the would-be seller. All this is possible because, while there's a land registry (*ypothikofylakío*) for each province (sometimes there are several), deeds and contracts on file before 1983 do not give the extent of the land or buildings on it, and even after that date are not explicit enough on that score. There is still no full nationwide cadastral survey for Greece; a national registry (*ethnikó ktimatolóyio*) was initiated in the late 1990s (*see* pp.118–19), with the threat to non-compliers of having their property forfeited to the government. However, so far only the Dodecanese and parts of Piraeus have been documented.

Finally, all potential sellers of real estate in Greece must have to hand seven required documents. If your would-be seller does not have a significant fraction of these ready, then he, she or they may not be the real owner(s) and you are quite possibly wasting your time. The seven magic documents are:

1 **The title to the property (*títlos ktíseos*). On a certain number of islands (e.g. Lésvos) that were part of the Ottoman empire until 1912, there may be no *bona fide* title deed (or rather, it is mouldering away in an archive in Istanbul). In such cases, the seller may have to get the mayor or village headman (*próedros*) to swear an affadavit stating that the property in question has been in a particular family for so many generations.**

2 **A site plan (*topografikó*). This describes what the seller claims is the exact extent of what you're buying and is useful (though not infallible) later if you get into boundary disputes with neighbours or to legitimise the extent of construction that you wish to carry out.**

3 **Notification of tax authorities (*foroloyikís enemerótitos*).**

4 **A certificate (*pistopiitikó*) stating how the property has been received, usually as an inheritance or granting as dowry.**

5 **A verification on sealed paper (*ypéfthyni dhílosi*) concerning Article 81 of Law 2238/94.**

6 **Another verification on sealed paper (*ypéfthyni dhílosi*) concerning Article 32 of Law 2459/97. *(These two have to do with satisfaction of any outstanding national tax liability of the seller.)***

7 **A declaration from the municipality (*vevéosi*) that any charges pertaining to the house are either paid up or, if it's just land, not applicable.**

Evaluating a Village House or Farmhouse

All of the above criteria apply, plus the following.

Avoid houses in the very centre of a village or on a busy thoroughfare, no matter how grand the building, unless it is set back from the street with a large front garden and/or has a rear garden with a separate entrance. Motorbikes will buzz by at all hours, despite recent police initiatives to combat 'boy racer' exhibitionism; the neighbours will use your front steps as a chatting venue or (worse) park vehicles to block your entrance; and privacy will be minimal. In fact, values with respect to what makes a house desirable have flip-flopped almost completely in the last half-century or so. Today, the grander structures well within a village, originally built by the most prominent local worthies as an expression of wealth, are shunned as they usually have no garden, balcony or courtyard, no possibility of parking and no views, as well as gloomy interiors and high maintenance costs – 'for sale' signs on them go unanswered for years.

The really valuable contemporary properties for both Greek and foreign house-hunters are at or near the edge of the community, where you often find abandoned houses with ample natural light, sweeping views, small courtyards or land adjacent and (assuming there's a road to it) parking. In the old days, they often belonged to the village eccentrics and outcasts; especially on the islands, such houses were not prime locations in the era of piracy because their inhabitants felt exposed. (High up is preferable to the lower edge of the village, which is apt to collect cold-air pockets, mosquitoes and rubbish.)

View the building at different times of the day and/or year, noting periodic noise patterns and exposure to the sun in particular. This, of course, means returning alone – an absolute necessity as eager sellers will, in the first encounter, be all too willing to shepherd you past problem areas that could use some prolonged mulling over. If you intend to only use the house as a summer residence, a northern or eastern exposure is best. For year-round residence, the house should be large enough and multi-directional enough to have a variety of rooms to move among depending on the season. Cave-like, ground-floor rooms are excellent as summer studies or bedrooms, while a west- or south-facing room retains heat in winter, after a sunny day.

Buy as freestanding a house as possible (a tall order, admittedly, in the Cyclades, where every house in the village may be in physical contact with several neighbours). Multiple common walls can produce acrimonious disputes even before you move in. The neighbour(s) may put in an appearance while you're renovating and demand that an extra partition wall be installed at the back of the closet, kitchen cupboard, bathtub or whatever is being improved (the inadvertently provocative routing of sewage pipes is an almost guaranteed way to – pardon the pun – flush out an irate neighbour). Attached houses are called *kolitó* in Greek; 'Siamese twin' or 'mirror-image' houses are called *adherfomeriá*. They result from a parent having built adjacent, identical houses for his offspring, who frequently fall out later (or *their* heirs do) or choose to sell to unrelated parties, who again commence arguing.

As you may have gathered, Greeks in general, and villagers in particular, are incredibly touchy (not to say litigious) on the subject of property boundaries and allowable liberties. This is exemplified by the customary law – enforceable in court – prohibiting the opening of windows on to a field or courtyard which does not belong to you. Occasionally, you may encounter a tiny window punched into a wall overlooking someone else's courtyard, the maximum aperture tolerated by that someone else to let a bit of light into the affected house (skylights weren't an option a century ago and still aren't much used). If you find such a window opening on to a property you are considering, you can safely conclude that there has at least been a loud discussion on the issue in the past – ask your seller if they have a copy of any court decision (*dhikastikí apófasi*) in their favour pertaining to the window.

Similarly, if a roofline drains towards a neighbour's property, by law you are not permitted to let rainwater drip onto their land or roof – if one is not already installed, you will have to fit a gutter and downpipe ending on your property, should you end up acquiring it. In the drier Cyclades and Dodecanese, this is less of a potential problem – roofs, whether flat or sloped, are expressly designed to channel precious water into the house's very own cistern (which should be inspected to see if it's usable). In a similar vein, no part of your roofline is allowed to overhang that of an adjacent house.

Buy as intact an old dwelling as you can afford – if possible, one that doesn't require anything more than a repair permit (*ádhia episkevís*). If improvements are internal, and do not affect the exterior profile of the building, no *ádhia* is necessary (but read on...). The minute you pull up roof tiles or erect scaffolding for a spot of exterior plastering, you can be denounced for not having a permit.

Innocent-looking tilts from the vertical or more obvious cracks in walls can turn out to be serious, costly problems that generally disqualify a house from consideration. If in doubt, have a civil engineer or architect inspect the premises. Very ruined ruins won't pass a verification (*vevéosi*) from the power corporation, who will then refuse to provide you with even a temporary power hook-up – leaving your restoration crew with no outlet to plug their tools into. In the case of shells or piles of rubble, you're in most cases essentially buying the site (*see next section*) – although you will see some ingenious constructions using old walls as a core or centrepiece, the result will end up containing a high proportion of modern materials (again, see below), unless you can persuade masons to re-erect stone walls, the most expensive procedure possible in Greece.

An example will make this clearer. Back in 1990, an acquaintance bought a 60-square-metre house with a small front courtyard (*avlí*) and an intact roof for 3.5 million drachmas (now equivalent to €10,300). So far, so good. But, although it had recently served as rental accommodation, she decided that the house needed to be completely gutted and replastered, and even with a boyfriend donating a year's labour the total outlay reached 7 million drachmas (€20,600). When the time came to sell the house six years later, she made a tiny profit and reckons that she would have been better off stretching finances to bag a slightly larger house in better condition for 5 million drachmas (€14,700), investing a million or so in improvements and coming out ahead.

Crying O'er the Chapel

Jack Holland, one of the original founders of the *Rough Guide* travel series, owns several properties on Kefalloniá. He bought first a post-earthquake house at the outskirts of a village on the Livathó plain in 2001. It had stunning views across to Zákynthos and up the side of Mount Énos, and came with a fair chunk of land – in one corner of which stood a nondescript chapel dedicated to the Archangel Michael, built by the grandfather of the seller on the site of a Venetian predecessor knocked down by the quake. Jack takes up the tale.

'I wasn't too concerned about the fact that the property I was buying included a chapel. I'd been assured by the vendor, my lawyer and the notary that the chapel was included in the sale, and that this was nothing unusual. My wife and I were enchanted by the idea of owning our own "private" chapel and signed on the dotted.

'A visiting UK friend with extensive knowledge of these matters pointed out that a little stairway leading up from the road indicated the chapel probably had customary public use. But since the house hadn't been extended yet, and my family of four was occupying three rooms, it was decided that the chapel would be the best place to put Mr Friend up for the night. So a mattress was dragged across the garden, along with a stock of candles and mosquito repellent, while my friend drove off for an afternoon of errands.

'There resulted one of the quickest-ever demonstrations of an iron-clad Greek rural axiom: Someone Is Always Watching. Within an hour, the invisible fervour of Greek Orthodoxy had been roused. Half the village turned up, with the sort of facial expressions of baleful, piercing devotion usually seen only on a Byzantine icon.

'Self-appointed Spokesman: "This is not your chapel."

'JH: "Actually it is, I bought it last month. I have the documents to prove it."

'SAS: "You are liar and not a religious man."

'JH: "I tell the truth and my wife, Nina Tsakarisianos, is of your church."

'This last bit was a fib, but her grandfather was a celebrated Communist agitator and exile whose family is well-known on the island; her Greek surname was my strongest suit. The tension momentarily lulled.

'JH: "Look, I can go and get the documents…"

'SAS: "We will get the police."

'Things were getting heated; I was now surrounded by screaming women and men were lining up, threatening to punch me. Two thuggish characters in plain clothes appeared and demanded to see his passport. Thug Number One prodded him in the ribs: "You – Passport!" "You – P*** Off!" I replied. "Me Big Policeman," he responded, meaningfully. "OK, I get passport."

'Showing an angry Greek crowd any form of official document is always a mistake. Sixty pages' worth of the contract of sale and supporting paperwork, including a huge *topografikó*, fluttered around the chapel. Everyone was shouting at me, and my Greek and my bravura were fading fast. The priest, without looking at me, removed the offending mattress. I phoned my lawyer and handed the Self-appointed Spokesman the handset. More screaming down the phone ensued, but the locals finally seemed pacified, if not placated, by my lawyer's assurances that I was *not* intending to bulldoze the chapel, erect "rented rooms" and turn this part of the island into a Greek Marbella. The plainclothes police I had mistaken for thugs shrugged their shoulders and vanished. I shook hands with the Spokesman, bowed to the priest, sauntered back to the house, and immediately rephoned my lawyer.

'JH: "Let's get this straight. I own this chapel and the land it's on, and – while we're on the subject – all its contents, correct?"

'Lawyer: "That is so."

'JH: "So theoretically I could demolish the thing tomorrow."

'Lawyer: "Yes, you could. But I would not advise this."

'JH: "Why the hell not?"

'Lawyer: "You wish to live here in Kefalloniá?"

'JH: "Well, perhaps a few months a year at this house."

'Lawyer: "And who will look after your house when you are away?"

'JH: [penny dropping] "So what do I do?"

'Lawyer: "Nothing."

'Actually, we did *some* things. We ensured my wife's maiden name was painted prominently on our letterbox. We ingratiated ourselves with the locals. My lawyer attended the Easter service at the chapel and spoke loudly of my dedication to the preservation of Greek monuments, of Lord Byron, etc. Very early one morning in November I awoke to the gorgeous sound of two monks chanting the Orthodox Mass, their *basso profundo* voices floating past the lemon trees into my bedroom. It was the feast day (*paniyíri*) for Mihalis and all the villagers of that name dutifully paid obeisance in the little chapel. I went up to its doors (for which I no longer had a key – the lock had been changed), where the local men gravely shook my hand. I hadn't been fully accepted but the villagers now realised I didn't intend to turn their church into a bedsit and that I was not the AntiChrist.

'Today, they treat me politely but still won't acknowledge that I technically own the chapel. Legally, they haven't a leg to stand on, but deep down, I know they're right: nobody can "own" a place of worship and a foreigner shouldn't even try to. Low-key skirmishes continue over minor matters like maintenance. We have offered to give them the chapel but they refuse to accept that we own it, therefore we do not have the right to give it to them (in fact, the Orthodox Church does not have the funds to pay the transfer tax such a gift would entail).

'Had I not sacrilegiously tried to put my friend up in my little chapel it's unlikely any of this would have happened. I learned a lesson in treating Greek traditions with proper respect – and the value of a wise local lawyer.'

Evaluating a Plot of Land

Again, all of the general criteria cited remain valid. The main specific factor to check with Greek building plots (*ikópedha*) is that they are genuinely suitable for building on (*ikodhomísimo*). If a plot falls outside the nearest municipal boundary (*dhimósio skhédhio*), throughout Greece the land must total a minimum of four *strémmata* (1 *strémma* = 1,000 square metres or approximately a quarter of an acre) for any structure at all to be legally built upon it (there is talk, but so far only that, of the minimum area being raised to six *strémmata* – watch that space!). Within the *dhimósio skhédhio*, the minimum is 250 square metres. The seller of any plot smaller than this should be able to satisfy you that it falls within the limits of a municipality, or for other reasons already has a building permit – which incidentally, are generally only valid for five years from the date of issue. Everywhere, whether within a *dhimósio skhédhio* or outside of it, there are variable restrictions on the maximum allowable footprint on the land and total square meterage of the structure. Examples include:

- on a 1,300-square-metre plot within a village on Lefkádha, a building of maximum 260 square metres may be erected;

- on Éyina, a plot outside a village just over the required four *strémmata* supports a structure totalling 175 square metres;

- on Sámos, an 80-square-metre plot within a village may have a 120-square-metre house built on it, on two (or if the slope allows) three floors;

- on Sými, a plot of 168 square metres within village boundaries may have an 84-square-metre structure on two storeys built on it.

There are further local wrinkles for areas under special regimes, which you should always appraise yourself of. Land abutting the coast is particularly subject to this – periodic threats are issued to bulldoze the vast number of illegal villas built too close to the sea. In Greece, a zone 50m inland from the median high-tide line is public property, while a strip 15m further inland from that – even if nominally private property – is subject to expropriation by the government if needed for military or developmental purposes. Furthermore, any structure built up to 500m inland is subject to severe controls concerning design and size, down to such details as the pitch of the roof. Incidentally, do not buy seashore property if you intend to live there year-round – the salt air ruins books and textiles, and makes for extremely dank winters.

Often the special local rules are counter-intuitive; Paxí in the Ionian Isles is a good example. In much of Greece, you cannot build on land which the local forestry administration (*dhasarhío*) has classified as forest, but on Paxí something like the reverse holds true. Many hopeful buyers there have come unstuck because they're bought rural land, secured a construction permit and then discovered that only plots with old-growth olive trees – presumably proving historical farmsteading – can now be built upon. We know of one cunning individual (local, not foreign) who constructed dry-stone planter wells, 'planted' sizeable sticks of recent olive prunings in said wells, and then photographed them as 'proof' of an existing olive 'grove' to support his claim.

Although you are generally not allowed to build in forest, you may be offered land adjoining Aleppo pine or olive groves. They are lovely to look at but both are highly flammable, and every summer arsonists take another chunk out of Greece's diminishing woodland. Make sure you will be able to build a safe distance from any stand of trees – insurance policies may be either void or carry a heavy extra premium for fire protection if combustible vegetation is deemed to be too close to your house.

It is far better to go for land that is flat or nearly flat, or already terraced if on a slope. Rocky hillside may be declared unsuitable for construction by the authorities or necessitate vast and expensive excavation to be prepared for building on. Plots sold outside of a *dhimósio skhédhio* are more likely to have road (often private) access, and obviously, parking – a major advantage, especially if a car is to be stored over the winter.

Evaluating a Modern Structure being Resold

There aren't, as yet, vast numbers of 'second-generation' resales of purpose-built homes in Greece – the market is still a bit young – as opposed to the burgeoning trade in brand-new developments. The main advantages are that they've usually snaffled a good site, may have such amenities as relatively mature gardens and a pool, and have had time to 'settle down'. This last will be a function of the original workmanship, which in Greece has historically left a bit to be desired. Kitchens and baths, even from the 1980s or early 1990s, are likely to be of the cheap-and-nasty variety and will almost certainly have to be refitted early on. Electrical wiring will also probably be deficient in some way – for a start, there were rarely enough power points in 1980s or early 1990s constructions, and materials tended to be poor Greek products rather than the imported French or German accessories that are now common. Buildings of the same vintage will probably have no provision for efficient heating, as local building strategies have in the past assumed summer-season-only occupation and acted as if winter did not exist. Hollow bricks and cement – the favoured structural materials – must be the two worst insulators known to man: stiflingly hot in summer, meat-locker cold in winter. Central heating is expensive and unsightly to retrofit (that is assuming that you can arrange for fuel-oil delivery) and many pre-fab fireplaces ordered from outlets in Athens have decorative value only. (We briefly rented premises where the pre-fab chimney had been installed backwards – it very efficiently smoked out the whole room and a stove pipe had to be pushed past the critical point to get the wood-burning stove to function properly.) Wall or roof insulation was until very recently almost unknown, and, rather than attempt to retrofit this, you would be advised to install double-glazing, as part of the horrible aluminium windows and doors that are rolling over most of Greece.

More recent villas may be partially or mostly stone-built, which has far better intrinsic thermal properties, and be fitted with central heating or truly functional fireplaces, permitting comfortable year-round use.

Property Types

Greece never had a proper Renaissance period or indigenous aristocracy (with the arguable exceptions of Crete, Corfu and Híos). Thus you will not find the broad range of historic properties that you would in Spain, Italy or France. Both history and nature have been hard on Greece, with frequent earthquakes,

Indigenous Architecture

If you are serious about acquiring a heritage property in Greece, and have narrowed your search down to a few regions or islands, it's well worth seeing if your chosen areas are covered by a monograph from the architectural series published by the **Melissa** publishing house in Athens (which has its own storefront on Navarínou 10, **t** 210 36 11 692). These slim, large-format books, available in Greek, English or German, cover the many distinctive indigenous architectures of island and mainland regions.Their disadvantage is that most of them tend to be written in a rather constipated style and date from the 1980s, with many of the islands and mainland towns profiled almost unrecognisable in their present-day form. Pluses include detailed plans of typical houses, good photos of individual specimens and usually a thorough glossary of specialised local architectural terms that are beyond the scope of this book. If you intend to undertake a detailed and authentic restoration of a ruin, they're invaluable for getting a notion of what the houses looked like in their original glory. Melissa titles exist for the following mainland regions and islands of principal interest to buyers:

- **Mainland**: Methóni-Koróni, Máni, Kynoúria, Monemvasiá, Fokídha, Mount Pílio, Zagóri.
- **Argo-Saronic Islands**: Spétses, Ídhra.
- **Cyclades**: Tziá (Kéa), Ándhros, Tínos, Mýkonos, Sýros, Páros, Náxos, Sífnos, Santoríni.
- **Dodecanese**: Rhodes, Kárpathos, Kálymnos, Astypálea, Léros, Pátmos.
- **Crete** (in one large volume).
- **North Aegean**: Skýros, Samothráki, Thássos.
- **East Aegean**: Sámos, Híos, Lésvos.
- **Ionian Islands**: Corfu (Kérkyra), Kýthira.

landslides and arson perpetrated during the Second World War and the civil war that followed. The result is that 150 years old is a respectable vintage for a property, and very few domestic structures predate the 1600s. Most of these are simple farmsteads or village houses serving the needs of the rural peasantry, rarely exceeding two storeys (the ground floor often originally housing animals), built ingeniously of cut stone and rubble stuck together with mud, straw or animal hair in the days before mortar. Places with a substantial period of Venetian, Genoese or other Latin occupation – such as Crete, Corfu, Híos and Rhodes – will show more elaborate architecture in a large-town setting. The Teutonic retinue that accompanied the court of King Otto – Greece's first, imported Bavarian monarch – spurred a craze for neoclassical architecture across the country among the aspiring bourgeoisie; even in the Cyclades, almost every important island has at least one example of a grandiose neoclassical mansion, complete with statue niches, fanlights and pilasters.

There are a number of abandoned villages on both the mainland and around the islands, but, as often as not, these have been vacated primarily for reasons of seismic or landslide threat, rather than (just) as part of the general rural depopulation that beset Greece throughout the 20th century. The logistics of restoring and reviving such a place, even on a house-by-house basis, are usually too daunting – and sometimes the archaeological service has stepped in and banned such initiatives. Finally, there are the fairly self-explanatory categories of rural, individual modern villas surrounded by land; purpose-built villa projects with a minimal garden space per unit; a flat in a two-storey apartment block near a beach (not nearly as common in Greece as on the Spanish *costas*); and, of course, empty land on which to build. Potentially more intriguing are hotels, restaurants or bars that occasionally come up for sale. The hotels will likely be freehold, the restaurants and bars not, which means you'll have a landlord in the latter case.

Guide Prices

This table of guide prices was compiled from information available in late 2003 and early 2004 and should be treated as a snapshot in time. Despite Greece's distance from northern Europe, prices are set to go in only one direction – up – so time is of the essence if you want to emerge from the buying process having made a significant savings compared to buying in Italy, Spain or France. Areas especially popular with foreigners, such as Crete, the Ionian Islands and the Dodecanese, are showing price growth well above the Greek rate of inflation, which most years is around four per cent. As a rough yardstick, and the one the local tax office (*eforía*) uses in evaluating properties that are changing hands, figure on a maximum of €3,000 per square metre in an expensive area (such as Kérkyra Town or the *hóra* of Ándhros), for a property in

Comparative Real Estate Values for Selected Greek Localities

Notes: All are given as minimum/maximum ranges. 'Rural' means outside the limits of the municipality, unless otherwise indicated. Sources: *Real Estate News* and *Akinita stin Elladha* supplement *Exohika se Oli tin Elladha*, mid-June 2004. 'N/A' means not available/not applicable.

Location	Dwelling prices /square metre	Rural building plots/ square metre
Halkidhikí (Sithonía)	€1,115–1,320	€8.8–29.3
Mount Pílio and Sporades		
Miliés	€838–2,100	€3–146
Skiáthos	€2,040+	€6–100
Évvia	N/A	€25–60
Peloponnese		
Náfplio	€1,173–3,000	€88–105 (in town)
Pórto Héli	€2,000–4,000	€7.50–200
Methóni/Koróni	€740–2,000	€6–30
Pýlos	€1,320–1,467	€6–44
Monemvassiá	N/A	€1,200–1,700 (in town)
Argo-Saronic		
Éyina	N/A	€15–50
Póros	€1,173–2,494	€30+
Spétses	€2,000–3,500	€30–400
Ídhra	€1,500–3,000	€60–500
Cyclades		
Ándhros	€1,000–3,000	€14–35
Tínos	€1,300–3,000	€14–20
Sýros	€2,000–3,000	€18–115
Mýkonos	N/A	€50–300
Páros	€1,465–3,000	€10–132
Náxos	€1,465–2,350	€45–74 (sea view) €9–12 (inland)
Santoríni	€585–4,400	€15–60
Sífnos	€1,200–1,500	€17.5–23.5
Mílos	N/A	€15–30
Crete		
Haniá	€1,100–2,000	€15–50
Réthymno	€1,000–2,000	€35–60
Áyios Nikólaos	€1,100–2,400	€15–50
Dodecanese		
Rhodes	€1,173–2,347	€15–50
Kós	€1,173–2,054	€6–12
Northeast Aegean		
Thássos	€1,000–1,500	€15–50
Límnos	N/A	€16–60
Lésvos	€1,320–1,614	€15–30
Híos	N/A	€50–150
Sámos	N/A	€10–22
Ionian Islands		
Corfu	€1,000+	€40–350
Lefkádha	N/A	€50–300
Kefalloniá	€1,600+	€14.70–100

move-in condition. Often the factor is much less – €1,000 or under per square metre in less prestigious areas.

If you can property-hunt in winter, do so – summer tourism distorts the economy in most places, and people badly need ready cash between Christmas and May. Alternatively, renting medium-term (*see* pp.95–6) in your chosen area can net you savings that far more than offset a few months' rent – once you become known (and presumably liked), you'll get a much better price than carpet-baggers from Athens arriving on flying weekend visits.

€15,000

• A ruined house on a hillside, in Ayía Triádha at the edge of the inhabited area of Sými, with no sea views – if you are very lucky and well-liked locally.

€20,000

• The upper storey only of a stone house in Lithí or Híos, with a sea view, structurally sound but needing modernisation.

• A buildable plot of 168 square metres with sweeping views, car access to within 3-minute walk, at the edge of Horió in Sými.

• Two-storey, 89-square-metre stone house in Strinýlas village, Corfu with garden and vehicle access, needing full renovation.

• A 100-square-metre stone house in Ayía Ánna village, northeast Évvian coast, with sea views but requiring updating.

€30,000

• A reasonably intact two-storey house for restoration with no land in the abandoned village of Emborió, Níssyros.

• A half-*strémma* (500 square metres) of land within village boundaries on Kefalloniá.

• A finished studio with a separate kitchen and bath in Pandélli, Léros.

• An 80-square-metre stone house with garden in a village just inland from Maléme, western Crete, limited sea view, in need of full renovation.

€45,000

• A two-storey, basically appointed studio cottage in Áno Vathý village.

• A two-storey, 98-square-metre stone house with view, veranda and garden, needing modernisation, in Áyios Pandelímonas, Corfu.

• A small apartment in the historic part of Náfplio, Peloponnese.

€53,000

• A two-storey, eight-room stone mansion in a village of Zagóri in Epirus away from the Víkos Gorge, requiring full renovation.

• A structurally sound shell of a house in Yialós, Sými with good sea views but requiring full renovation.

€60,000

- A stone-built olive-grove cottage, half-finished, near the cliffs on Paxí.
- A very small (50-square-metre) two-bedroom flat in a purpose-built development at Kallithéa, Kassándhra Peninsula, Halkidhikí.

€70,000

- A one-bedroom stone cottage, restored but needing finishing touches, in a village 4km inland from the sea (of which distant views) in the Inner Máni.
- A 70-square-metre house on a 304-square-metre plot, needing some TLC but great sea and mountain views, in the village of Valerianó, Kefallloniá.
- A large one-bedroom stone house 8km inland from Kíssamos, Crete, almost completely restored to retain period features, no view.

€75,000

- A structurally sound stone ruin to restore in Vrýsses, Crete.
- A large galleried studio, one of five in a converted stone building, in Stoúpa, Inner Máni.

€80,000

- A 97-square-metre cottage on Ídhra with views, electricity and water connected, walls sound but needing thorough modernisation.

€85,000

- Two-bedroom, upper-storey apartment in a purpose-built development in Kriopiyí village, Kassándhra Peninsula, Halkidhikí.
- Old house, 80 square metres on 1.5 *strémmata* overlooking Lákka, Paxí, habitable but needing modernisation.
- Restored, two-storey stone house (not a medieval mansion) in Pinakátes, Mount Pílio, ready for habitation.

€100,000

- A six-room medieval fixer-upper in Rhodes Old Town.
- A modern two-bedroom apartment in or near Rhodes Old Town.
- Large, two-storey ruin off the Kalí Stráta in Sými, with harbour views.
- A galleried studio, already furnished, in the *kástro* of Astypálea.

€115,000

- A fully restored two-storey neoclassical house in the countryside of Léros.
- A ruined, seven-room vintner's farm in an inland village of Santoríni, with good views but requiring full renovation.
- A new-built one-bedroom apartment, fully equipped, in eastern Crete.

€120,000

- A new-built, compact, two-bedroom house with garage in Hóra, Alónissos.

• A watermill converted into a 70-square-metre dwelling in Mési Potamiá village, Náxos, with a streamside garden.

• An old inland dwelling on Paxí, upper storey converted to a small two-bedroom flat with good views, lower floor could be workshop or extra bedroom/bathroom; large overgrown garden.

€125,000

• Five-room house, habitable but kitchen/bath needing modernisation, on half a *strémma* of land in a village 700m from the sea, southern Kefalloniá.

• A large one-bedroom apartment on the hillside overlooking Papá Neró beach, northeast Pílio coast.

• A 140-square-metre stone house with interior arch near Kolmbári, western Crete, limited sea view, needs full restoration.

€130,000

• Village house in Steniés, Ándhros, 100 square metres on a 500-square-metre plot, in one piece but needing restoration work.

• Detached three-bedroom house, modern but tasteful take on Cycladic style, near Kiónia, Tínos.

€140,000

• Utterly derelict but unique seafront property in Kalámi, Sámos: two-storey, six-room house with outbuildings suitable for conversion on two *strémmata* of land. Access by path or boat to private dock only.

• A two-bedroom, fully converted village house with a garden of 270 square metres in Karyá village of central Lefkádha.

• Converted two-bedroom stone house, 150 square metres, plus one-bedroom guest cottage, outside Sitía, Crete, with partial sea view.

€145,000

• A partly renovated two-storey, 132-square-metre house in the Kástro of Náxos, with sea view.

€150,000

• A complex of five conjoined one-bedroom bungalows on the Messenian coast, Peloponnese.

€160,000

• Three-bedroom semi-detached villa on the beach in Pefkohóri, Halkidhikí.

• A luxury three-bedroom villa in Pessádha, Kefalloniá, near the coast.

€175,000

• Two-bedroom villa in mock-traditional style on Páros with garden and limited sea view.

€180,000

- An 180-square-metre old house in Magaziá, Paxí, a fixer-upper but includes 6 *strémmata* of land.

€200,000

- A three-bedroom beachfront apartment, ground level, at Platanídhia, 14km out of Vólos on Mount Pílio.

€220,000

- Two-level maisonette, modern construction, 88 square metres, in view setting on Éyina.
- An old neoclassical two-storey mansion, habitable, in Ándhros *hóra*.

€230,000

- Two structurally sound but derelict houses on a single plot with gardens and well, in Nimborió, Sými.
- 18th-century tower-house in Kardhamýli, Inner Máni, fully restored.

€240,000

- Prefabricated four-room villa with pool, several *strémmata* of land and views to Epirus, near Lákka, Paxí.

€250,000

- A small (57-square-metre) four-room house with four *strémmata* of land at the edge of a village in southern Kefalloniá.
- Beachfront, three-bedroom house in Kalámi, Corfu, with small garden/courtyard, needing modernisation.
- 12.5 *strémmata* of rural land with sweeping views in eastern Crete.

€300,000

- Modern, 185-square-metre house in nearly five *strémmata* of walled mature orchard and garden at the edge of Náfplio with fine views to town.
- Modern, four-bedroom house with separate in-law apartment in Áyios Nikólaos, Crete.

€320,000

- A four-bedroom, 130-square-metre house on Ídhra, with large garden and views of Kamíni, in move-in condition.

€350,000

- Two-storey house with basement, 236 square metres in total, in Vári area of Sýros, suitable for conversion into separate flats.

€450,000

- Modern, two-bedroom apartment over 150 square metres in central Athens, with panoramic roof terrace taking in Acropolis views.

- A 1982-built, box-like 10-room pension with a ground-floor restaurant and large garden, currently operating, in the beachless coastal village of Áyios Konstandínos, Sámos.

€470,000

- A five-bedroom, 200-square-metre old mansion with unimpeded harbour views on Spétses.

€500,000

- Seven-room, two-storey villa (160 square metres) on 4.3 *strémmata* of land near Longós on Paxí.

€550,000

- Ten-room hotel occupying a fairly undistinguished 1970s building in a strategic location of a northeastern Pílio village, with all operating licences current. (NB This eventually sold after a year on the market for €400,000.)

€750,000

- Three-bedroom mansion on Ídhra, renovated to high standard with walled garden and knockout views.

€1,000,000 and upwards

- Converted eight-room Venetian farmhouse in secluded location over-looking Rópa Valley, with pool, two-bedroom guest annexe, orchard and olive grove.

- Venetian-era mansion of 540 square metres near the old harbour of Haniá, permission on file from the archaeological authorities to renovate.

€4,500,000

- Your very own 1,000-*strémmata* island in the Ionian Sea between the Ahelóös River Delta and Itháki; rather bare but with a permanent spring.

Research and Information Resources

An Internet search for property in Greece will throw up plenty of links, but a large proportion of these will be concerned with estate agencies. The property supplements of UK weekend newspapers, such as those found in the *Sunday Times*, have limited listings under 'Greece', largely Crete. Similarly, the property exhibitions and seminars that do the rounds of the UK tend to pay very limited attention, if any at all, to Greece. Consult **www.inter nationalpropertyshow.com** for the next date and venue of this major exhibition organiser, though chances are that only Crete will be featured. The 'Greece' link of **www.real-estate-euro-pean-union.com** has general but accurate guidelines, though nothing you won't find within this book.

You'll have better luck with print media specifically devoted to Greece. The bi-monthly *Greece* (£3.50, **www.greece-magazine.co.uk**), 'The Magazine for People Who Love Greece', published in Bath, has extensive property features and adverts in every issue, and each issue generally profiles a different region of the country. *The Corfiot*, 'Corfu's English Language Monthly Magazine' (€2), has extensive adverts for both buying and renting property and regular features on renovation. The extensive property classifieds of the *Athens News* (weekly, Friday; €1.80) not surprisingly are devoted overwhelmingly to property in and around Athens, but occasionally there are listings for sales on the islands and in prime mainland areas. The annual paperback compilation *Greek-o-File* (£9.50 in the UK, **www.greekofile.co.uk**), issued every autumn, is a bit of a mixed bag but has invaluable round-ups on property themes, as well as periodic features on topics such as retiring to Greece and collecting unemployment there (!), as well as repertory, where-I-spent-my-holiday pieces.

Other, Greek-language resources could be worth having a Greek-reading friend scan for you, but again they are largely fixated on property in and around Athens. Try *Real Estate News* (every Saturday, **www.propertyae.gr**) and the *Miniaio Periodhikó yia tin Akíniti Periousía*, issued on the second Tuesday of the month free with *Kathimerini* newspaper, or sold separately for €3 at kiosks. *Akinita stin Elladha* (**www.homeads.gr**) appears weekly on Thursdays with *Ta Nea*, or separately at kiosks for €1.

Estate Agents

Until the early 1990s, estate agents (*mesitiká grafía*) were largely confined to Athens and Thessaloníki and you could count the number of serious provincial players on your fingers and toes – many of whom were just civil engineers or other merely tangentially qualified folk who hung out a shingle. Most property, if it wasn't sold by the traditional red-on-white stickers or crudely painted signs as noted above, changed hands via the classified ads of major urban and island newspapers with no intermediary involved, though foreign buyers could hardly be expected to wade through the Greek-language small adverts. Times have changed, with an explosion of estate agencies, and the Greek propensity for buying property as investment, especially in the wake of the crash in the Athens stock market around the millennium.

Estate agents' commissions are high by EU standards, in the range of 2–5%. Agents are supposed to be government-regulated, but membership in such professional bodies as the **SEK** (Greece) or the **CEI** (Europe-wide) is strictly voluntary and not usually something that is brandished with pride. Another body with perhaps a bit more cachet is the international **FIABCI** (**www. fiabci.com**); most Greek members tend to be in Athens and Crete, but it's a good way to find more agencies in areas not featured in the listings.

Greek, or Greek-related, estate agencies vary widely in efficiency – you will form your own impressions with a few phone calls or e-mail queries – foreign-owned and -managed ones are not automatically better, though the websites tend to be more informative. Many of the larger estate agencies on Crete, Rhodes, Corfu and Kefalloniá, in particular, also double as building contractors, and claim to be able to deliver a finished product to your specifications.

The estate agents listed in the **References** section are known to be active in various locales of particular interest to foreign property-buyers and include a brief description of their likely offerings. There is a direct correlation between the number of estate agents operating in a place and its popularity with outsiders and the available land/housing stock. With more agencies opening all the time, this list cannot claim to be exhaustive and is given for information purposes only. Because of the rather tentative nature of certification in Greece, inclusion here does not constitute an endorsement, and the authors and publishers of the guide cannot be responsible for any mishap or disappointment arising from patronage of these estate agents.

If an estate agent is registered with the local tax office, he will require the potential buyer to sign a commission agreement (normally 2–4 per cent of the price of the property) upon purchase. The commission will be subject to 18 per cent VAT unless the contract takes place in one of the areas where VAT is applied at a lower rate. If no receipt is provided, no VAT will be charged.

Although sometimes stated on the agreements presented for signature by the estate agents, an issue can arise of whether the commission is based on the price that was agreed upon the purchase contract, either a declared value for tax purposes or the real amount of money that exchanged hands between purchaser and seller (*see* pp.122 and 132). It is usual for the agent to demand that the commission be based on the true value of the sale and not the amount declared on the contract, which might be substantially less than the true value of the agreed price. It should be stressed at this point that the purchaser and seller are legally obliged to declare the true value of the transaction.

Renting before Buying

If you have a hunch that an island or mainland region is for you, but aren't ready to commit to buying, it might be a good idea to rent first locally, for six months to a year. And if you buy a property that's not yet habitable, but need to stick around to supervise renovation or construction, again you'll need to find temporary premises. In either case, renting makes a good 'dry run', not only for the chosen region, but just to get a feel for day-to-day life. It also gives you a head start for things like residence permits, post office boxes (there are usually waiting lists for these) and telephones (which can fairly easily be transferred to your bought premises within a short time). Many of the estate agents listed on pp.263–6 will be happy to help you find temporary medium-term accommodation while your permanent home is being restored or built.

Bear in mind the seasonality of the rental property market in and around major resorts. Because of the rich pickings to be had for daily or weekly lets in such places, individual landlords or villa agencies will be extremely reluctant to give you a good monthly rate between May and October (though of course they'll be falling over themselves to rent to you during the winter when many of their premises are, in fact, very uncomfortable to live in). Properties in and around resorts are always let furnished and (after a fashion) with equipped kitchens. If you opt for a provincial capital (e.g. Lefkádha Town or Rhodes Town) while your property is being finished, you'll have a much better chance of securing a decent monthly rate for a period of a full year. Such properties are, however, much more likely to be unfurnished (no big issue here, especially if you can take all purchased appliances and furniture with you to your purchased home). For a medium-term commitment, you don't want to rent sight unseen, so you'll want to arrive first on a flying visit or conventional package holiday and find your rental in person, at some leisure. A studio (*garsoniéra*) is generally about 22–29 square metres, a one-bedroom apartment (*dhiamérisma*) starts at around 40 square metres. You often see the words 'two-roomer' (*dhyári*) or 'three-roomer' (*triári*) in adverts, but it's often not entirely clear whether the kitchen is counted as a fully fledged 'room'. Monthly rents in a medium-demand area start at about €250 for a smallish one-bedroom apartment, but in the largest towns or most popular islands, it can easily exceed €400.

You will almost always be required to sign a contract (usually written in impenetrably formal Greek) – for example, the generic ones available from stationers entitled *Idhiotikón Symfonitikón Misthóseos Dhiamerísmatos* – and hand over a security deposit, typically some multiple of a month's rent, which should be returned upon vacating the premises in good condition.

One-year contracts often require you to pay six months' rent in advance, with the second instalment halfway through the term. There may be revenue stamps (*hartósima*) to pay, which are traditionally split 50:50. There are also generally clauses prohibiting the keeping of pets and limiting the number of persons who can stay in the premises. Make sure that the sense of 'family members' includes an unmarried partner. One month before the term of the lease expires, you must either signal your wish to renew the contract or give notice – and reasonable access to the landlord for viewings by new prospective tenants.

The rent must be paid in euros unless the owner of the premises is a foreigner. If there is any dispute, you can't just withhold rent – it must be deposited in the Legacies and Loans Fund (Tamío Parakatathikón ke Dhaníon) in central Athens, and notices served stating that you are doing this. It makes eviction more difficult. The only grounds for non-payment of rent is if the premises are rendered uninhabitable by fire or flood; prolonged, unrepaired failure of major appliances, such as the water heater, does not count.

Making the Purchase

Frank Kydoniefs
Barrister at Law and International Lawyer

Buying a property in Greece is as safe as buying a property in England. On reading a book such as this – which must explain the potential pitfalls if it is to serve any useful purpose – it can seem a frightening or dangerous experience. If you go about the purchase in the right way, it is not dangerous and should not be frightening. The same or similar dangers arise when buying a house in England. If you are in doubt, look briefly at a textbook on English conveyancing and all the horrible things that have happened to people in England. You don't worry about those dangers because you are familiar with them and, more importantly, because you are shielded against contact with most of them by your solicitor. The same should be true when buying in Greece. Read this book to understand the background and why some of the problems exist. Ask your lawyer to advise you about any issues that worry you and leave him or her to avoid the landmines!

Law

This book is intended primarily for people from England and Wales. For this reason, we have drawn comparisons with English law.

Disclaimer

Although we have done our best to cover most of the topics of interest to the potential buyer of property in Greece, a guide of this kind cannot take into account every individual's personal circumstances, and the size of the book means that the advice cannot be comprehensive. The book is intended as a starting point that will enable people who are thinking of buying a property in Greece to understand some of the issues involved and to ask the necessary questions of their professional advisers. **It is no substitute for professional advice**. Neither the author nor the publishers can accept any liability for any action taken on not taken as a result of the sport.

The Property Market in Greece

As in England, there are great variations in property prices both for land and houses, depending on the particular area in Greece concerned. Over the past 20 years, property prices in Greece have been steadily rising but still represent good value compared to prices in England. With literally thousands of islands, a buyer is spoilt for choice. It used to be the case that, in the major cities and more popular islands, new-build properties sold almost as quickly as they were built. There has been a recent slowdown since then. Nowadays, land which is viable for building tends to be sold at a slower pace, although 'beachfront' property or property with exceptional views always tends to be in high demand. It is not unusual for people to go on holiday to Greece, be enchanted by their surroundings and purchase property on the spur of the moment. This type of instinctive purchase has the potential for many future problems and it is always advisable to make preparations prior to committing your finances to a piece of land which, as it may turn out, may not be viable for building.

In Greece, once you have located a property to buy and agreed the price, the purchasing process can proceed relatively quickly. The buying of property (especially by non-residents) tends to be seasonal. It is not unusual for prospective buyers and sellers to be in negotiations over matters such as the price in the period between April and August before the actual process of purchasing commences in September. Good preparation and a clearly thought-out plan of what you think is essential can save you euros in the long run.

The Greek property market is no exception to the rule of supply and demand. Overall, there is a slight surplus of property in the Attica region at present, where the granting of new licences for buildings was down 24 per cent in the period between January to May 2004; in the rest of Greece, the downtrend was equivalent to 8.3 per cent. If this continues, it may minimise the negative consequences of oversupply. The Greek market, however, is a relatively closed market which is fed on the whole by internal demand. It is currently estimated that there are 5.5 million residences in all of Greece and that one million of these are second residences or holiday homes.

Despite increases in asking prices, investment returns from owning property in Greece continue to be relatively good. Given that an investment in property is normally treated as a zero-risk investment, it is not uncommon to see a return of three to five per cent annually, which is pretty good value compared with 10-year government bonds with a return of four per cent, or 2.3 per cent interest rates (at the time of writing).

The signs of wavering in property prices, however, cannot be ignored. Sellers can no longer confidently affirm that they 'will not budge a cent'. Undoubtedly, there is scope for haggling in the currently difficult economic climate. As a consequence, the asking price should now be treated as an initial point for negotiation and nothing more.

Over the past few years, there have been noticeable changes emerging from mainstream tourism: the cost of a standard package holiday once or twice a year for a family of four, for example, is at least equal to the repayment of a low-interest loan which would allow them to buy a permanent holiday home at a place of their choosing.

The following list provides other very good reasons for choosing Greece as the location of your holiday home over other European countries.

- **There are large areas of Greece which are completely unspoilt, places where one can simply get away from it all and enjoy clean air, good food and very high-quality sea and sand.**

- When compared to other Mediterranean countries, Greece offers holiday homes at considerably lower prices.

- Over the coming years, the market trends predict that the value of a second home in Greece will increase significantly by comparison with other Mediterranean countries.

- The Greek tax system is more favourable as there is no capital gains tax to pay. In Spain, for example, this tax is set at 35 per cent and in France it is levied at 25 per cent.

What Preparation Should You Make?

Understand the System

The system of buying and selling property in Greece is different from that of England or Scotland but bears similarities to the French system and that of other continental countries. Furthermore, although the core ingredients of the system are the same all over Greece, there are regional variations to consider. For example, in certain areas close to Turkey such as Rhodes, a non-Greek national must first obtain a residence permit for Rhodes before he can purchase property on the island. These permits are issued by local tribunals which meet every two weeks, and non-EU nationals are not allowed to purchase property on the island. Such individuals must resort to company schemes or proxy ownership. It is, of course, essential that you seek appropriate professional advice before doing so. It is not unusual for the seller to offer the purchaser the use of his own lawyer (*dhikigóros*) to represent both parties in the sale, but it is always advisable to obtain independent legal advice as there are many expensive traps.

Professional guidance from a legal expert helps avoid additional bureaucratic problems. Because of this book's limited scope, it can only offer general guidelines and will not be able to cover all types of situations, particularly those concerning the complex areas of international taxation and property law. It aims only to put you in a position to ask the necessary questions of those advising you, who will have a broad general understanding of the processes.

See a Lawyer

Consulting a lawyer before you find a property or at least before agreeing the price will save you a lot of time and trouble in the long run. A number of preliminary but important issues can be discussed and considered before you find yourself under pressure to sign the contract. These issues include:

- **Whether to consider mortgage finance and, if so, in which country.**
- **What to do about converting the money to buy the property into euros.**

• Who should own the property, bearing in mind Greek inheritance rules (which apply to Greek or dual nationals), inheritance tax provisions and the Greek and British tax consequences of ownership.

• Advance tax planning, especially as regards possibly avoiding transfer tax (*fóros metavívasis akiníton*) for first-time buyers and a potentially large income tax liability the year following the purchase.

Only lawyers who specialise in Greek real estate will be able to assist you adequately. Your standard English solicitor will know little or nothing of the issues involved, in the same way that a Greek lawyer is unlikely to have a great deal of knowledge about the British tax system and all the issues pertaining to English or Scottish law which may affect the way the transaction is carried out. *See* pp.120–21.

Decide on Ownership

Initially, this is an important decision to make when buying a property, because although Greek inheritance laws preventing you from leaving your property as you please (*see* pp.151–2) only apply to Greek and dual nationals, tax rules intended to 'encourage' you to follow these laws can lead to an increased inheritance tax burden upon your death. *See* pp.110–14.

Get an Offer of Mortgage/Finance

At present, interest rates in Greece are lower than equivalent rates in the UK and more and more people borrow at least part of the money needed to buy their home in Greece. In some cases, it is possible to get clearance from a lending institution before you start looking at property. *See* pp.103–10.

Think About How You Will Pay the Deposit

It is not unusual to be asked to put down a preliminary deposit of between 5 and 10 per cent of the price of the property. The usual way of paying a deposit is by cash or banker's draft (*trapezikí epitayí*) issued from a Greek bank in euros. Another option is to leave the amount likely to be needed as a deposit with your lawyer in the UK, if you are using one. Once you have found the right property and the local estate agent is pressuring you into signing a legally binding contract, you can tell him that it is your lawyer who has the money and that you will only sign upon his approval before then transferring the funds into the seller's account by electronic transfer. This has a number of advantages. The lawyer should be able to check a contract that is faxed to him or her while you wait and be able to advise you that its terms appear reasonable and that any necessary special clauses have been included. He or she will also be able to inform you about the nature of the contract that you are signing and briefly explain its legal consequences.

Property Inspection

There is no tradition in Greece of formally inspecting property prior to its purchase. Indeed there are no property surveyors as such.

Architects and civil engineers can be commissioned to carry out surveys on the structural integrity of a property, something which can be exceptionally useful in some of Greece's earthquake-prone zones. Although the seller is obliged to provide an up-to-date topographical plan, in many cases what is provided is out of date and therefore inaccurate. A buyer should insist on having a current topographical plan to ensure that the boundaries of the property are well-defined and that there is no discrepancy in the measurements quoted in the seller's title documents (*symvólea ktiséos*).

An estate agent can be instructed to value a property, but such a valuation is of limited use as he cannot offer any professional advice on the buildings and their structural integrity.

If the purchase is subject to finance from a bank, the bank may commission an engineer to inspect the property, but normally most banks will limit themselves to calculating the tax value under the objective tax value system (*see* p.132) and therefore such a survey is also of limited value.

A buyer can take other steps to ensure that a property has no hidden defects. For example, it is always worthwhile speaking to the administrator of the building when buying a flat to check whether the other owners have had any problems with the building in the past. Local research through neighbours can also be useful.

If you are going to do a virtual demolition and rebuild then it might make more sense to get a builder or architect to do a report on the property. A reputable and experienced builder will also be able to comment on whether or not the price is reasonable for the property in its existing state. Make sure you ask for a written quotation for any building work proposed. As in any country, it is worth getting several quotes, although this can be tricky.

A very few UK surveyors – usually those with a love of Greece – have seen a gap in the market and have set themselves up in Greece to provide UK-style structural surveys. As in this country, they usually offer the brief 'Homebuyers' Report' or the fuller 'Full Structural Survey'. This is not as simple as it would first appear. To do the job well, they must learn about Greek building techniques and regulations, which are different from those in Britain. Without this knowledge, the report will be of limited value. Your UK lawyer might be able to recommend a surveyor able to do a survey in your area. Alternatively, look for advertisers in the main Greek property magazines. Check they have indemnity insurance covering the provision of reports in Greece. Check also the person's qualifications and experience in providing reports on Greek property and get an estimate. The estimate will only be a rough calculation because a surveyor will not know for sure the scope of the task until he actually visits the property. The travelling time involved means that visits such as these just to give estimates are not usually feasible.

Some UK surveyors provide reports from a base in the UK. These can be very good but travelling time often makes them impractical – especially in remote areas – and expensive.

You could also at least try to make a thorough check yourself, using the checklist supplied in **References**, pp.272–7.

There is no process of 'contracts subject to survey' in Greece. However, from a legal point of view, there is nothing to stop a Greek preliminary contract (*prosýmfono*) containing a clause stating that the sale is conditional upon a satisfactory survey being obtained. Such a term is unlikely to meet with the approval of the seller, his lawyer or the notary involved.

Raising Finance to Buy a Property

In these days of variable interest rates, many more people are taking out a mortgage in order to buy property abroad. If the property is viewed simply as an investment, a mortgage allows you to increase your benefit from the capital growth of the property by 'leveraging' the investment. If you buy a house for £200,000, and it increases in value by £50,000, that is a 25 per cent return on your investment. If you had only put in £50,000 of your own money and borrowed the other £150,000, then the increase in value represents a return of 100 per cent on your investment. If the rate of increase in the value of the property is more than the mortgage rate, you have won. In recent years, property in most popular areas has gone up in value by much more than the mortgage rate. The key questions are whether or not this market trend will continue and, if so, for how long. If you decide to take out a mortgage you can, in most cases, either mortgage (or extend the mortgage on) your existing UK property or you can take out a mortgage on your new Greek property. There are advantages and disadvantages both ways.

Many people buying property in Greece will look closely at fixed rate mortgages so they know their commitment over, say, the next 5, 10 or 15 years.

Mortgaging Your UK Property

Owing to the fierce competition in the market to lend money, there are some excellent deals to be had, whether you choose to borrow at a variable rate, a fixed rate or as part of a mixed scheme. There are a number of mortgage brokers who are experts on lending money for the purchase of property abroad. It is outside the scope of this book to go into detail about the procedures for obtaining a UK mortgage. A number of people have found that, in today's climate of increasing interest rates, remortgaging their property in the UK has increased the cost of their existing borrowing significantly.

Advantages

• **The loan will probably be very cheap to set up.** You will probably already have a mortgage. If you stay with the same lender, there will be no legal fees or Land Registry fees for the additional loan. There may not even be an arrangement fee. If you decide to go to a new lender, many of the special deals involve the lender paying for the fees involved.

• **The loan repayments will be in sterling.** If the funds to repay the mortgage are coming from your UK earnings, then the amount you have to pay will not be affected by fluctuations in exchange rates between the pound and the euro. Equally, if sterling falls in value, then your debt as a percentage of the value of the property decreases. Your property will be worth more in sterling terms but your mortgage will remain the same.

• **You can take out an endowment mortgage or pension mortgage or interest-only mortgage, some of which may not be available in Greece.**

• **You will be familiar with dealing with British mortgages and all correspondence and documentation will be in English.**

• **You will probably need no extra life insurance cover.** This can add considerably to the cost of the mortgage, especially if you are getting older.

Disadvantages

• **You will pay UK interest rates, which at the time of writing are higher than the rates available in Greece.** You should ensure that you compare the overall cost of the two mortgages. What is the total monthly cost of each mortgage including life assurance and all extras? What is the total amount required to repay the loan including all fees and charges?

• **If sterling increases in value against the euro, a mortgage in euros would become cheaper to pay off.**

• **If you are going to let the property, it will be difficult or impossible to get Greek tax relief on mortgage interest.**

• **Many people do not like the idea of mortgaging their main home when they may only just have cleared the debt after 25 years of paying a mortgage.**

• **Some economists argue that, in financial terms, debts incurred to buy assets should be secured against the assets bought and that assets in one country should be funded by borrowings in that same country.**

In general, a UK mortgage is generally the better option for people who need to borrow relatively small sums and who will be repaying the mortgage out of UK income.

Greek Mortgages (*Stegástika Dhánia*)

This type of mortgage is one taken out over your Greek property, either from a Greek bank or a British bank that has registered and does business there.

The basic concept of a mortgage is the same in Greece as it is in the UK or Scotland. It is a loan secured against land or buildings. Just as in England, if you do not keep up the payments, the bank will repossess your property. In Greece, if they do this, they will obtain a judicial order for the forced sale of the property at public auction.

All the major Greek banks offer various types of mortgages. In most cases, the basis is a capital and interest repayment taken out over a number of years. The purpose of the loan is the purchase, building, extension or repair of a residence, as well as the purchase of a plot of land that is viable for building. As in the UK, the loan may be at a variable rate of interest or a fixed rate for a number of years.

The term of the loan varies from bank to bank, and whether the loan is at a variable or fixed rate of interest, and may be offered for terms up to 30 years with the proviso that the borrower has not reached the age of 70 by that time. The amount of the loan can be 100 per cent of the value that is declared on the purchase contract and/or the cost of the building or repairs, etc. Furthermore, the amount of the loan can reach 100 per cent of the commercial value of the property involved.

In all cases, the loan depends on the personal or family income and credit-worthiness of the applicant. The repayment of the loan is by monthly payments.

Main Differences Between English and Greek Mortgages

- Greek mortgages are almost always created on a repayment basis. That is to say, the loan and the interest on it are both gradually repaid by equal instalments over the period of the mortgage. Endowment, pension and interest-only mortgages are not known in Greece.

- The formalities involved in making the application, signing the contract subject to a mortgage and completing the transaction are more complex and stricter than in the UK.

- The way of calculating the amount the bank will lend you is different from in the UK. As you would expect, there are detailed differences from bank to bank but most banks are not allowed to lend you more than an amount the monthly payments of which amount to 30–33 per cent of your net disposable income (see 'How Much Can I Borrow').

• There will usually be a minimum loan (say £20,000) and some banks will not lend at all on property less than a certain value. Some will not lend in rural areas.

• The paperwork on completion of the mortgage is different. There is often no separate mortgage deed. Instead the existence of the mortgage is mentioned in your purchase deed. It is prepared by and signed in front of a notary public.

How Much Can I Borrow?

Different banks have slightly different rules and ways of interpreting the rules. Generally, they will lend you an amount giving rise to monthly payments of up to about 30–33 per cent of your net available monthly income.

The starting point is your net monthly salary after deduction of tax and National Insurance but before deduction of voluntary payments, such as to savings schemes. If there are two applicants, the two salaries are taken into account. If you have investment income or a pension, this will be taken into account. If you are buying a property with a track record of letting income, this may be taken into account. If you are over 65, your earnings will not usually be taken into account but your pension and investment income will be. If your circumstances are unusual, seek advice, as approaching a different bank may produce a different result.

e.g.	Mr Smith – net salary per month	£3,000
	Mrs Smith – net salary per month	£2,000
	Investment income per month	£1,000
	Total income taken into account	£6,000 per month

The maximum loan repayments permitted will be 30 per cent of this sum, minus your existing fixed commitments, i.e. £1,800 per month.

Regular monthly commitments would include mortgage payments on your main and other properties, any rent paid, HP commitments and maintenance (family financial provision) payments. Repayments on credit cards do not count. If there are two applicants, both of their commitments are taken into account.

e.g.	Mr and Mrs Smith – mortgage on main home	£750
	Mrs Smith – HP on car	£200
	Total pre-existing outgoings	£950 per month

Maximum loan repayment permitted = £1,800 – £950 = £850 per month.

If you are buying a property for investment (rental), the bank may treat this as commercial lending and apply different criteria.

Applications for a Greek Mortgage

Although the information needed varies from bank to bank, there are a number of core documents that are required:

- The bank's application form.
- A photocopy of the applicant's identification card or passport.
- For the self-employed, tax statements (*ekkatharistiká simiómata*) from the tax office for the past three years.
- For persons employed or retired: a) tax statements for the past year and b) a computer-generated receipt for the salary or pension in the past month or a certificate from your employer regarding salary which will confirm the length of employment, gross and net remunerations and the fact that no part of your salary is being held back for the repayment of another loan.
- A sworn declaration (*ypéfthyni dhílosi*) by the applicant that there is no other outstanding debt to other banks or lending institutions in connection with other loans or guarantees.

If the loan is for the purchase of a property, then the bank will also need the following documents:

- A copy of the vendor's purchase title (*symvóleo ktiséos*).
- Certificates of land registration, ownership (*pistopiitiká metagrafís*) and a certificate that there are no encumbrances or any other claims (*pistopiitikó váron ke katskhéseon*) against the vendor's name and that of his predecessors in title for loans up to the amount of €30,000. For loans over €30,000 and up to €150,000, the title documents and certificates which cover the period of the previous 10 years. For loans over €150,000 titles and certificates which cover the previous 20 years.
- A copy of the planning permission licence (*ádhia ikodhomíseos*) together with architect's plans (if applicable).
- For apartments: a copy of the act of horizontal ownership (*sýstasi orizóndiou idhioktisías*) and a certificate of registration.
- A copy of the National Land Registry certification (KAEK), if applicable.
- For land viable for building – a topographical plan with an endorsement by a civil engineer or architect that the land is viable for building.

Most banks will only give an offer of a mortgage once the property subject to the loan has been identified by the borrower. Variable interest rates at present offered by banks come in at around 5.25 per cent, while many banks offering fixed rates of interest for a period of one, two, three, five, 10 or 20 years come in at rates of between 3.75 per cent through to 6.7 per cent, depending on the length of the loan.

The Mortgage Offer

Allow four weeks from the date of your application to receiving a written mortgage offer as getting the information to the bank sometimes takes a while. It can take longer than four weeks. Once you receive the offer, you will generally have 30 days from receipt in which to accept it, after which time it will lapse. Have the mortgage explained in detail by your lawyer.

The Cost of Taking Out a Mortgage

The cost of setting up the loan depends on the amount taken out, but most banks usually have a minimum charge of €450 at the time of writing. The cost of the bank charges for taking out a loan will vary from bank to bank but are usually between 1 and 2 per cent on the value of the loan. This does not include the Land Registry fee for the registration of the charge securing the loan.

The loans are granted following the registration of a mortgage on the property which is the subject of the loan or against another property belonging to the borrower for a sum equal to 125–140 per cent on the sum of the loan. A number of banks will agree to the registration of a preliminary notice of mortgage (*prosimiósi*), which incurs a smaller land registration fee (0.8 per cent) compared to that of a standard mortgage charge.

You will probably be required to take out **life insurance** for the amount of the loan, though you may be allowed to use a suitable existing policy. You may be required to have a medical. You will be required to **insure the property** and produce proof of insurance – but you would probably have done this anyway.

Mortgaging Your Greek Property: A Summary

Advantages

• **You will pay Greek interest rates which, at the time of writing, are slightly lower than UK rates.** Make sure you compare the overall cost of the two mortgages. Crude rates (which, in any case, may not be comparable as they are calculated differently in the two countries) do not tell the whole tale. What is the total monthly cost of each mortgage, including life insurance and all extras? What is the total amount required to repay the loan, including all fees and charges?

• **You will be able to get tax relief on mortgage interest if you can prove residence in Greece.**

• **The loan repayments will usually be in euros.** This will be useful if you are letting the property and the funds with which to repay the mortgage are being generated in Greece.

Disadvantages

• **The loan will probably be relatively expensive to set up in comparison with a UK loan.**

• **You will incur further fees to clear the record of the mortgage from your title once it has been paid off.**

• **The loan repayments will usually be in euros.** If the funds to repay the mortgage are coming from your sterling earnings, then the amount you have to pay will be affected by fluctuations in exchange rates between sterling and the euro. If sterling falls in value, then your debt as a percentage of the value of the property increases in sterling terms. Your property will be worth more in sterling terms but your mortgage will also have increased in value.

• **You will be unfamiliar with dealing with Greek mortgages and all correspondence and documentation will be in Greek.**

• **Usually only repayment mortgages are available (mortgages where you pay off the capital and interest over the period of the mortgage).**

Generally speaking, Greek euro mortgages will suit people who intend to reside in Greece permanently and who intend to repay the mortgage from income generated in Greece, for example from lettings, or from working.

Saving Money on Your Euro Repayments

Your mortgage will usually be paid off directly from your Greek bank account. Unless you have a substantial rental or other income in euros, you will need to supply your Greek bank account with sterling. Every time you send a payment from the UK to Greece, you will face two separate costs – the cost of the exchange and the cost of the transfer.

There are steps that you can take to keep check on these charges. As far as the exchange rate is concerned, you should ask to receive the so-called 'commercial rate', which is a better rate of exchange than the tourist rate which is published in the papers. Some banks will only apply the commercial rate to larger amounts of transfers so it may be advisable to send funds to Greece three or four times per year as opposed to every month. This has the added advantage of reducing the transfer costs. As far as the exchange rate is concerned, it is a matter of common knowledge that Greek banks offer a substantially better rate of exchange for sterling if the exchange is carried out by a Greek bank than by an equivalent UK bank. In other words, the bank mandate which you will be giving to your UK bank should ensure that the funds are transmitted in sterling and not changed into euros prior to their transfer. The Greek bank then will, upon receipt, exchange the funds into euros. Over and above the exchange rate benefits, the bank will also issue a certificate confirming the import of a foreign currency into Greece (commonly known as a pink slip). This registers the amount as declared income and therefore does not raise any income tax liability, which is very important (*see* box, p.127).

Foreign Currency Mortgages

It is possible to mortgage your home in Greece borrowing not euros but sterling or US dollars. The rates of interest will be sterling rates not euro rates and this, at the present, means that you will be paying more. Also the rates that Greek banks offer are not as competitive as those you could obtain if you remortgaged your property in the UK. In some cases, the administrative and legal costs will be substantially more than those raised on a euro mortgage.

Who Should Own the Property?

As in the UK, property ownership can be structured in a variety of ways, with the right structure potentially saving you thousands of pounds of tax and expenses during your lifetime and upon your death. In Greece, unlike some continental systems, such as France, total control of how one disposes of property after death is not restricted for foreign nationals who own property in Greece, though Greek and dual nationals do face restrictions. However, not leaving your property to your offspring or spouse can incur significant taxation where inheritance tax is concerned; *see* pp.151–3 and 147–9. You should therefore take professional advice as to which option suits you best.

Sole Ownership

In certain limited situations, it may be worthwhile to put the property in the name of only one person. This is advisable if your spouse runs a high-risk business with uncertain future prospects or is of an advanced age and you are far younger. Another reason might be for tax purposes – if you envisage letting the property and want all of the income allocated to your tax-free allowance.

Joint Ownership

Joint ownership is when two people purchase a property together, usually in both their names. There is only one way of achieving this in Greece. You purchase indivisibly or *ex adiaretou* and normally in equal shares. The result is joint ownership of an indivisible whole. This is similar to the English concept of a tenancy-in-common. Upon the death of one of the co-owners, whether the Greek law of intestacy or the English rules apply depends on the nationality of the persons involved. Upon your death, your portion will be disposed of in accordance with your last will and testament or, if there is no last will and testament, in accordance with the English rules of succession (intestacy). Unlike joint tenancies under English law or in the case of some other continental systems, your indivisible share does not pass automatically to the surviving joint owner upon your death but rather to your beneficiaries. Those beneficiaries or successors will be liable for Greek inheritance tax on the value of your share. The amount of tax payable is regulated by the closeness of their relationship to you. For example, if you decide to leave your property to your children, they will pay far less tax than if you decided to leave your share of the property to a partner to whom you were not legally married at the time of your death.

Adding Your Children to the Title

If you give your children the money to buy part of the property and therefore place them on the title at the time of the purchase, you may save a substantial amount of inheritance tax in the future. On your death, your share of the property will be smaller and only that portion will be taxable. Its value may be so negligible as to fall within the tax-free threshold of inheritance tax – the result will be a tax-free inheritance for your survivors! The drawbacks are that if, for example, you fall out with your children, they can insist on an enforced sale of the property and receive their share from proceeds of sale.

Putting the Property in the Name of Your Children Only

Under the Greek legal system there is a mechanism whereby legal ownership can be placed in the name of your children while you and your partner retain a life interest on the use of the property (*epikarpía*). This is the right to use the property during your lifetime and for all the proceeds which may be generated by that property to be yours during your lifetime. Only upon your death will the property pass to the heirs in full. This device not only protects your right to use the property and benefit from the income it generates but can also save on large amounts of income tax or inheritance tax. If, however, you need to dispose of the property sooner, you must first obtain the agreement of the legal owners, who will be entitled to the proceeds of the sale.

Greek Limited Company

For some people, owning a property via a limited company can be a very attractive option. You own company shares, not a property in Greece. If you put the house up for sale, you will be selling the shares of a company rather than transferring the ownership of the property itself. It is, however, very unusual for this mechanism to be employed, because of the associated costs of owning and running a company.

Buying through a Greek company gives rise to a host of potential problems as well as benefits. The plan needs to be studied closely by your advisers so that you can decide whether or not it makes sense in the short, medium and long term.

Ownership via a Greek company will mean that the income from letting the property is taxed in the way usual for companies – basically, you pay tax only on the profit made – rather than at the flat rate applicable in the case of an individual owner who is not tax resident in Greece. This can reduce your tax bill. Ownership in the form of a company also gives rise to certain expenses – accountancy, filing tax returns, etc. On the other hand, it may be advisable if, for example, you will be using the property to generate income, and especially if it is one of several properties owned.

Set-up costs are not insubstantial and there will be annual management and maintenance costs, but savings from allowances set off for income tax purposes and later inheritance taxes can outweigh initial cost disadvantages.

There are different company entities available under Greek law, each one with its own plus points and drawbacks. Which one is likely to be suitable if you choose the company route of ownership will depend on your circumstances.

The first type of company is the **O.E. company** (*omórythmi etería*), which loosely translates as a **general partnership company**. The partners are responsible to each other in all their assets, including personal gains from the activities and debts relating to the company. They are also liable to imprisonment if they are unable to pay their creditors.

Another form of company is the **limited partnership** or **E.E.** (*eterórythmi etería*), where at least one of the partners is responsible for the extent of all his assets from the activities and debts relating to the company and is therefore liable to imprisonment if he is unable to pay off the debts.

Most medium to large commercial enterprises use the **limited company** or **A.E.** (*anónymi etería*), which is similar to S.A. companies in continental Europe. Such companies are share-based and shareholders are responsible only in proportion to their shareholding. They vote on the management of the company, etc. according to the number of shares held. In the case of liquidation, they are only responsible for the amount they paid for their shares; in the worst-case scenario, their shares would lose all their value.

A halfway house between general partnerships and limited partnerships and companies is the **limited liability company** or **E.P.E.** (*etería periorisménis efthýnis*). Its main advantage is the low initial capital required for its incorporation and the limited responsibility of the company owners for the amount of deposited capital.

All of the above corporate entities are subject to certain formalities for their incorporation. Although it is beyond the scope of this book to go into great detail regarding the prerequisites and the procedures involved, the incorporation of a limited liability company or E.P.E. will be briefly discussed here, as this is the one most likely to suit an English buyer contemplating ownership by way of a company.

The prerequisites for setting up a limited liability company are as follows:

- **The minimum capital required is approximately €18,000 which must initially be deposited in whole at the time of signature of the articles of incorporation of the company.**
- **This type of company can generally be founded only by one person.**

The basic characteristics of such a company are:

- Capital control by way of contributory shares, each of which consists of a company share which cannot be less than approximately €30.
- Certain rules regarding publicity at the time of its incorporation but also during the term of its existence.
- Limited life of the company.
- Limited responsibility of the owners.
- Decision-taking by simple majority when at least half or all the capital of the company is represented.
- Organs of control to safeguard the owners' General Assembly and that of the management.

The major steps in the formation of such a company are as follows:

- Drawing up the articles of incorporation.
- Getting the company's trading name approved.
- Signing the articles of incorporation before a notary public and a lawyer. The lawyer will charge one per cent for the first €14,673 of capital and 0.5 per cent thereafter for the remaining amount.
- Filing a copy of the articles with the Chamber of Commerce.
- Paying a one per cent tax on the company's capital to the tax authority governing the area where the company will be located within 15 days of signing the articles.
- Paying fees on 0.5 and 1 per cent of the capital of the company into the lawyer's fund and his insurance fund.
- Submitting the articles of incorporation to the Court of First Instance for approval, within one month of signing.
- Waiting for the publication in the gazette issued by the government publication office, the public authority which issues a decision approving the articles and corporation.
- Registering the company with the local Chamber of Commerce within two months of its incorporation.

A commencement of trading must be filed with the tax authority within 15 days of the public authority's approving the company's incorporation.

UK Company

It is rare for a purchase through a UK company to make sense for a holiday home or single investment property. This is despite the fact that the ability to pay for the property with the company's money without drawing it out of the company and paying UK tax on the dividend is attractive. Once again, you need expert advice from someone familiar with the law of both countries.

Offshore (Tax Haven) Company

These types of companies were widely used in the past but have recently incurred a special tax of three per cent on their objective value (*andikemeniki axía*) per annum. This compensates the Greek state for all the inheritance, transfer and large property tax which it would otherwise have received from the owners of these properties.

The Process of Buying a Property in Greece

The standard procedure for buying property in Greece appears at a first glance to be similar to that in the UK but this is a false impression. The procedure is actually quite different and it is therefore advisable to seek professional legal advice before proceeding further.

The Law

The main legal provisions relating to property law are found in the Greek Civil Code (*Astykós Kódhikas*) which was based on the French code but has since been modified. It declares that all non-Greek nationals be treated in the same manner as Greek nationals as far as the law is concerned.

Greek law divides property into two categories – movables and immovables. The basis of ownership and the transfer of ownership rights depend on the category in question. The distinction is similar to the English concept of real and personal property but is not identical.

Greek law must always govern the sale and purchase of a property located in Greece. The form of land ownership is similar to the concept of freehold. It is possible to own the buildings or even part of a building on a piece of land under a different law to the land itself. This is of particular relevance in the case of flats which are owned with full ownership similar to the English concept of freehold.

Where two or more people have a piece of land or other property in common they will always own it in undivided shares. The piece of land is not physically divided between them. Each owner may, in theory, sell his share without the consent of the other.

Greek Legal Concepts and Terms about Property (Immovables)

In accordance with Article 948 of the Greek Civil Code, an 'immovable' is the soil and its component parts, such as buildings. It therefore follows that a movable is anything that is not an immovable. 'Soil' in this case means a defined and unique part of the earth's surface, and a property is rendered unique by the definition of its borders and dimensions, all of which should be set out in the topographical diagrams prepared by specialist engineers.

The component parts of an immovable are those items defined in the general criteria of Article 953 of the Greek Civil Code, according to which a component part is part of a whole which cannot be separated from the whole without damage to itself or the whole, or without a change in the substance and the items that are considered to be component parts in accordance with Article 954 of the Greek Civil Code. These are:

- Things fixed to the soil in a sturdy fashion, such as buildings, the removal of which would be extremely difficult.

- Products of the immovable connected with the soil (for example, trees and minerals, etc.).

- Subterranean water and wells.

- Movable items used to complete a building or in connection to it.

The temporary removal of a component part from the whole does not change its character. The description of such has the following legal consequences:

- For as long as the connection of the component part to the whole lasts, there cannot be separate ownership or separate restricted right on that component part. On the contrary, the ownership and other rights on the whole are extended to the component part.

- Any transaction which concerns the exclusive right where the whole is concerned and includes the component part (even if it was added after the transaction).

- Any pre-existing real rights (see below) that were in existence on the component part are cancelled permanently with its connection to the combined part.

Where a building or a piece of land is physically divided between several people, a condominium is created. The land is divided into privately owned parts, such as individual flats and communally owned areas. The management of these communal areas is determined by the owners of the privately held areas (see pp.118–20) but can be delegated to someone else.

The agreement for the transfer of ownership of a property can be by private agreement – written or otherwise. This is a contractual agreement which may bind both parties to it but is not effective for third parties, who are entitled to rely on the contents or registers of the Land Registry. Between buyer and seller

- The real rights on the component part remain unchanged even after its removal from the combined whole.
- No separate claim is permitted on the component part.
- No separation or division of the component from the whole is permitted.
- Taking a component part is not permitted. On the contrary, the seizure of the immovable is extended to its components.

Real rights (ownership, service charges, pledges and mortgages) are legal forms of the owner's control over the financial entitlements, which in accordance with Article 973 of the Greek Civil Code generate immediate authority insofar as a third party is concerned. They include:

- **Full Ownership** (*Kiriótita*)
  A person's immediate and absolute authority on a property.

- **Usufruct or Usefruit** (*Epikarpía*)
  A person's exclusive right to use a property which does not 'legally' belong to him. The user (*epikarpótis*) does not have legal title yet is allowed to enjoy the property in full but without being able to change the nature of it. This right cannot be transferred unless it has been defined differently. However, it may be transferred for a period of time not exceeding the duration of the usufruct (in accordance with Article 1166 of the Greek Civil Code).

- **Residence** (*Íkisi*)
  A person's exclusive right to use a residence, building or premises which do not belong to him (Article 1183 of the Greek Civil Code). This right cannot be changed and is cancelled upon the death of the person who exercised it.

- **Legal Ownership** (*Psilí Kiriótita*)
  The exclusive right once full ownership no longer has the right of usufruct – that is to say, the use of the property. All that therefore remains is the power to dispose of the property.

- **Services** (*Pragmatikés Dhouliés*)
  In accordance with Article 1118 of the Greek Civil Code, services and restricted rights on a property created for the servicing of the needs of another property (e.g. a flat) and which grant a benefit to the owners of that other property.

the ownership of land is transferred by the signing of a sale contract (*symvóleo*) before a notary public (*symvoleográfos*) and its registration at the Land Registry. Ownership can also be acquired by possession under 10- or 20-year rules of use (*khrisiktisía*).

There are other rights which fall short of full ownership and which can also exist over land. Some of these have been identified in the box above and include services, such as rights of way, tenancies, life interests, mortgages, etc. All require some sort of legal formality to be valid against third parties but are always binding between the people who made the agreements.

- **Restricted Personal Services** (*Periorisménes Prosopikés Dhouliés*)
  Exclusive rights on the property which are created in favour of a person and which grant that person a certain authority or use over the property.

- **Right of Possession** (*Nómi*)
  The exclusive right of a person on an immovable over which he exercises ownership (in accordance with Article 974 of the Greek Civil Code).

- **Mortgage** (*Ypothíki*)
  The exclusive right on a property as security in connection with a specific claim that grants the creditor favour or satisfaction from the property (Article 1257-1345 of the Greek Civil Code).

- **Compulsory Expropriation** (*Anangastikí Apallotríosi*)
  The removal of ownership of a property by a unilateral administrative action in return for the payment of a sum of compensation, which is judicially calculated for the public good as defined law. The opposite is compulsory addition (*anangastikí proskírosi*) which takes away ownership of a property from one person and adds it to the ownership of another person.

- **Horizontal Ownership** (*Orizóndia Idhioktisía*)
  The exclusive ownership of a floor in a building or an apartment which also contains some co-ownership of the land and the common parts of the building.

- **Vertical Ownership** (*Kathetí Idhioktisía*)
  Co-ownership of a building, which could be built alongside other building/s on the same plot of land, and is combined with the co-ownership of the plot of land, the common parts of the building and that of the other beneficiaries and their vertical ownerships.

- **Field** (*Yípedho*)
  An area of land which comprises a whole and self-contained property and which belongs to one or more owners indivisibly.

- **Land Viable for Building** (*Ikópedho*)
  A plot of land that lies in an approved planning area or within the boundaries of a residential area but is without approved planning permission from the competent planning authority.

There are two land registers in Greece. There is the newly created **National Land Registry** (*Ethnikó Ktimatolóyio*) and the relatively more established (as the National Land Registry does not extend to all Greece) **Local Land Registry** (*Ypothikofilakio*) which also acts as a register for mortgages. The latter uses the names of owners as an index for recording the deeds and mortgages or other claims relating to the land as well as land ownership. Where an area is covered by both registers, the sale contracts are registered in both. When the process of the National Land Registry has been completed in a specific area, then you only register with the National Land Registry.

The National Land Registry (Ethnikó Ktimatolóyio)

Since 1995, the European Union has funded the creation of a National Land Registry in Greece. The purpose of this system was to collate all necessary information regarding land ownership in Greece into a single and unified central system instead of having a system of localised land registries which did not share information with one another. Another reason behind this new system was to simplify and render more secure the process of a conveyance in Greece.

Irrespective of the practical difficulties involved (unavoidable in such a large-scale endeavour), everyone agrees that the creation of National Land Registry was vital, in terms of both social and legal objectives. The present system, which sees publication in the registration books at the Local Land Registry, is ineffective and contains many hazards for the transactions taking place. The National Land Registry will cover all the shortcomings of the present system by ensuring a fully public system of land ownership in Greece.

The registration system at the Local Land Registry is centred on the owner's details, while at the National Land Registry it is centred on the plot of land in question. The foundations of the national land registration system are not built on changeable landowners (although there will be an alphabetical cross-index at the National Land Registry) but on the characteristics of the property (immovable) itself. Each piece of property will have its unique code or number. This type of system secures far better transactions when compared to the present registration system and mortgages based on topographical diagrams.

The Land Registry issues a formal and substantive publication which is useful for any purchaser acting in good faith. This is established by the objective or *prima facie* assumption that any land which has been properly registered with the National Land Registry will lessen the risks faced by a bona fide purchaser when buying land from an owner not registered yet claiming ownership simply by using the land (*khrisiktisía*).

The Community of Owners

A community of owners is a situation whereby a number of people own land or buildings in such a way that they have exclusive use of parts of the property but shared use of the communal areas. This is a device familiar in continental Europe but fairly unusual in the UK.

Houses built on their own individual plots with no shared facilities will not be a member of 'the community'. Other property, such as an apartment and a building with other apartments, will be. It is not only the shared parts of the building that are jointly owned but all the lift shafts, roofs, foundations, entrance areas, parking zones, etc. Other members of the community will each be responsible for their own home. They will collectively agree on the works that are needed on the common areas and budget for all those works. They are then responsible for paying their share of those common expenses as

The creation of such a national registration system cannot happen all at once. It has been designed to gradually take place in stages across different regions of Greece. Eventually, all property in Greece will be dealt with in this way, but the country is, at present, some way from attaining this goal. Until then, parts of Greece will continue to be subject to the National Land Registry while the rest will remain under the system of registration operating with local land registries and others, notably the Dodecanese Islands which already have a system of land registration in place similar to that of the National Registry.

The first stage of the introduction of the system of National Land Registry includes the procedure of identifying a large area of Greece which is subject to the process. The first stage is therefore the declaration by the government that an area is subject to this system. The second stage is the stage when the government's appointed agency accepts filed declarations from the persons wishing to register their property ownership with the system. The third stage is the creation and completion of the relevant maps and tables of ownership. The fourth stage is the formal registration of the property in the National Land Registry database.

As this is not yet a national system, the general rules applied by the Greek Civil Code as regards the registration of purchase contracts at the Local Land Registry are still effective, even in those areas where the National Land Registry has been introduced. T

he formation of the National Land Registry does not affect the substantive law presently in force in relation to the manner in which real property rights are obtained or transferred. It simply records those rights. The only substantial change in the law is that, once registered with the National Land Registry, land is presumed to have been correctly filed.

The National Land Registry registers full ownership of property as defined by Article 948 of the Greek Civil Code in conjunction with Articles 953 and 954.

stipulated in their title. There are detailed rules as to how these communities should be run. They are normally set out in the act of horizontal ownership (*sýstasi orizóndias idhiokisías; see* p.117) and in the regulations of use of the community or constitution document (*kanonismí polikatikías*). The act and rules deal not only with technical matters about how the community should be governed and managed but also with rules of conduct that must be followed by the owners. They also set out how your share of the expenses is to be calculated.

The supreme ruling body of any community is the general meeting (*yenikí synélefsi*) of its members. It must be held at least once a year to approve the budget and deal with any other business. Voting for most issues is by a simple majority vote. If you cannot attend, you can always appoint a proxy to vote on your behalf. Day-to-day management is usually delegated to an administrator. The relevant service charges are divided in the proportions stipulated by the deed creating the community of owners – horizontal ownership in a special table allocating the percentages of ownership (*pínakas katanomís posostón*). These have normally been calculated in relation to the size of each apartment, with a larger fraction going to any commercial area included in the community. You will pay fees whether you use the place all year round or for only two weeks of the year. The rules set out by the community's regulations (*kanonismí polikatikías*) are intended to improve the quality of life for its residents. They could, for example, deal with concerns about noise, or prohibit the use of communal features such as a swimming pool after a certain hour, ban the hanging of washing on balconies, etc., limit the keeping of pets or forbid certain types of commercial activity in the building or even short-term holiday letting. It is therefore very important to consider thoroughly these obligations before making any purchase. If you do not speak Greek, you should have any documents summarised in English.

Choosing a Lawyer

The Notary Public (*Symvoleográfos*)

The notary is a special kind of lawyer or solicitor. He is in part a public official but he is also in the business of making his living from the fees he charges for his services. There are about 3,070 notaries in Greece.

Under Greek law, only purchase deeds (*symvólea*) approved and witnessed by a notary can be registered at the Land Registry. Although it is possible to have a contract agreeing the transfer of a property, such an agreement would only bind the two parties involved and not affect the rights of third parties (including people who wanted to make a claim against the property or banks wishing to lend money on the strength of the property). If you are not registered as the owner of the property, you will always be at risk. For practical reasons, all sales of real estate in Greece must be carried out in the presence of a notary public, who is also entitled to charge for issuing the certified documents. His fees are fixed by law: 1.2 per cent on the value of the contract, as well as a charge for every separate sheet contained in the contract, plus any copies and other documentation submitted to the Land Registry.

The notary is usually appointed by the buyer, although in some cases it makes sense for a notary to be appointed by the seller. In many situations, the notary should not be connected to the seller (e.g. where the seller and notary have a long business relationship together, in which case it may be prudent to have an independent notary who may be the more willing to scrutinise the various documents provided by the seller).

The notary is a neutral party in the transaction. His duties are to ensure the documentation is complete, that documents comply with the strict rules that are applicable to the transaction and that the sale contract is properly drawn up so as to be accepted by the Land Registry for registration.

It is not uncommon to find that Greek notaries do not speak English or certainly do not speak it well enough to give advice on difficult and complex legal issues. In any case, the buyer will seldom meet the notary before the signing of the contract and there is little reason for seeking advice from him.

Greek Lawyers (*Dhikigóri*)

In cases where the value of a transaction exceeds a given amount in euros, it is absolutely crucial that a Greek lawyer be present at the signing of the purchase contract. The values that are applicable vary in different parts of Greece. For example, the limit in the Athens area is €29,347 while, in some of the more rural areas, it is as low as €11,738. The lawyer will charge you at least the minimum fee, which is usually scaled at 1 per cent up to approximately €44,000 euros and thereafter at 0.5 per cent. These fees are set by the Bar Association, which will keep a large chunk of this fee, which they, in turn, distribute annually to all members in equal shares.

Especially in rural areas, a local lawyer is appointed or recommended by the seller, and his role in the transaction is generally limited to a quick perusal of the Local Land Registry on the morning of the signing when his presence is required. This, in many cases, falls short of the advice required by a UK buyer.

English Lawyers (Solicitors)

For English people, the services of the notary are unlikely to give them all the information or help they need to buy a home in Greece. They will often require advice about inheritance issues, the UK tax implications of their purchase, how to save taxes, surveys, mortgages, currency exchange, etc., which is outside the scope of the service of the notary. If possible, they should retain the services of a specialist UK lawyer familiar with dealing with these issues. He will also be able to offer a full proxy service whereby the physical presence of the buyer in Greece is not required and everything can be dealt with through correspondence. The buyer's usual solicitor is unlikely to be able to help, as there are only a tiny handful of English law firms with the necessary expertise.

The Price

This can be freely agreed between the two parties. Depending on the economic climate and the location of the property, there may be ample or little room for negotiating a reduction on the asking price. It is common for there to be a good deal of haggling involved.

At the moment (2004), the market in major cities, such as Athens, is saturated, but there is always strong demand in the outlying areas, especially those frequented by tourists and serviced by an airport. There is, nevertheless, a great deal of scope for purchasing property in 'undiscovered' Greece, particularly if the property needs repair. If you are unsure of the value of the property (especially if you're buying during a short trip to Greece), it is worthwhile to ask your professional adviser to find out the objective tax value of this property (*see* p.132). This can be a useful starting point in calculating its overall market value. Your professional adviser can also do some research at the Local Land Registry and find similar properties for price comparisons. This is standard practice in Greece, especially when the actual agreed purchase price exceeds the value calculated for tax purposes (*andikimeniki axía*). This leads to issues of legality and issues of how the portion that is not recorded is to be paid.

How Much Should be Declared in the Deed of Sale?

As already mentioned, there is a tradition in Greece of under-declaring the price actually paid for a property when signing the deed of purchase. This is because the taxes and other fees such as the notary's and local lawyer's fees are calculated on the basis of the declared price. A lower price means less taxes to pay for the buyer. In certain situations, the seller may be under pressure to declare the full price, as he wishes to purchase another property.

At the time of writing, the current government is considering a future increase in the tables by which the value for tax purposes (*andikimeniki axía*) is calculated. There is an incentive therefore for prospective buyers to move relatively quickly and take advantage of the lower rates presently available.

Which Currency?

The price of the property will be recorded in the purchase contract in euros. In the past, it was quite unexceptional to enter agreements whereby the purchase price was deposited directly into the seller's UK bank account. This was largely due to the weakness of the Greek drachma at the time, and such agreements are now rare due to the existence of the euro. However, ensure that you as a buyer do not prejudice your position before the Greek tax authorities as regards declaring the funds used for the purchase of a property when accepting such terms. **Such funds must have been declared during the previous financial period or certificated as imported currency or they will be subject to income tax; *see* box, p.127**. It is therefore very important to take professional advice before agreeing to deposit the sale price abroad.

Where Must the Money Be Paid?

The asking price, together with the taxes and fees payable, is usually paid by the buyer with a banker's draft or cash at the time of the signing of the purchase contract. Usually as part of an under-declaration, a portion of the money is handed over in cash but, apart from this being illegal, it can be risky on a practical level. If you are going to under-declare, you should pay the money directly into the seller's account.

General Enquiries and Special Enquiries

General enquiries include a check to see whether the seller is actually the registered owner of the property and that it is being sold (if this has been agreed in the contract) free of mortgages or other charges. Other standard enquiries include a check on the planning situation of the property to ensure that the building plot is viable for building and not subject to any rights of way, etc. In order to advise you of what other enquiries may be appropriate to your circumstances, your lawyer will need to be told of your intentions for the property. Do you wish to let it out? If so, will this be on a commercial basis? Do you intend to use it for business purposes? Do you want to extend or modify the exterior of the property?

Planning Permission

Information relevant to planning permission rules and permitted use which affect the property (both within or outside planning zones) can be provided by the planning authority (*poleodhomía*) or the planning office which issues the building licences in the area where the property is situated.

In certain cases, it is worthwhile checking to see whether a plot of land is liable to be included in planning zones in the near future, as this not only affects the size of the building which can be built but also its overall value and the use to which the land may be put. This information can be provided by the local municipality (*dhímos* or *kinótita*), which should be able to give some basic details and will certainly be able to provide the enquirer with information as to which public authority should be approached for the specific details.

In many cases, a prospective buyer will be offered old farm buildings and old stone buildings. These are likely to offer attractive conversion prospects and the purchaser should be aware that there are incentives for the protection of preserved (*dhiatirítea*) buildings, especially of traditional hamlets. The incentives are both financial and administrative, including low interest loans and tax benefits; for example, a 30 per cent reduction on transfer tax (*fóros metavívasis akiníton*), inheritance tax (*fóros klironomías*) and gift tax (*fóros dhoréas*) applicable to protected buildings. To reap these benefits, an owner must first ensure that the property is actually a registered protected property.

The procedure involved is as follows:

- **An application must be made by the individual owner of the property.**

- **The application must include the relevant structural study and topographical plan, details of ownership, photographs, etc.**

- The planning authority will also carry out a relevant study and report its findings.

- The result is then published in local newspapers or magazines.

- There are certain criteria which must be met so that rebuilding meets the requirements of a protected building.

- It must have certain architectural components which give it specific architectural and historical value as a building in relation to the area where it is located.

- The specific situation of a building may render it necessary for it to be protected if it comprises a composite whole together with other similar buildings.

Your Personal Details

When preparing documents in Greece, you will be asked for a full set of personal details. This will comprise your full name, address, occupation, nationality, passport number, the names of your parents, the date and place of your birth and your civil state (whether you are married or single). Your tax registration number will also be included (*A fi Mi*). Most, if not all, of this information will be included in the purchase contract. Normally a solicitor will need to see your passport at the time of signing.

Tax Registration Number

To own a property in Greece you need to obtain a foreigner's tax registration number (*see* p.143). Alternatively, your lawyer can obtain this for you.

Initial Contracts

In Greece, most sales start with a **preliminary contract**. The type of contract will depend on whether you are buying a finished or an unfinished property. The signing of this document will have far-reaching implications which are sometimes different from the consequences of signing similar documents in the UK. Seek legal advice beforehand.

Finished Properties

A **promise to sell** is a written contract or document in which the seller offers to sell a named property at a named price to a named person at any time within a named period. The seller will usually require that the person taking up his offer pay a **deposit**. The amount is not fixed by law but is usually five or 10 per cent of the property price.

Once he has received the deposit, the seller must reserve the property for you until the end of the period specified in the contract. This has similarities to an English option contract. If you do want to go ahead and buy the property, you can but you are not obliged to do so. If you do not go ahead, you lose your deposit. These contracts can contain special get-out clauses stipulating circumstances in which a buyer is entitled to the refund of his deposit if he or she decides not to go ahead. If the seller refuses to go ahead, the buyer is entitled to claim compensation, which is normally double the amount of the deposit paid.

This type of contract can either be a **formal contract** (*prosýmfono*) before a notary public, or simply a contractual agreement drawn up by the two parties involved. In the formal contract, it is possible to include terms where the buyer contracts with himself at the time of the final sale agreement, thus enabling the contract to be executed without the seller actually being present.

Unfinished Properties or Land Only

If you're buying an unfinished property or a plot of land and have negotiated with the builder the completion of a building on this land, there are two different options available to you.

The first option is to purchase the plot of land from the seller. After this is complete, you, as the new owner of the land, may make an application to the local planning authority for planning permission and a building licence to be issued. The paperwork required for the submission of an application is normally prepared by an architect or a civil engineer and the fees involved will vary, starting from €5,000 minimum, depending on the size of the building to be constructed. Once the planning and building issues have been dealt with by the planning authority, a building licence, initially valid for two years, will be issued. You must then either contract a builder who will undertake the construction or, as is more usual, contract with the various sub-contractors involved. It is advisable to commission an architect or a civil engineer to oversee the project, and they will normally charge a fee of approximately 15 per cent of the construction costs.

You could also enter into a contract with a builder that involves stage payments according to the progress reached at specific points of the project. This second option, which normally applies when the builder also happens to be the owner of the plot of land, is for a pre-contract before a notary public, whereby a full description of the property to be built is given, along with its size, the number of rooms, quality of the finish, etc. The scheme for stage payments must also be stipulated. The full transfer of title will take place one or two months before the building is complete.

Steps Between Signing the Contract and Signing the Deed of Sale

Assigning Power of Attorney

Very often it will not be convenient for you to go to Greece to sign the purchase contract in person. Sometimes, there may be other things that in the normal course of events will require your personal intervention but where it would be inadvisable to deal with them yourself. Just as often, you will not know whether you will be available to sign in person. As completion dates are notoriously fluid in Greece, you may not be able to be present as planned for the signing of the contract. The solution to this problem is the power of attorney. This document authorises the person appointed to do whatever the document authorises on behalf of the person granting the power. The most sensible type of power to use will be an English power of attorney that has been amended to include the Greek style of power of attorney appropriate to the situation.

If this is the option used, the power of attorney also needs to be legalised by the Foreign and Commonwealth Office in London in order for it to be acceptable by the Greek authorities; they will issue a certificate (apostile) to be used internationally. This should take one day of processing and costs £12.

Another option is to use a Greek power of attorney and for an interpreter to be present at the time that it is put into practice. Your specialist lawyer can discuss your requirements with you and prepare the necessary documentation.

A power of attorney can occasionally state that it cannot be revoked. If this is not mentioned, power can be withdrawn in a number of ways. It can be granted so that it is only valid for a limited period of time (for the purchase of the property). Alternatively, it can be cancelled by giving written notice to the person appointed. The power of attorney is a powerful tool. It gives this person a great deal of authority to do things on your behalf that could prove very costly. Therefore it should only be given to people whom you trust implicitly: a close member of your family, such as your partner or child, or your lawyer.

Getting the Money to Greece

Electronic Transfer

The most practical is to have it sent electronically by SWIFT transfer from a UK bank directly to the recipient's bank in Greece. This costs about £30, depending on your bank. It is safest to allow two or three days for the money to arrive in a rural bank, despite everyone's protestations that it will be there the same day!

Europe has now introduced unique account numbers for all bank accounts. These incorporate a code for the identity of the bank and branch involved, as well as the account number of the individual customer. These are known as **IBAN numbers**. They should be quoted on all international currency transfers.

Means Test (Póthen Éskhes)

In order to put a stop to the rampant tax evasion by the Greeks, the government introduced a series of measures based on obvious signs of wealth such as property, expensive cars, yachts, etc. A person must be able to show when purchasing any one of these luxury items that the income used to effect the purchase was declared to the tax authorities in a previous tax year. If they cannot do so, the tax authority will charge income tax on the amount that has not been declared. This can turn out to be a substantial amount of money and is of great relevance to the foreign buyer of Greek property because, under normal circumstances, he or she would not have been able to file a tax return in Greece in the year previous to his purchase. The way around this fix is to be able to prove that the income used to effect the purchase originated from the buyer's country of residence and was effectively 'imported' as foreign exchange into Greece. It is therefore vital that the money sent for the purchase of a property is sent as sterling and exchanged by the Greek bank into euros. The appropriate **certificate of exchange** (the **pink slip**) will then be issued and attached to the income tax return for the following year, thus avoiding any income tax liability for the would-be buyer.

You can also send the money from your own bank via your lawyers or via a specialist currency dealer. For the sums you are likely to be sending, you should receive an exchange rate that is more favourable than the going 'tourist rate' quoted in the press. It is also a well-known fact that Greek banks tend to offer a better exchange rate when receiving sterling. Make sure you get a pink slip.

Banker's Drafts

You can arrange for your UK bank to issue you with a banker's draft (bank certified cheque) which you can take to Greece and pay into your bank account. Make sure that the bank knows that the draft is to be used overseas and so issues you with an international draft.

Generally this is not a good way to transfer money. It can take considerable time – sometimes weeks – for the funds deposited to be made available for your use. The recipient bank's charges can also be surprisingly high. The exchange rate offered against a sterling draft may be uncompetitive.

Cash

This is not recommended. You will need to declare the money on departure from the UK and on arrival in Greece. You must do so by law.

Exchange Control and Other Restrictions on Moving Money

For EU nationals, there is no longer any exchange control when taking money to or from Greece. There are some statistical records kept showing the flow of funds and the purposes of the transfers. When you sell your property in Greece, you will be able to bring the money back to the UK if you wish to do so.

Fixing the Completion Date

The date stated in the contract for signing the deed of sale could, most charitably, be described as flexible or aspirational. Often it will move, if only by a day or so. Avoid booking your trip to Greece until you are certain that matters will proceed on a given day.

Buyer's Checklist

- Prepare power of attorney.
- Check which documents must be produced on signing the contract.
- Confirm that all outstanding issues have been complied with.
- Confirm that all other important enquiries are clear.
- Check that the seller has presented all the documents required at the time of the signing.
- Confirm all the arrangements (date, time, place) for completion with your lender if you have a mortgage.
- Arrange for the filing of a transfer tax declaration with the solicitor which must be signed by both buyer and seller or the persons holding the appropriate powers of attorney.
- Arrange for the transfer tax to be paid and the receipt made available to the solicitor.
- Send the necessary funds to Greece.
- Confirm all the necessary arrangements (date, time, place) for completion with the solicitor.
- Receive the other documents which may be appropriate such as the Rules and Regulations of Use when buying a flat.
- Obtain a tax registration number from the tax authority (*A-fi-Mi*).

Documents Provided by the Seller

- A certificate or a declaration under Article 81 of law 22388 /1994 that the property has been declared for the past two years (if a certificate is issued) or that it has not generated income for the past five years (if a responsible declaration is filed).
- A declaration that there is no Large Property Tax (*see* pp.146–7) owed for the property to be transferred under Article 32 of law 2459 /1997. If the seller is obliged to pay Large Property Tax, then you must obtain a certificate to confirm he has paid the appropriate tax for the property he wishes to sell.
- A certificate to show you that there is no national insurance fund monies owed from the IKA, if applicable.

- A tax clearance certificate (*pistopiitikó foroloyikís enimerótitas*).
- A copy of the building licence if the property was built after 1983.
- A certificate from the local municipality stating that there are no property dues owing (TAP).
- A certificate from the National Land Registry if the property is located in an area where the National Land Registry is enforced.
- If the plot of land where an apartment block has been built falls under the regulations of Law 1337/1983, a certificate from the municipality is required to confirm there is no contribution in land owing or in money or that any such amounts have been deposited.
- If the title documents of the seller are by parental contribution, or by gift which has taken place after 1 January 1985, or by an inheritance where the person died after 1 January 1985, then a certificate will be issued, stating that there is no pending tax of parental contribution, gift or inheritance tax.
- If dealing with a gift, dowry or inheritance which has taken place before 1 January 1985, then a copy of the notarised document of gift or dowry or a copy of the Registered Act of Death in the case of inheritance.

The Purchase Contract (*Symvóleo Agorás*)

This document must be signed in front of a notary either by the parties in person or by someone holding power of attorney on their behalf. It is broken down into separate sections and will normally contain the following details:

- The date of execution of the contract.
- The name and address of the notary.
- Full details of the buyer and seller and the same details of any person/s appearing on their behalf on Greek power of attorney, plus the conditions of that power.
- Full details of the interpreter commissioned where the buyer or seller does not speak Greek.
- A full description of the property (including its size, Land Registry details, borders, owners of the adjacent land, plus details of the topographical plan prepared by the civil engineer).
- There will be a history of ownership and possession. This will justify the current claim to ownership of the property and state the date when the buyer will take over possession of the property (usually on that same day). It will also contain various guarantees to confirm that the property is free from any claims or other encumbrances.
- The price and methods of payment.

• A declaration regarding the type of property involved in the transaction. This will also deal with issues of tax to be paid and the amount.

• An itemised list of all the various certificates (*pistopiitiká*) and confirmations (*vevéoses*) provided by the buyer and the seller.

• A statement that both parties have confirmed the truthfulness of all their statements and are acting in good faith.

Formalities

Most signing ceremonies follow a certain procedure. The parties are identified by their passports (for non-Greek nationals) or identity cards. This will initially be done by the notary's clerk and thereafter by the notary himself. He will read out the purchase contract in Greek. It is therefore important for an interpreter or someone who is fully qualified in legal terminology to be present to ensure that an accurate translation is available. In addition to the buyer and seller, it is usual for the two lawyers to be present, and occasionally the estate agent may be involved. Any amendments to the purchase contract which have been agreed by the parties and their lawyers are made there and then and the final contract is printed out. The purchase monies are handed over and the notary then makes a note on the contract of the method of payment and any banker's draft number. Both parties and their lawyers will sign every page of the contract. Initialled signatures by all parties involved will also be needed alongside amendments made to the contract by hand. All parties also sign the notary's book of contracts and the buyer will need to pay the notary his fees and dues and arrange to have the contract registered at the Land Registry when it is made available.

All taxes must be paid. Once these have been paid, your title and any mortgage should be presented for registration at the Land Registry. Individuals who register first get priority. If the purchase title is not registered within 12 months of the purchase, the contract must be revalued by the tax authorities and any further transfer tax paid prior to registration.

After a week or so, the Land Registry will issue a certificate of registration to the effect that the title has been registered. Until then, you are not considered the rightful owner of the property, so it is important for registration to take place as soon as possible.

The Cost of Buying a Property in Greece

These are the fees and taxes payable by a buyer when acquiring a property in Greece. They are normally impossible to predict with total accuracy at the outset of a transaction. This is because it is not always clear whether the property involved will be liable to the objective value for calculating tax (*see* p.132).

These costs are calculated on the basis of the price that is declared as the price paid for the property on the purchase contract, and the size of these expenses, coupled with the Greek dislike for paying tax, has led to the habit of under-declaring the price on the purchase contract.

In Greece, **VAT** is levied at 18 per cent in most areas but is not currently being imposed on transactions for the purchase of properties. In certain cases, VAT is payable – where, for example, you have purchased a plot of land and agreed the purchase of a prefabricated house to be placed upon the land. VAT will normally be payable to the supplier of the prefabricated property.

The buyer will also be responsible for the land registration fee, notary's fees, property transfer tax, mortgage costs and estate agent's fees. If an estate agent has sold the property, his fees will usually be between two and four per cent depending on the location and the value of the property and are usually paid by the buyer. These will be subject to VAT. The price of the property will always be recorded on the purchase contract in euros.

It is a prerequisite that the payment of the transfer tax be made prior to the signing of the purchase contract.

Notary's Fees

These are at least 1.2 per cent of the value that is on the contract and a further small charge is made for each sheet of the contract as well as for any certified copies provided. It is not unusual, however, for the notary to charge slightly more especially in more complex cases.

Local Lawyer's Fees

These are set by the Bar Association and vary according to the value of the contract involved. The minimum fees are:

Up to €44,020.54	1%
€44,020.54–€1,467,351.43	0.5 %
€1,467,351.43–€2,934,702.86	0.4%
€2,934,702.86–€5,869,405.72	0.3%

The scale continues further so that the minimum fee is set at 0.01% at the very top of the range.

Land Registration Fees

These are calculated up to the value of €30 at a rate of 1.5 per cent; from €30 to €60 the rate applied is 1.2 per cent; while for sums over €60, it is 0.45 per cent. For example, if the value of the contract is €100,000, the registration fee will be €450. A small charge is also paid for the standing charges of the registrar.

Property Transfer Tax
(*FMA* or *Fóros Metavívasis Akiníton*)

The main tax which will concern a buyer of property in Greece is transfer tax (the rough equivalent of stamp duty in the UK). Perhaps not unsurprisingly, the Greek tax system is unfamiliar to English buyers, and is made more confusing by the fact that the value quoted on the contract of purchase is rarely the amount of money that actually changes hands but rather a figure known as the **objective tax value** (*andikimeniki axía*). Transfer tax is then paid on this value.

The system of objective tax values is applied to determine the tax value of immovable property in connection with the taxation of capital, which includes transfer tax and the taxation upon large property ownership. The tax authorities have various tables which categorise and apply values to 14 different categories of property based on their nature, location and size. The different categories include buildings used as residences, apartments, commercial property, plots viable for building, storage buildings, parking spaces, and buildings used for agricultural purposes, etc.

The categorisation of a property is proved by the following:

- **the building licence for its construction**
- **the act of horizontal ownership**
- **its title of ownership**

When none of the above-mentioned documents is available, then the category is determined by the income tax declaration. For each category of property, and in accordance with where it is located, a different document is required to value a property under the objective tax value system.

Forms are completed at the time of purchase by the notary in conjunction with the lawyers acting for the purchaser and the seller and submitted to the relevant tax authority, who will determine the tax value on the property before calculating the appropriate tax which must be paid prior to the signing of the contract.

For property situated in areas where the system of objective values is enforced, the monetary value of the property is determined by that system. For property on which buildings have been constructed and which is located in areas where there is no system of objective values, the value of the building/s is calculated by applying the system of objective values but the financial worth of the actual plot of land is calculated through a comparative criteria system (*sýstima synkritikón stihíon*) which exists within the relevant local tax authority. In other words, the plot of land will be given a value which is comparable to similar plots of land that have been valued beforehand and which are situated in the same area.

Fields (plots and agricultural plots) located in areas which have not yet applied the system of objective values are valued by their commercial or market value as defined by the comparative criteria system.

Calculating Transfer Tax

Transfer tax is calculated in the following manner.

For values on property determined up to €15,000 in places where a fire station is located, a tax of 9 per cent is raised and where no fire station is present only 7 per cent. For values over the sum of €15,000 in places where a fire station is located, 11 per cent tax is applied and where no fire station is present only 9 per cent tax is applied.

Let's take two examples. In the first example, A purchases a plot of land valued at €8,800 in an area where there is no fire station. The tax that is levied will be calculated at 7 per cent. In the second, B buys a plot of land valued at €16,000 in an area where there is a fire station. Up to €15,000 of the tax will be applied at a rate of 9 per cent while a rate of 11 per cent will be applied to a further €1,000.

Once the tax has been calculated, a further municipal tax of 3 per cent is applied on the main transfer tax which has been calculated. For example, if the tax is €5,000, a further tax of 3 per cent on that value will be applied. In other words, €150 of municipal tax will also be charged which then gives a total of €5,150 in tax which must then be paid.

In areas (such as the islands) where the residents number less than 3,100 people, a reduction of 40 per cent is made on the tax charged.

In certain cases, advance tax planning can provide a mechanism whereby a purchaser may be exempt from the transfer tax applicable and this usually makes economic sense where the tax raised is over €7,000.

The law requires that, where the purchase price is greater than the objective tax value, the greater value must be declared and a tax levied upon that greater value. However, it is common practice for people to simply declare the objective tax value and for the buyer to save himself a substantial amount of money in transfer tax. Where no objective tax system is applied to property, the purchaser is obliged to pay tax on the value he has declared. The tax authority then carries out its own investigation and the buyer may be obliged to pay further tax.

Paying Transfer Tax

The purchaser of a property is obliged to file a declaration of transfer tax (*FMA* or *Fóros Metavívasis Akiníton*) and to pay the tax that is due in advance. This declaration is filed jointly with the seller of the property and must be signed by both seller and purchaser or by their proxies. The purchaser may be partially or wholly exempt if he satisfies the respective preconditions (such as the fact he is a first-time buyer, etc.). Furthermore, if the buyer does not agree with the amount quoted on the transfer tax, he has the right to apply to the financial courts within 60 days of the filing of the tax declaration.

The transfer tax declaration is filed by the purchaser (or his representative) with the capital department of the appropriate tax authority. The appropriate tax authority is that which governs the area where the property is situated.

In order to submit a tax declaration, these documents may be required concerning both the property in question and the purchaser:

- A building licence, if applicable.
- Certificates from the planning offices/municipality, Forestry Commission, electricity supplier, etc.
- Notarised documents.
- Plans and tables from the technical offices (e.g. engineers, architects).

The documents which concern the purchaser may include:

- A certificate of family status.
- A copy of the filed income tax declaration, if applicable.
- A copy of the E9 form.
- Certificates from municipalities, land registries and consular authorities.
- Notarised contracts.

The documents that will actually be required depend very much on whether the purchaser is liable to be exempt from the transfer tax on account of the fact that he is, say, a first-time buyer, and on whether the transfer tax is fully payable, in which case most of the above mentioned documents will not be required to be produced with the filing of the tax declaration.

The tax declaration is filed along with two copies, one of which is returned and attached by the notary to the purchase contract which is then registered. The relevant tax authority will issue a document confirming the value of the property for tax purposes and a document stating the amount of transfer tax that must be paid. The transfer tax is usually paid by way of banker's draft, as there are usually limits on the amount of cash (normally €1,500) that a tax authority is willing to accept. The receipt of payment of the transfer tax is then annexed to the purchase contract by the notary.

It is an absolute prerequisite that both the purchaser and seller have tax registration numbers (*see* p.143).

INDEPENDENT LEGAL ADVICE

Specialist legal advice for purchasing property in Greece

Helen G Kydoniefs & Co
Attorneys at Law & International Lawyers
42 Cranbourne Gardens
London NW11 0HP
Tel: +44 (0)20 84553488 Fax: +44 (0) 20 84580932
Email kydonief@otenet.gr

Financial Implications

Frank Kydoniefs
Barrister at Law and International Lawyer

Taxation

All tax systems are complicated. The Greek system is no exception. Fortunately, most people will only have limited contact with the more intricate parts of the system. For many owners of holiday homes in Greece their contact with the system will be minimal.

It is helpful to have some sort of understanding about the way in which the system works and the taxes that you might face. Be warned: getting even a basic understanding will make your head hurt. You also need to be particularly careful about words and concepts that seem familiar to you but which may have a fundamentally different meaning in Greece than from in the UK. Of course, just to confuse you, the rules change every year. This general introduction does little more than scratch the surface of an immensely complex subject. It is intended to allow you to have a sensible discussion with your professional advisers and, perhaps, to help you work out the questions that you need to be asking them. It is not intended as a substitute for proper professional advice.

Your situation when you have a foot in two countries – and, in particular, when you are moving permanently from one country to another – involves the consideration of the tax systems in both countries with a view to minimising your tax obligations in both. It is not just a question of paying the lowest amount of tax in, say, Greece The best choice in Greece could be very damaging to your position in the UK. Similarly, the most tax-efficient way of dealing with your affairs in the UK could be problematic in Greece. The task of the international adviser and his client is to find a path of compromise which allows you to enjoy the major advantages available in both countries without incurring any of the worst drawbacks. In other words, there is an issue of compromise. There is no perfect solution to most tax questions. That is not to say that there are not a great many bad solutions into which you can all too easily stumble.

What should guide you when making a decision as to which course to pursue? Each individual will have a different set of priorities. Some are keen to screw the last ha'penny of advantage out of their situation. Others recognise that they will have to pay some tax but simply wish to moderate their tax bill. For many, the main concern is a simple structure which they understand and can continue to manage without further assistance in the years to come. Just as different clients have different requirements, so different advisers have differing views of the function of the adviser when dealing with a client's tax affairs. One of your first tasks when speaking to your financial adviser should be to discuss your basic philosophy concerning the payment of tax and management of your affairs, to make sure that you are both operating with the same objective in mind and that you are comfortable with his approach to solving your problem.

Are You Resident or Non-Resident for Tax Purposes?

An important factor in determining how you will be treated by the tax authorities in any country is whether you are resident in that country for tax purposes. Tax residence is a question of fact. The law sets out certain tests that will be used to decide whether you are tax resident or not. It is your responsibility to declare tax each year. The decision of whether you fall into the category of resident is made by the tax office with which you choose to file your tax return. If you disagree with the decision made, you can appeal through the courts.

You'll have to consider two different questions concerning tax residency. The first is whether you will be treated as a tax resident in the UK and the second is whether you will be treated as a tax resident in Greece.

Tax Residence in the UK

In the UK, there are two tests that will help determine where you pay tax. These assess your domicile and your residence. Under UK law, there is a test of simple residence – actually living here other than on a purely temporary basis – and of ordinary residence.

Domicile

Domicile is a general law concept. It is not possible to list all the factors that affect your domicile, but some of the main points are explained below. Broadly speaking, you are domiciled in the country where you have your permanent home. Domicile is distinct from nationality or residence. You can only have one domicile at any given time.

You normally acquire a **domicile of origin** from your father when you are born. It need not be the country in which you are born. For example, if you are born in Greece while your father is working there, but his permanent home is in the UK, your domicile of origin is in the UK.

Until you have the legal capacity to change it, your domicile will follow that of the person on whom you are legally dependent. If the domicile of that person changes, you automatically acquire the same domicile (**domicile of dependency**) in place of your domicile of origin.

You have the legal capacity to acquire a new domicile (**domicile of choice**) when you reach age 16. To do so, you must leave your current country of domicile and settle in another country. You need to provide strong evidence that you intend to live there permanently or indefinitely. Living in another country for a long time, although an important factor, is not enough in itself to prove you have acquired a new domicile.

Your domicile is the place that is your real home. It is the place where you have your roots. You can change your domicile but it is often not easy to do so.

Changes in domicile can be useful tax reduction tools, for example if your new country of domicile has no capital gains tax, like Greece.

Residence and Ordinary Residence

To be regarded as **resident** in the UK, you must normally be physically present in the country at some time in the tax year. You will always be resident if you are here for 183 days or more in the tax year. There are no exceptions to this. If you are here for less than 183 days, you may still be treated as resident for the year under other tests. Even if you are resident (or ordinarily resident) in the UK under the UK rules, the terms of a double taxation agreement with another country might affect your final tax position if, for example, you are resident in both that country and the UK.

If you are resident in the UK year after year, you are treated as **ordinarily resident** here. You may be resident but not ordinarily resident in the UK for a tax year if, for example, you normally live outside the UK but are in this country for 183 days or more in the year. Or you may be ordinarily resident but not resident in the UK for a tax year if, for example, you usually live in the UK but have gone abroad for a long holiday and do not set foot in the UK during that year.

A person is ordinarily resident in the United Kingdom if his presence is a little more settled. Residence will normally have gone on for some time. The most important thing to understand is that, once you have been ordinarily resident in this country, the simple fact of going overseas will not automatically bring that residence to an end. If you leave this country in order to take up permanent residence elsewhere, then by concession the Inland Revenue will treat you as ceasing to be resident on the day following your departure. But they will not treat you as ceasing to be ordinarily resident if, after leaving, you spend an average of 91 or more days per year in this country over any four-year period.

You are resident and ordinarily resident in the UK if you usually live in this country and only go abroad for short periods – for example, on holiday or on business trips.

If you leave the UK to work full-time abroad under an employment contract, you are treated as not resident and not ordinarily resident in the UK if you meet all the following criteria:

- **Your absence from the UK and your employment abroad both last for at least a whole tax year.**

- **During your absence, any visits you make to the UK total less than 183 days in any tax year and average less than 91 days per tax year. The average is taken over the period of absence up to a maximum of four years.**

If you meet all the above conditions, you are treated as non-resident and not ordinarily resident in the UK from the day after you leave the UK to the day before you return to the UK at the end of your employment abroad. You are treated as coming to the UK permanently on the day you return from your employment abroad and as resident and ordinarily resident from that date.

Tax Residence in Greece

Tax residence in Greece is treated by a number of rules:

- If your centre of economic interests is in Greece, you are tax resident in Greece. Your centre of economic interests is where you have your main investments or business or other sources of income and, usually, where you spend much of your money.
- If you work in Greece, except where that work is ancillary to working elsewhere, you will be tax resident in Greece.
- If you have a Greek residence permit, you will be assumed to be resident in Greece unless you can demonstrate otherwise.
- If you spend less than 185 days in Greece and have a home elsewhere, you will be treated as non-resident in Greece.
- If your main home and family base is in Greece, you will be treated as a tax resident of Greece.

Tax Residence in More than One Country

It is possible to be resident or ordinarily resident in both the UK and Greece at the same time under the respective rules of those countries. For example, you might spend 230 days of the year in Greece and 135 days in the UK. In this case, you could end up being responsible for paying the same tax in two or more countries under the rules of each country. This would be unfair, so many countries have signed reciprocal 'Double Taxation Treaties'. The UK and Greece have such a treaty. It contains 'tie breakers' and other provisions to decide, where there is the possibility of being required to pay tax twice, in which country any particular category of tax should be paid.

Taxes Payable in the UK

If you are only buying a holiday home and will remain primarily resident in the United Kingdom, your tax position in the UK will not change very much. You'll have to declare any income you make from your Greek property as part of your UK tax declaration. The calculation of tax due on that income will be made in accordance with the UK rules, which will result in a different taxable sum from that used by the Greek tax authorities. The UK tax man will give you full credit for any tax that has already been paid in Greece.

On the disposal of the property, (*see* 'Capital Gains Tax, below) you should disclose the profit made to the UK taxman. He will again give you full credit for any Greek tax paid. Similarly, upon your death, the assets in Greece must be disclosed to the UK (*see* 'Inheritance Tax', below). But, once again, you will be given full credit for any sums paid in Greece.

If you leave the UK to live in Greece:

• You will continue to have to pay tax in the UK on any capital gains you make anywhere in the world for as long as you are ordinarily resident and domiciled in United Kingdom (*see* below).

• You will continue to be liable to British inheritance tax on all of your assets located anywhere in the world for as long as you remain domiciled in the UK. This will be subject to double taxation relief (*see* below). Other, more complex rules also apply in certain circumstances.

• You will always pay UK income tax on income arising from land and buildings in the UK – wherever your domicile, residence or ordinary residence.

• You will pay UK income tax on the following basis:

  • Income from 'self-employed' trade or profession carried out in the UK – normally taxed in the UK if income arises in the UK.

  • Income from interest, annuities or other annual payments from the UK – normally taxed in the UK if income arises in the UK and you are ordinarily resident in the UK.

  • Income from investments and businesses outside the UK – normally only taxed in the UK if you are UK domiciled and resident or ordinarily resident in the UK.

  • Income from government pensions (fire, police, army, civil servant, etc.) in all cases taxed in the UK.

  • Sundry profits not otherwise taxable arising out of land or building in the UK – always taxed in the UK.

• You will pay income tax on any income earned from salaried employment in the UK only in respect of any earnings from duties performed in the UK unless you are resident and ordinarily resident in the UK – in which case you will usually pay tax in the UK on your worldwide earnings.

Capital Gains Tax

If you are either resident or ordinarily resident in the UK, you may be liable to capital gains tax on gains arising when you dispose of assets situated anywhere in the world. Disposing of an asset means selling, exchanging, transferring, giving it away or realising a capital sum from it. Usually you will not pay capital gains tax on:

• the transfer of an asset to your spouse.

• the disposal of private motor vehicles.

• the disposal of household goods and personal effects up to a value of £6,000 per item.

• the disposal of a private home which has been treated as your main or only residence during the time you have owned it.

'Overseas assets' are assets located outside the UK under capital gains tax rules. For assets such as land, and most types of immovable property, the asset is situated where it is located. If you are resident or ordinarily resident in the UK, and dispose of such assets, you will normally be liable to capital gains tax on any gains arising from them. But if you are not domiciled in the UK (i.e. if you have elected to take Greek domicile), you are taxed on such gains only to the extent that they are brought in or 'remitted' to the UK in a tax year during which you are resident or ordinarily resident in the UK. There is no capital gains tax charge on gains remitted to the UK before you become resident in the UK.

There is no capital gains tax in Greece.

Inheritance Tax

Domiciled in the UK

Liability to UK inheritance tax depends on your domicile at the time you make the transfer. For inheritance tax purposes, there is the concept of '**deemed domicile**'. Even if you are not domiciled in the UK under general law, you will be treated as domiciled in the UK at the time of a transfer if you were domiciled in the UK within the three years immediately before the transfer or if you were ordinarily resident in the UK for at least 17 of the 20 income tax years of assessment, ending with the year in which you made the transfer.

You or your personal representatives may be liable to UK inheritance tax if you transfer anything of value, such as a lifetime gift or a willed transfer to your personal representatives on your death.

Which Assets are Taxable in the UK?

Generally, if you are domiciled or deemed to be domiciled in the UK, inheritance tax applies to your assets wherever they are situated. If the value of your gift or the assets in your estate is above the threshold then you may be liable to inheritance tax.

If you are domiciled abroad, inheritance tax applies only to your UK assets. However, if you are domiciled abroad there is no charge on excluded assets, so the taxman may remove certain other types of UK assets from the tax charge.

The location of the assets is decided according to general law but is subject to any special provisions in a double taxation agreement. The normal rules are:

- **Rights or interests in or over immovable property (such as land and houses) and chattels are situated where the property is located.**

- **Coins and bank notes are situated wherever they happen to be at the time of the transfer.**

- **Registered shares or securities are situated where they are registered.**

- **Bearer securities are situated where the certificate of title is located at the time of the transfer.**

- Goodwill is located where the business to which it is attached is carried out.

- An interest in a partnership is situated in the country whose law governs the partnership agreement.

- Debts are situated where the debtor resides.

- Bank accounts are situated at the branch where the account is kept.

Double Taxation Relief

If you have income or gains from a source in one country and are resident in another, you may be liable to pay tax in both under their tax laws. To avoid 'double taxation', the UK has negotiated double taxation agreements with countries like Greece. The agreement has been in effect since 1953. Relief in so far as Greece is concerned is offered for income tax. In so far as the UK tax is concerned relief is offered for income tax and capital gains tax.

Taxes Payable in Greece

Income Tax: Non-residents

If you are not resident in Greece, and do not generate any income in Greece, your contact with the tax authority will be limited to the filing of a first income tax return after the purchase of your property.

Under Greek law, every person is obliged to file a tax return if his or her annual taxable income is over €3,000. There is a further obligation to file a tax return even if the annual income is under €3,000 if this income is a net income from commercial activities (in other words, it has taken into consideration the losses of the business). If a person is resident abroad, he or she is obliged to file a declaration if he or she owns property in Greece, has a private car or an income of over €600 per annum from rental of property.

The income which remains after taking into consideration certain allowances is then subject to income tax. Income which remains after these sums have been calculated is taxable based according to the following scale:

Income Tax Rates

Category A (Employed People and Pensioners)

Scale of Income (€)	Tax Band Applied (%)	Tax Scale (€)	Total Income (€)	Tax Due (€)
10,000	0*	0*	10,000	0*
3,400	15	510	13,400	510
10,000	30	300	23,400	3,510
Excess	40			

Tax Registration Number *(Arithmós Foroloyikó Mitróön)*

One of the initial steps which must be taken prior to the purchase of a property in Greece is the issue of a tax registration number (or *A-fi-Mi* as it is widely known). This unique number is issued to anyone who needs to carry out transactions with the Ministry of Finance and any other public authority. The tax registration number identifies a person and is used in transactions with public and private bodies wherever it is necessary by law.

Whether resident in Greece or abroad, a person has to obtain a tax registration number when he or she:

- Is obliged to file an income tax return.

- Obtains any assets which define indicators *(tekmíria)* of tax liability, such as a motor vehicle, a boat, or a motorcycle over 50cc, etc.).

- Requires a tax clearance certificate *(pistopiitikó foroloyikís enimerótitas)*, or other certificates or confirmations from the various tax authorities.

- Is a business member or a partner.

- Is obliged to file a declaration of capital (due to the acquisition of assets).

- Is the representatives of persons liable to pay tax (e.g. guardians, liquidators, tax representatives, etc.).

The competent tax authority (DOY/Dhimósia Ikonomikí Ypiresía) for the issue of a tax registration number is the tax authority that governs the area where the person is resident. For persons who are non-resident in Greece, the appropriate tax authority is normally the non-resident's tax authority in Athens.

For the issue of a tax registration number, the presentation of an identification card or passport for non-Greek nationals is a prerequisite. If a third party applies for the issue of a tax registration number, he must have with him the appropriate document of authorisation. The tax authority will provide two forms which must be then completed and which will contain all the necessary details required for issuing a tax registration number.

Category B (Self-Employed People)

Scale of Income (€)	Tax Band Applied (%)	Tax Scale (€)	Taxable Income (€)	Tax Due (€)
8,400	0*	0*	8,400	0*
5,000	15	750	13,400	750
10,000	30	3,000	23,400	3,750
Excess	40			

It should be noted that for non-residents the first band of tax is not zero but five per cent unless 90 per cent of their income is generated in Greece. Furthermore, no tax-free allowances or allowances for certain types of expenses are permitted for non-residents unless 90 per cent of their income is generated in

Greece. It should also be noted that the above rates and tax-free amounts are subject to change in the annual budget presented by the government.

Filing of Tax Returns

It is an absolute prerequisite that non-residents nominate a **tax representative** in Greece, both for the receipt of the tax demands which are issued by the various tax authorities and as a point of contact for any queries that arise. The tax representative basically acts as a go-between between the tax authorities and the persons who are resident abroad.

The appointing of a tax representative takes place by power of attorney, which is submitted at the same time as the application for a tax registration number (*A-fi-Mi*) for a non-resident.

After 2000, the appropriate tax authority for the receipt of the income tax returns for non-residents of Greece who have income generated in Greece is determined by the place of residence of their tax representative. In other words, if their tax representative is resident in the Attica prefecture, then the appropriate tax authority is the non-residents' tax authority in Athens.

The annual income tax declaration must be filed in May of the following financial year with an absolute deadline of June 4 for that particular year. The declaration (income tax return) must be submitted in two copies, either personally by the non-resident or by his or her tax representative.

Different rules apply in determining the appropriate tax authority for the receipt of the Large Property Tax (*FMAP*), parental contribution (*fóros gonikís parohís*), gift (*fóros dhoréas*) or inheritance tax (*fóros klironomías*) declarations.

- **For the filing of the Large Property Tax declaration, the tax authority is that which governs the income tax return for the person involved.**

- **For the filing of declarations concerning gifts, parental contributions and inheritance tax in the case where the persons involved are non-residents (the person making the gift, the parent making the contribution or the deceased person), the appropriate tax authority is the non-resident's tax authority in Athens.**

- **If, however, the deceased was a non-resident but died in Greece, then the competent tax authority is the one nearest the town or city where he or she died.**

For non-residents, the time limit for the filing of an inheritance tax return is one year from the date of the death of the person involved and, if there is a will involved, then it is one year from the date of its publication if the beneficiaries or the deceased were resident at the time of death abroad.

Income Tax (*Fóros Isodhímatos*): Residents

For all matters relating to income tax, the appropriate tax authority is the local tax authority near the person's residence and the Ministry of Finance thereafter. As in the UK, income is divided into various categories, such as pensions and employment income which is taxed at source.

Income Tax Rates

Category A (Employed People and Pensioners)

Scale of Income (€)	Tax Band Applied (%)	Tax Scale (€)	Total Income (€)	Tax Due (€)
10,000	0	0	10,0000	
3,400	15	510	13,400	510
10,000	30	300	23,000	3,510
Excess	40			

Category B (Self-Employed People)

Scale of Income (€)	Tax Band Applied (%)	Tax Scale (€)	Taxable Income (€)	Tax Due (€)
8,400	0	0	8,400	0
5,000	15	750	13,400	750
10,000	30	3,000	23,400	3,750
Excess	40			

The citizen's gross income is subject to certain **deductions** which reduce the amount of income which is eventually taxed. The list below is not exhaustive.

- **Any rental expenditure in the case where a person resident in Greece lives in rented accommodation.**
- **The costs associated with life insurance.**
- **Any expenses incurred for tuition for any children of the marriage.**
- **The equivalent of National Insurance contributions to the social security funds in Greece.**
- **Costs in connection with medical care (such as visits to the doctor or hospitalisation).**
- **Interest charges for mortgages (mortgage interest tax relief).**
- **The purchase of Greek shares or investment funds.**
- **The cost of purchasing a computer.**

Agricultural income must be declared by all persons who do not keep Category B books.

The annual income tax declaration must be filed in May of the following financial year with an absolute deadline of June 4 for that particular year.

Income generated and received abroad is also taxed. Initially, the tax authority will consider the treaty of double taxation that applies and then calculate whether any surplus tax is payable.

Means Test (Póthen Éskhes)

In order to put a stop to rampant tax evasion by the Greeks, the government has introduced a series of measures based on obvious signs of wealth such as property, expensive cars, yachts, etc. A person must be able to show when purchasing any one of these luxury items that the income used to effect the purchase was declared to the tax authorities in a previous tax year. If they cannot do so, the tax authority will charge income tax on the amount that has not been declared.

Large Property Tax (FMAP/*Fóros Megális Akinitís Perousías*)

Regardless of their nationality and their residence status, everyone is liable for Large Property Tax if their immovable property on 1 January 2003 was in excess of €243,600 (for unmarried people) or €487,200 (for married people). This tax is also extended to legal entities or corporations who own immovable property in Greece. The declaration of Large Property Tax is filed with the tax authority responsible for receiving the annual income tax return for the person affected.

The value of property for the purposes of this type of tax is calculated in reference to the **objective tax value system** in those areas where this system is enforced (*see* p.132). If the property is mortgaged, then the value of the loan is taken into consideration, with an appropriate reduction in the value of the property concerned. The tax thresholds mentioned above increase by €61,650 for a married couple with two children and by a further €73,400 for every additional child.

Tax is calculated in the following manner:

Large Property Tax Rates

Scale (€)	Tax Scale (%)	Tax According to Scale (€)	Total Taxable Assets (€)	Tax Due (€)
146,750	0.3	440.25	146,750	440.25
146,750	0.4	587	293,500	1,027.25
146,750	0.5	733.75	440,250	1,761.00
293,500	0.6	1,761	733,750	3,522.00
293,500	0.7	2,054.50	1,027,250	5,576.50
Excess	0.8			

Given that the government faces large public funding issues, it does not appear likely that there will be significant changes to Greek property taxation in 2005. Only the relatively minor incentive of increasing the amount of mortgage tax relief for mortgages taken out after 1 January 2004 seems likely to change.

However, in the next three-year period, the government is planning changes to how property is taxed. As regards the information presently being made available, the Greek government intends to inject some life back into the market by lowering taxes, increasing tax-free amounts and taking other measures designed to encourage the numbers of new-build properties.

There are also plans to lower transfer tax and increase tax-free amounts for gifts and parental contributions, as well as for inheritance tax. A proposal is in place by which the Large Property Tax would be discontinued and no VAT imposed on new-build properties in 2005. It also seems unlikely that objective tax values will be increased in 2005.

The government raises objective tax values from time to time and an increase occurs after January 1 of the year in which the tax declaration for large property (*FMAP*) must be filed. The tax value which will be applied is that which occurred on January 1 of the year in which the tax declaration was made.

Local Taxes

Both residents and non-residents pay these taxes.

You will have the following taxes to pay as the owner of a property in Greece: local **municipality dues** calculated at a fixed rate, which are then multiplied by the size (square meterage) of the building concerned; a **property tax** levied against the size of the property (e.g. building) and the pricing zone in which it is situated; and a small charge made for the **national radio and television corporation**.

All of the above taxes are relatively small and are usually incorporated in your electricity bill. It follows that if you are not connected to the grid, such as in the case of the owner of the plot of land with no buildings on it, you pay a smaller amount direct to the municipality. It will also make an annual charge for **water and sewage disposal**, which varies from area to area and is based largely on the size and nature of the property involved.

Capital Gains Tax

There is no capital gains tax in Greece.

Inheritance Tax

A declaration of inheritance tax must be filed with the relevant tax authority by the beneficiary or his or her legal representative. If the deceased died in Greece, the time limit for filing the inheritance tax return is six months, whereas if the deceased was non-resident or died out of Greece and all the beneficiaries were resident abroad at the time of death, the time limit is then one year. The time limit is calculated from:

- **the time of the death of the deceased person.**
- **the publication of the deceased person's will, if there is one.**

The above time limits may be extended by a further three months by the decision of the director of the relevant tax authority if there are important reasons for the extension to be granted.

At the time that the inheritance tax declaration is filed, a number of other important documents must also be submitted:

- **A certified copy of the death certificate.**

- A copy of the will (if applicable).

- A certificate of inheritance or a certificate from the appropriate municipal authority regarding the time and closeness of the relationship of the relatives of the deceased.

- A certificate from the secretariat of the Court of First Instance regarding the non-publication of a newer will or in connection with the non-publication of any will in relation to an intestate succession.

- A certificate regarding the age of the person who is entitled to the use (*epikarpótis*) of a property when his age is taken into consideration for the calculation of the value.

- A copy of the power of attorney authorising a legal representative to file the inheritance tax (if applicable).

- Any documents in support of the burdens of the estate.

The inheritance tax return must be filed with the tax authority responsible for the area where the deceased person had his last residence, or with the tax authority for non-residents if the deceased person was a resident abroad. If the deceased person was resident abroad but died in Greece, the appropriate tax authority is that which covered the place of death.

Tax that is imposed on the assets of an inheritance is banded not only according to value but also according to the closeness of the blood ties of the deceased to his or her beneficiaries. It follows that the relatives in **Category A** (including the children and spouse of the deceased) are liable to pay five per cent tax on the amount between €20,000 and €60,000. For the first €20,000, the amounts are taken tax-free, while the tax band is 10 per cent for sums between €60,000 and €220,000. For sums over €220,000, tax is applied at 20 per cent. For relatives in **Category B**, the following tax rules apply. For the first €15,000, the amounts taken are tax-free. For sums between €15,000 up to €60,000, a 10 per cent tax is applied. For sums between €60,000 up to €220,000, tax is levied at 20 per cent. For sums over €220,000, tax is set at 30 per cent. For persons in **Category C**, any sums received between €5,000 (up to the first €5,000 the amount is tax-free) up to €60,000 have 20 per cent tax applied. For sums between €60,000 up to €220,000, the band applied is 30 per cent while for sums exceeding €220,000, the tax band is 40 per cent.

Inheritance Tax Rates

Category A

Scale (€)	Rate of Scale (%)	Tax scale (€)	Taxable value (€)	Tax Due (€)
20,000	0	0	20,000	0
40,000	5	2,000	60,000	2,000
160,000	10	16,000	220,000	18,000
Excess	20			

Category B

Scale (€)	Rate of Scale (%)	Tax scale (€)	Taxable value (€)	Tax Due (€)
15,000	0	0	5,000	0
45,000	10	4,500	60,000	4,500
160,000	20	32,000	220,000	36,500
Excess	30			

Category C

Scale (€)	Rate of Scale (%)	Tax scale (€)	Taxable value (€)	Tax Due (€)
5,000	0	0	5,000	0
55,000	20	11,000	60,000	11,000
160,000	30	48,000	220,000	59,000
Excess	40			

More recent legislation (Law 3091/2002) states that a spouse (married for at least five years prior to the death of her husband) and her children are exempt from inheritance tax up to €300,000.

There are certain tax-free allowances when certain prerequisites are fulfilled in connection with the inheritance tax when the tax applied is in connection to what is known as a first residence allowance. For example, if the beneficiary, his spouse or their children do not have legal title or use of the right of residence in another building or apartment which is adequate for the housing needs of their family, then an amount is applied tax-free in connection with their inheritance.

For an unmarried person, the tax-free amount in connection with a plot of land viable for building is €30,000; for a building the amount is €65,000. For a married person, these amounts are increased to €55,000 for the plot of land (increased by €8,000 for the first child, a further €8,000 for the second child with a further €10,000 for each additional child). For a building or apartment, this amount is €100,000 with increases of €20,000 for the first child; a further €20,000 for the second child; and a further €30,000 for the third and any more children.

Inheritance tax may be paid in 24 equal monthly interest-free instalments if the amount of tax is to be calculated based on the filed declaration. Alternatively, inheritance tax may be paid in six equal interest-free monthly payments if the tax calculated is based on a judicial decision from the administrative court or has been calculated following a judicial compromise. If the beneficiary is a minor, these monthly payments are doubled.

Taxes Payable upon Parental Contribution and Gift (*Fóros Dhoréas Ke Fóros Gonikís Parohís*)

A declaration of gift tax or parental contribution tax (i.e. where a parent contributes to the purchase of a child's property) must be filed by the parent and child concerned or, in the case of the non-formal gift, by the beneficiary of the gift. The appropriate tax authority for the filing of the gift tax or the parental contribution tax is the tax authority which governs the area of the person making the gift.

The declaration must be filed prior to the execution of the notarised contract and, where a non-formal gift is involved, within six months from the award of the object of the gift to the person receiving it. Gift tax is calculated on exactly the same basis as inheritance tax. Parental contribution tax is half of gift tax.

Where parental contributions are concerned, the maximum amount of parental contribution for tax purposes is €90,000 for each parent. This amount may be increased to €130,000 if one of the parents is deceased. For values over this amount, the tax applied is the greater whole amount of gift tax.

There are certain tax-free allowances for obtaining a first residence by way of parental contribution. These amounts are identical to those which govern the inheritance tax allowances noted above.

Parental Contribution

The following documents are required by the donor:

• A certificate or declaration under Article 81 of Law 22388/1994 that the property has been declared for the past 2 years (if a certificate is issued) or that it has not generated income for the past 5 years (if a declaration is filed).

• A declaration that there is no Large Property Tax owed for the property to be transferred under Article 32 of law 2459 /1997. If the seller is obliged to pay this type of tax, then you must obtain a certificate to confirm that he or she has paid the appropriate tax for the property that he wishes to sell.

• A certificate to show that there is no national insurance fund monies owed from the IKA.

• A tax clearance certificate.

• A copy of the building licence if the property has been built after 1983.

• A certificate from the local municipality stating that there are no property dues owing (TAP). The certificate must bear the names of both parents if they are both donors. Care must also be taken to ensure that the correct size of the property is noted. If a parking space or a store room is being transferred, their square meterage must also be recorded.

• The title documents for any parental contribution or gift after 1 January 1985, or by an inheritance where the deceased person died after 1 January 1985. In this case, a certificate that there is no outstanding tax of parental contribution, gift or inheritance tax must be issued.

• If the case is a gift, dowry or inheritance which has taken place before January 1, 1985, then a copy of the notarised document of gift or dowry or, in the case of inheritance, a copy of the registered act of death must be provided.

Inheritance

The Greek Inheritance Rules

Unlike some continental systems, such as the French one, Greek inheritance rules are only applied to Greek nationals. This is fortunate, as the Greek rules are much more restrictive than the rules under English law. Certain groups of people have automatic rights to inherit at least a part of your property. If you are a Greek national, even if you are resident abroad, or even dual nationality, your property must be disposed of in accordance with the provisions of Greek law. However, even if the Greek inheritance rules do not apply, for instance if the deceased person was not a Greek national, Greek taxation rules in a round-about way offer an incentive for the property to be left in a specific way. For example a spouse or a child is likely to pay far less tax upon inheritance than a friend unconnected by blood ties, or a distant relative. This has specific importance in cases where partners are cohabiting and have not formally married.

Who Gets What under Greek Law

The regulations which govern succession and inheritance provide for a minimum legal share to be left to certain classes of persons. These provisions only apply in cases of assets which had been left by will; the intestacy provisions of Greek law provide for a larger share to be left to the persons protected under the minimum legal share provisions.

Beneficiaries are identified into various classes. The **first class** are the children and the spouse who survive the deceased. Where no children survive, grandchildren comprise this class. Children inherit in equal shares. Also included are children born outside the bonds of marriage but who have been formally recognised by their father, as well as children formally adopted by their parents. The **second class** of beneficiaries are the parents of the deceased and his or her brothers or sisters, as well as the children and the grandchildren of the deceased's brothers and sisters. The parents as well as the brothers and sisters inherit equally; any stepbrothers or stepsisters are entitled to 50 per cent of the share that a full brother or sister would have been entitled to. The **third class** of beneficiaries includes the grandparents of the deceased as well as their descendants. The **fourth class** includes great-grandparents of the deceased.

A beneficiary will only be called to inherit if there is no beneficiary available from the previous class. The surviving spouse is entitled to all the personal possessions of the deceased spouse. If no beneficiaries are available from the first four classes, then the spouse will be entitled to all the assets of the deceased. Where there are no beneficiaries, all the assets go to the state.

Where a spouse and children survive, all of the first class, then the spouse is entitled to one quarter of the estate, with the remaining three-quarters being divided equally by the other beneficiaries of the first class. When the spouse survives with beneficiaries of the other classes mentioned above, then she or he will inherit 50 per cent of the assets with the beneficiaries sharing the further 50 per cent. In accordance with Article 1825 of the Greek Civil Code, the direct descendants (children, grandchildren as well as the parents and the surviving spouse of the deceased) have a right to a minimum legal share which is calculated to be 50 per cent of the provisions under the rules of intestacy.

Therefore in order to identify and calculate the amount of the minimum legal share first we must identify the amount that the beneficiary would have been entitled to under the intestacy provisions.

For example:

- **A man dies leaving a single child: under the rules of intestacy the child would be entitled to at least 100 per cent of all the assets, so his minimum legal share (in the case where the deceased left a will be leaving the asset to a third party) would be 50 per cent of all the assets.**

- **A person dies leaving a spouse and two children: the spouse would be entitled to one quarter of all the assets under the rules of intestacy, so one-eighth would be home protected minimum legal share. Each of the children would be entitled to three-eighths under the intestate provisions, so three-sixteenths would be there protected minimum legal share.**

Any provisions in a will which conflict with the minimum legal share provisions are deemed not to be valid. When making a will it is essential that a testator provides that the beneficiaries who are protected in law receive at least a sum equal to that provided for by Greek law.

As already referred to above, these provisions only apply to Greek nationals, and even here there is an exception to the general rule whereby Greek nationals who have lived abroad for a continuous period of over 25 years are not subject to these provisions in so far as their property which is located abroad is concerned. An English purchaser of property in Greece, unless he or she is also a Greek national, will be permitted to freely dispose of property, and where no will is made, the English rules of intestate succession will apply.

However, as already stated, inheritance tax plans which are applied upon succession take into consideration the closeness of the relationship (blood ties) of the beneficiary and the deceased, and this can therefore have a significant financial effect and is an effective way of limiting a the choices available to the non-national testator. *See* 'Inheritance Tax', pp.147–9.

Making a Will

It is always best to make a Greek will. If you choose not to do this but rely on your English one, this may cause more problems in the long run than the money saved from drawing up a Greek will in the first place. There is a process for validating an English will, but the costs involved making a Greek will represent the more attractive option. If you are not resident in Greece, your Greek will should state that it only applies to your property in Greece. The rest of your property will be disposed of in accordance with English law and under the provisions of your English will. If you do not make a will and are an English national, your property will be disposed of in accordance with the English rules of intestacy.

In most cases, a Greek will is merely a notarised document signed before a notary public. If there is the option of a handwritten will, it must be done in the hand of the testator, dated and signed by him. The will must show the day, month and year. Any additions to it must be signed by the testator, otherwise they will not be considered to have been written by him. The handwritten will may be deposited with a notary public for his safekeeping and eventual publication. The preferred route, however, is that of a public will composed following a declaration by the testator of his last will and testament before a notary public and three witnesses or a second notary and one witness. The advantages of a public will override its disadvantages. For example, it is very difficult to challenge the originality or validity of a public will because it has the proof of a public document. A notary public is also usually better able to precisely express the intentions of the testator in legal terminology. The safekeeping of the document in the hands of the notary public guards it from destruction or loss.

There is a simple procedure to follow in order to publish a Greek will and obtain the relevant certificate of inheritance which will enable any assets left in the will to be dealt with. The notary (or the attorney acting for the estate) will send the will to the secretary of the competent court of first instance (such a court being the place where the notary has his seat for publication). The court will draw up a special memorandum which will include the will and confirmation of whether or not the will has been drawn up in line with the rules described. Once publication is complete, the beneficiaries can also apply for a certificate of inheritance which will set out their rights to the assets of the estate.

Investments

If you are moving overseas, you *must* review your investments. Your current arrangements are likely to be financially disastrous and may even be illegal. For most British people, the Big Issue is whether to continue to keep their interests in England in sterling. Trusts have a limited use in Greece unless your income is very large or unless you will remain resident in the UK.

What Are You Worth?

Most of us are, in financial terms, worth more than we think. When we come to move abroad and have to think about these things, it can come as a shock.

Take a pen and fill in the chart below. Do this to give yourself an idea of the amount you are worth now and, just as importantly, what you are likely to be worth in the future.

Where Should You Invest?

For British people, the big issue is whether they should keep their sterling investments. Most British people will have investments that are largely sterling-based. As the value of the euro fluctuates against sterling, the value of your investments will go up and down. That, of itself, isn't too important because the value won't crystallise unless you sell. What does matter is that the revenue you generate from those investments (rent, interest, dividends) may fluctuate in value. In general terms, investments paying out euros are preferable if you live in a European country.

Asset	Value – Local Currency	Value – £s
Current Assets		
Main home		
Holiday home		
Contents of main home		
Contents of holiday home		
Car		
Boat		
Bank accounts		
Other cash-type investments		
Bonds, etc.		
Stocks and shares		
PEPs, Tessas, ISAs		
Value of your business		
Other		
Future Assets		
Value of share options		
Personal/company pension – likely lump sum		
Potential inheritances or other accretions		
Value of endowment mortgages on maturity		
Other		

Restoration and Building

Building Codes and Costs

Despite the recent wave in purpose-built developments, outside of Crete and Kefalloniá a small majority of properties bought by foreigners are still older buildings ready for restoration. Across Greece, vernacular one- or two-storey houses almost always have stone-built walls of 55–60cm thickness (the ancient *píhi* or distance from elbow to fingertips), though grander multi-storey buildings typically attain ground-floor wall thicknesses of 80cm. As noted above, they are far superior to most new-build for temperature control, remaining cool in the summer until the afternoon, retaining appreciable heat in winter until well after dark. A civil engineer or architect will, upon inspection of the premises, tell you how sound the walls are, whether they just need pointing or re-rendering, and whether they're strong enough to support the addition of an extra storey. If you want to do this without unsightly extra columns, consider using lightweight materials, such as pumice blocks, or artificial-pumice blocks (Ytong brand), which will not unduly stress the lower storey – though your architect will stipulate a narrow course of cement with rebar at the top of the original wall to stabilise it. Old houses, however superficially sturdy, have no foundations to speak of, the stonework being typically dug into the surrounding ground level not more than two or three courses. Inside a village, you will generally only be allowed to go up two storeys or, if on a slight slope, 9–10 metres up from the lowest point on the plot, 7.5 metres up from the highest point. Again, there are local wrinkles and exceptions, especially for preservation areas, which you must investigate before commencing any works.

In May 2001, former PASOK Minister of the Aegean Nikos Sifounakis announced the imposition of a strict new building code for the smaller islands of the Cyclades, Dodecanese and east Aegean, to check the spread of concrete monstrosities. With too many voters to be antagonised, most of the larger islands were excluded from the plan, as well as Mýkonos, where Sifounakis' father-in-law wished to build a mega-hotel – but it was, at least, a step in the right direction. In addition to height limits similar to those cited above, obligatory guidelines were included for the number of windows, doors and balconies on the façades of buildings, and the height-to-width proportion those windows and doors should have – something approximating to the *golden mean* of the ancients (that is, 1.618:1). It's still too early to tell if the new Néa Dhimokratía government, in power since March 2004, will maintain, strengthen or altogether drop this code. As ever in Greece, keep your ear to the ground.

For an elderly house in good shape, with easy road access, needing only modernised plumbing, kitchen units, wiring, a new roof and a spot of plastering, the renovation multiplier ranges from three to five times the base purchase price, assuming a modest permit for the roof and scaffolding, and IKA payments – analogous to Class 4 DSS contributions in the UK, which average around one-third the total cost of the works.

Builders and Budgeting

Any sort of construction work in Greece is fraught with pitfalls for the novice, exacerbated by the probable language barrier. There is no system for formal certification of specialist craftsmen, as in Italy or France, and workmanship is, to put it politely, highly variable. Aegean builders tend to think they know it all and have seen it all, and it can be difficult to persuade them to do something out of the ordinary in terms of their experience. The rapid modernisation (and touristification) of Greece has had a deleterious effect on both restoration and new-build with a current overriding emphasis on pre-fab materials (*prókat*) and patchwork (*proherodhouliá*). Other idioms you'll hear and learn soon enough include shoddy work (*mápa*) and pseudo-craftsmen (*pseftomástori*). In 1992, a free, EU-funded course in stonemasonry failed to commence on Sámos owing to lack of enrolment – not an isolated event and emblematic of the plight of traditional methods throughout Greece, where most young people prefer the easy pickings of the tourist industry.

All that said, there are still numbers of skilled builders around, on almost every island and in almost every mainland region. If you see finished results in your neighbourhood that you like the look of, don't be shy about asking the owners who they used – referrals are always appreciated, and get you off on good footing with the worker in question.

If your restoration property only requires the contracting of specific, individual jobs (such as electrical rewiring or modernisation of plumbing), you should

---

Violations and Denunciations

Even with the proper permit in hand – and prominently displayed on the work-site in the format 235/04 (meaning the 235th local approval for 2004), builders and renovaters still run the risk of denunciation for alleged violations. Denunciations – often anonymous – can be made to the local *poleodhomía* or IKA, and are a quick and painful way to find out how many enemies you've made locally. Neighbours have the right to inspect copies on file of your permit, and can snitch on alleged contravention of the agreed plans. Even if you do all of the labour yourself, in theory you have to make IKA payments *as if* you were paying the going rate to outside workmen, and you can even be denounced for carrying out internal works which don't require a permit (this rarely happens, however).

Just what lengths petty malice can go to is illustrated by the experience of a successful taverna keeper – we'll call him Makis – on the Epirote coast near Párga. When I commented that his roofline, with a ratio of height-to-base of 1.3:1, looked odd, Makis filled me in on the tale of how a jealous rival had denounced him twice, reducing the pitch from the intended 1.8:1 to 1.5:1 and then 1.3:1. Having failed to deter Makis, the rival topped off his performance by spiking Makis' reservoir tank (*vítio*) with kerosene, then chopping up a dog and disposing of the remains down his well.

Not for the Faint-hearted...

Jill Sleeman is the proprietress of the Old Silk Store, a small guesthouse in Moúressi, Mount Pílio (www.pelionet.gr/oldsilkstore), acclaimed in *The Best Small Hotels of Greece* and the *Alpha Guide to the Best Hotels and Restaurants in Greece*. She bought what was then a private dwelling in 1988 from an elderly French woman who had used the place as a summer residence for 27 years. Though structurally sound, the house – a 19th-century mansion which had indeed been built by a wealthy silk magnate – had no mod cons whatsoever, certainly no hot water or proper heating. The wiring was so dodgy that if one tried to boil an electric kettle, the fuses popped out of the wall. Using the one cold-water bathroom that existed in the building was a Siberian ordeal as the first winter of renovations was bitterly cold (–10°C at times). Jill and her partner journeyed to Vólos once a week to buy supplies, as almost nothing was available in the village back then. They often had to stay overnight (enjoying a hot bath at the Park Hotel) because they couldn't finish everything by 2pm when the shops closed at the end of their morning shift. 'When we had workmen due,' she continues, 'I used to lie in my early morning bed shredding petals from an imaginary daisy: "Will he come, won't he come..." Whoever shouted loudest at the workmen to appear on their doorstep won the day.'

In no particular order, Jill's worst renovation nightmares were:

• Having the roof repaired while she was away (big mistake); all the slag and debris was left on the roof and she spent five days together with a helper removing it in a bucket lowered down with a rope.

• Sandblasting off the old exterior paint. Seemingly the whole of the nearest beach found its way into every corner and every item of the interior. While polythene sheeting had been put up on the outside of the windows, nobody had warned Jill to put another layer on the inside, too.

• Installing central heating, which dragged on over four months that winter, with several setbacks and a huge mess at the end that required three people ten days to clean up, working in shifts. The result, however, was worth it as central heating is much more practical than the romantic wood stoves, which are now only for decoration.

Jill concludes, 'Anyone who likes old houses loves the Old Silk Store, which is no longer a semi-ruin – though I am. A dream enterprise like this takes plenty of sweat, nerves and patience, as well as a network of supportive nearby friends when things run into the ground.'

allow €60–70 per day for an unskilled labourer (*ergátis*) and €90–100 per day for a specialist craftsman (*tekhnítis* or *mástoras*), including IKA and *Tamío Epangelmatión ke Viotekhnón Elládhos* (TEBE) payments. You will be expected to stump up an advance (*prokatavolí*) of perhaps a quarter of the agreed total, ostensibly for the purchase of raw materials; never hand over the final instalment until you are satisfied with the work. You may find your job subject to strange suspensions and halts; this is owing to the common practice of 'rolling financing' – that is, your advance is actually facilitating the completion of a previous task, while your job will not really proceed until the builder has found a subsequent job to take on, and so on.

Plumbing and electrical works are, by northern European standards, very affordable in Greece, and it's possible to plumb and wire a 125-square-metre house (external dimensions) with two bathrooms and one kitchen for about €1,000–1,200 total labour. (This includes switches and power points, which you're unlikely to source yourself, but excludes sanitary and kitchen fixtures.)

If you acquire a shell with perhaps two or three reusable walls standing to head height and no easy road access, you should expect to pay up to 10 times the base price for a result that will effectively be new-built. Reinforced cement work, masonry – even if carried out by the famously cheap(er) Albanian immigrant craftsmen – and plastering are the three most expensive operations you can have done, far exceeding plumbing and wiring in cost. Structural carpentry is not far behind, though joinery and cabinet-making – a separate discipline in Greece – are usually more reasonable. Put another way, a useful rule of thumb in budgeting for new-builds across Greece is €880–1,250 per square metre measured externally (*not* the net internal usable area), which figure should include the IKA payments for the work crew, though not necessarily the building permit. The higher base figure will apply to constructions with special difficulties (such as poor access), where remedial reinforcement is required, or a high quotient of stone masonry, cement work or carpentry is needed.

Demolition and Clearing

You can save a lot of money when restoring a ruin by carrying out much of the demolition and preparation yourself. This is filthy, unskilled work which most outside workmen – except Albanians – are not keen to take on. Also, by preparing the ground (and walls, as plaster-stripping is a common operation), you will increase the likelihood of getting a constructed result you want, not the one of maximum convenience for the hired help. You will need a traditional Greek wheelbarrow (the same sturdy model is sold nationwide), thick planking for ramps as necessary, lots of thick plastic and heavy paper bags (discarded plaster and cement sacks are ideal), a crowbar, mallets (both short- and long-handled), a long cold chisel, (de)plastering spatulas (both broad and narrow), a pickaxe, quality goggles and sturdy all-leather gloves (for welders), although these last are difficult to find in Greece and should ideally be brought from overseas.

You will also require access to a pickup truck or *tríkyklo* (motor-trike with payload space) that is capable, if necessary, of manoeuvering into narrow village lanes. As in most countries, construction debris cannot be disposed of as conventional household rubbish, but must be conveyed to the local rubbish tip (*homateri* or *skoupidhótopos*). You should also not accumulate rubble on a public pathway or street pending its evacuation, or you can be denounced; you are also not allowed to wheelbarrow or bang away noisily between 3 and 5pm, or between midnight and 8am (you will quickly notice that Greek work crews commence operations at 8.01am or even 7.50am on the dot). If you can work only during the summer, the heat will likely dictate an after-dark schedule.

Be There or Else...

With my first ruin, which I had restored in 1995–96, the time came to run the kitchen waste-pipe along the outside wall down to the village lane to join up with the main sewage outflow. I usually packed a picnic so that I could hover all day at the house taking shape, which was a good 8km from where I was renting, but that day I'd forgotten and was getting dizzy with hunger. With (apparently) at least a couple of hours remaining before the pipe was to go in, I elected to bike back to my temporary apartment and have lunch. When I returned two hours later, there the grey PVC pipe hung in all its glory, two feet above the level of the notional foundation, nailed with flimsy brackets to the wall and with an insufficient slope to insure efficient drainage. Strong language erupted. With a great deal of grumbling, sawing and reglueing – the joints on the existing scheme had already set – the piping was rerouted.

You would have thought that I'd have learned a lesson. But six years later, one hot September afternoon, the beach beckoned to my partner and me. We left an electrician – who had worked unsupervised for us before and whom we felt we could trust – to get on with the task of running high-load cable from the fuse box of the existing house to the four-room extension, a renovated ruin immediately adjacent. At the beach, we realised that he'd probably not understood our explicit instructions to recess the cable as discreetly as possible along the length of the cypress trunk that formed the longitudinal roof beam (*amorgá*) or on the inside of our roof, which also did duty as the ceiling. We crossed our fingers and hoped for the best. Upon our return, we were greeted with the dismal sight of the garish cable, visible from just about every point of the open-plan combination kitchen-salon. The white wire began its trajectory according to plan, tucked nicely onto the face of an angled log running up from the corner of the house where the fuse box lay and obediently curling over a lateral trunk. But when he'd reached the *amorgá*, electrician Yiórgos had decided to run the cable in a straight line, failing to push it up on to the top of the log where it would have been out of sight except for when it dipped down to cross over a lateral beam – and incidentally requiring perhaps a metre and a half more material. I remonstrated – nay pleaded – with Yiórgos to reroute the offending wiring, but it was too late. The cable had already been cut and connected to the extension, there was no more spare, and the electrician adamantly refused to go and get a new length.

Unless you are a certified architect yourself and/or speak fluent Greek, it is advisable to engage the services of a trained local architect (*arhitéktonas*) as opposed to one of the far more numerous civil engineers (*politikí mihanikí*) for ground-up construction or major restoration work. In Greece, an architect will probably combine the functions of architect, civil engineer and site manager, which elsewhere would be exercised by three separate people. A good one, preferably trained abroad and fluent in English, is worth his (or sometimes her) weight in gold. The architect should draw up a contract of works, specifying exactly what is to be done, for how much money, and by when, perhaps stipulating financial penalties or bonuses for non- or early fulfilment. You may only get a general total figure rather than a breakdown of individual tasks, but be sure to agree on *exactly* what is included in the price – Greek ideas of 'finished' rarely tally with foreign ones (e.g. are the ornamental stone pediments in the bedroom to be pointed or left with gaps?) The architect will submit plans to the city planning department (*poleodhomía*) for approval and oversee the process of obtaining any necessary permits. And he or she will know of good local craftsmen and assemble a construction crew, will be your eyes while you are away, and will make sure the work is completed to your satisfaction.

Even with a good architect as watchdog, it is strongly advisable to be present while critical works are carried out. This can speed up construction remarkably – though many workmen refuse to work if someone is watching them continually, considering it an affront to their pride – and lessens the risk of paying for works not done (e.g. two coats of paint on the shutters rather than the promised four), plus, most importantly, ensures that you get it the way *you* want it, not the way the work crew wants it. You may be briefly (or perhaps not so briefly) unpopular, but remember that you may never see the work crew again, but you will have to deal with your house as it is for a long time to come.

Be warned that Greek workmen never clean up after themselves – neither their own construction debris nor damage to a previous craftsman's accomplishments – unless obliged to. The UK concept of 'making good' simply doesn't exist, unless included in the contract (rare). Budget many days of your own labour to remove wood-chunks and sawdust, bits of wire, pipe fragments and insulation; swabbing down cement dust from every surface; and repainting/revarnishing/rewhitewashing anything and everything that someone was foolish enough to 'finish' before a messy task took place.

Building Materials and Restoration Techniques

If you're of the DIY disposition, every sizeable town has an assortment of hardware shops (*ídhi kingalerías*) selling a range of hand and power tools, as well as plumbing parts, nails, screws and the like. The best tools are reckoned to be German-, Italian- or American-made and are priced accordingly; cheap and nasty Chinese-made tools are considered fit for a job you'll do only once. Materials other than lumber and paint are bought at building-supply yards (*mándhres*), or found at the outskirts of major towns. You're unlikely to see the inside of these except for special purchases, such as paving stones, as contractors like to make a bit of mark-up on materials, concealing this in the final grand total. Lumber is sourced separately, from a *xylapothíki*, as are paints, varnishes and wood treatment reagents (from an *ídhi khromáton*). Paint manufacturing was one of the first Greek industries established, back in the 1920s, and there are numbers of decent factories; however, for certain applications (especially varnishing), most agree that British or Danish formulas are far superior.

Cement Work, Plastering and Masonry

These are the most expensive part of your building job, but for obvious reasons this must be got absolutely right. The most (depressingly) common cause of cement-work failure is the use of un-rinsed sea sand – or worse, mixing up concrete with seawater! The latter 'technique' corrodes the internal rebar extra quickly, and was a major contributing factor to the seriousness of damage in both the 1999 Athens and Istanbul earthquakes. If you visit Kastellórizo Island, you can view an entire social housing project that has been condemned for use of seawater concrete (the contractor faces criminal charges, while the government decides whether the derelict terraced houses can be salvaged). Proper concrete is mixed using various proportions of Portland cement (*tsiménta*), 'blue', actually grey, concrete sand (*ámmos betoú* or *galázia ámmos*) and gravel (*halíki*), plus fresh water.

Creeping damp is a major problem in certain situations, specifically in hillside structures where at least one wall is recessed into the surrounding terrain. Damp-coursing, as standard in UK properties, is not widely known; the usual strategy is to mix some liquid insulator (*monotikó*) in with the concrete. One product that has been recommended as more effective than many is Drylok Masonry Waterproofer.

If you have a garden terrace abutting a wall of your house, and you don't wish to cease watering and using that particular area, one relatively simple technique will cut 90% or more of the damp damage to the inside of the wall. Dig a trench as deep as you can go – the closer to bedrock, and past the foundations of your dwelling, the better the result. Treat the exposed outer surface of the wall base with a waterproofing product. Fill the resulting trench with not-too-fine gravel – 2–3cm diameter chunks are ideal. Optionally, line the garden-ward side of the trench with fine chicken wire to keep the gravel from dispersing itself slowly into your planted area. Cover the gravel with flat, mortared fieldstones, which make an attractive walkway around the garden plot and also serve to stabilise the waterproofing layer.

Moisture wicking its way into a house from outside cannot be stopped by attempting to treat the inside surface alone – the hydrostatic pressure will overpower anything you do, and you are just wasting time and money by removing sloughed-off plaster and optimistically replacing it with fresh. If there's a stone wall underneath of reasonable quality, it is better to point the interstices and let the wall 'breathe', dealing with the resulting water vapour instead (*see* below). Once a building has been plastered on its exterior, the use of heavy-duty acrylic-based paints – essentially akin to swimming pool paint – effectively waterproofs it for many years, at least above ground.

As a rule of thumb, new-build stone walls (e.g. for garden terracing) should cost about €100 per square metre, assuming 50cm in thickness and the foundations sunk in two courses' worth, resting on a concrete bed. Dry stone walling (*xirolithiés*) is cheaper but essentially a dying art; the walls are beautiful but have a distressing tendency to collapse from the weight of saturated soil behind them during rainy winters. For bearing walls in the house of the standard 80cm thickness, you'll pay much more.

On existing house walls fit for restoration, you'll find that many so-called 'stone' walls are, in fact, swallow's-nest-type agglomerations of mud and crude rubble, with properly cut stone only at the corners. Accordingly, pointing (*sklívoma* or *armolóyima*) is not much resorted to unless the quality of the masonry merits it (e.g. in Zagóri, Lésvos/Límnos, Híos, many of the Dodecanese). Mortar (*láspi*) consists of variable proportions of Portland cement, *ámmos thalássis* (sea sand, also used when setting *plákes*), a bit of lime (*asvésti*) and usually another binding agent (*marmaroskóni*, or marble powder, available from any marble quarry for the asking, is the best). 'Sea sand' here is a generic term; never use actual, unwashed beach sand! Rinsed and sieved river sand is what is usually sold as *ámmos thalássis*.

If you're going to engage in a spot of DIY repointing, use a wire brush to clean out the interstices of the stone beforehand, then dampen any exposed mud still holding the wall together with a spray mister of the sort used on house plants – this will keep it from crumbling further and ensures that the new mortar adheres. For most masonry work, use the usual proportions of cement: sand: binder (approximately 60:35:5) by volume. Strictly lime-based mortar is virtually unknown in Greece (a cement-mad country), except in conservation areas like Rhodes Old Town, where the archaeology authorities require it. Wear a mask when working with Portland cement, as it's very nasty stuff to breathe in; no Greek plasterer of my acquaintance does, and their macho denial means that most, by their late thirties, find themselves in the early stages of silicosis or emphysema. If you use lime as a binding agent for mortar, it will severely irritate your hands and promote infection in every open cut and nailbed – wear medical exam gloves (available at any Greek pharmacy) while at work.

Rendering or plastering (*souvátisma*) of walls is the most popular strategy, whether the underlying stratum is stone, brick or cement. The brown sand used is called 'dirty' or 'dump' sand (*homaterí*) and cannot be employed for masonry work exposed to the elements. After the first, rough (*petakhtó* or 'flying' in Greek) coat, it's time to mark out the guides for electrical wiring (*see* below); then there's a second coat to even up the wall and cover the wiring, and a final layer prior to painting relying mostly on gypsum (*yípsos*) and lime. You may be given a choice on the final coat of *lío* (smooth) or *mykoniátiko* (rough-mottled, so-called 'Mýkonos' style). The latter looks better, but is costlier and has a distressing tendency to shed bits continually. If you are renovating an old house, you might forgo expensive acrylic paint on the inside in favour of whitewashing (*ásprisma*), the traditional Greek strategy. This is based on bags of lime that burst, lost their fluid and are no longer suitable for plastering – but, rehydrated, they are perfect for whitewashing. If stone and/or wood floors are already down, cover everything with newspapers, taped at the junctions with the wall. There will still be puddles of dribbled whitewash afterwards at the edges, but they will at least be manageable.

Field-stones/flagstones (*plákes*) are widely used to surface both exterior courtyards or terraces, and interior spaces (especially kitchen floors). Grey-green *piliorítiko* stone from Mount Pílio is the most prized and charged for accordingly; *karýstou* from Évvia is a budget approximation of the same, and not nearly as attractive or versatile; while *galazópetro* is blue-black slate. Our favourite – produced in very limited quantities – is *kariótiko* from Ikaría, a wonderful, warm-toned rock with orange, grey, red and yellow accents. Sámos and Híos *plákes* are also good for flat surfaces, and, as with wall-building, it's always worth researching to see if there's a tradition of usable local rock. Linseed oil (*linéleo*), besides its uses on wood (*see* below), is recommended for stonework – it partly waterproofs it and subtly highlights the mineral colours. If you don't want to pave over every inch of an outdoor terrace, fine gravel (*garbíli*) is excellent and cheap; strewn an inch or so thick, it keeps weeds down.

Elsewhere in the world, marble may be a trademark of ostentation or vulgarity, but in Greece, it's a part of normal life, normally priced and abundant. The best is reckoned to come from Pendéli (outside Athens) and Thássos, but almost every region or large island has its own quarry. Marble (*mármaro*) is widely used for countertops, garden tabletops, door thresholds and the like. Every batch, even from the same quarry, is apt to differ, so order what you think you need all at once unless you don't mind variation across the house. Even large countertops and their flange pieces are typically set into the wall with strong tile glue (*kólla*) rather than mortar, best mixed from powder rather than used as ready-liquid (*revstí*). Marble's main disadvantage is its extreme sensitivity to degradation and staining by any acidic foodstuff, whether lemon juice, tomatoes, vinegar, tea or coffee. Various formulas (*adhiovrohopiitikó*), based on white spirit and buffed in with a rag, are sold to make the surface impermeable.

A fairly limited range of tiles (*plakákia*) for bathrooms and kitchens, almost exclusively imported from Spain and Italy, is available in bathroom and kitchen shops, as well as select hardware stores. It has become difficult, especially for bathrooms, to find much choice in the traditional square 12cm by 12cm or 15cm by 15cm wall tiles; rectangular sizes such as 25cm by 15cm are now all the rage. Unlike other raw materials, you will rarely, if ever, find what you need in stock; the rule is to choose from a sample board, order from Athens, and wait a week or three for delivery.

Central Heating, Insulation and Ventilation

Especially in summer homes, provision for central heating is not the norm unless you request it. If you think your seasonal use of the property may change in the future (e.g. after retirement), it is wise to plumb in everything except the furnace and the actual radiators, leaving the intake and exit pipes for the latter sticking out of the floor – it looks ugly in the short-term but is preferable to tearing up the walls and floors to retrofit later. Central heating systems in Greece use fuel oil (*petréleo thérmansis*), and if the tanker truck can't get to your house to fill a bunker, there's little point in contemplating it. The only available alternative is underfloor electrical heating in every room, which is expensive to run, though quite effective. Most people, frankly, will be more concerned with keeping cool than keeping warm; wall-mounted air-condi-tioning systems sold in Greece are generally 'two-way', that is, they can double as heaters during your winter visits.

Wall insulation is also a relatively new phenomenon, consisting of blue-foam sheeting inserted between layers of bricks, or inside the lath supporting the plaster. Fenizol brand is obsolete, next to useless and to be avoided (as the author found out the hard way). It has now been superseded by Dow-brand sheeting, but even better is yellow-fibre insulation (*petrovámvakas*) produced to US standards in matted sheets, sometimes with an aluminium backing sheet. This is more versatile and can be used in subflooring, in wall cavities, and (especially) in attics.

It is important to ventilate your house in some fashion while you are absent, especially if there is any problem with damp. If you have a working chimney, passive ventilation can be provided by a 'storm hat' (*kapéllo thyéllas*) – this looks like a metal chef's hat with slots, and, mounted at the top of a chimney, whirls around by itself in the slightest breeze, creating a powerful updraught. Otherwise, two-way air conditioning units as described above can be programmed to kick in for an hour every week to circulate the air in the house (make sure the timer has some backup power source to withstand power cuts). If you do nothing in this regard, at the very least the house will smell bad every time you return, and at worst you may find yourself with a severe mildew problem.

Wood

In Greece, wood is sold by the cubic metre, not in board feet as in Britain and the USA. There may be more choice on the mainland, but generally, the following catalogues what's available, in roughly ascending order of price:

- *Souidhikó* (**'Swedish' pine**): A blond, soft, if not to say spongey pine, much of it plantation-grown in central and eastern Europe, not Sweden. Suitable only for interior cabinets and floors if you're really budget-conscious.

- *Pítspyn* (**pitch pine**): A hard, yellowish pine from Canada which is well worth the extra cost for its durability, though it's brittle, prone to cracking and requires regular oiling if used for doors and shutters (its main role).

- *Kyparíssi* (**cypress**): An extremely hard, knotty wood, common in the Mediterranean zones of Greece. Woodworkers hate it – you may have to indemnify yours against a new set of saw blades or even lathe bearings! That said, it's unsurpassed for flooring, round beams (*dhokária*) and stair-way balustrades. Despite its hardness, cypress cannot tolerate prolonged exposure to moisture, so is unsuitable for exterior-facing surfaces. Beware that cypress, *dhokária* especially, are often infested with the grubs of boring beetles, which as the trunk dries out, chew their way (noisily) to the surface and fly/crawl away in search of live cypress trunks to lay eggs in. The resulting exit hole should be doused with worm-killing fluid as a precaution and filled in, after which there should be no further problems.

- *Iróko* (**iroko**): An extremely hard, light chocolate-coloured tropical wood. Like many such, it gives off a toxic dust when cut or sanded and, like cypress, breaks saw blades, making it unpopular with craftsmen. It's reserved for limited areas of heavy use, such as steps on spiral metal staircases, banisters and door sills.

- *Kástano* (**chestnut**): A strong, dense hardwood, no longer systematically harvested; most commonly found on the mainland, but also in some Sporadean houses and on the larger east Aegean islands. It formerly enjoyed widespread use in stairways, cupboards, and ornamental constructions; also prominent in structural support (e.g. as the beams or *dhokária* supporting floor planks), though the beams are too slender to support modern weights of furniture and planking. Chestnut virtually petrifies with age and retains most of its strength even when the surface is worm-damaged; unsound areas should be removed with a scraper (*xýstra*) and the remainder treated with worm-killer and a linseed oil/turpentine mix (*see* below).

- *Élato* (**fir**): A pale-coloured conifer, found only on the mainland in older houses, used as planking (*sanídhoma*) for floors and doors.

- *Origón* (**Oregon spruce**): A reddish-tan, medium-hard conifer; too expensive for shutter sets, but planks make wonderful flooring or coffered ceilings for small rooms, as well as steps.

• *Katráni* (incense cedar, cedar of Lebanon): Knotty, often disguised-by-paint wood which, when cut or sanded, shows a rich orange colour and gives off a pleasant, distinctive aroma, even when a century old. And it's likely to be – katráni grows only in southwest Turkey and has been essentially unavailable since 1923 (though the Turkish government has auctions of the limited annual harvest). This wood is still found as flooring and panelling in old houses across east Aegean and Dodecanese – treasure any sections you have and rehabilitate them as necessary. The persistent resin makes it very resistant to attack by insects or fungus, unless it's been buried in mud.

• *Dhrýs* (oak), *karydhiá* (walnut), *péfko* (native pine) and *oxiá* (beech): Mostly encountered in antique furniture. All of these woods are subject to attack by small woodworms, as found in northern Europe; unlike with cypress trunks, the problem gets worse over time as the wood dries out and must be robustly confronted with worm-killing solution (*see* below). **Teak** (*tík*) and **mahogany (***maóni***)** are popular for modern doors.

Beware of badly cured (green) or improperly kilned (*fournistó*) wood – shutters and doors made from such will swell, warp and stick horribly, forever. (This accounts in large part for the popularity of prefabricated aluminium doors and windows in Greece.) You have only your woodworker's (*marangós*) word for it that your designated batch of wood is ready for use. To be extra sure, pay for your batch, take delivery and let it sit for a few months in dry, well-ventilated conditions.

Windows, Doors, Floors and Ceilings

The first step in installing traditional wooden windows and doors will be the fitting of frames (*kásses*) in the appropriate apertures *before* the final plaster layers are applied. Polyurethane foam (*afrós*) should not be a cure-all for sloppiness with a tape measure. Ideally, the *kásses* should fit snugly at most points; foam is only for deviations from true – more likely with openings in masonry walls. When the house is finished, install a flange (*perváza*) at the transition point between the *kássa* and the surrounding plasterwork; without one, rain and damp leak in and distemper the surfaces of the wall perpendicular to the window.

If the window is not deeply recessed in a well (which should slope downward at the bottom), you will also probably need a zinc awning (*tzíngo*) just above. A narrow one just 10–15cm wide keeps rainwater from penetrating the top of shutters and percolating inside the window, flooding and staining as it goes. Wider *tzínga* (up to 1.25 metre outward overhang) are mounted on wrought-iron brackets above doors to prevent rain pummelling these and getting through fitted windows. Zinc awnings are commissioned either from iron works or tinsmiths, who also specialise in constructing fume hoods for tavernas.

For traditional wooden shutters, windows and doors, a double-leafed design is the norm, even for quite narrow apertures. Doors, at least double ones, typically have windows commencing at about waist height, which open inward on hinges. Speaking of which, always opt for bronze (*broúntzines*) rather than steel (*atsálines*) ones; the latter are not rust-proof and are prone to snapping.

Your woodworker will probably suggest the easiest-to-make, bevelled-square panels for the surfaces of both doors and windows. If you want something more elaborate or traditional (lozenges, diagonal slats, arrowhead, etc.) you will have to take photographs of older examples in your neighbourhood and persuade him to copy these. Don't expect too much, however – the intricate techniques for producing these, essentially akin to parquet, are beyond the skills or patience of most contemporary *marangí*, who rely predominantly on electric routers and one-piece (*monokómmato*) assembly.

Nowhere is the decline in wood craftsmanship more evident than in the mania for *rambouté* (tongue-and-groove flat-pack kits) ceilings and floors. They are, admittedly, the technique of choice for floors – even planks from an unusual wood like cypress will be run through a router to produce the necessary tongues-and-grooves. It is suggested that the planks be screwed, not nailed to the beams below, with the screw-heads counter-sunk and then covered with wood-filler; this way, you can disassemble the floor without damaging the planking in the event of a subsequent problem with the beams.

If your living area is limited, you might want to consider the traditional solution of a trapdoor (*glavaní* or *katapaktí*) at the head of a stairway up from a lower floor. The trapdoor should not be so large that its weight makes it problematic to lift, but not so small that coming up the stairway you knock your head on the frame-struts of the trapdoor opening. A bit of preliminary experimentation with the pitch of the proposed stairway will help you and your builder get it right. Yacht chandleries will sell you the necessary recessed ring pulls for lifting the trapdoor, and you can prop the door open with a hinged strut system, with the lower end resting on the rim of the trapdoor opening, or (using another eyelet screwed into the edge) hold it vertical with a chain-and-karabiner suspended from a cross-beam in the ceiling. It's not difficult to assemble a traditional coffered ceiling. First, construct a moulding akin to a picture frame on all four sides, a tad lower than you want the actual ceiling planking to be. Then insert half the planks above the moulding (you'll need some play to wiggle them back and forth so that both ends are in place), screwing through the moulding if desired, spacing them about half a plank-width apart. Finally, the remaining planks are installed, flush with the moulding, covering the gaps between the first series of planking and screwed securely to them.

Biffs, defects, wormholes and the like can be disguised with water-based wood filler (*neróstohos xýlou*). This comes in little plastic pots supposedly colour-graded to different types of wood – cypress, pine, oak, oregon spruce, etc. – though experience shows the identifications to be a bit arbitrary and eccentric. Always test a small area, allowing it to dry and applying varnish or oil as planned, before committing yourself.

Protecting Wood

All exposed wood, especially on a house exterior, must be treated in some way if you don't plan to paint it. The main pests are superficial fungus (*mýkitas*) and assorted wood-borers (*saráki*). Rain splash-up on the lower half of unpainted wooden doors is the most common cause of fungus attack. Unfortunately, it doesn't sand away easily and the best cure is prevention in the form of tin shields made to the necessary height by the same person who makes your awnings (*tzínga*). Simply attach them to the *kássa* with self-drilling screws before you leave for the winter, or, if they're designed with a 'foot' flange, just weigh them down with rocks. The Greeks tend to 'winterise' their door and window openings with nailed-in extents of plywood.

To treat prevent woodworm, UK-made Cuprinol is available in sizes ranging from ¾ litre up to 25-litre drums. Xylodecor is the cheaper, vastly inferior local equivalent. It is prudent to apply Cuprinol to flooring and shutters, in particular, before varnishing or oiling.

Linseed oil (*linéleo*) mixed 60:40 with pine turpentine (*néfti*) is the traditional treatment of choice for unpainted shutters; the grain (*nerá*) remains attractively exposed but this blend attractively darkens the wood, and unlike varnish, actually penetrates a few millimetres in. Reapply as needed – usually every six months – and the wood becomes progressively harder, pest-resistant and slightly less prone to swelling. You may baulk at doing it twice yearly, but *linéleo-néfti* is far cheaper, easier and neater than painting. Do it during a warm, still period; otherwise clouds of dust and debris stick unattractively to the surface and can be difficult to sand off.

Painting

Some doors and shutters, however, sustain too much punishment from the weather and must be painted. The best months for doing this are warm but not too much so, relatively windless and dustless, so that the paint cures evenly and without extraneous surface matter; on average, this means May and October, subject to variations for each year and where you are located in Greece. Messy as it is, this is one thing really worth doing yourself – you'll pay over the odds to hired labour and probably discover later that they've skimped on materials and the promised number of coats. This should, at a minimum, be three: one of lead oxide primer (*mínio*) which gives Greek boatyards their distinctive orange signature); white undercoat (*velatoúra*); and the desired colour (*khróma*), optionally two coats of this. Especially out on the islands, 'Aegean blue' (*Egeopelayítiko*) is ever-popular for doors and shutters – Ena-Sigma is the code for this colour with main brand Neochrom, but almost every manufacturer makes a near-equivalent.

The best way to support shutters or doors when painting them is to lay your hands on some old bed trestles (found in antique shops, etc.) of the sort that supported the typical plank bed in Greece until the 1950s – purpose-designed painting easels are astronomically priced in Greece. When you turn the painted items to do the other side, small mar marks will inevitably result, but these can be sanded and touched up later upon hanging. You can buy electrically powered spray guns for about €60, which leave a nice, even coat, but they are so fiddly to work (the nozzle part must be disassembled and soaked in nitro-thinner every time you pause for more than an half an hour or so) that most folk just resign themselves to using brushes. Don't economise on paintbrushes (*pinélla*) – the cheap ones just shed bristles constantly and ruin your surface.

If you're removing old paint (e.g. restoring old shutters or doors) be aware that there's no dipping service available in Greece. Buy a few cans of imported paint-stripper (*dhiavrotikó*) – Nitromors and equivalents are easily available, and also do wonders for caked-up, expensive paintbrushes – and set to work with a scraper (*xýstra*), wire brush (*broútsa*) or steel wool (*atsalómalo*), sand-paper (*yialóharto*), goggles and rubber gloves. Once the wood is exposed, treat any minimally damaged sections with wood-filler and worm compound. More severely damaged items can be taken to *marangí* who specialise in skilful repair of such, using prostheses attached to the remaining sound wood by mortice-and-tenon technique.

Wrought Iron

Wrought-iron work is reasonably priced and popular in Greece, frequently used for balcony railings, window grilles and perimeter fences. There are good, talented iron workers (*sidherádhes*) around, but, unfortunately, modern designs can be less than inspired, and competition from cheap-and-nasty aluminium prefab railings is a constant invitation to cut corners further.

Antique dealers are a good source of salvaged, century-old metalwork, ranging from grilles for door windows to considerable lengths of veranda railing. All of this is rather more ornate, and considerably heavier, than anything produced today – you will need lots of help transporting the larger pieces. Also to be found are neoclassical balcony supports with dolphin rampants, apparently cast at a single foundry in Piraeus in the 1880s and 1890s.

To rehabilitate corroded wrought iron, small objects like shutter clamps can be soaked for a few hours in a pink, mild hydrochloric acid solution, Feroxal brand or equivalent. Rusted railings or balustrades can, in theory, be paintbrushed with this stuff as well, but it's more effective to rub them down with a wire brush or steel wool, and then paint the cleaned surface with metal primer (*astári*) and then the final colour. Paints (e.g. Hammerite) combining the primer and pigment in one solution claim to be applicable directly to rusted parts, but you'll always get much better results if you brush or buff the corrosion away. The traditional colours for railings are black, shades of blue, and occasionally turquoise green; window grilles are found in these colours as well as white.

Roofs

Except in various islands where flat roofs for houses were the rule, Greece traditionally displayed a range of materials for pitched roofs. Across much of the northern mainland, Thássos and the Sporades, slate or schist slabs were employed; on many of the Dodecanese and Ionian Islands, flat clay pan tiles (*keramídhia massalías*) were the norm; while in most other places, atop neo-classical houses and the humblest chicken coops alike, the pan-Mediterranean canal tile (*keramídhia vyzantiná*) performed yeoman service for centuries. Such roofs had a wonderful, undulating visual aspect, owed in part to the often rough-hewn framework supporting them, but also to the uniqueness and small flaws in each tile, which in times past were shaped over the maker's thigh before being baked.

Sadly, old-fashioned canal tiles are disappearing rapidly, swept aside by a seemingly unstoppable tide of truly hideous modern flanged tiles that increas-ingly make Greek villages resemble low-income housing estates somewhere in Southeast Asia. Their use honours no tradition other than the Greek propensity for convenience-seeking, stinginess and disparagement of their architectural heritage. No other Mediterranean or south European country – not Italy, Spain, France, Portugal, Croatia, or even Turkey – dispenses so cavalierly with its canal tiles; only in a few protected settlements, and in the case of certain old churches, can the Byzantine archaeological authorities require the use of tradi-tional methods.

It is true that canal tile roofs require somewhat more maintenance, but that should not be an insurmountable barrier to their existence. Many claim that they always leak, but with adequate protection against cats and the wind displacing them, and a waterproof layer of tarpaper (*pissóharto*) or a synthetic membrane underneath, this simply isn't so. Should you decide to repair or install such a traditional roof, your main battle may be to find a builder willing and able to lay canal tiles correctly; the deceptively simple technique has been forgotten in many regions, and often only one elderly craftsmen still practises it.

Traditional canal tiles are still manufactured in small quantities but you will probably end up collecting second-hand ones as these tend to be thicker and have all the lovely idiosyncrasies described above. You'll probably have to look no further than the next house where an old roof is being removed – the tiles will be yours for the asking, though you need between 600 and 900 for the average-sized roof. They come in two types: *strósi* (wide, gently parabolic tiles meant to be laid upside down as the bottom layer) and *kapáki* (the narrow, tightly curved specimens laid right side up atop the meeting-point of two *stróses*). A sound tile will produce a bell-like tone when tapped; a defective tile with microscropic cracks will go 'thwack, thwack' when struck.

Every row of tiles should be anchored with mortar; it's costlier but the roof lasts a lot longer. For a bit of whimsy, you can affix *akrotíria* or ceramic plates at the end of the *amorgá* or roof ridge, and/or so-called *koukouváyies* ('owls') at the roof corners. The latter, *akrokerámata* in proper Greek, are stylised Medusa figures dating from ancient times which warded off evil. Or you can imitate your neighbours with a kitsch white ceramic pigeon or two.

Whatever type of traditional roof you install, your carpentry crew will prepare a framework (*traváka*), either of round cypress corms or squared conventional timbers. Cross-beams (*latákia*) will be balanced on a parapet (*patoúra*) at the top of your walls, culminating in the *amorgá*. Then, a 'skin' (*pétsoma*) of thin planks – most likely a *rambouté* flat-pack kit – will be applied and the tarpaper (preferably two layers, or a synthetic membrane) tacked on to this.

Last but not least, if you buy a property with an Ellenit corrugated roof (Eternit in the UK), these are now illegal within municipal boundaries throughout Greece, owing to their high asbestos content. They should be removed and disposed of carefully.

Electricity, Wiring and Illumination

For most residential applications, single-phase (*monofasikó*) current is sufficient and what will be offered by the DEI unless you propose otherwise. Once the DEI has supplied the electrical meter, your electrician will devise a temporary hook-up for the construction crew to use power tools pending the actual wiring of the house and installation of the circuit-breaker box (*pínakas*). Wiring commences with the marking out of guides (*odhigí*) for the cable tubes in the first, rough coat of plaster. Before this is done, you or your general contractor should make a definitive plan for the location of all power points and switches. Better yet, be there with some pieces of coloured chalk or spray paint to indicate *exactly* where you want them to go – there is nothing more frustrating than plugs or switches that will be too high or too low relative to furniture you may have already purchased, or hidden when they're supposed to be exposed (or vice versa). Once the guides are finished and the next two layers of plaster applied over them, the wiring will actually be passed through the tubing. Always specify the heaviest-gauge wiring feasible so that your lights don't dim 20 watts every time your electric water heater kicks in.

All power points currently installed are *soúko*-grade, accommodating two fat round pins (as found on irons, heaters, washers, etc.), with earthing provided by two metal clips at the top and bottom. Formerly, *prízes*, with three narrower pin-holes (one the earth) in a triangular array, were also fitted but this practice has largely ceased; if you buy a property with these already in place, you'll be easily able to find small adaptors at electrical-goods shops allowing you to use appliances with two fat pins. Every third *soúko* or so should be 'reinforced' or high-load circuits (*eniskhiiméni*), capable of taking a space heater or even a welder. Two-ways switches at either end of a stairway are referred to *à la français* as *aller retour*. Like in England, but unlike in America, Spain or France, full-amperage power points capable of running a hairdryer, etc. are generally not installed in Greek bathrooms. However, there is no law against it, and after a bit of grumbling most workmen can be persuaded to do so, though they may insist on a spring-loaded cap to cover it. No such hang-ups apply to power points in kitchens, though it's still a good idea to keep a minimum distance away from water sources (one metre as required in the UK is prudent).

Light bulbs (*lamptíres*) come with bayonet (*bayoné*), threaded (*vidhotó*) and mini-threaded (*minioné*) bases. Low-consumption bulbs (*lamptíres hamilís katanálosis*) are all the rage but they're as ugly – and initially expensive – in Greece as anywhere else. They're really only for when they can be concealed with a lampshade or globe (*ambazouár*), not overwhelming a chandelier! They are also quite a bit longer than conventional bulbs and will not fit in many of the standard closed fixtures sold.

Lightning Protection and Voltage Regulation

Lightning-strikes on unprotected electrical systems are an ever-present threat in Greece, especially for houses that are isolated, elevated or for other reasons a choice target. Burying the cable supplying the house from the nearest power pole, as done in other countries, is not generally an option. The feed-line from the pole is supposed to have fusible links, which melt within a few milliseconds of a strike, stopping the flow of current down line into the house, but this doesn't reliably happen in Greece. Lightning rods (*alexikéravna*) work by providing a 'cone of protection' from the tip of the pole as a right circular equilateral conical solid section. In Greece, they're usually reserved for hilltop mobile phone antennae, which have very powerful systems pushing the strike threat into the circular area immediately outside the conical section – as happened to a rental premises the author once inhabited. A properly designed array of *alexikéravna* for private residences runs into thousands of euros, and an improperly applied system is worse than none, serving as an attraction to your house rather than repulsion. A far more practical alternative is to fit a heavy-duty surge-protector master fuse (manufactured by Legrand) in your circuit-breaker box. They'll cost about €150, but it's a lot cheaper to replace one of these than all the melted wiring (and ruined appliances) in your house should you sustain a strike. The only disadvantage with installing one is that you won't be able to operate electric water heaters and an electric oven at the same time – the lightning circuit 'sees' all this amperage as a strike-surge and will probably fuse, leaving you without power.

Moreover, when you leave for extended periods, pull the plugs for *everything* out of the wall – especially items with always-on capacitors inside like faxes or televisions. Don't forget the phone cables, too – lightning likes to travel up these as well. The only exception you might make is the fridge, which should be fitted with its own surge protector.

A 10-euro surge protector box won't suffice to protect televisions, videos, computers or fancy stereo equipment from the vagaries of everyday current, which can deviate as much as 25 volts either way from the nominal 240 AC supplied. For these, you will need a heavy-duty regulated voltage supply box, about the size of a police radio and costing €80–110. You can find these at major electrical widget shops, like Radio Katouma in Athens.

Plumbing and Sanitary Fixtures

Rather surprisingly, all couplings, piping and joints for plumbing are sold in inches (*íntses*) rather than metrically – a lasting tribute perhaps to the Victorian obsession with sanitation. Copper piping is universally used for water intake, while various widths and shadings of grey PVC piping are installed for draining grey water and sewage. Metal screw fittings are lined with hemp thread (*kanávi*) to stop any leaks, while plastic threadings are instead lined with sheer teflon tape. All bathrooms tend to be fitted with central floor drains; this has the advantage of protecting you against flooding, but the disadvantage (especially evident after a long absence) is that these can pong until and unless the other drainages linked to them get used copiously.

A certain amount of shock-horror verbiage is devoted in all travel guides to Greece on the topic of the peculiar local custom pertaining to used toilet paper. As in much of Latin America, you are instructed *ad nauseam* in Greece to place it in the adjacent bin, not in the bowl. However, this is something of a Greek urban myth, especially if you have the opportunity to design your own plumbing system. If you install wide (*c.* 20-cm) PVC piping to the sewage hookup, with no really sharp turns, and buy toilets without tight S-bends, you are unlikely to experience any problems with modest amounts of paper down the drain (unless you're hooked up to a digester cesspit, in which case consult the installer). If you dispense reams and reams of toilet paper at one go and follow it on directly with toothpicks, dental floss, tampons, etc., you are almost certainly going to have blockages – but in all fairness, if you did this in northern Europe the same thing would happen!

Having dealt with sewage and drainage, there's the more refreshing matter of water supply. Whenever and wherever interruptions in the mains supply can be expected, water-storage tanks (*dhepósita*) made of galvanised steel are popular. One-tonne capacity (1 metre by 1 metre by 1 metre) is the norm; properly treated with anti-rust primer (especially at the weld-joints), a *dhepósito* should last 15 years at a minimum. If the municipal mains fail, a tonne of water should supply the average adult couple for about 5 days. You should always hook up a pressure pump (*piestikó*) in series, between the tank and house; set to between two and three atmospheres, such a pump will guarantee decent water pressure up in a second-storey bathroom. The central axles of the pumps are prone to sticking in cold weather, especially if you're away, and the electrical control box is sensitive to wet weather, so make a protective housing for them both. The *depósito* itself should be as elevated as local regulations permit so that you still have some water pressure from gravity when the power fails.

Vast megastores (*ídhi iyenís*) are devoted to bathroom fixtures, of which there is a veritable cult in Greece (probably a reaction to the outdoor, hole-in-the-ground privies that were the rule almost everywhere until the 1970s). Most items are made in Greece, Spain or Italy, with name brands like Roca, Vitruvit and Ideal Standard at the fore. You can spend as little or as much as you like – there are Bulgarian-made toilets costing a few tens of euros, scarcely fancier than the tatty plastic models used in beach tavernas – all the way up to items costing close to €300 with sophisticated flush cycles and styling. Porcelain sinks come in a similarly astonishing variety, fitted either with standard mixer taps or a single mixer lever – separate UK-style taps are unknown. It's worth spending the bit extra on the tap set (e.g. solid brass rather than brass-plated) as these are the parts most likely to fail or corrode. Sets for showers (*bateríes*) are almost invariably of the flex-hose type (*tiléfono*), though you can now find power showers, adjustable sliding mounts and the like. You can also find apparati for Jacuzzi-type bathtubs.

Water Heating Systems

The choice in water heating systems is basically between electric and solar. Electric water heaters (*thermosífona*) are nothing like the expensive, cumbersome immersion heaters of England. The Greeks have this down to a fine art: they're reasonably priced, easy to install and (if you choose a good brand) long-lived – and the pressure chambers inside have an interesting use once they do die (*see* below). In areas with hard water, which means almost everywhere, Elco Glass brand comes highly recommended for shedding limescale effectively and a longer working life. The most common sizes are 40, 60 and 80 litres, available as vertical (*kathetó*) and horizontal (*orizóndio*) models convenient for putting in lofts. If you want to reliably fill a large bathtub, then you'll need 120 litres (generally what a hotel uses for each floor). If your house has two bathrooms some distance apart, consider installing a second, smaller (40-litre) heater with its own power supply. Solar, roof- or terrace-mounted water heaters are popular and eco-friendly, but they're useless in winter without an electrical backup (essentially a heating element threaded inside the solar panel). Solar units are much more expensive to purchase and install, offsetting their cheaper running costs; if you're going to be using the house for only a few months annually, it's probably simpler to go with a *thermosífono*.

Chimneys, Fireplaces and Wood Stoves

Considering that fireplaces and wood stoves (*sóbes*) were the only heating options available in Greece for decades, there's often a surprising inability to construct properly working chimneys on the part of local fireplace technicians (*tzakádhes*). This may have something to do with the fact that proper firebricks (*pyrótouvles*) are no longer manufactured in Greece and almost impossible to find second-hand. These are essentially the same as used to build any Victorian building in England, so it is well worth bringing a load of such bricks down with you if you're driving to Greece. Do *not* attempt to construct a chimney with the hollow-channel bricks used for construction in Greece, or the modern so-called firebricks with recessed surfaces, meant for paving terraces or building pedestals for modern barbecues – the trapped air will expand upon heating and the brick(s) may well explode.

The old folk wisdom of the chimney rising above the level of the roof ridge should be abided by – one metre over the rooftop wouldn't hurt. Otherwise, you'll have a smoky backdraught into the room with every strong gust of wind. Some regions (e.g. the Cyclades) have traditional chimneypots, while elsewhere a chimney is formed by nothing more than two roof tiles leaned together. In any event, rain from all but the freakishly strongest of storms should be excluded.

Cast-iron wood stoves are available from better appliance stores and agricultural supply depots, occasionally from iron workers themselves; most of them are manufactured in northern Greece. There isn't the wide variety that is available in northern Europe or New England, but you should find something suitable; the most popular, basic, vertical model with mica windows, an ash pan below and removable round plate at the top should cost from €150, nicely heat a space of 20–30 square metres and last at least three winters. It is almost impossible to find stove blacking or heat-resistant paint in Greece – the most you'll be offered upon sale of the stove is some graphite powder in solution – so if you're keen on this, bring it from elsewhere. Stovepipes (*bouriá*) are sold in one-metre lengths, plus angle sections, in two standard widths – make sure you've got the right one for your stove. You should also buy some aluminium foil adhesive tape (*alouminiotenía*) to apply to the pipe-joints everywhere the *bourí* is cool enough to touch while in use; this will keep them from dripping messily if you get a load of green wood.

The most sought-after firewood is olive, with pear, apricot or almond trimmings a good second choice. On wooded islands or regions, sources of firewood advertise themselves through wall notices with peak demand in October. A little over 100 euro should enable you to a pick-up-truck full of trimmed logs that will last a good six weeks, assuming a fire from 5pm to 10pm, and perhaps for an hour or two in the morning.

Settling In

Now that you own a habitable property in Greece, it's time to consider all the implications of life there, whether you plan to be there on a seasonal basis or as the result of a permanent relocation. If it's the former, then you won't be dealing with the full gamut of removal strategies and employment/retirement issues, but you will still need to master certain essentials: the shopping routine (rather different from most of northern Europe); getting utilities connected; the type of banking services provided; deciding on what sort – and what registry – of vehicle to keep in Greece; and learning enough about the culture to avoid being labelled an Ugly Whatever ('Ugly Britons' being much in the news of late since the summer 2003 excesses at Faliráki, Rhodes and Kávos, Corfu). Whether you establish part-time or full-time residence, begin learning proper Greek as soon as possible – and that doesn't mean the pidgin restaurant-Greek you may have got by on during a package holiday. It will make all the difference, especially if you're living in a village setting, where it's vital to avoid misunderstandings.

Removals versus Buying Anew in Greece

British, Irish and other EU nationals will be able to import their household chattels into Greece without paying taxes or customs duties (though *see* the note on cars, pp.215–19). Non-EU nationals, except for those of Greek descent, should brace themselves for delays and sequesterings; more likely than not at least one shipment will end up in a customs compound in a dreary part of Piraeus, and, especially if you're monolingual, it's a fairly futile exercise trying to clear the items yourself – engage the services of a customs broker (*ektelonistís*). Many overseas and Greece-based companies alike claim to act as such or at least arrange customs brokerage for you. No matter what they say – in particular any door-to-door quote – all overseas removal companies will only ship as far as Athens; from there on, the shipment is handed over to a local affiliate. Every large island or region has such a company doing removals (*metaforés*) and they're not known for displaying much duty of care. So, be sure that fragile goods are carefully packed at the start point of the journey, either by you or by the company. Shipping quotes from Germany and the UK, in particular, can be so stratospheric that with a modest amount of domestic kit it could well be worth buying a van or truck, cramming it to the gills and driving it down (two round-trips if necessary) in spring or autumn to take advantage of cheap low-season ferry fares across the Channel and the Adriatic, though, again, *see* the warnings on pp.215–19 about foreign-plate cars in Greece.

Don't drag large appliances into Greece – the warranties (if any time is remaining) will be voided, the models will be unfamiliar to local servicemen, and spare parts are likely to be unavailable. The Greek furnishings market remains highly uneven; quality, tasteful sofas, sofa-beds, bookshelves and

Case Study: Furnish in Greece or from Abroad?

It came to the time for Jack Holland – he of the contested chapel (see pp.82–3) – to furnish the extended house he'd had built for himself, his wife and two young sons. After a week spent scouring every furniture store in the Kefallonian capital of Argostóli, he despaired of finding any bedroom and dining room sets he – and equally importantly, his wife Nina – could live with. 'The price of a crappy, so-called "designer" bed with a poor mattress was about €1,500, and they were all revolting, at every price level; add a wardrobe plus delivery charge, and the total was getting on for €2,000.' Checking the Internet, Jack found an outlet of Praktiker, the German DIY chain, in Pátra, but they didn't sell furniture. There was a Habitat branch, too, but their Greek web page was coy as to exactly what furniture they actually stocked (e.g. no catalogue pages for viewing). 'Nobody would rent me a van on Kefalloniá and allow it off the island, and even if they did, I'd be looking at two ferry fares and a night in a Pátra hotel because of the way the boat schedules were.' IKEA in Athens would not deliver, hold furniture for third-party collection, or guarantee the availability of items. Jack would need to fly to Athens, buy furniture on spec and have a delivery company's truck on the spot ready to freight his stuff to the island. 'Can you imagine any Greek removals company turning up on time at IKEA's loading bay? Then I would have to continue by domestic flight from Athens–Kefalloniá (more expense!) while the truck crew treated my furniture like crash-test dummies.' In the end, Jack took a deep breath and went to IKEA in the UK, and bought a very acceptable 1.8-metre-long bed, a superb mattress, three chests of drawers, a 2-metre wooden bench, an extendable 2.2-metre, 10-person dining table, six chairs, plus sundry bedding, for £1,000. 'I'd initially been quoted £300 for shifting 100kg of flat-packed furniture, door-to-door, but discovered it was much cheaper to ship by container volume – we managed to find someone who would do five cubic metres for £800, as against the usual sum of £1,300–1,500. All that furniture weighed 670kg and we still hadn't used up our space allowance. Also, rather than just slinging the flat packs in the back of a van, my freight company repacked every item and wrapped it on a pallet. All the goods arrived safely.'

dining room sets, often made in Italy or Scandinavia, can be fairly easily found, while conventional beds, desks, nightstands and dressers tend to be horrible and overpriced. You may find it well worth making a trip to IKEA or Habitat in the UK, stocking up on flat-packs, and bargaining with a shipping company.

Moving Checklist

Don't let the hassle and ferment of having boxes packed and disposing (by rental, house-sit or sale) of your house in Britain make you neglect these points.

- If you are intent on a permanent relocation, is your paperwork in order, specifically residence permits (see pp.12–13)? Or rather, do you have all the necessary paperwork assembled to get a residence permit when you arrive, with no essential supporting document forgotten back home?

• Is your home passport valid for the whole of your intended stay in Greece, and ideally six months beyond that date? A couple of extra photocopies are a good idea – you'll need them to get a residence permit, or to prove to your consulate who you are if for any reason your original passport goes missing.

• For appliances with modular plugs, such as laptop computer transformers, be sure to bring a good supply of two-to-three-pin plug adaptors from the UK. They are nearly impossible to find in Greece and you do not want to be snipping off modular three-pin plugs to fit a continental-style one (this will void the warranty, if any remains). North Americans, however, will find two-rectangular-pin-to-two-round-pin adaptors (*prosarmostés*) easier to find.

• If you are moving permanently, notify your subscriptions, credit card companies and current account banks of your change of address. However, many financial institutions can be awkward when informed of this – you can possibly anticipate a decrease in credit limit from credit card issuers, and many banks require that you maintain a UK address for current account facilities. You may have to switch to an offshore subsidiary of the same bank.

• Whoever you end up banking with, make sure that any periodic debts of yours in the UK (such as the mortgage and utility payments on a rental property) continue to have valid direct debits linked to them.

• If you spend less than six months of the year at your Greek home, you will still be fully liable for UK taxes. You can downland Inland Revenue forms anywhere, in time to file, or you can leave this to your accountant.

• Bring books or sheets of UK postage stamps with you, not with any actual financial denomination, but marked 'E' for mail to Europe. These are essential if you have to send stamped addressed envelopes to the UK.

• Most private medical insurance will not cover you for any stay in Greece, whether for holiday or residence. You may want to buy a UK-based plan specifically geared for expats, not a traveller's plan which has strict limits on the amount of time spent overseas, both total in one year and per trip.

• Medications in Greece are cheaper than in the UK or the USA, and also often available over the counter rather than just by prescription. However, do bring a container of any medication currently prescribed for you in the UK, complete with the literature or printed carton, so that you can match the active ingredients with the help of a pharmacist – trade names and exact formulas in Greece may not be the same. One glaring gap is in the field of cold and flu remedies – if you swear by Lemsip or Night Nurse, take along a supply sufficient for the impending winter.

Case Study: Miranda's Nightmare

Miranda, proprietress of a small hotel in the medieval city of Rhodes, wasn't quite so fortunate as Jack. In early 2004, she paid US$1,000 to ship her personal effects – clothes, books, CDs, musical instruments – from California to Athens. The shipping company had demanded approximately another $1,000 to send the goods onwards to Rhodes, but Miranda demurred, especially after she found a Greek company, Hellas Express, which claimed to be able to complete the journey for just €68. As a precaution against sequestration, she declared her belongings as second-hand goods, not for resale, with an uninsured value of €400 (US$500); additionally, the consignee was to be Hellas Express, not Miranda, and provision was supposedly made for the shipment to clear customs in Rhodes, not Athens. The items arrived in Greece at the end of April and Miranda was asked to pay an extra fee of €59 for customs brokerage in Athens; at the end of June, her boxes were still sitting in Piraeus and Hellas Express proved unwilling or unable to move the goods any further (perhaps they regretted the exceptionally advantageous quote of €68). At the time of writing, Miranda is contemplating having to go to Athens from Rhodes – an expensive, time-wasting trip at peak season when she should be running her hotel – or (probably more productive and cheaper) retaining an independent customs broker (*ektelonistís*) to escort the goods out of the compound in Piraeus.

Several morals can be extracted from this story. Be very clear about just what is included for the sum you've paid for 'freight'. Think very hard about what you're going to ship and whether you need *any* of it. Yes, books have sentimental value, and foreign-language ones aren't cheap in Greece, but quite a few can be replaced economically via the Internet, and it's probably only worth shipping rare out-of-print or first edition items. As for clothes, they too are expensive and of variable quality in Greece, but you should exclude anything that has the least bit of shrinkage, wear or fading – it won't last long enough in Greek summer conditions to make their freight charges worthwhile. Miranda can justify shipping the musical instruments – enough to equip a small band – because she got them cheaply and could sell them for a good price if necessary in Greece.

- All name-brand continental cosmetics, perfumes and sundries, from Clarins to Issey Miyake, are available (at a price) in Greece. Bring a good supply of anything very British that you can't live without, but the Hondos nationwide chain of cosmetics and sundries is likely to stock anything you need at competitive prices; they're in almost every provincial capital.

- Greek computers tend to have dual keyboards for the Greek and Roman alphabet. Bring any software you have, as English language programmes can be hard to find outside of the largest cities.

Antiques and Salvage Yards

Given the shortcomings of the Greek domestic furnishings market, and especially when restoring a derelict traditional house, many Athenians and foreigners entertain the notion of decorating or even furnishing their home with antiques. If you're lucky, an old house may come complete with a substantial complement of abandoned rural impedimenta, ranging from olive-oil urns (*kioúpia*) to steelyard-type scales, by way of copper stewpots (*tenzerédhes*), bread-dough moulds and wooden block-planes. Were you to buy any of these separately, they would each run into many tens, if not hundreds, of euros. The fact that such articles are left behind speaks volumes about the often schizophrenic local attitude towards 'old things': scorned as reminders of drudgery and hard times in the rush to acquire kitsch substitutes as 'décor' or the most ostentatious 'modern' furnishings possible; or something to be extracted from ruins and sold to silly foreigners and Athenians for silly prices.

There are a limited number of organised antique flea markets in Greece. In Athens, they are to be found around Platía Avyssinías in Monastiráki district, and most of the wares – primarily wooden furniture and light fixtures – are overpriced and over-restored. The Piraeus flea market, along Skylítsi parallel to the metro tracks about 500m inland from the seaside metro station, is more what's called *hýma* in Greek – a true jumble of unsorted, uncleaned items – but, with persistence, you can net some reasonable, unusual things, though it's by no means undiscovered and prices are inching up. Both markets are at their peak at weekends from about 7am to 2pm. In Thessaloníki, the rather expensive antique district – mostly old lamps, bedsteads and wooden furniture – lies along and just off Tossítsa. Builder's salvage yards are even fewer and further between; the main ones we know of are in western Athens, at Ierá Odhós 134, corner Ayías Ánnas – the places to go for iron grilles, old doors, paving bricks and tiles, etc.

Pickings are slim in the provinces; the closest one to Mount Pílio is Païteris, outside Vólos on the road between Dhimíni and Sésklo; this is really *hýma* (you have to provide your own restoration elbow grease) but relatively cheap – mostly scrap iron but also a bit of wooden furniture. In Mytilíni on Lésvos, there's a whole row of antique dealers on the northern reaches of Ermoú street, but these are pretty picked over and expensive. A much better island shop, with a reasonable in-house restoration service and a growing clientele from across the country, is Miltiades Makris' Aiones on the island of Sámos (t 22730 28121 or t 693 285 8068); Miltiades speaks almost no English, but he stocks just about everything you need to decorate a home in old-fashioned rustic style, from window grilles to rag rugs to Singer sewing machine trestles to dining room sideboards, from as far afield as Thrace and Turkey.

Given the Greeks' often contemptuous local attitude towards their domestic heritage, trips to the local rubbish dump (*homaterí* or *skoupidhótopos*) can be surprisingly rewarding, though permission from (or a gratuity to) the warden to 'raid' the premises may be needed, and posted signs occasionally forbid the practice. Urban myths of great treasures to be had for the taking at Greek dumps contain more than a kernel of truth; the author, through regular repeat visits, has scooped up a couple of traditional wicker chairs with minor, reparable defects, and an Anatolian cedar bedroom door.

After a while you'll realise that rural Greece is one great outdoor antiques showroom, in the form of thousands of derelict houses adorned with shutter clamps, balcony railings and supports, door knockers or pull-handles, wagon wheels, hand-operated flour grinders, *kioúpia* and the like. As tempting as it may be to go and 'liberate' such items *in situ*, this is inadvisable: though the owner may have long since died and the heirs be scattered across the globe, Greek Rural Rule Number 1 stipulates that Somebody is Always Watching. The police will be summoned and you will quickly find yourself in an awkward situation. Asking permission of the owners (if they can be located) or guardians is likely to result in an automatic refusal, even if the items concerned are of no use to them. It's an intensely frustrating situation, especially (as often happens) if the building is demolished and the coveted articles are smashed to bits or instantly carted away to the dump rather than salvaged. If the building collapses of its own accord after a winter storm (not unknown) and scatters its endowments to all points of the compass around the foundations, DIY 'salvaging' is another matter...

Day-to-day Shopping

For years, the traditional village or big-city corner general store (*bakáliko/ pandopolío*), invariably family-run, was one of the mainstays of Greek life. Picturesque outdoor hanging displays of coiled rope, braided garlic and brightly coloured 'monkey-cups' (*kantária*) for measuring out wine would be fronted by huge burlap sacks of dried grains, beans and animal feed, while inside was a veritable Aladdin's cave of goods, from bricks of green olive oil soap to great brine vats of cheese, to which only the proprietor had access. Since the 1990s, however, and the effect of full effective membership in the EU, supermarkets and out-of-town megastores – many of them franchises of northern European chains – have become well-established players, slowly but surely driving most *bakálika* out of business. They survive, however, in the remoter villages and on small islands where, owing to emigration patterns or more inexplicable factors, you may find exotic Egyptian tropical juices or Madagascan tea bags on sale – just one of those endearing quirks that keeps life in Greece interesting.

Despite the advent of giant discount stores and the presence of the odd mango or pineapple at fruit stalls, Greeks still prefer to eat by the calendar, and moreover locally produced fresh food. Even major supermarket chains will give their local outlets the discretion of buying some of their cheese and meat locally rather than from some central Athenian depot. You'll quickly learn the eagerly awaited seasonal progression of the various fruits and vegetables as Greece generally doesn't import things from much further away than another Mediterranean country or West Africa: strawberries in April and May; apricots in May and June; cherries in June and July; fat peaches and figs during July and August; grapes from August through September. The selection of fresh fish and seafood is very limited from June 1 to September 30, when trawling with drag-nets is forbidden and only multi-hook lines (*paragádhia*), doughnut-traps (*kýrti*) and small drift nets may be used.

It's suggested that you avoid stockpiling more cereal, flour or other grain-based foodstuff than you can eat within a couple of weeks during summer; moth-weevils are very active at this time and you may find the packaging for these products changed over from plastic or paper containers to metal in an attempt to prevent these bugs getting in. Spices and herbs also deteriorate very quickly in the Mediterranean summer and you will find it best either to buy these whole and grind them as needed or to store hard-to-find items in the freezer.

Given some years now of Greek participation in the single market, it's possible to find a wide variety of foodstuffs and other products from northern Europe in Greek shops. However, stocking remains haphazard, unpredictable, seasonably variable and often just plain arbitrary. If a product of any kind proves useful, good value, of exceptional quality or all three – whether it's a brand of sandal, Italian-made glass food containers, non-bleaching detergent for colour clothes, an exotic herb/spice, or an arcane tool – go back as soon as possible and get more. Rather perversely, if something sells out, most merchants seem to take this as an indication not to re-stock it, and producers or distributors as a sign not to re-manufacture or re-import it.

Types of Food Shops

As on much of the European continent, in Greece, food shops are highly specialised. Butchers (*hasápes* or *kreopolía*) generally sell only meat, and fish-mongers (*psarádhika* or *ikhthyopolía*) only fish and seafood, while *manávika* (*oporopolía* in formal written Greek) are usually restricted to fresh fruit and vegetables. *Galaktopolía* sell yogurt, *xynógalo*, rice pudding and usually a selec-tion of cheeses. You may see more versatile, self-styled 'delis', essentially butchers who've decided to carry a few eggs plus a chiller cabinet full of milk and butter, as well as more esoteric combinations like fishmongers-cum-green-grocers, but as a rule the boundaries are respected. A *foúrnos* (oven) is a bakery, though the sign will read *artopiíon*; they may also have a few Middle Eastern sticky cakes and biscuits, though those are more reliably found at a cake shop (*zaharoplastío*). Last but not least, a *káva* sells only alcoholic drinks – bottled wine and perhaps their own in bulk, *oúzo*, beer and hard spirits, plus perhaps a few mixers and juices.

Special or Exotic Foods

If you have special dietary needs or cravings, you should be aware beforehand of what the Greek market can and cannot supply. Diabetics and health food junkies are fairly well provided for; there are special lines of fructose-based products and non-wheat-based crackers, many of them produced by Fytro, a nationwide brand devoted to health products and supplements. But there are frequent gaps: for example, you might find soya milk but not rice milk (or vice versa), you can easily get white basmati rice but not wholegrain, and overall brown rice is a tough proposition. Wholegrain pasta is marginally easier, though again, stocking is inconsistent – you may find spinach noodles or *tricolore* instead. Burnt sesame oil is rather easier to find than unroasted oil, while soy sauce is now almost universally available. Mediterranean herbs and spices (with the conspicuous exceptions of tarragon and chives) are easy to obtain, but Indian spices are almost impossible to get hold of except in Athens (though wherever large numbers of Dutch are in residence you can pick up raw materials and condiments for Indonesian cuisine). Wholemeal flour and wholeroot ginger are often only seasonally available. Greece is hardly known as a tea culture, but you can get several varieties of Twinings, more frequently in bags than loose, as well as the ubiquitous Liptons.

Arabica coffee beans suitable for Western filter coffee, cappuccinos and espressos – as opposed to the robusta variety which can only be used for making Greek coffee – are exceptionally hard to find, except at the Coffeeway chain, with about 30 outlets nationwide; otherwise, you may get pre-ground vacuum-packs, usually Jacobs brand, from a large supermarket. Accordingly, you can easily find drip-filter apparati and their replacement filters, but coffee grinders *per se* are thin on the ground. Most foreigners learn pretty quickly to avoid Nescafé, whose stranglehold on the market up to now has been so all-encompassing that 'Nes' has become Greek shorthand for any instant coffee. The formula is much stronger than in the UK.

On a small island or in a remote area, you'll probably resign yourself to stocking up on exotics at outlets of Alfa Vita Vassilopoulos when passing through the largest towns – their motto is *'Keh tou poulioú to gála'* (And [we've even got] bird's milk) – or to enlisting friends to bring special goodies when visiting.

Larger towns may have a designated central *agorá*, a French-style *halle* (the ones at Haniá on Crete, in Athens, Thessaloníki and on the Argo-Saronic Islands being especially famous) where the various kinds of food stalls are gathered in one place. Elsewhere, you will find street markets (*laïkés agorés*) which, depending on the town, may appear only once a week or almost every day, featuring an excellent selection of (usually) locally grown produce. Their downside is that these small producers are not subject to any sort of quality control, and (though they will usually boast to the contrary) pesticides are often applied

> ## Shopping Hours
>
> Greek shopping hours are fairly predictable, though, outside Athens, subject to local idiosyncrasies. In general, small shops are open Monday, Wednesday and Saturday from 9am to 2.30pm, but on Tuesday, Thursday and Friday from 9am to 2pm and again from 5.30pm until 8.30pm. In summer, the morning opening may take place at 8.30am and the evening schedule may shift to 6pm to 9pm to avoid the worst of the heat. Fishmongers and butchers do not open and are not allowed to sell meat on summer afternoons; pharmacies (*farmakía*), except for the duty/rota outlet (a list is posted on the door), never open Saturdays. Supermarkets, found at the outskirts of most sizeable towns, keep long, continuous hours: 8am to 9pm Monday to Friday; 8am to 6pm on Saturday. *Laïkés agorés* begin at around 7.30 or 8am, and by 1.30pm, the stalls are being folded and the trucks loaded.

indiscriminately, with the reasoning that if five grammes of poison per 10 litres is good, then double that concentration is great. The *laïkí agorá* (in the singular) is also the only place to find wild, dawn-gathered greens, which the Greeks generically call *hórta*; these, of course, will not have been sprayed and are a major feature of cooking in winter. (A cookbook nostalgically devoted to *hórta*-based recipes, unsurprisingly entitled *Ta Horta*, is now in its fifth edition.) In the larger towns, *laïkés agorés* will also usually have a large and less-interesting section of tatty goods: out-of-style underwear and socks, bootleg CDs, plus other household goods, such as pots and pans, brooms, bin liners, etc.

Pavement Kiosks (*Períptera*)

Pavement kiosks (*períptera*) have been a part of Greek life for nearly a century, and are found everywhere except the smaller islands and mountain villages. They were originally started by the government as a programme to help disabled veterans of the 1912–13 Balkan Wars and then the First World War; the lucrative concession is jealously guarded by their descendants or sold on for a good price. They're open continuously until late, stocking items such as news-papers, mobile phone top-up cards, glue, tape, condoms, cigarette lighters, sweets, nuts, tissues, pens, pencils, key rings with football team logos, and (if equipped with a chiller cabinet) ice cream, cold drinks, maybe even milk and yogurt. Bigger *períptera* are not free-standing but essentially shopfronts; they may not have chilled items but will have all the above, plus things like laundry detergent, cat food in bulk, cleaning products, toilet rolls, tampons, nappies, etc.

Roving Pedlars

You will have chosen a spot either terribly remote or served by appalling roads if you do not hear, at some time in the span of a week, the loud-hailer of an itin-erant, truck-bound pedlar. These are typically produce-vendors and fishmongers operating out of small pickups; the wares may well be local and/or own-grown, but the disadvantage is that you tend to be pressured to buy more than you need. In the case of repeat visitors, discreet enquiries will establish who's flogging the real deal and who's trying to offload stuff that won't pass muster at the nearest *laïkí agorá*. Larger trucks and the proverbial white vans with out-of-area licence plates invariably belong to gypsies selling live poultry, garlic braids, plastic chairs, melons, clothing seconds, budget cookware and occasionally more desirable basketry which can be very good indeed – though not cheap.

Megastores and Supermarkets

The European chains **IKEA** (**www.ikea.gr**; Athens Airport and Thessaloníki), **Praktiker** (**www.praktiker.com**; Pátra, Lárissa, Thessaloníki and four outlets across Athens) and **Habitat** (**www.habitat.co.uk/greece.htm**; various locations) maintain a presence in Greece. IKEA sells its usual range of items, Habitat to a lesser degree, while Praktiker is more like the UK chain Homebase, best for things like garden trellises and shower curtains. There is also a Greek quality furniture chain, **To Epiplo** (**www.toepiplo.gr**; three outlets in suburban Athens, plus Kalamáta, Spárti, Sérres, Réthymno and Hánia), worth considering.

Major supermarket chains include **Atlantik**, **Bazaar**, **Champion-Marinopoulos**, **Lidl** and **Spar**; any island or mainland town of more than about 10,000 population will have at least one. They sell everything imaginable except fresh fish – any seafood they do have will be frozen and either farmed or imported – while their produce sections vary widely in quality and scope. In tourist areas, they may also have a catering section aimed at restaurateurs, should you wish to procure jumbo-sized tubs of pickled red peppers, sardines or margarine.

Other Shops

You will also periodically make use of other shops, such as a a **bookstore-cum-stationers** (*vivliopolío/hartopolío*), which will sell you things like fax rolls, pens, paper, envelopes and so on (the books will be almost exclusively Greek and geared to kids' school needs), as well as making photocopies for you; a **dry cleaner's** (*stegnokatharistírio*); a **hardware store/ironmonger'**s (*ídhi kangelarías*) for all your DIY needs; a **pharmacy** (*farmakio*); and a **florist** (*anthopolío*).

Kitchenwares and Electrical Appliances

One (heavy) category that you could happily omit from your load of shipping from overseas is that of kitchenwares. You can buy almost any baking or cooking implement in Greece (including such items as flour-sifters, lobster pots and pastry syringes) except enamelled, cast iron stewpots of the Le Creuset type. Good, thick potholders (*piástres*) are also curiously hard to find and worth bringing from overseas. There will be independent retailers in every sizeable town. The best chain for practical, quality items is Cook Shop, rather superior to the more publicised Vefa's House.

For cookers, washing machines, refrigerators, vacuum cleaners and the like, there are again numerous independent retailers, but outside of Athens and Thessaloníki no real chains. Always buy as locally as possible. Yes, it may cost a few euros more than if you order from Athens, Thessaloníki, Iráklio or Pátra, but the shipping costs will likely wipe out any savings. Moreover, warranty service will be next to impossible to obtain unless you've purchased the appliance in a nearby town. Many appliances are made in Greece under licence – e.g. Bosch, for which there is a sharp price difference between 'Made in Greece' and 'Fabrik aus Deutschland' – and in the former case you will definitely make use of the warranty, whether a one-year or three-year one. Most of the major European brands, such as Zanussi, Siemens, Miele, AEG, Panasonic, Bosch, Candy and DeLonghi, are represented, though British ones like Electrolux are rarer. There are Greek home-grown brands, too, like Pitsos and Izola, but few people buy them any longer except for the occasional fridge.

Washing machines are generally plumbed in and found in a bathroom or separate utility room, not the kitchen (that's where *nouveaux riches* Greeks like to put their dishwashers), and given the climate, combination washer-driers are not the norm (Americans must get used to the fact that washers are almost always front-loading). Fridges are generally freezer-on-top, two-door models in a range of sizes. Cookers can be bought as all-gas (not popular as the oven consumption is significant), all-electric or with an electric oven and a gas hob (but including one electric ring or *máti*), the most common and most practical solution. This allows you to keep cooking something both during power outages or when your gas bottle unexpectedly runs out. Buy as good, and large, a cooker as you can afford and have space for – the smaller, cheaper models tend to maintain oven temperatures below the promised rating, and erratically at that, which makes problem-free baking almost impossible.

Large-appliance shops are often quite distinct from other electrical retailers, which sell only bulbs, switches, plugs, phone sockets, hairdryers, toasters, clock radios, irons and an improbable assortment of light fixtures, most in questionable taste. For those, you are better off going to shops that sell primarily light fittings, with switches and the like as an afterthought. Again, you will have to wade through a fair amount of dross but, with a large enough selection, you're almost certain to hit on something acceptable or even positively covetable. Don't hesitate to scour every such shop in the region or island – given the erratic ordering and stocking policies prevalent, this may be the only way to assemble a decent range of fixtures.

Clothing and Shoes

Greeks are Mediterranean fashion victims second only to the Italians, such that even the smallest island will have a handful of clothing and shoe stores and a large town will have literally streets-full. Outlets are specialised: menswear, womenswear, kids' shops, baptismal and wedding dresses, even shop-fronts selling nothing but women's lingerie – provocative and otherwise. You are allowed to try on outerwear and obviously footwear. Most articles, either obscure local labels or international brands like Levis made under licence, are manufactured in Greece, and the quality is reasonable (no undue fading or shrinking) but, that said, they're not great value given prices at or beyond northern European levels. Sales, typically January–February and August, make the wares a bit more attractive. Alterations are never included or even available – get acquainted with the local tailor, who will do the necessary for a few euros.

Appreciating and Learning Greek

So many Greeks have lived abroad in North America, Australia and Britain that you will find someone who speaks English in even the tiniest island village. Add to these returned emigrants the thousands of young Greeks attending language schools or working in the tourist industry, and it's understandable that so many visitors never get past the few words and phrases necessary to order food and drink. What's less understandable is how some second-home owners, let alone full-time foreign residents, think that they can get by indefinitely in such linguistic poverty. It's not only arrogantly ethnocentric but potentially dangerous – you won't be able to summon help in an emergency or fill out the necessary insurance declaration forms should you smack into another vehicle.

The Greek language has a reputation for being fearsomely difficult, something that the Greeks themselves are partly responsible for, insomuch as they promulgate a mythology that few foreigners are capable of learning it properly, and treat those who are fluent or nearly so as freaks of nature. In fact, judging by what translators' unions in the UK suggest that their members charge clients per page, Greek is rated as harder than German but much easier than Russian, let alone Arabic or Chinese. Most novices are daunted by the unfamiliar alphabet, but this is, in practice, fairly quickly mastered within a couple of weeks and, frankly, is the least of your troubles – though certain combinations of letters have less than obvious results. Greek grammar is undeniably tricky: nouns are divided into three genders, all with different case endings in the singular and plural, and all adjectives and articles have to agree with these in gender, number and case. Just to keep you on your toes, there are a few feminine nouns that masquerade under masculine declensions but, of course, must take feminine adjectives, plus numbers of neuter words that, at first glance, look like masculine ones. Verbs are even more complex; they come in two conjugations, in both active and passive voices, with passively constructed verbs often having transitive sense.

Now the good news: most Greeks are highly flattered by anyone who bothers to learn the language beyond ordering a beer and will encourage any and all of your faltering steps with copious corrections (though bad, ungrammatical Greek spoken by Greeks abounds, so don't take everything you're told as gospel). There's rarely any of the snappy impatience you might encounter in France when attempting French, though you may find that the conversation is quickly steered back to English or that you may have provided your hosts with a certain amount of inadvertent or deliberate amusement. Foreigners' linguistic *gaffes* have acquired the status of legend: who could forget the family of Germans who bemused all they met in Santoríni by intoning squid (*kalamári*) instead of good day (*kalí méra*)? Or the comely young Scandinavian lass who was instructed to go to the baker's and ask for *éna kiló psolí* (a kilo of cock) rather than *éna kiló psomí* (a kilo of bread)?

What can't be overemphasised about spoken Greek is the correct stress on a word. Since a 1981 language reform (the last, one hopes, in a series; *see* below), this has been marked on one of a word's final three syllables by a single acute accent or a dieresis. With the right sounds but the wrong stress, people will either fail to understand you or else hear something quite different from what you intended. There are numerous pairs of words with similar spellings and identical phonemes, distinguished only by their stress (e.g. *mílo*, 'apple', versus *miló*, 'I speak', or the classic, naughty example of *gámo*, 'a wedding' in the accusative case, versus *gamó*, 'I f***'). Correct use of accents is often counterintuitive and, judging from the mangling given to words by many visitors, something simply not audible to most Anglo-Saxon ears. To add to learners' miseries, the use of accents is not constant – in the singular and plural genitive cases, the stress usually (but not always) shifts back a syllable towards the end of the word.

Once you begin to acquire a substantial vocabulary, you'll notice the debt most western European languages owe to ancient Greek, particularly with respect to medical and philosophical terms. But the modern Greek language has been heavily influenced by its neighbours and conquerors, who all left loanwords, such that perhaps only 70 per cent of the contents of the average dictionary is incontestably of Greek origin. The rest, in roughly decreasingly order of importance, is originally Turkish, Venetian (who contributed almost everything pertaining to nautical life), Albanian, Slavic, French or even Arabic or Persian (either direct or via Turkish). Of late, despite the existence of perfectly good Greek words for computer and electronic technology, there are numbers of English contributions – everyone says '*email*' and '*kompúter*' rather than '*ilektroniki allilografía*' and '*ypoloyistís*'. Often there are three or four words for the same thing, of different provenance: for example, *katsíki*, of Albanian or Turkish origin, is the most used term for 'goat', especially the live animal, but you will also need to understand the demotic-Greek *gídha* (as in *gídha vrastí*, goat stew), while the sign at the butcher's will likely say *erífi*, which is the same as the term for the beast in New Testament Greek.

The issue of foreign 'contamination' of Greek is not new and, in fact, has exercised linguistic purists with an ideological axe to grind, as well as out-and-out nationalists, since the early 19th century. When Greece became independent in 1830, its inhabitants were almost universally illiterate, and the language they spoke – *dhimotikí*, 'demotic' or 'popular' Greek – had evolved considerably from New Testament Greek (*koine*), let alone Classical Greek. Besides the accrual of vast numbers of loan words, the grammar had been considerably streamlined compared even to mid-Byzantine times.

The inspiration for the revolution, as well as many of Greece's early leaders, came largely from a diaspora of wealthy, cosmopolitan Greeks who had been living in the sophisticated cities of central and eastern Europe. Stung by the accounts of Grand Tourists who disparaged the peninsular Greeks as visibly degenerated descendants of a lofty past, the diaspora Greeks set to work erasing the evidence of subjugation to foreigners in every possible sphere. And where better to start than by purging the language of its foreign accretions and reviving its Classical purity?

The new mandarins accordingly went about creating an essentially artificial language: 'cleansed' Greek (*katharévoussa*). The complexities of Classical grammar and syntax were largely reinstated and long-forgotten Classical words were reintroduced. To Greece's great detriment, *katharévoussa* became the language of the schools and the prestigious professions, government, commerce, the law, newspapers and academia. Everyone aspiring to membership in the new, self-appointed élite strove to master it and to speak it – even though there was no consensus on how many words should be pronounced. Those who couldn't or wouldn't adopt the rules of something even battier than Esperanto were effectively cast into outer darkness as far as the gatekeepers to success and advancement were concerned. Thus arose the *dhiglossía*, a situation where two parallel linguistic universes existed in Greece, the great mass of 'non-U' *dhimotikí* speakers juxtaposed against a far smaller body of 'U' *katharévoussa* speakers. However, *katharévoussa*'s very nature militated against anything like fluency in conversation and most people chose to occupy an intermediate point on the continuum between the most pompously classicised *katharévoussa* and the most 'vulgar' demotic. The conflict between the partisans of each side of the linguistic issue remained a hot-button issue continuously until the 1980s, with riots and broken heads on occasion. Popular writers – from Solomos, Makriyiannis and Papadiamantis in the 19th century, to Seferis, Kazantzakis and Ritsos in the 20th – all championed demotic Greek, or some approximation of it, in their prose or poetry. From the early 1920s onwards, advocacy of the demotic became increasingly linked to left-wing or at least staunch Republican politics, while crackpot right-wing/Royalist governments forcibly (re)instated *katharévoussa* at every opportunity. The colonels' junta (1967–74) reversed a decision of the previous civilian government to use *dhimotikí* as the medium of instruction in schools, bringing back *katharévoussa*, even on cereal boxes, as part of their delusions about racial purity and heroic ages. Two examples gleaned from the utterances of the Ubu-esque head colonel Papadopoulos, still used in parlance today, suffice to illuminate the all-but-untranslatable, quasi-Teutonic constipation of *katharévoussa*. It wasn't enough to refer to *Elládha*, 'Greece', it had to be *o elladhikós hóros*, or 'the Helladic *lebensraum*'; strikes, illegal in any case under the colonels, were not *aperghíes*, but *aperghiakés kinitoopíises*, approximately 'strike-ish mobilisations'.

Dhimotikí returned, once and for all, after the fall of the colonels; perhaps the final blow to the classicisers was the official decision in 1981 to do away with the ancient breath marks (which, in fact, no longer signified anything, certainly not the 'H' used in the more eccentric transliteration schemes) and abolish the three different stress accents in favour of a single acute accent (though there are still plenty of pre-1981 road signs displaying the older system). *Dhimotikí* is used in schools, on radio and television, and in newspapers (with the exception of the extreme right-wing *Estia*). The only institutions that have declined to update themselves are the Church and the legal professions – so beware rental contracts and official documents.

Traces of *dhiglossía* and nationalistically motivated 'cleansing' still linger elsewhere, however. The Metaxas dictatorship of the 1930s, elaborating on attempts at the same by previous regimes, changed scores of village names from Slavic, Turkish or Albanian words to Greek ones – often reviving the name of the nearest ancient site – and these official place names still hold sway on most road signs and maps – even though local people stubbornly continue to use the *dhimotikí* or non-Greek form. Thus you will see 'Leonídhio(n)' or 'Spétsai' written, while everyone actually says 'Leonídhi' or 'Spétses'; Pándhrossos on Sámos, Platáni on Kós and Ayía Paraskeví in Epirus are still preferably known to locals as Arvanítes, Kermedés and Kerásovo respectively.

Minority Languages and Dialects

Along with (more or less) standard Greek, Greece still displays considerable linguistic diversity in both regional dialects and minority languages. Ancient dialects, some of them quite incomprehensible to outsiders, are alive and well in many remote areas. The dialect of Sfákia in Crete is one such; Tsakónika (spoken in the east-central Peloponnese) is another, while the dialect of the Sarakatsáni shepherds is said to be the oldest, a direct descendant of the language of the Dorian settlers.

The tongue of the Sarakatsáni's traditional pastoral rivals, the Vlachs, on the other hand, is not related to Greek at all, but is a derivative of early Latin, with strong affinities to Romanian. In the regions bordering the FYROM and southwestern Bulgaria, there are around 40,000 speakers of Macedonian (a Slavic language) resident, while dwindling numbers of Sephardic Jews in Thessaloníki speak Ladino, a medieval form of Spanish. Until a few decades ago, Arvanítika, a dialect of medieval Albanian, was the first language in many villages of inland Attica, southern Évvia, northern Ándhros and much of the

Argo-Saronic area; it is still (just) spoken (and sung) by the oldest generation. Since the early 1990s, modern Albanian has become prevalent, as throngs of Albanian immigrants circulate in Athens and other parts of the country, so that at least one bank has seen fit to provide ATM instructions in Albanian. In Thrace there is also a substantial Turkophone population (between 60,000 and 100,000), as well as some tens of thousands of speakers of Pomak (an offshoot of Bulgarian with a large Greco-Turkish vocabulary). Across the mainland, you'll find itinerant communities of Gypsies (80 per cent nominally Orthodox, the rest Muslim), thought to total 150,000, whose first language is Romany.

Out in the islands, Náxos and Lésvos possess strong dialects, which owe much to migration from Crete and influences from Asia Minor respectively. The dialect of Sámos and that of adjacent Híos are completely different from one another, Híos being considered a more pure 'Ionian' (and this thousands of years after the Ionians arrived from the mainland), while the rough 'Samian' variant owes much to the diverse origins of its settlers. On Rhodes and Kós, there is a dwindling Turkish-speaking population, probably not at present in excess of 6,500 persons.

Recommended Greek Courses

In Greece, the **Athens Centre**, Arhimídhous 48, Pangráti (**t** 210 70 12 268, **f** 210 70 18 603) is the granddaddy of schools in the capital geared to teaching foreigners Greek. There are others, both in Athens and the provinces, but these tend to have a short lifespan – to find ones currently operating, consult the display adverts in the weekly *Athens News*.

In the UK, you can locate a range of Greek courses through **Learn Direct** (**t** 0800 100 900, **www.learndirect.co.uk**). Two prestigious Greek courses are run respectively by the **Brasshouse Language Centre** in Birmingham (**t** (0121) 303 0114, **www.birmingham.gov.uk/brasshouse**) and **Lancashire College** in Chorley (**t** (01257) 260909, **www.lancashirecollege.com**).

Home Utilities and Services

With the exception of certain phone and Internet services, provision of utilities is still by various monopolies or quasi-monopolies in Greece. To open accounts, you'll need to bring documentation to the office of the respective utility: definitive identification (either a foreign passport or a Greek residence permit), your Greek tax ID registration number or *A-fi-Mi* (*see* p.143), if you've obtained one, and the passbook for your Greek bank account.

Bills are still paid by the vast majority of customers at the office of the particular utility, in cash, in person, from Monday to Friday until 1pm only. Queues can be very long in the first few days after bills are issued, so look for the date given in the box after the citation *líxi párondos logariasmoú* ('last day to pay the present bill'), which is usually some weeks in the future. Throughout Greece, **cheques** are deeply mistrusted and not much used for consumer purposes. You can, increasingly, also pay through the **web banking** facilities of various Greek banks, but you must have the hard-copy bill to hand with its all-important *kodhikós logariasmoú* at the top of the page in order to do this on-line, as you cannot access your account status on the utility's own website (assuming it has one). You might also set up a **standing order** (*páyia endolí*) with your bank to pay each utility bill automatically when due but, unlike in Britain, these cost money – generally more than the minuscule late-payment fees – and, moreover, if there's any risk of running the account into the red, it's not really worth it; overdrafts don't exist in Greece.

Water

Throughout Greece, provision of water and (if applicable) disposal of sewage is administered by your local **DEYA(X)**: Dhimósia Epihírisi Ydhrévseos ke Apohétevsis ('X' often standing for the locale, e.g. Ródhou for Rhodes) or Municipal Water and Sewage Enterprise. Bills come either once a year in autumn or winter, or twice (one in the spring). If you get two bills, the first will likely be the standing charge (*páyio*), the second for your consumption (*katanálosi*). Water bills are typically paid at the town hall (*dhimarhío*) or perhaps the community office (*kinótiko grafío*) in smaller places. Late payment fines are so small as to not be worth fretting over – you simply can't count on being there when bills are issued. If your water meter packs up (not unknown), you'll be notified in writing and told to buy a new one (budget €30–35 for this) on pain of disconnection, but the municipality has to install it.

Mainland supplies, especially if mountain-spring-fed, are often excellent, as are those on large islands, such as Crete, Évvia, Kárpathos, Sámos and Híos, though occasionally – as on Corfu, Kálymnos and Sýros – overzealous drawing down of the water supply has caused the sea to invade and rendered municipal wells brackish. On really arid islands, like many of the Dodecanese, supplies are brought in by tanker from the nearest 'wet' island (in this case, Rhodes), augmented by municipal rain cisterns – though, in some years, these have been contaminated by livestock droppings, with warning notices posted. If a property you buy has its own cistern (*stérna*), cherish it and keep it in good repair – rain water is lovely to drink and, should it become tainted, you can still garden and wash with it.

Even when ostensibly drinkable, Greek **tap water** tends to be very hard (*éhi pollá álata*) and best filtered before being drunk. Otherwise, in the more hydrologically blessed regions, there will always be at least one spring where the locals go to fill up huge, plastic jerry cans (*bidhónia*) for table use – ask which is the good one or just look out for the roadside queues.

Gas

Piped-in natural gas is available only in Athens and Thessaloníki; elsewhere, the norm is 10-litre bottles (*boutília*) of '**Petrogaz**' butane with a fitting that takes a hexagonal nut at the end of a rubber hose serving the appliance in question. Getting a bottle at the outset of your stay is a bit of a Catch-22: you can't just go to get a full *boutíli* without handing in an empty one in exchange, and laying hands on an empty one means going to the nearest Petrogaz depot, begging for an empty, and paying a fairly chunky 'deposit' for it (technically, the bottle remains their property but they never expect to see it again). You will also need to buy a regulator (*rythmistís*), a length of rubber hose, a few washers (*rodhélles*) made of compressed chipboard, not rubber, and a crescent wrench to tighten and undo the regulator. Beware – if the washer is too thick or too worn, the gas bottle will leak out its contents within a week or so. In many island villages with narrow streets, full bottles are delivered by motorised tricycle or small vanette – well worth the small extra fee if you're without a vehicle. Gas bottles come in squat (*hondhró*) and narrow (*stenómakro*) varieties, designed for different cupboard dimensions. The squat ones primarily power catalytic space heaters, but at about €16 per can this isn't an efficient way to warm a house in winter as you'll go through one every few days just using it four or five hours in the evening. Used only to power three or four hobs on a stove top (assuming an electric oven, the most common option), a bottle should last you a couple of months.

Electricity

The **DEI** (Dhimósia Epihírisi Ilektrismoú) or Public Electrification Enterprise has a monopoly on the provision of electric power in Greece and any competition or privatisation in the near future is unlikely; DEI's powerful unions have seen to that. At the start of your service contract, you'll be obliged to leave a small deposit in the region of €20 for a residential service.

Meter readings are taken every three months and the resulting bills are frankly gobbledygook, making phone bills models of clarity by comparison.

Along with your power consumption charges are collected various others: a municipal tax (*dhimotikós fóros*) based on the external 'footprint' of your house; a form of property assessment (*télos akinitís periousías*), again based on the size and age of the house; the television and radio licence fee for ERT, the state-run network in instalments roughly every four months; and anything else (*idhikó télos* or 'special charge') they can think of. Odd amounts are rounded up or down and the resulting credit or deficit carried over to the next bill; the amount to pay (labelled *posó pliromís*) is in the box at lower right, above the detachable payment stub. As with the water bill, late payment penalties are trivial; unless you're absent for a few consecutive periods, the DEI is unlikely to tap into your initial deposit or disconnect your service.

Post and Telecommunications

Post and Couriers

The Greek postal service, known by its acronym **ELTA**, is fairly efficient, especially for outbound international mail – delivery times of two to three days to the UK and the Republic of Ireland are not unknown and delays beyond this are as likely to be owed to deficiencies at the receiving end as in Greece. **Post offices** are open Monday to Friday 7.30am to 2pm; there are no longer Saturday morning hours except in the largest cities. A range of delivery options (surface-air lift is the most efficient for moderate weights) is available for overseas parcels, and boxes (but not tape or twine) are sold at major post offices. There are also small branch postal counters (look for the yellow-on-blue logo with the stylised Hermes head) installed in newsagents and stationers, which keep longer hours, though, of course, they won't offer anything like the full range of surfaces.

In terms of incoming post, if you have picked a remote site beyond municipality limits there may be a delivery only a few days a week – or not at all. You can either buy an approved-design post box from a hardware shop, mounted on a pole at the top of your access drive, or consider renting a post office box (*tahydhromikí thyrídha*) in the nearest large town. If you're intent on the latter option, you should make enquiries as soon as you decide on your preferred region for purchase – box quantities are limited and waiting lists are often long. Unless you receive mountains of correspondence, a typical box can hold about three months' worth of bills, magazines and the like. You should always ask for a long-term rate for PO boxes: major branch managers are authorised to make you an offer – three years of rental for about €80 is a good benchmark to aim for.

Ordinary Greek domestic post can be more erratic than overseas deliveries, and accordingly, **courier services** are popular with business folk. If you set up an enterprise that involves shipping paperwork securely, you will probably make their acquaintance. All provincial capitals and any island of over about 5000 population will have at least one outlet. **ACS** is the local affiliate of DHL, while **Speedex** is the local correspondent of Fedex. They will honour any international account numbers, whether your own or (more importantly) that of the person or organisation you're shipping to. A sample rate for up to half a kilo from the provinces to Athens is about €7–8, to northern Europe over €20. ELTA has its own competing **Express Mail Service (EMS)**, run as a subsidiary; t 800 11 83 000 for further information.

Telephones

Basic telephony is still largely the province of the **OTE** (Organismós Tilepikinoníon Elládhos) which, goaded by the two prongs of part-privatisation and competition from mobile networks, has transformed itself beyond recognition from the bad old days (as recent as the early 1990s) when crossed lines were the norm and it could take years to get an analogue home subscriber number. For an ordinary PSTN connection, the line-rental charges (*vasiká téli*) are about €21, plus VAT at 13 per cent, per two-month period, paid in advance; actual call charges are paid retrospectively. If you have a digital line (this can be provided in most of Greece now), you should request a free breakdown of all charges on your bills. Your calls will be separated into local (about 2.5 euro-cents per minute plus VAT); Greek inter-city (about 6 euro-cents per minute plus VAT); overseas (varies by destination and time of day – roughly 25 euro-cents per minute to the UK); Internet dial-up; calls to mobile numbers; and Greek lo-call services (numbers prefixed by 801, about 2.5 euro-cents a minute plus VAT). As with DEI bills, rounding up or down to even figures is the rule, with carry-over to the next period; again, the amount to pay is shown as *posó pliromís*, in the box at lower right, above the detachable payment slip.

If you plan to leave Greece before receiving an anticipated large bill, it's easy enough (and free) to go down to the OTE premises and request an up-to-the-minute meter reading. You can then leave an amount at the cashier's sufficient to cover your estimated liability until the time you return. If a 'minus' figure is subsequently showing in the *posó pliromís* box and the payment slip is blank, that means you've left an overly generous amount, have a credit and need do nothing until the next billing period.

OTE offers one fairly useful discount plan for overseas calls, called OTE *piloyés* for residential numbers (there's a separate scheme for business lines). You elect a frequently called country and save a minimum 5–25 per cent on call charges, depending on the time of day. If your usual monthly phone expenditure falls in the range of €60–90, you save 10–30 per cent. But if you pick more than one country (up to three are allowed), the discount falls considerably to 3–15 per cent and 8–20 per cent respectively. This programme is free so far – there's no subscription to pay; you just fill out a form. As well as the basic line, OTE provides a range of optional services on digital lines, notably the *prosopikós tile-fonitís* (a network answering service similar to BT's 1571), call waiting, temporary incoming call bars, outgoing call bars, and so forth. The local OTE premises will also sell you a range of phones and faxes, though their subsequent responsibility for their welfare stops at the outer wall of your house unless you buy further service plans or warranties.

Competition to OTE for the provision of long-distance service is furnished by **Tellas** (**www.tellas.gr**), a subsidiary of the DEI, and **Forthnet** (**www.forthnet.gr**), which began life as an Internet service provider. Each claims to undercut standard OTE rates by 25–40 per cent on international calls and by smaller discounts to mobile numbers, with itemised billing by the second for qualifying calls. However, they are both piggybacking services – you must still have a basic line provided by OTE, and dial a prefix (1738 for Tellas; 1789 for Forthnet) to access their network unless you make special arrangements with them to be automatically connected. The Tellas Call and Surf programme has much the same charges as OTE for local and intercity calls, but is noticeably cheaper for most calls to mobiles and overseas; however, their discount plans (called My Mobile, My City, My Country) charge a monthly subscription fee for percentage savings on the basic Tellas rates rather less than OTE *piloyés*.

Mobile Phones

Greece has the highest per-capita rate of mobile phone ownership in the world, aside from Italy and Cyprus; there are more (approximately 7 million) mobiles than fixed phones in the country and you can't go anywhere – not ferry boats, remote beaches, or even churches – without hearing the incessant twittering of incoming calls. There are four domestic networks, with **Cosmote** (a subsidiary of OTE) reckoned to have the most thorough coverage for really isolated areas; the others are **TIM** (ex-Telestet), **Vodafone** (ex-Panafon, which still shows as the network ID on your screen) and relative newcomer **Q-Telecom**. Vodafone has its own chain of storefronts; Cosmote is, of course, handled primarily through OTE premises; the post office (among others) represents TIM; while Q has random outlets, primarily the ACS courier chain. They're all pretty much of a muchness, and which network you choose will probably depend on the prevailing handset deals and time plans available. If you're in Greece for only a few months every year, you'll probably opt for a pay-as-you-go plan; the top-up cards (in denominations of €7–9 and upwards) are available from any *períptero*, though with per-minute charges to national fixed lines of about 40 euro-cents, and to mobiles of about 70 euro-cents, you'll run them down quickly. Discount plans are now available to approximately halve these rates but there's often a minimum three-minute charge. For periods of residence more extended than six months, and/or if you have reason to travel extensively within Greece, you're better off with a monthly call plan.

In any case, you should choose one or other type of Greece-based mobile, even if you only use your Greek residence for a few months per year: if you are so rash as to attempt 'roaming' on a foreign-based mobile, you'll be stung with approximately a one-euro-per minute tariff, which most of the major northern European networks have agreed on, whether you ring across the island or across the continent. The EU is said to be investigating this price-fixing cartel; in the meantime, act to protect yourself against this rip-off.

Internet Services

Greek Internet access and e-mail services are primarily PSTN (ordinary dial-up, 56Kb/sec) or ISDN-based (both 64Kb and 128Kb per second; broadband is still on the horizon for most of the country and there are a few remaining primitive exchanges, e.g. in eastern Zagóri in Epirus, where not even simple e-mail transmission is supported). The most popular and widespread ISPs are **Forthnet, Otenet, Tellas, Yahoo.gr, Germanosnet** and **Panafonet**. Most of them actively court short-term business from seasonal foreign residents and tourists; you can get anything from a one-month subscription up to a year, often with special deals like nine months for the price of six. Subscription fees for periods longer than four months average about €12–14 per month, though these usually have to be paid in advance. Tellas offers an always-on service, with speeds of 64Kb/sec and 128 Kb/sec, plus a 10Mb/sec service for businesses; for their voice-phone customers they also have a monthly subscription-free (*páyio*) programme but the per-minute charges on this are horrendous, and it's not cost-effective if you spend more than about six hours monthly on-line. With Otenet (**www.otenet.gr**), the dial-up charges for PSTN are quite affordable, 20–38 euro-cents per hour (plus VAT), depending on the time of day; Forthnet's are similar. The Germanos chain of shops selling batteries, mobile phones and other electronic accessories is the most impartial vendor for all the plans, and can fill you in on the most current offers.

The Media

While Greek press and airwaves have been ostensibly unrestricted since the fall of the colonels' dictatorship in 1974, no observer would ever propose the Greek media as a paradigm of responsible or objective journalism. Many news-papers are inflammatorily sensational, state-run radio and television often biased in favour of the ruling party, and private channels imitative of the worst American programming. Even if they have good comprehension in Greek, most foreign residents tune all this out, seeking solace in the music of private, local radio stations, or the very limited number of English-language publications.

Newspapers and Magazines

English-language

British newspapers are fairly widely available in Greece at a cost of €1.75–2.50 for dailies or €4 and upwards for Sunday editions. You'll find one-to-two-day-old copies (same day by noon in Athens and the largest tourist centres) of *The Times*, the *Telegraph*, the *Independent* and the *Guardian*'s European edition, plus a few of the tabloids. American and international alternatives include the banal *USA Today* and the slightly more readable *International Herald Tribune*, the latter including as a major bonus a free though somewhat abridged English translation of the respected Greek daily *Kathimerini* (online at **www.Kathimerini.com**). Rather than forking out coins regularly at a newsstand, you will probably elect to subscribe to something like the *Guardian Weekly* (**www.guardianweekly.com**) or the *Weekly Telegraph*, though by the time they reach you the 'news' is one week old.

There are precious few surviving locally produced English language magazines or papers. Expensive, glossy *Odyssey* (**www.odyssey.gr**; €6), produced every other month by and for wealthy diaspora Greeks, has improved markedly under new ownership and an editorial board, and often has good book and events reviews. Best of the English language newspapers, available in most resorts, is the full-colour *Athens News* (weekly every Friday, online at **www.athensnews.gr**; €1.80), with good features and Balkan news, plus entertainment and arts listings for Athens and Thessaloníki (and sometimes for special events in the provinces as well).

Greek-language

Many newspapers have ties (including funding) with specific political groups, which bias tends to decrease the already low quality of Greek dailies. Among these, only the centrist *Kathimerini* – whose former proprietress Helen Vlahos attained heroic status for her defiance of the colonels' junta – has anything approaching the status of a paper of record, though left-of-centre *Eleftherotypia* has excellent Sunday supplements, while *Ta Nea* is a highly popular centrist daily. On the far Left, *Avyi* is the Synaspismós (Euro-communist) forum with literary leanings, while *Rizospastis* serves as the organ of the KKE ('unreconstructed' Communists). At the opposite end of the political spectrum, *Apoyevmatini* generally supports the Néa Dhimokratía Party, while *Estia's* no-photo format and reactionary politics are both stuck somewhere at the beginning of the 20th century. The ultra-nationalist lunatic fringe is staked out by paranoid *Stohos* ('Our Goal: Greater Greece; Our Capital: Constantinople'). With the birdcage-lining quality of most newspapers, you wouldn't imagine there would be room for a designated tabloid press, but there are two papers: *News Traffic* and *Espresso*. There are also half a dozen or so daily papers devoted exclusively to sport.

Among magazines that are not merely translations of overseas titles, *Takhydhromos* is the mainstream news and features weekly, *Ena* is more sensationalist, *Klik* a crass rip-off of Britain's *The Face*, while *To Pondiki* (The Mouse) is a satirical weekly revue similar to Britain's *Private Eye*; its famous covers are spot-on and accessible to anyone with minimal Greek. More specialised niches are occupied by low-circulation titles, such as *Adhesmatos Typos* (a slightly right-wing, muck-raking journal), and *Andi*, an intelligent bi-weekly similar to Britain's *New Statesman and Society*, with links to the Synaspismós Party.

Radio and Television

Playing dial roulette on your radio has its rewards. Greek music programmes are always accessible (if variable in quality), and, since the breaking of the government's former monopoly on wavelengths, regional stations have mushroomed – the airwaves are now positively cluttered as even the tiniest island village sets up its own studio and transmitter. The two state-run channels are **ER1** (a mix of news, talk and popular music) and **ER2** (strictly popular music).

On islands like Rhodes, Corfu and Crete, with a substantial expat and tourist presence, there will usually be at least one station on the FM band trying its luck at English-moderated programming by and for foreigners. The Turkish state radio's **Third Channel** is also widely (if somewhat unpatriotically) listened to on east Aegean border islands for its classical, jazz and blues programmes. The **BBC World Service** broadcasts on short wave throughout Greece; consult **www. bbc.co.uk/worldservice** for the current frequencies used.

Greece's centralised, government-controlled television stations, **ET1**, **NET** and (from Thessaloníki) **ET3**, nowadays lag behind assorted private channels – **Antenna**, **Mega**, **Star**, **Alpha**, **Alter**, **Eurosport** and **Makedonia TV** – in the ratings. Programming on all stations tends to be a mix of soaps (Italian and Latin American more than home-grown); game shows; talk shows; 'reality' Big Brother-type programmes; 1950s and 1960s movies; and sports. All foreign films and serials are broadcast in their original language with Greek subtitles. Most private channels operate around the clock; public stations broadcast from between 7am or 8am until around 3am. Cable television is rare to non-existent in Greece, but satellite subscription is avidly pursued, with expensive decoders locally available which will give you access to nearly 400 channels; one bonus is that you can receive many overseas radio programmes via your satellite receiver.

Money and Banking

Whether you establish part- or full-time residence in Greece, you will need to open some sort of euro account locally; transactions exclusively based on a UK- or North America-based account will rapidly become too unwieldy and expensive, especially for things like paying utility bills. At the very least, you'll want a **savings account** (*tamievtírio*) linked to an ATM card; this should prove sufficient for most expat needs. Greek **ATM cards**, if part of the Visa Electron network (certainly true in the case of the Alpha, Pireos and Emboriki banks), can act as **debit cards** for purchases, both within Greece and abroad – within Greece, there should be no fee levied for such use. Never discard cancelled passbooks (*vivliária*), as they are vital for proving your financial solvency when applying for or renewing residence permits.

You can, subject to variable minimum initial deposits, also open a **dollar or sterling account**, though it will pay almost no interest, and what does get paid is – like interest on your passbook account – taxed at source immediately. Having a foreign currency account allows you to speculate somewhat against the euro, changing dollars or sterling (for no charge) when the rate proves favourable. You can deposit sterling or dollar cheques received from overseas in your foreign currency account free of charge (or nearly so), though allow three weeks for the funds to clear. For a small fee, and with a couple of days' advance notice, you can also get cash sterling or dollars prior to travelling abroad. For higher fees, you can have pensions or other regular remittances sent directly into your foreign currency account.

There are currently around twenty separate **banks** operating in Greece but you are unlikely to see most of them outside the largest cities. Across the country, the four biggest and most widespread banks are **Ethnikí Trápeza tis Elládhos** (National Bank of Greece; **www.nbg.gr**), ponderous and state-dominated with take-a-number queues the rule in many branches; privately run Alpha Bank (**www.alpha.gr**) and **Trápeza Piréos** (Piraeus Bank; **www.piraeusbank.gr**), together reckoned the most efficient and innovative; and state-dominated **Emborikí Trápeza** (ex-Commercial Bank; **www.emporiki.gr**), in which Crédit Agricole currently has a 23 per cent stake. The government hopes to increase the degree of private investment in Ethnikí and Emborikí but don't hold your breath. There is also the **Agrotikí Trápeza** (Agricultural Bank) but you must be a certified farmer to open an account – perhaps worth investigating if your property has a few productive olive trees or grape vines.

Greek banks are normally open Monday to Thursday 8.30am–2.30pm, Friday 8.30am–2pm, though they may close not only for the national holidays but also for local saint's day feasts (*see* pp.267–9). Private banks, in particular, encourage ATM use and discourage personal visits with US-style tricks, for example, by charging you a euro or so for every counter transaction above four per month. If you maintain an average balance over a six-month period below a certain amount (usually about €300), you will also get hit with a stiff monthly 'maintenance' charge until you top up the account.

With Greek tax residence officially confirmed, you can obtain locally adminis-tered **credit cards** through almost every bank; interest rates have tumbled compared to former times, though not quite to UK or US levels as yet. Any credit card denominated in dollars, sterling or euro is usable in an increasing number of places, but always ask first – electronic swipe machines at the till are a good indication that it's okay but some merchants and (especially) travel agencies will pass on the card issuer's three per cent charge to you.

At present, Emborikí is the only bank that will offer consumer **loans**, including mortgages, to non-residents, subject to verification of income. All other banks will require a Greek residence permit and your last annual tax return, filed in Greece. **Internet banking** and **telephone banking** are offered by all the major Greek banks. Some sites are ostensibly PC-compatible only, though OSX Panther should solve any problems for Mac users.

Property Insurance

Insurance in Greece is provided either by companies operating in-house from, or affiliated with, all the major banks, or by independent entities. One potential problem with securing it through a bank is that their insurance division can, in some cases, just be a single desk staffed part-time by somebody who's only reliably contactable by mobile. You might feel better about contracting insurance through an independent broker working reliably from their own premises. This may be an accountancy office or even an auto parts store, so don't be surprised – the important thing is that you can find them when you need them.

Most owners of property in Greece take out a multi-risk household policy. This covers the fabric of the building, its contents and any civil responsibility landing upon the owner of the property. At a minimum, a house policy should cover flood, meteorological events (e.g. a lightning strike), acts of God (such as meteor landings), and acts of man (such as crashing aircraft). In wooded areas, always get coverage for 'fire from the forest'. Otherwise, you are insured only against fire caused from within the property (e.g. an electrical fault, accident with an open hearth, or a garden rubbish fire). You may be asked if you lie within a certain distance of an olive grove (*eleónas*) – count on a premium hike if you do, as these trees are especially flammable. For all of these types of coverage, count on Greece-based premiums of about (for example) €100 per year for €115,000, the value of the structure and its contents combined; the breakdown will be cited at the front of the policy.

You cannot as a rule obtain theft protection unless you are resident full-time or nearly so, and you cannot get earthquake cover unless the house has been new-built to verifiable anti-seismic standards.

Always make a copy of your policy document (*asfalistírio*) and keep this copy *out* of the insured dwelling – in a safe deposit box and/or in the UK. If the house burns down with the only insurance certificate in it, you will just have added to your woes.

Many foreign residents are daunted by the prospect of having a Greek-language policy, and want the luxury of 'plain English'. It is possible to contract UK-based insurance for Greek holiday homes, but of course you will pay extra for the privilege. Two English brokers worth contacting for quotes are **Copeland Insurance** (**t** (020) 8656 8435, **www.andrewcopeland. co.uk**), who offer cover for earthquake, subsidence and tenants' liability, and Insurance for **Homes Abroad** (28 Waterloo Street, Weston-Super-Mare, BS23 1LN, **t** (01934) 424040).

There are three important points to consider when choosing a policy.

• **Make sure that the level of cover is adequate.** Just as in the UK, if you under-insure the building and the worst happens, the company will not pay you out for the full extent of your loss. The amount you should be covered for as far as civil liability is concerned should be a minimum of one million euros and prefer-ably higher. The amount of cover for the building itself should be the full cost of the reconstruction. If you own an apartment, then the cost of the building's insurance for the whole block of apartments should be included in your service charge. You will then only need contents and public liability insurance.

As far as contents are concerned, you should make a detailed estimate of the value of your furnishings and possessions likely to be in the property at any time. Remember to allow for items, such as cameras, that you may take with you on holiday. Notice, in particular, whether there is a requirement to stipulate items of high value. If you have any items of high value, it is worth having them photographed and possibly valued. The insurance company might specify secu-rity measures that must be in place in your home.

• **If you are using the property as holiday accommodation (or spend long periods away from home), you must specify a policy which is a holiday policy.** If you do not, you are likely to find that one of the conditions of the policy is that cover will lapse if the property is empty for 30 or 60 days. Premiums will be higher for holiday homes because the risk is higher.

• **If you intend to let your property, you must notify the insurance company and comply with any requirements of the insurance company with regard to the lettings. Otherwise, your cover could be void. Your premiums will be higher.**

If you have to make a claim, note that there are usually time limits for doing so. If the claim involves theft or a break-in, you will usually have to report the matter to the police. This should normally be done immediately after discovery of the incident and within 24 hours in any case. The claim should be notified to the insurance company without delay. Check the maximum period allowed in your policy, which could be as little as 48 hours. As with all-important docu-ments in Greece, the claim should be notified by recorded delivery post.

Working and Employment

Bluntly put, few northern Europeans come to Greece with the intention of becoming the employee of someone else, unless they are working for the local branch of a major multinational, with the post prearranged from overseas. The basic unemployment rate is around nine per cent, but among school-leavers it easily exceeds 20 per cent in some regions. Most unskilled labour is performed by Greece's growing immigrant communities, first and foremost Albanians, Russians, Ukranians, Bulgarians and Pakistanis. Many of these workers are 'off the record' and the government is ostensibly keen to get them documented and contributing to the tax and social security systems, though two successive amnesties for illegal entrants have produced disappointing results.

Greeks can make excellent hosts but, alas, experience shows that they are apt to be less than brilliant bosses. Many, many, many foreigners have fallen out with Greek employers over the latter's failure to pay their contributions to the **IKA** (*Ídhryma Kinotikón Asfalíon*) or Social Insurance Foundation scheme, without participation in which you are not eligible for unemployment and a number of other social benefits, such as healthcare and disability payments. It is, in fact, illegal for employers not to pay for IKA, but so many foreign staff have worked without proper contracts of employment that it's easy for them to get away with it. Assuming that you do obtain a contract worth the paper it's written on, you'll find that your salary is set by the Greek government or unions (whichever is applicable), and is based on your job title, experience and length of service (wages go up automatically every year you are continuously employed with the same outfit). Employer reluctance to pay IKA contributions – and the difficulty of getting rid of contracted employees of long standing – are the main reasons why so many Greek businesses are 'family-run' – proprietors aren't obliged to pay IKA for immediate family members, with whom there will, of course, be no formal contract of employment.

Thus self-employment among foreigners is the rule and this is confined to professions where either Greeks won't compete effectively (e.g. translation) or where you can satisfy the requirements of the Greek state for equivalent qualifications to native Greeks plying the same trade (e.g. veterinarian or physiotherapist). Greek-to-English translation work is almost entirely based in Athens and runs the gamut from tourist literature to highly technical material for financial institutions and think-tanks. The basic minimum rate for translations is €15 per single-spaced A4 page, increasing in relation to your experience and the difficulty of the text.

Bureaucratic Requirements for Self-employment

If you intend to pursue a profession that requires qualifications, you can obtain an assessment of your foreign degrees compared to those recognised in Greece from the Dhiapandepistimiakó Kéndro Anagnórisis Titlón Spoudhón tis Allodhapís (Inter-University Centre for the Recognition of Foreign Educational Qualifications) at Syngroú 112, Athens 117 41 (**t** 210 92 22 533).

In any case, you'll need to sign on with the local branch of **TEBE**, the national insurance scheme for self-employed people – which doesn't, however, give you the right to unemployment benefits or on-the-job accident compensation. If you are continuing to contribute to any social insurance scheme in a country that has reciprocal agreements with Greece (all EU states do), this must be proved in writing – a tedious and protracted process. Specifically, the document from the Department of Work and Pensions in England stating what your current contributions are will have to be translated into Greek and certified –

most easily done through your Greece-based solicitor. However, there are reports that this only gives you up to three years' exemption from double contributions; after that you will have to participate in the Greek scheme, no matter what you are still doing in your 'home' country.

Once you're set up with TEBE, you visit the tax office (*eforía*) to be issued with a tax number ('*A-fi-Mi*' – *arithmó foroloyikó mitróön*, akin to the UK's national insurance number) which must be cited in all transactions. To be issued one of these, you need to present a birth certificate (certified copies are usually acceptable) which shows the full unmarried names of *both* your parents. Once in business, you will be required to keep receipt and invoice books with your tax number professionally printed on them, or have a rubber stamp made up for applying that number to every sheet. The tax office will determine which **VAT rate** (abbreviated as *fi-pi-ah* for *fóros prostithémenis axías*) you should pay for each kind of transaction; VAT returns must be filed every two or three months depending on the type of business, for which you will need an **accountant** (*loyistís*).

Your accountant will also advise you on which, if any, of the types of incorporation are to your advantage compared to doing business as a sole proprietor; incorporation is much more expensive but provides some protection in case of bankruptcy, as well as potential tax advantages. The most popular alternative is to trade as an E.P.E. (*etería periorisménis efthýnis* or limited-liability company), which must consist of at least two partners holding share certificates worth approximately €20,000; each partner is liable for the debts of the company up to the face value of the share certificates.

Last, but not least, retain a good **solicitor** (*dhikigóros*) – you will eventually need one even if everything is relatively plain sailing. Energetic, effective and bilingual ones are rare beasts in Greece – if you secure one, be sure to cherish him or her.

Tourism-related Businesses

Because (up to now) no certification or qualification is needed to engage in such businesses, various tourist-related enterprises are the most popular options for self-employment among foreign residents: yacht charter, windsurfing schools and, of course, providing hospitality in the form of hotels, pensions and restaurants. Most foreigners managing accommodation opt for a **rented furnished rooms licence** (*enikiazómena epiplómena dhomátia*) rather than one for a hotel. Application and renewal costs (every five years) are cheaper, you're not obliged to offer breakfast (though most foreigners do), inspections are quarterly rather than monthly, and accounts are rendered to the local tax authorities similarly less frequently. If you are running a restaurant, bar or lodging out of premises that you have not actually purchased, the standard business lease terms are either one year or twelve years – obviously you want to go for the longer period.

Operating a Pension/B&B/Rooms Establishment

For anybody who runs a **pension** (*dhomátia*) as a sole proprietorship business, profits are linked to one's *A-fi-Mi* number (*see* p.143). Besides this and your residence permit, as a prospective proprietor you will need to present:

- **An official copy of your secondary school and/or university diploma.**
- **An official copy of a police report from your home country, showing that you are not wanted on any criminal charges.**
- A health certificate verifying negative TB and HIV antigen tests, performed at the local hospital.
- A certificate (*pistopiitikó*) showing that you do not have any unpaid private debts or back tax assessments in Greece.
- A certificate from the municipal fire department stating that the building is equipped with the appropriate extinguishing equipment and fire exits.
- A certificate from an engineer stating the building is structurally sound.
- A certificate from the local health department verifying that the sanitary system is hygienic.

Once the operating licence is granted, you will be issued with **placards** (*kartéles*) to be posted in each room, stating the official price of the room at low, middle and peak season. It is illegal to charge more than the posted price for the appropriate season. Depending on the number of rooms, you may be required to pay a small annual fee to the municipality (*dhímos*) for each of the *kartéles* at the start of each season; rented rooms are usually open only from April to October, but in places with longer seasons – like Crete and Rhodes – this can be stretched to March–November. Room rates include 13.5 per cent VAT (*fi-pi-ah*), which are payable in quarterly instalments. Establishments with eight or more rooms must pay an additional 2 per cent municipal tax on the room rates.

Utility bills are a major hidden expense; even during the months when a pension is closed, you will still have to pay the standing charges on the phone and electric bills (which include various other charges based on the area of the building) which can be considerable, even when there are no appliances running.

Besides employee wages, you will have to pay IKA contributions each month, which can be almost half again as much as the actual salary. Your employees will probably want to file for unemployment at some point during the six or so months when the pension is not operating. Employers are also obliged to pay bonuses (*filodhórima*) at Easter and Christmas. Don't forget the TEBE contributions for yourself – about €140 per month – although the new government elected in March 2004 is proposing to make participation in this scheme optional for *dhomátia* owners.

All records of room receipts and business expenditures have to be forwarded to your accountant weekly; she or he, in turn, passes on all VAT and municipal

Case Study: Miranda's Pension

Miranda bought a pension in a privileged location of Rhodes Old Town in 2001 from the previous owner who had converted a private dwelling into tourist accommodation. Although Miranda is American by birth, she was married to an EU citizen, which allowed her to obtain both a residence permit and a business licence to run a pension. For the moment, the physical premises are owned by an EU-based company created for the purpose (English as a rule, as the tax is lowest), though when Miranda shortly receives her EU passport, she will sell the property to herself and own it directly.

Miranda says – and this is corroborated informally by several other pension owners: 'If you have only five to seven rooms, you can just manage by yourself, along with a cleaner who comes in at mid-morning. You can't be mopping and making beds – your job is to keep the bookings straight, interact with guests and otherwise keep the business on the rails. Keeping 10 to 13 rooms going is really a full-time job for a married couple, plus a cleaning lady. Somebody needs to be on the case from just before breakfast time until around midnight, that is 16 hours a day. I'm currently single but don't want to spend all my time working, so there are three of us here working variable shifts. Philippe serves breakfast from 7.30am until about 11am or so. Then I take over, doing office work and greeting any arrivals until about 7pm, when another person relieves me at the front desk, also serving drinks from the bar until late.'

Before pursuing her dream to run a smallish B&B in the Greek islands, Miranda spent 25 years as a high-powered designer and textile representative in the New York and Paris fashion business. 'Most of my contact with people in the rag trade was competitive and adversarial. Owning this pension has given me an entirely different view of the human race. Most travellers are in a good mood and want to communicate and explore. They do need attention and service but that's more than offset by the really interesting people I've met – some of whom have become friends – that I'd never have come in contact with in my previous life.'

So much for the intangible rewards; show us the money. During a seven-and-a-half-month season (mid-March to the end of October) in a busy year, Miranda's eleven-room pension grosses about €90,000. Deducting the cost of VAT on the room rates, municipal tax, fire insurance, accountancy fees, TEBE for Miranda, staff salaries, IKA, holiday bonuses, breakfast and cleaning supplies, plus utilities, still leaves a handsome profit of just over half that amount. Not bad for the attendant quality of life.

taxes owing and makes the annual tax declaration for the business every March. For accountancy services, budget €500–800 annually.

Finally, there are insurance premiums – at a minimum fire but also possibly liability if you have lots of steep stairways and the like. Again, budget €500 for an establishment of under a dozen rooms.

Health and Emergencies

Since 1983, Greece has had a semblance of a public healthcare system, dispensed through a network of outpatient clinics (*iatría*) and state hospitals (*kratiká nosokomía*). It is, however, grossly under-funded and considered by far the worst in the EU (as it was before May 2004); many doctors opt to work in their own private, pricey clinics or hospitals, despite repeated government efforts to control such moonlighting. Treatment models tend to be antiquated, hidebound and pill-mad. In the mental health field, for instance, psychiatrists dominate at the expense of counsellors or therapists; drug- or alcohol-related problems tend to be referred to neurologists as symptoms of a 'nervous disorder', given the complete absence of any rehabilitation/treatment centres; and powerful tranquillisers are routinely prescribed for back or neck pain that anywhere else would result in a referral to a physiotherapist.

Reputations of the **state hospitals** vary considerably – just as they do in the UK and the USA – from the competent and salubrious to the House of Horrors/ Grand Guignol variety. Discreet local enquiry will quickly rate the one nearest you: as examples, the hospitals at Ioánnina (partly affiliated to a medical school) and Híos have good reputations, while Rhodes has a decidedly mixed one. Casualty wards are excellent for acute traumas – motorbike accidents, broken glass in your foot, fractures, etc. – well used as they are to the grisly, war zone-type injuries common on work sites (Greek work safety consciousness not being a strong point). But in-patient wards are not good for extended care – families typically haul in extra bedding and food, and take turns doing shifts that the demoralised staff nurses can't be bothered to perform.

EU nationals, on presentation of identification (either passport, identity card or residence certificate) plus form E111 (though this is shortly scheduled to be replaced by an EU-wide benefits 'smart card') are entitled to treatment in the state-run clinics and hospitals on the same basis as locals. However, if you're not signed up to either the IKA or TEBE systems, you'll have to pay for pharmacy medicines and special tests – though medical attention itself remains free. The E111 form, while it lasts, is only intended for EU citizens travelling (not residing) in other EU countries and isn't valid for time away from your home country exceeding three months. Non-EU/EEA nationals are entitled only to free emergency care in Greece.

All things considered, you should consider taking out private **medical insurance**, which will cover you regardless of the duration of your stay in Greece or the number of sojourns there per year, if not permanent. Most so-called travel policies will not cover you for more than a certain number of journeys of a modest duration per year and may refuse to pay out at all if they learn you have a second residence abroad. All the big UK-based names such as BUPA, WPA and PPP offer policies specifically tailored to suit long-term expats. Publications

Case Study: The Revenge of the Fig

When I bought my second ruin on Sámos, contiguous to the first one that I'd already restored, there was a huge *agriosykiá* (wild fig) growing out of the northeast corner. Wild fig trees infest many ruins across the country and this one had to go before any substantial renovation could take place. So I set to work with my trusty Stihl chainsaw, as this specimen was clearly beyond what strong herbicides could be expected to deal with. Unfortunately, rather than early morning or evening, I chose midday during a hot June for the task, dressed in old cutoffs and an old T-shirt. A huge plume of sawdust sprayed over my bare, sweaty legs and arms as the papery wood of the trunk defied the saw chain. With the branches finally in neat chunks, and the stump thoroughly doused in herbicide, I quit for the afternoon, washed off thoroughly and had lunch with some visiting friends.

By the next day I was itching and scratching, and thinking I'd caught a bit too much sun. By the second day, I looked as if I was auditioning for the lead in *The Elephant Man*. Huge, puffy welts covered every square inch of my forearms and thighs. Swimming offered only temporary relief; my guests, greatly alarmed, insisted I go straight to hospital. In the casualty ward, they immediately popped me on to a gurney and began pumping me intravenously with powerful steroids to get the welts down while the duty doctor began exploring whys and wherefores. I already suspected that the fig was my adversary, though for the sake of thoroughness admitted that I'd been using Roundup. A quick call to the Poison Control Centre in Athens established that there were no such reactions known to glyphosate (the active ingredient in Roundup). The lady doctor, a

such as the *Guardian Weekly* periodically run special advertorial supplements on the topic. However, those aged over 60 may find that the premiums asked are so horrific (e.g. £1,000 per annum per person with a £1,000 excess on claims) that they might well be better off paying on a case-by-case basis for private treatment, which still costs much less in Greece than it does in northern Europe.

Throughout Greece, the phone number to summon an ambulance is t 166. If for any reason this doesn't work, try the Europe-wide emergency number t 112.

Social Services, Benefits and Retirement

Enforceable reciprocal EU/EEA rules mean that a person moving from one EU/EEA state to another should not lose his or her entitlement to certain benefits by having done so. Specifically, if you have earned a pension from years of work in the UK, you should be able to receive it while retired in Greece. Similarly, if you are unemployed in the UK and elect to look for work in Greece, you can (with the necessary paperwork prepared) collect unemployment benefit for up to three cautious sort, refused to accept the most obvious explanation, ordered a battery of tests for typhus and other systemic nasties, and tried to persuade me to check in as an in-patient for at least one night. I demurred, not wanting to impose visiting and nursing duties on friends who were supposed to be on holiday.

After the welts began subsiding a bit, I was paraded before the head internist who immediately pronounced me the worst case of fig poisoning he'd ever seen. The typhus-plus tests were, of course, all negative, and I was out of pocket about £24 equivalent because a) they cost well below the excess on my travel policy and b) I wasn't signed up to IKA or TEBE. Some four hours after checking myself in, I was finally sent on my way with prescriptions for two batches of Betnovate cream and Clarityn pills to continue treatment (another £12 or so). Redness, itching and discomfort continued for another six weeks, and to this day, even the least bit of wild fig sap provokes a strong reaction in me.

Overly conservative testing aside, this is a prime example of what a provincial Greek hospital is good at – I doubt I would have received as prompt, heads-up care in northern Europe, not least because the condition wouldn't be recognised quickly enough. In Greek folklore, people are warned against sleeping under the shade of a fig because it is 'heavy'. More to the point, it is a massive irritant – wake up after a nap with fallen fig leaves as a cushion, and one's face will look the way my limbs did. To add insult to injury, the saw-chain was horribly dulled, and a few days later, I went to the Stihl dealer to have it sharpened. The owner took one look at me and, without preamble, said, 'You've been sawing fig, haven't you?' 'How did you know?' I replied. 'Oh, my grandmother died of fig allergy,' he exclaimed, cheerfully.

months in any other EU member state. However, lingering Greek obstructiveness and xenophobia can mean that this is sometimes easier said than done.

To make your entitlement to UK unemployment benefit portable, you have to make an application for 'Export of Benefit'. Many local Job Centres do not regularly stock the pertinent form, so you may be referred to the Department of Work and Pensions (Overseas Benefits Directorate, Exportable Jobseekers Allowance, Room TC001, Whitley Road, Benton, Newcastle-upon-Tyne, NE98 1BA). Once you get the form and fill it in, you send it to your local Benefits Agency for processing. After a few weeks, you should receive an E303, which is a sheaf of forms used by Greece to claim back from the UK any benefits that they pay you. You should also get a letter of introduction in Greek explaining what you're after.

Once in Greece, you head for the nearest **OAED** office (Organismós Apaskhólisis Ergatikoú Dhynamikoú; roughly equivalent to a UK Job Centre – they're in the phone book), where you register as unemployed, get an ID card and undertake to look for work. Your first benefit cheque will come through four to six weeks after you've signed on. The E303 can also be used to claim sickness and maternity benefits in Greece.

In smaller places, certain social services and benefits can be overseen in the first instance by the clerk of the local town hall (*grammatéas*). These are, sadly, keeping their jobs only by virtue of seniority and can be unhelpful to foreigners when not actually dismissive and racist. The best strategy when faced with oral rejection is to make a written petition (*étisi*) for whatever it is you want, preferably on a sheet of revenue-stamped paper (*ypéfthyni dhílosi*), available

Case Study: When is a Resident not a Resident?

During spring 2003, it was announced on the island of Sými that all those living there with permanent residence status would be entitled to half-price fares on the various scheduled ferry boats calling on the island. Since nearly everybody there needs to get to Rhodes for shopping or official errands at least twice weekly, and two round trips at full price costs about €50, this is a not inconsiderable benefit. Jean Manship, owner of a popular bar in Horió since 1984, reckoned she had an airtight case for the permanent-residence certificate necessary to obtain this discount, but upon application to the town hall was brusquely told by the *grammatéas* that such certificates would be issued only to native-born Symiots. Jean, having paid municipal tax and TEBE locally through her business for so many years, wasn't going to take this lying down, and on 1 July (along with 45 other foreign signatories), petitioned the mayor and the municipal council to provide permanent residence certificates to any EU national residing on the island. No written reply was received, but through an informal interview in August the mayor reiterated that the council had no intention of issuing the desired certificate to foreigners. The indomitable Jean made an appeal to the Ombudsman for Human Rights in Athens, and shortly thereafter, obtained satisfaction in the form of a letter informing her that the mayor of Sými had also been written to and told to mend his ways. He was reminded by the Ombudsman that 'according to Law 2647/1998, Articles 3 and 4, when persons prove, through authentic documents, their permanent residence in Greek territory, they should be provided with the relevant certificate. Furthermore, Greek nationality is not a precondition to this result, since this certificate may be used in various ways, for example, to obtain a driving licence.'

It would seem that the Symiot authorities were not (just) being xenophobic or discriminatory in their reluctance to grant the residence certificate. Residents of frontier municipalities such as Sými, with populations of under 3,000, enjoy significant rebates on income tax, in an effort by the Greek central government to encourage year-round habitation. Should the official population rise above 3,000, however, this privilege would be likely to be withdrawn. So the Symiot town hall has a vested interest in limiting the numbers of permanent residents, by fair means or foul. Jean and several other petitioners have now obtained their official residence certificates – but not (yet) their right to reduced income tax; Jean has a discrimination case pending at the court in Strasbourg and is preparing to wait three years for a hearing.

from stationers and kiosks, being mindful to retain a photocopy for yourself. By Article 4, Paragraph 1 of Law 2690/1999, public authorities are required to respond within 60 days to such a petition. If you do not hear from them within this time period, the next step is to make a complaint to the Office of the Ombudsman for Human Rights and/or the Office of the European Commission Lawyer in Athens. Usually this will obtain satisfaction, but some individuals have seen themselves obliged to lodge cases with the European Court of Human Rights in Strasbourg. To begin getting in touch with any of these bodies, contact the **Citizen's Signpost** service (**t** oo 800 6789 10 11 in any EU country).

If you are due a UK-based pension, you should be able to receive it in Greece with relatively few complications. The Department of Work and Pensions in the UK issues various leaflets and maintains telephone helplines and a website, to assist you in understanding your benefits entitlement should you go abroad. For EU states, the relevant leaflet is GL29. Concerning a UK state pension, you have a number of choices:

- **You can have it paid directly into a UK bank account and then transfer money to Greece as and when you need it.**
- **You can have it paid directly into your Greek bank account, but set wire-transfer fees and exchange commissions will considerably erode small sums so it's best to have this done quarterly rather than monthly.**
- **You can have a sterling cheque sent to you, or to someone you nominate, every one to three months (possibly the best choice, especially if you open a sterling account in Greece, *see* p.201).**

Some UK-based private pensions will pay directly into a UK-based bank only. You should also enquire as to whether the pension will be taxed in the UK or in Greece – there may be a significant advantage to one or other option.

Until and unless the UK adopts the euro, your net pension will obviously vary with exchange rates. And even if the UK does joins up, you cannot count on being completely free of bank charges, as banks within the euro zone are still levying charges on interstate transactions (e.g. €3 on a wire transfer of €250 from Italy to Greece).

Those receiving US or Canadian pensions will also find that payment can be made by the three ways specified above – but, of course, there is no possibility of it ever being in euros, so you will always have to deal with exchange rate fluctuations.

Education

If you relocate year-round to Greece with school-age children, you'll be confronted with a public education system that is uniform nationwide – the curriculum is mandatory and centrally generated. The Greek school system, described in 2003 by *Athens News* as 'fragmentary, competitive, repressive and thought-stifling', is geared to the senior-year exam sessions, which determine a teenager's fate in higher education, emphasising the ability to parrot reams of memorised trivia at the expense of any lateral or creative thinking.

The only variable is in the physical state of the school and the teacher-pupil ratio; even Montessori or other 'innovative'-method schools are required to follow the state syllabus, with a mandated, single textbook for each course. There are rays of light in the gloom, however, and not always where you'd expect them: should you be raising children on tiny Kastellórizo, for instance, they will bask in a teacher-pupil ratio of about 8:1 and state-of-the-art computer equipment – all part of the government effort to maintain this remote territory as a going concern.

Under-fives can attend state **crèches** (*pedhikí stathmí* or *nipagoyía*), one of the few enduring achievements of the 1980s PASOK governments. Schools themselves are divided into *próto dhimotikó* (primary school for those aged 6–11), *yimnásio* (akin to the UK or US middle school) and *lýkio* (for ages 14 to 17). At the moment, there are also vocational schools (abbreviated 'TEE') as an alternative to the *lýkio*, but these are set to be scrapped and a network of technical *lýkia* created in their stead. The school year starts on the Monday of the second complete week in September and finishes at the end of the second complete week in June for the *próta dhimotiká* and *yimnásia*; however, *lýkia* classes are let out in late May as seniors must sit exams in nine subjects for three weeks.

The only way to exempt your children from (most of) this ordeal is to enrol them in a private, foreign-curriculum academy designed primarily for the offspring of diplomats and multinational employees, who will be going on to university in the UK or North America. They are found, however, only in the Athens and Thessaloníki area at present. Notwithstanding any nominal national affiliation, all the schools listed below accept students from a wide variety of nationalities and backgrounds, and award the widely recognised International Baccalaureate diploma. British-orientated schools will have their students sit GCSE and A-level exams.

- **American Community Schools of Athens**, Halándhri district, **t** 210 63 93 200, **www.acs.gr.**
- **Byron College**, Garyitós Yéraka, near Athens, **t** 210 60 47 722, **www.byroncollege.gr.**
- **Campion School**, Pallíni Attikís, **t** 210 60 71 700, **www.campion.edu.gr.**
- **Pinewood**, Piléa, Thessaloníki, **t** 231 03 01 221, **www.pinewood.gr;**
- **St Catherine's British Embassy School**, Lykóvrissi Kifissiás, Athens, **t** 210 28 29 750, **www.stcatherines.gr.**
- **St Lawrence College**, Ellinikón, **t** 210 89 81 537, **www.st-lawrence.gr.**
- **Tasis International School**, Kifissiá, **t** 210 62 33 888, **info@tasis.edu.gr.**

Keeping a Car in Greece

All things considered (especially the text following), it is easiest to buy and licence a left-hand-drive car once in Greece, especially if you will be resident full-time. Although Greece is still (almost) the only country in Europe that does not manufacture automobiles, prices and taxes have dropped considerably since the 1980s when they were deemed 'luxury items' and were heavily taxed; new Japanese- or Korean-made runabouts, the usual entry-level models, start at about €6,000 before taxes and licensing fees.

If you as an EU citizen drive a car into Greece from another EU country, most obviously when using it to bring household chattels to your new home, you are allowed – in common with the rules of many EU nations – to drive it for six more months from the date of entry, provided the road tax in its home country is paid up and insurance (third party at a minimum) is valid. As EU passports are no longer routinely stamped upon entry to Greece, some other proof of the entry date is necessary – most usually, the ticket stub for the Adriatic ferry that brought you into the country. After that, matters get decidedly peculiar and you must choose between a number of unsatisfactory options.

Many second-home owners have, in the past, used the 'six-on, six-off' system. This involves taking one's car off the road for six months annually – easiest if you have private parking – and having it placed under seal by the nearest customs office. A customs official is summoned the day before you leave in, say, October and a cable threaded through the steering wheel and brake pedal to immobilise them, and a record of the deed made. You or a caretaker should still, however, be able to turn the engine over periodically during the winter to keep the battery from going flat; you might also want to put the car up on blocks to keep the tyres from sustaining irreversible damage. When you return the following April, you merely inform the customs in person or by phone that you're 'reactivating' the car and clip the cable yourself.

Recently, however, serious threats to the viability of this regime have arisen. The car must be road-taxed and insured during its six months of activity but you can no longer secure UK tax discs without having a current MOT certificate, which you cannot obtain without driving the thing back to Britain. In Greece, the local *eforía* is no longer accepting part-year payments for road tax and most Greek insurers will not issue policies for foreign-plate cars. Ethniki was the last known company to do so, but you had to buy 12 months at a time, at Athens-based rates, and in early 2004 reliable reports indicated that they had stopped granting new policies to foreign-registered vehicles, and that, in case of accident, they would not pay out to policy-holders whose basis of circulation was illegal in any way. You could attempt to insure the car through a British entity but they will probably demand documentation (e.g. an MOT certificate), which may not be available, and they are likely to charge British home rates. It is unlawful to drive in Greece without third-party insurance at a minimum and paid-up road tax.

The second option is total, all-year illegality. Greece, especially the smaller, remoter islands, swarms with foreign-plate cars that have been there since Noah stepped off the ark. Few of these have any sort of current insurance or road tax, but relatively few of them have been bothered as long as the owners are well-liked locally and they don't ever take the vehicle off the island concerned. However, once these cars and their owners leave their home turf, they're liable to scrutiny – especially at busy ferry docks, such as Pátra, Igoumenítsa and Piraeus – by plain-clothes SDOE officers, a body recently formed by the merger of certain divisions of the customs and tax offices. If they have any reason to suspect that a car has entered Greece permanently, or at least been there in excess of six months, they will demand evidence of valid, paid-up insurance and road tax in the country of the car's registration and/or documentation of the vehicle's entry into Greece within the past six months; if none of this is forthcoming, the vehicle will be seized immediately and its erstwhile owners literally left standing by the side of the road – in my experience, this has happened to two people. To free it from impoundment, you'll have to pay a huge, arbitrary fine plus customs duties; failure to do so results in the vehicle being quickly auctioned. The 'auction' dates are known only to customs officials, the police – and their friends...

The main reason that driving 'black' has (up to now) proved such a popular option among foreign residents in Greece is a particular, wholesale defiance of EU law by the Greek state itself. Directive 83/181/EEC states that cars domiciled in one EU state can be imported VAT-free into another EU country if VAT has already been paid in the country of original purchase. Moreover, by the terms of other EU directives, if the Greek VAT rate on cars of 18 per cent is lower than that prevailing in the country of the car's original purchase and registry (e.g. Denmark, at 25 per cent), the customs service is actually obliged to refund the difference between the two rates – though don't hold your breath waiting for this to happen, as it never does. The Greek customs service has always insisted on illegally charging 18 per cent VAT again upon a vehicle's import, based on an assessed value that is often wildly higher than the market value. The only discount or concession given is if the car is more than 15 years old, in which case, VAT is levied on just 20 per cent of the assessed value, but even in such cases, expect to pay total import fees roughly equal to the street value of the car. Greece has been hauled into the European Court of Human Rights in Strasbourg repeatedly over this by irate motorists coming to live in the country. It usually takes three years for cases to be heard, and though the Greek authorities (who always lose or make no representation) are obliged to yield in the individual case, they continue to violate the law every week. The Greek exchequer simply raises too much money through this practice to stop it and old punitive habits – engendered in the days when every Greek who could manage it sneaked off to Italy to buy a much cheaper car there – die hard.

Officially Importing and Registering a Foreign-plate Car

So you've read all the foregoing but decided anyway that you can't bear to be parted with your beloved northern European buggy. What to do? First, you should go to a good **customs broker** (*ektelonistís*) within six verifiable months of having entered Greece with the car in question. They will quickly do some rough calculations based on your estimate of the car's value to see if importation is financially feasible. Then you bring the car to the customs compound where officials will note the engine and chassis number, count the seats, and give a valuation of the tyres and any expensive peripherals (remove any fancy sound systems if possible). Then a sheaf of paperwork, including your **personal petition** (*étisi*) to import the vehicle, is sent to the head office in Piraeus, which will respond within 10 working days, saying what their definitive evaluation is (against which there is no appeal), and how much in VAT and import fees you have to pay. That same day, you'll have to give, or deposit in the bank account of, your *ektelonistís* the amount demanded, along with his fee. The car is now lawfully imported into Greece. Next you go to a mechanic for two batteries of tests: one for exhaust emissions, another for basic roadworthiness. Your carburettor or fuel injection system will be tinkered with until the emissions are legal, and a **smog card** (*kárta kavsaeríon*) is issued. This must eventually be shown to get Greek car number plates and should stay in the glove box for ever after. The appropriate mechanic will also have a device that performs a mock braking-pressures test, designed to ensure that you pass the rather less rigorous one that will be done at the nearest provincial **KTEO** (Kéndro Tekhnikó Élengho Ohimáton) or Vehicle Technical Control Centre. Go early in the day to the KTEO, where queues can be long; they will also check that your horn, lights, wipers and

Sample Calculations for Importing a Used Car

These figures are based on the author's 1975 VW minibus, UK plates. Clearly, £2,700 is almost double the van's street value in the UK; the only justification for doing this (besides its being a very reliable and useful vehicle) is that savings on the insurance of about €300 per year will allow the author to claw back the money paid over seven years.

Customs evaluation: £2,700 (the author had, in good faith, declared £2,000).
Less 80% discount for being over 15 years old: £540
Converted to euros: €774.75
Plus flat import fee: €500
Subtotal: €1,274.75
Multiple factor of 142% (based on size of engine and year of manufacture; ranges
   from 5% to 346%): €1,810.15
Plus Greek VAT of 18%: €229.45
Grand total to pay into customs broker's account: €2,039.60
   (including his fee of about €115).

A Potential Happy Ending for Importing a Used Car

According to a couple I met in an ancient Land Rover with GB plates, if you formally declare your intention to take up permanent residence in Greece at the Greek embassy of the northern European country you are leaving, and secure a residence permit, the paperwork (duly forwarded to a solicitor in Greece) and consular fees (which won't exceed a few tens of pounds) will protect you from the worst stratagems and intentions of the Greek customs service – just drive the thing down and wait to be issued with your local number plates. NB: This won't, *repeat*, won't work for folks just maintaining a holiday home in Greece a few months annually.

turn signals work. A follow-up **KTEO test** (approximately €23) is required every two years in provinces where they exist; the presence (or otherwise) of a KTEO is a hot political issue as, if there's not one in your home province, you're not obliged to submit to inspection and, unsurprisingly in such places (e.g. Lésvos), unroadworthy bangers happily multiply.

With your customs paperwork, *kárta kavsaeríon* and KTEO 'pass' certificate in hand, you then go to your nearest Grafío Synkinoníon (Transport Office) to obtain your local number plates and **diptych circulation permit** (*ádhia kyklo-forías*). The latter must live permanently in the glove box, with the *kárta kavsaeríon* and (once the Grafío Synkinoníon has made a photocopy of it) the KTEO certificate. There will be some to-ing and fro-ing to the tax office (*eforía*) for the payment of a one-off charge or two and the annually renewable **road circulation tax** (*téli kykloforías*). The latter depends on the size of the engine and number of seats; most fees are in the range of €90–150.

Currently, Greek-generated car plates are in a three-letter-plus-four-number format; Athens-based plates start with Y or Z, Thessaloníki's with N, but all other locations utilise two letters from the province name common to both the Latin and Greek alphabet, plus an accession letter; thus XNE 1287 is from Haniá province, Crete, third series (after XNA and XNB, gamma and delta being not usable as they're not in the Latin alphabet).

Upon payment of the *téli kykloforías*, you will be issued with a scored, re-use-proof adhesive disc showing the year, to be attached to the inside of the windscreen. Irrespective of the date of original registry of the car in Greece, you must renew this within a very narrow time-window of a few weeks around the beginning of December – whenever the Ministry of Transport gets around to announcing its charges for the coming year. Fines for missing the deadline are pretty hideous, so if you're not going to be around at that time of year, it's worth getting a friend or acquaintance to do this for you.

With the *ádhia kykloforías* in hand, you are free to contract **insurance**, for either six or 12 months at a time, with the Greek insurer of your choice. Part of the insurance certificate is a detachable stub, which you must display in a plastic pocket on the opposite corner of your windscreen from the circulation tax sticker. One of the benefits of registering an overseas car in Greece is that insurance premiums immediately plunge to a fraction of what you'll have been paying on an overseas-based policy, and if you end up keeping the car for five or six more years, this saving can, in fact, largely offset the cost of importing the vehicle.

Keeping a Scooter or Motorbike

If you're on a small island, and/or you just can't face the hassle involved in maintaining a car, an automatic scooter (*papáki*) or geared small motorbike (*mihanáki*) is an excellent mobility solution. You can get a decent new one for around €1,500 (new), though numbers of second-hand ones also circulate. It is unwise to buy a scooter of more than 50cc unless you have the appropriate driving licence from your home EU country; without it, you won't be able to get insured – yes, third-party insurance is required for all bikes, even those of only 50cc – or to pay the annual *téli kykloforías* (about €16 for a 90cc bike).

In Greece, scooter/motorcycling licences come in three grades: 50–125cc, 125–250cc, and over 250cc displacement. The Grafío Synkinoníon keeps stocks of blank forms to request the granting of such licences, but don't even bother completing it until or unless you've had a couple months' worth of lessons with a local driving school (instructors drive behind you as you scooter along) – and your Greek is fluent enough to take the written test. Budget €400–500 for lessons and bureaucratic fees to obtain a licence.

You'll quickly notice that, while most holidaymakers rent low-slung, relatively unstable, fuel-thirsty Piaggio or Peugeot scooters as a fashion statement, many locals prefer a more rugged, manual-transmission motorbike with safer, large-radius tyres. The favourite workhorses, in descending order of reliability, are: the Honda Cub 50, Yamaha Townmate and Suzuki FB Birdie. Gears are shifted with an easy-to-learn left-foot pedal action and (very importantly) these can all be roll-started in second gear if the starting crank fails. They can all (just) carry two passengers on the flat, though if you have a choice, the Honda Cub 90 gives more power at nominal extra cost, as does the Yamaha 80 Townmate. Best of all, and most up-to-date, is the attractive Honda Astrea 100 and its rival-brand clones, very powerful but scarcely bigger than the older models. With most of these bikes, you can mount a locking plastic payload box on the rear rack, which greatly facilitates errand-running and shopping – and is an excellent place to keep your *ádhia kykloforías* and insurance certificate.

Violations and Fines

It is an offence to drive either a car or a motorcycle without the appropriate licence, tax disc, circulation papers or evidence of insurance on your person or in the vehicle – driving without a licence will net you a fine in excess of €80. Helmet-wearing while driving a scooter is required by law, again with fines of about €80 levied for failure to do so. You can always tell when the municipal coffers are running dry: police set up roadblocks at the outskirts of major towns, especially during the summer, and do a brisk commerce in citations, from which foreign drivers are most definitely not exempt, whether in vehicles with local or overseas plates. For the most egregious parking offences (such as blocking an emergency exit), the police will unscrew your number plates and you'll have to go and ransom them for whatever price they choose to ask.

Fines for moving violations must be paid within 10 working days at the municipal cashier (*dhimotikó tamío*); take proof of payment to the police station to have the citation cancelled, keeping evidence of such for six months in case record of payment is lost. Scofflaws inclined to tear up tickets and aim them at the bin be warned: non-payment means a court date being set and the Greek authorities – so dilatory in other respects – are amazingly efficient at translating summonses into foreign languages and forwarding them to your overseas address, if you've given them that instead of your local one to throw them off the scent. No-shows are automatically convicted and a conviction could make your re-entry to Greece awkward at best.

Pets and Animal Welfare

If you are bringing pets into Greece, there are no specific formalities for importing animals. Bringing your pet back to the UK is, however, another matter: you will have to comply with the British rules for the importation of pets into the UK, which are more stringent than the rules about the importation of pets into Greece. Greece does not currently belong to the PETS (pet passport) scheme, so your animal will be required to go into quarantine on its return.

No single issue potentially pits foreign home-owners (especially English ones) in Greece against their locally born neighbours more than the status of pets and animal welfare in general. Abuse, especially in the rural areas, is rife, and the Athens Olympic year saw mischievous journalists, both local and overseas, whip various incidents up to scandal proportions ('Filipino sailors eat dogs in Piraeus' went one headline). In the run-up to the Games, rumours persisted that the estimated 70,000 feral dogs and cats in the capital would be rounded up and done away with before the start of the event. In spring 2004, American and Australian animal welfare groups attempted to organise a boycott of the Olympics in protest against Greece's decidedly chequered record on animal welfare, a tactic averted only by the organising of an emergency evacuation of strays to new homes around Europe.

Juxtaposed against a growing number of Greek animal-lovers and pet-owners, with veterinary practices and pet-supply shops in every provincial capital, are the age-old Greek attitudes towards animals. They are seen as part and parcel of the rural economy, with a job of work to do: donkeys to carry loads;

dogs to help hunt; cats to catch rodents. When their usefulness is over, they are apt to be disposed of without sentimentality; in the days of poverty, there simply wasn't spare food available to keep an unproductive animal as a pet. Many islands have a remote valley where it was the custom to set old donkeys loose to starve; hunting dogs are kept chained to outdoor stakes in all weathers, rarely with enough water or food, and surplus kittens are routinely drowned in a weighted sack. Money spent attempting to treat a sick animal – even if only to have it humanely put down – is regarded as completely wasted and you may be openly ridiculed by villagers should you take a stray to the vet (assuming there is one nearby). An almost orientally fatalist stance reigns, in that the beast's fate is seen as in the hands of God. Many older people, annoyed by all-night barking or strays rampaging through their chicken coops, engage in wholesale strychnine poisoning of 'undesirables'...and of no insignificant number of foreign-owned pets who, in the absence of any leash laws, are off roaming by themselves. So *never, ever* let your dog run loose! At all social levels there is a great aversion to neutering animals, something going back to Classical times – a dog or cat may be kicked, starved or killed, but while it lives it should engage in unlimited fornication and must meet its maker intact.

Greek urban pet-owners are slowly coming around to 'western' values on the topic. However, irresponsible abandonment of rambunctious dogs and cats who no longer fit into apartments is common, and in the deep country you are just wasting your breath – and raising the blood pressure of everyone concerned – by proselytising to change opinions. If you ask, 'Why don't you feed your strays?' the response will likely be, 'You care more about animals than people. Why don't you feed your homeless on the streets of London?' If you query, 'Why don't you neuter strays and keep their numbers down to a reasonable level?' you might be told, 'Our cats are beautiful and sleek, English ones are fat, lazy and ugly, that's why.'

Greece is full of admirable laws (albeit more honoured in the breach than the observance), and, under Law 1197/3.9.81 of Greece, as well as 2017/1992/A-31 of the European Convention for the Protection of Domestic Animals, it is an offence to poison, torture or otherwise mistreat animals, on pain of a six-month jail sentence or fine. Additionally, the outgoing PASOK government in 2003 introduced legislation mandating fines of up to €1,000 for owners caught abandoning unwanted pets. That's the theory anyway but it hasn't stopped mass poisonings, in particular, especially in winter when there are no longer soft-hearted foreigners around to leave food out for street animals.

If you feel strongly about all this, there will be an animal welfare organisation anywhere there are large numbers of expats in residence – Rhodes, Corfu, Ídhra and Sámos are prime examples. These groups organise mass neuterings by visiting vets, maintain feeding stations and organise the adoption of strays by overseas families. In this last instance, they are always looking for air passengers returning to northern Europe willing to accompany a caged animal to the destination airport, where it will be met by representatives of the eventual owner. There are several overseas and Athens-based animal welfare groups:

- **Greek Animal Welfare Fund, t** (020) 7828 9736, **admin@gawf.freeserve.co.uk.**
- **Greek Animal Rescue, t** (020) 8203 1956, **gar-uk@dial.pipex.com.**
- The **Greek Cat Welfare Society, t** (020) 8998 6867.
- **Friends of the Cat**, PO Box 18192, 116 01 Athens, **www.friendsofthecat.com.**

Police and Crime

There is only one police force for the whole of Greece: the **Ethnikí Astynomía** (National Police). The former distinction between *gendarmes* (*horofýlakes*) and separate urban forces is now a relic of the distant 1980s. The one sub-force that you're most likely to come in contact with is the **traffic police** (*Trohéa*). Many policeman (there are just a few policewomen, mostly in traffic control duties) are grumpy, all but monolingual and (especially if they've had to deal with lager louts in established resorts) xenophobic; at other times and places they are young, relatively approachable and skilled at defusing tense situations. Nationwide, they are summoned on **t** 100.

Greece has a well-deserved reputation for being one of the safest countries in Europe, a legacy of its former homogeneity and strong family values. Since 1990, this record has been tarnished somewhat by a rise in crime, universally attributed to numbers of desperate central and eastern European male immigrants – certainly the population of the prisons at present comprises over half Albanian, Romanian and Moldavan inmates. Violent crime against persons remains rare, though burglary and petty street crime or beach bag-rifling are now unfortunately an established fact of life.

The crime rate in rural areas, where you're most likely to have a property, remains gratifyingly low, though it's best not to tempt fate with lax security; 'Trust in Allah and keep your camel tied' is the watchword here. For obviously posh villas at the outskirts of major towns, vendors of alarms (both real and fake) do a roaring trade; armoured front doors are all the rage; and 'Beware of Dog' or (more to the point) 'The Dog Bites' signs are popular, regardless of whether there's a canine in residence. If you have an isolated property, ensure it has a strong perimeter fence – preferably wrought iron, with spears or spikes at the top – and a stout gate for the driveway, and that the windows have substantial shutters that can't easily be prised open with a crowbar. Spanish-style grilles are not common in Greece but can be ordered. Do not leave bags of potting soil, large and valuable pot plants, garden tools and deck furniture – the sorts of things most likely to sprout legs – exposed in such a way that opportunistic truck- or van-equipped thieves could make off with them unnoticed in a few moments. It may be worth hiring a trustworthy local guardian (*fýlakas*) to make regular rounds and keep the garden looking neat so the place doesn't appear obviously uninhabited. In a village setting, getting known and relying on your neighbours' natural suspicion of outsiders is probably the best system of protection.

Greek Cuisine

The primary virtues of Greek cooking are fresh, mature raw materials and simple presentation; it's not a cuisine that gains much in elaboration, though there are plenty of more involved recipes, especially from Asia Minor, reliant on multiple steps, special treatment of ingredients, and layering with filo dough. Peninsular Greek cuisine has evolved under the exigencies of mealtimes on a fishing boat, in an olive grove or in an alpine shepherds' colony – what you can do with a frying pan or stewpot on a crude hob made of stacked stones and a few smouldering twigs, or (at best) a baking tray in a domed wood-oven. Olive oil was a nearly universal ingredient and every family made its own from even a bare handful of trees.

Traditionally, nothing of any nutritional value went to waste, not even the insipid fruits of the *koúmaro* (arbutus) – fermented into a sort of moonshine – and the white mulberry, which could be made into more appetising preserves. Snails emerging after a rain, *vólvi* (the edible, onion-like bulbs of a meadow flower), *hórta* (usually radicchio or chicory) plucked from a hillside, purslane sprigs weeded from the garden – all was fair game to the resourceful and hard-pressed country dweller, and a world away from the *kalamári*-and-chips fare of the typical contemporary holidaymaker. If you haven't noticed, such *echt*-Greek cooking is the 'new sex'; not a season goes by in London without yet another published cookbook purporting to have the lowdown on titivated Greek peasant food, or another weekend supplement magazine feature on the cuisine. Crete, with its abundance of fresh produce and long growing season, has been one of the main motivating forces in Greek *nouvelle cuisine*.

Fresh *kalamári* is, in fact, now a distinct rarity in Greece, and seafood in general – as across the Mediterranean – is pricey. You're far better off setting your sights on humble, seasonally migrating fish than the gilt-head bream and sea bass familiar from northern European supermarket counters, which are just as likely to be farmed here as there. Greece is where many of the Mediterranean's fish farms are located, and the less said about them, the better. Shrimp and sole in the spring, swordfish in early summer, anchovy, silver smelt and sardines in late summer are typical delights of the east Aegean, the richest fishing grounds in the country owing to the nearby Dardanelles and Anatolian river mouths. Elsewhere, *gópes* (bogue), grilled or wine-stewed *soupiá* (cuttlefish) and grilled octopus are reliable seafood platters. For the adventurous, there are unusual shellfish: *petalídhes* (limpets), *yialisterés* (smooth Venus), *kydhónia* (cockles) and *petrosolínes* (razor clams) must be eaten alive to avoid poisoning – their twitching when dribbled with lemon juice is a sure test. To really acculturate, tuck into a banquet of (allegedly aphrodisiac) sea urchin roe, or for the truly hardened, perhaps the most externally disgusting denizen of the deep, the *foúska* – a favourite snack of the Dodecanese – that looks distinctly like a hairy turd. Slice it lengthwise to reveal the orange-and-yellow innards, though, and opinions change markedly: the flavour is not unlike oysters. Real oysters (*strídhia*), small, round but tasty, also exist in limited numbers.

Grilled meat is another strong point. Lamb chops often come from New Zealand so go for goat instead, possibly the healthiest choice at the butchers: invariably free-range, antibiotic-free, less fatty than lamb and redolent of the herby hillsides on which it grazed. Pork is also excellent, whether as chops (*brizóles*), spare ribs (*pantsétta*) or sausages (*loukánika*). Greeks aren't quite so fond of beef, and chicken tends to be raised at battery farms in Évvia and Epirus. However, rabbit, whether hunted or farmed, has an honoured place at butchers – and as *kounélli stifádho* on restaurant menus. Despite inroads made by western-style fast food, *yíros* and *souvláki* are still popular carniverous meals on the hoof. Traditionally *souvláki* is pork-based between November and April but made of lamb the rest of the year.

Until the 1960s, however, meat was a luxury for most, eaten a couple of times a month at best, while fresh vegetables, dried pulses or rice, cheese and potatoes made up the staple diet of most people. Minor miracles were, and still are, performed with okra, courgettes, aubergine (eggplant), tomatoes, garlic and onion, in various combinations, or all together as *briám* or *tourloú* (ratatouille). Potatoes, often harvested in May (it needs six weeks of winter and six of summer, according to an old saying) remain gloriously defiant of EU size-standardisation rules, and no restaurant worth its salt will demur from the task of preparing hand-cut chips, fresh, daily.

Angináres ala políta (artichoke hearts, carrots, dill and potatoes) is undoubtedly the best way to treat that glorified thistle. Lentils and chickpeas are soaked as needed and reconstituted into hearty soups, especially on the mainland, while *mavromátika* (black-eyed peas) are served cold nationwide, garnished with parsley. *Lahanodolmádhes* (stuffed cabbage leaves, usually meaty) make a nice change from the somewhat clichéd stuffed (vegetarian) vine leaves, which go by various names (*yaprákia, yalantzí dolmádhes*) depending on the region.

Tomatoes, cucumbers, peppers, olives and feta cheese are, of course, the components of the so-called peasant's salad (*horiátiki*), mainstay of a thousand tavernas. In the winter, when most foreigners are absent, the Greeks revel in medleys of various lettuces, cabbage, grated carrots and dill. As in much of the Mediterranean, olives are harvested between November (whacked off the trees) and January (gathered from the ground; the so-called *hamádhes*). There are over a dozen varieties in Greece, from green to black to purple, which attain idiosyncratic sizes and flavours according to local conditions; some are esteemed mainly for oil, others – such as the famed *kalamatas* and *amfissas* – are deemed too good to use for anything but munching.

Féta is merely the most famous of numerous Greek cheeses and almost every region of the country produces something – perhaps surprisingly, Greeks are Europe's top per capita annual cheese-eaters. Cow, goat and sheep milk, alone or in unpredictable combinations, are the basis of these. They run the gamut from hard *kefalograviéra*, just about suitable for grating, to the soft *myzíthra* and *anthótyro*, ideal for spreading or stuffing. *Halloúmi*, the classical Cypriot grilling cheese, is known but the Greek preference is for *saganáki* – the term for any suitable cheese, fried. Local yogurt, especially sheep-milk-based, is famous across Europe; in some locations, it can be difficult to get between June and November, when the lambs have been weaned. Desserts of the pudding-and-pie variety are a recent introduction and a nod to western tastes. The traditional Greek *epidhórpio* is limited to the stereotypical oriental sweetmeats like *baklavás* and *kataïfi*, milk-based dishes like *ryzógalo* (rice pudding) or *kréma* (custard), *smigdhalísios halvás* (semolina halva) or – increasingly rare these days – *kydhóni sto foúrno* (baked quince) in the autumn.

Almost every region or island has its local specialty. To some outside tastes, Greek food can be rather bland, but not so in the north mainland, where the cult of the chilli pepper is observed and the recipes of the Asia Minor refugees can be distinctly on the hot side – as in *mýdhia saganáki* (mussels in red sauce), making use of that mollusc that's gathered and farmed along much of the Macedonian coast. From the lagoon at Mesolóngi in central Greece come smoked eels and *avgotáraho* (pressed grey-mullet roe). Corfu boasts *sofrítto* (wine-braised veal) and *bourdhétto* (white-fleshed fish in a red sauce), while Zákynthos *mandoláto* (almond nougat) is that island's calling card. *Krítamo* (rock samphire) is gathered from the shoreline and pickled in all the east Aegean islands, while the Dodecanesians have made a virtue of necessity by similarly treating the *kápari* (caper bushes) which sprout from every wall. *Dákos* (a salad based on barley rusks) is effectively the 'national dish' of Crete, while *fáva purée* with chopped onions performs the same role on Santoríni. *Bouyourdí* is a Samian dish of baked peppers topped with cheese. On Lésvos especially, September sees squash blossoms – especially the fruitless male ones – stuffed with rice, herbs and often cheese. Most locales, especially on the mainland, have some sort of favourite *pítta*. More universal are *bourekákia* (little filo turnovers filled with cheese and herbs).

Greek Wine, Spirits, Beer and Novelty Drinks

Wine-making in Greece has a distinguished pedigree, going back nearly four millennia, but currently, Greek wines do not have much of a reputation abroad for two principal reasons. The small production capacity of the quality vintners ensures that very little of the best stuff leaves the country, and the prevalence of retsina-based experiences among the backpacking crowd from the 1960s onwards has closed foreign minds to the possibility of anything better.

After a nadir during the early 1990s, when snobbery dictated that it almost disappeared, 'house' wine is back in fashion – the magic words are *varelísio* (barrelled) or *hýma* (in bulk), traditionally kept in barrels and sold by the quarter, half- or full litre, served either in glass flagons or the brightly coloured tin 'monkey-cups' called *kantária*. The quality is pot luck, but when it's good, it's more than decent. *Retsína* – pine-resinated wine, a somewhat acquired taste – is also often available in bulk, though the bottled brands Yeoryiadhi from Thessaloníki, Liokri or Malamatina from central Greece, and Cambas from Attica, are all quaffable and usually more consistent in quality.

Among bottled mass market wines available across Greece, Cambas Attikos, Boutari Lac des Roches, any white from Zítsa and the Rhodian CAIR are good, inexpensive whites, while Boutari Naoússa and Kourtakis Apelia are decent, mid-range reds. If you want a better, but still moderately priced red, go for the merlot of either Boutari and Tsantali, or Averof Katoï from Epirus.

Stocking and availability of the best wines, however, can be very regional indeed; for example, wines from Límnos seem to have a following only in the far north Aegean and Macedonia. The best available guide to the emerging Greek domaines and vintners, though now overdue for an update, is Nico Manessis' *The Illustrated Greek Wine Book* (easy to order via **www.greekwineguide.gr**). Out in the islands, almost anything produced on Límnos is decent; the Alexandrine muscat is now used for whites, the local *límnio* grape for reds and rosés. Thíra, another volcanic island, has a number of premium white products, such as Ktima Arghyrou and Boutari Nykhteri, and the Gentilini Robola white of Kefaloniá is justly esteemed. Páros (Moraïtis) and Náxos also both have acceptable local vintages, while Crete is now beginning to have labels superior to its supermarket-grad Logado plonk, such as Economou (Sitía) and Lyrarakis (Iráklio). On Rhodes, Alexandhris products from Émbonas are well thought of, as is the Emery label with its Villaré white, and CAIR's dry white '2400'.

Curiously, island red wines are generally mediocre; you're usually better off choosing reds from the mainland. Carras from Halkidhikí does the excellent Porto Carras, while Ktima Tselepou offers a very palatable cabernet-merlot blend. Antonopoulos Yerontoklima (Pátra), Ktima Papaïoannou Nemea (Peloponnese) and Tsantali Rapsani (Thessaly) are all superb, velvety reds – and likely to be found only in more upscale tavernas or *káves*. Antonopoulos, Tselepos (Mantinia *domaine*), Spyropoulos (again Mantinia) and Papaïoannou also do excellent whites, especially the Spyropoulos Orino Mantinia, sometimes found organically produced.

Other premium micro-wineries on the mainland whose products have long been fashionable, in both red and white, include the vastly overrated Hatzimihali (Atalánti, central Greece); the outstanding Dhiamandakou (near Naoússa, red and white); Athanasiadhi (central Greece); Skouras (Argolid); and the two rival Lazaridhi vintners (Dhráma, east Macedonia), especially their superb merlots. For any of these, you can expect to pay €7–10 per bottle in a bottle shop or supermarket, double that at a taverna.

Last but not least, CAIR on Rhodes makes its very own 'champagne' ('naturally sparkling wine fermented *en boteille*', says the label), in both brut and demi-sec versions. It's not about to make the French quake in their boots, but at less than €6 per large bottle, it does nicely for special occasions.

Oúzo is the national aperitif, along with its variants *tsípouro* (in the north mainland, Thássos, the Sporades) and *tsikoudhiá* (Crete). They are simple spirits of 40–48 per cent alcohol, distilled from grape mash residue left over from wine-making, and then usually flavoured with herbs such as anise or fennel. There are nearly 30 name brands of *oúzo* or *tsípouro*, with the best reckoned to be from Lésvos and Sámos Islands, or Zítsa and Týrnavos on the mainland.

When you order, you will be served a glass with a few fingers' worth of *oúzo*, plus a bottle or carafe of tap water to be tipped into your *oúzo* until it turns a milky white. It is also increasingly the rule to add ice cubes (*pagáki*), a bowl of which will be supplied. The next measure up from a glass is a *karafáki* – a deceptively small 200ml vial, and the favourite means of delivery for *tsípouro* – which will quickly render you legless if you don't alternate tippling with snacks.

A much smoother variant of *oúzo* is *soúma*, found chiefly on Rhodes and Sámos, but again, in theory, anywhere grapes are grown. The smoothness is again deceptive; as with *tsípouro*, two or three glasses of it and you had better not have any other firm plans for the afternoon.

Oúzo or *tsípouro*, and the *mezedhákia* or *tapas*-like titbits that traditionally accompany them, form the backbone of the *ouzerí* or *tsipourádhiko*, the trendy eateries that, since the 1990s, have taken urban Greece by storm. The idea is to go in a group and pick from the tray (*dhískos*) on which the waiter will display the cold platters, dipping into these while your hot entrées are being prepared. If you're not up for the full works, *oúzo mezédhes* is a menu item that will get you a glass plus some bits of cheese, cucumber, tomato, a few olives, and maybe even an octopus tentacle or a couple of picarel (*marídha*).

Beer in Greece has traditionally been foreign-label made locally under licence at just three breweries on the mainland. Innocuous Amstel is the long-standing cheapie; the Dutch themselves claim that it's better than the one available in Holland, and Amstel also makes a very palatable, strong (seven percent) bock. Heineken, still referred to as a *prássini* by bar and taverna staff, after its green bottle, despite the advent of Mythos, is too harshly sharp for many tipplers. Kronenberg 1664 and Kaiser are two of the more common quality foreign-licence varieties, with the latter available in both light and dark.

However, several genuinely local new formulae have appeared since the late 1990s, rapidly capturing a large market share: Mythos, a smooth lager in a green bottle, put out by Boutari; Veryina, brewed in Komotiní and found in eastern Macedonia and Halkidhikí; Alpha, highly variable in taste; Zorbas, a not-too-bad 2004 entrant (worth it for the tacky label alone); and last, but not least, the resurrected Fix, until its demise in 1980 Greece's only beer, though not (according to those who remember) vastly better the second time around than the first. Greece also finally has a micro-brewery, the Athens-based Craft: they make a tasty pilsner and an amber lager, but for obvious reasons, distribution is not wide. Additionally, the fancier bars and any major supermarket in places where foreigners congregate will stock a range of imported German or British beers.

Finally, besides the usual spectrum of cola, lemonade and orangeade **soft drinks** – among which Vólos-based Epsa has earned a cult following – there are a number of **novelty refreshments** worth seeking out. *Soumádha* (almond syrup) is made on Níssyros, Lefkádha and reportedly Skópelos; diluted four or five to one with chilled water, there is no more satisfying drink on a summer's day. Another refreshing curiosity – confined to Corfu and Paxí – is *tsitsibýra* (ginger beer), a holdover from the 19th-century British occupation of the Ionian Islands; cloudy, greyish-white and fizzy, it tastes vaguely of lemon and the sour beginnings of fermentation in its little bottle.

Gardening

Maintaining a garden or orchard is another of the pleasures of the Greek summer (and winter too, if you're able to raise citrus and salad greens). Whether it's just a few pot plants on a Cycladic roof terrace, or an entire olive farm on Corfu, the temptation to partake may prove irresistible. The climate – as discussed on pp.65–7 – is generally forgiving, but subject to freak freezes. The citrus and olive zone extends as far north as southern Lésvos in the east Aegean and the Amvrakian Gulf in western Greece, plus all points on a rough line connecting these two spots, as well as sheltered locations on Corfu. Microclimates abound, however, so always ask locally before planting something with demanding requirements.

There's one highly recommended guide to gardening in Greece: Mary Jaqueline Tyrwhitt's *Making a Garden on a Greek Hillside* (published by Denise Harvey, Limni, Évvia). Some of the text is specific to conditions in Attica but the majority applies to much of Greece, and it's a delightful month-by-month summary of the Greek rural year, touching on festivals, plants in bloom or fruiting, active fauna, and typical gardening jobs.

If you have reasonably reliable mains water, automatic drip-irrigation computers powered by a nine-volt battery are a godsend if you're going to absent during the hottest weather. Any well-stocked garden-supplies store should be able to sell you one, as well as all the black plastic piping and drip-nipples (*bekákia*) you could desire to coil around your garden and keep both pot plants and bedding plants alive. Ordinary garden hoses do not come pre-sized as they do in Britain or the USA, but are sold to order by the metre; Claber brand couplings are reckoned the best for both automatic irrigators and the nozzle end of hoses. Almost any gardening tool you're used to in Britain or the USA is available – save for a few strange omissions. You can find spades, in British parlance, but not a proper garden shovel; similarly, you cannot get a proper, blunt-pointed, curved gardening trowel, only something approximating a mason's flat, diamond-shaped mortar trowel (*mystrí*). Bring these items from overseas to avoid intense frustration.

Ornamental Specimens

If you're not going to be around consistently – or you are possessed of two brown thumbs – oleanders (*pikrodháfnes*) and geraniums (*yeránia*) are ideal for you. They are both drought-resistant and salt-tolerant. Geraniums can be irrigated with brackish water, though they're quite frost-tender. Hibiscus (*íviskos*) is temperamental and apt to die on you with little warning; it needs full sunlight and seems to do better with its roots somewhat confined. *Rodhokaliá* is a half-wild shrub native to the southeast Aegean; its multicoloured flowers give off a lovely after-dark scent, but the plant itself is extremely invasive – don't put it anywhere where the root corms can escape confinement. More usual choices for nocturnal odours are jasmine, honeysuckle and a distantly related plant the Greeks call *nykhtoloúloudho*. Jasmine (*yiasemiá*) is a good climber and can get huge, so it needs regular discipline; the scent of *nykhtoloúloudho* is too strong for some and has been likened to a bathroom deodoriser. For daytime colour, the classic shrubs are bougainvillea in a variety of shades, light blue plumbago and orange trumpet vine. Bougainvillea acquires monstrous dimensions if left unchecked, is nasty to prune because of its thorns and has messy blossom-drop; trumpet vine is nearly as messy but is thornless and relatively well-behaved. For small pots or bedding use, marigolds (*tsohákia*) are reliable favourites, as are carnations (*garýfalla*).

Vegetable Gardens

Peppers of various kinds are probably the most reliable summer vegetable, thriving in limited space, producing into November (weather permitting) and needing only steady watering. Tomatoes are nearly as consistent, with two or three plants supplying your needs for a couple of months in late summer;

take care not to overwater them, as the blossoms then drop without setting fruit. Aubergines (eggplants) are not a good choice unless you have lots of space, as the yield per plant can be poor; likewise melons and cucumbers. In terms of cool-season crops, rocket is nearly idiot-proof, producing in such weed-like profusion from late August and February sowings that you'll marvel at how you ever paid so much for a tiny bag of 'wild rocket' at a UK supermarket. Unfortunately, it bolts quickly with the first hot days of May. Various lettuces produce over the winter, ending (in protected, cool locations) in late May or early June. Radishes and onions (spring and bulb) are other reliable row favourites for the cooler months, but your soil must be soft and well-tilled.

Fruit Trees

A gazetteer of the most commonly planted orchard fruits follows. It is not possible in Greece to obtain paraffin/petroleum oil, the best dormant spray for fruit trees, so bring it with you. Greek horticulturalists are poison-crazy and will sell you any pesticide you desire, as well as more useful fertilisers.

- *Lemoniá* **(lemon):** Has the lowest heat requirement of all the citrus trees, but is also the most frost-tender; quite fast-growing, begins bearing fruit (which ripens February to April) at about three years of age.

- *Mandhariniá* **(mandarin):** A handsome tree, very slow-growing but attains large size; temperamental fruit set (after six or seven years of age); crops around Christmas and New Year.

- *Portokaliá* **(orange):** Both navel and Valencia are planted. Large trees; crops in February.

- *Gréypfrut* **(grapefruit):** Small, almost round, pale-yellow fruit, if grown in a sun trap will hardly need added sugar. Medium-sized; not that fast-growing, but begins fruiting at about three years of age; crops January.

- *Lotiá* **(persimmon, sharon fruit):** An excellent choice; pest-resistant and the fruit is seldom found in shops. Begins producing at three years of age; crops October–November; needs frequent watering during summer.

- *Akhladhiá* **(pear):** The variety most peddled tends to be a well-naturalised type known as *krystalliá*. Produces at four years of age; small but very juicy, sweet, greenish pears in October.

- *Verykokkiá* **(apricot):** A very temperamental producer, most successful in dry climates; enquire locally as to the feasibility of planting. Begins producing after four years; crops May–June depending on the variety. In the east Aegean there is another, larger-fruited, cling-stone type called *kayisiá*.

- *Sykiá* **(fig):** Best planted some distance from structures as the tree is not small and the roots famously invasive. Begins producing by three years of age; main crop is August. In much of Greece, the luscious purple Smyrna fig (*boukhniá*) is found.

- *Eleá* (**olive**): Several varieties sold, but all save one are not self-fertile, so you'll need a minimum of two trees. They take a long time to begin bearing – up to 10 years – and are subject to attack by the *dákos* fly, which causes fruit-drop. An olive grove is something of a lifestyle choice, so you'll need to decide if you want to be around between November and January to benefit from them or let a caretaker 'sharecrop' them.

- *Klimatariá* (**grape vine**): It's unlikely you'll plant a whole vineyard, but more probable that you'll set out a couple of vines to cover a pergola. Shade they will produce in abundance, but actual grapes are very much subject to the degree of harsh pruning you're willing to perform in winter, and the spraying or sulphuring against pesticides done constantly from spring to summer. Messy leaf-drop from June to October; a high-maintenance choice.

- *Mouriá* (**mulberry**): Comes in red or white varieties. The red is a smaller tree with a more esteemed (and highly staining fruit); the white makes a superb shade-tree, formerly much planted to feed the leaves to silkworms, though the fruit is insipid and rains, messily, throughout May and June. White mulberries can attain great age – up to 500 years – and their some-what anarchic growth habit benefits from careful yearly pruning.

Barbecues

A courtyard barbecue (*mangáli*) is one of the joys of the Greek summer. You can buy factory-produced, rectangular galvanised steel ones, but these are shabby and flimsy, rarely lasting more than a single season. It's far better to have one custom-made from the horizontally orientated pressure chamber (*bómba*) of a burnt-out 40- or 60-litre *thermosífono*. These can often be had for the taking, discarded by the roadside, and any competent iron worker will slice the *bómba* in half lengthwise and fit it with hinges and legs to bring it to the right height. Besides lasting just about forever (they usually have a nice protective layer of limescale inside), they're also very economical with charcoal – just close the lid when you're done grilling and the coals (with a bit of topping up) can be reactivated at the next use.

Charcoal (*kárvouna*), ideally made from kermes oak, are usually sold at any large supermarket. Ten-kilo sacks start to appear during May or as soon as the weather has stablised and evenings are comfortably warm. To get coals to ignite reliably and quickly, drizzle them with denatured alcohol (*inópnevma*) rather than white spirit – it's far less carcinogenic and tainting of the food. Also buy, or have made, a tin-sheet 'chimney' in the shape of a funnel to assist the coals to catch; alternatively, a paint can with both ends removed does the trick or (in stubborn cases) use a blow-dryer – this is what most tavernas do. A variety of hinged, stainless steel grilles for safely positioning your meat or fish are sold.

Greek Nation-building and Politics

Modern Greece dates only from 1832, when a two-year series of international conferences codified the end of the Greek War of Independence and confirmed the borders of the new nation state. However, its territory occupied just a fraction of the historical extent of the ancient Greek world and the Byzantine empire, which lasted in some form from the 4th century AD until the 15th century. From 1460, when Mystra, the last Byzantine outpost in the Peloponnese, surrendered to the Ottomans, what is now Greece was a collection of backwater provinces within far vaster, imperial Turkey.

The guiding principle of fledgling Greece was *Iy Megáli Idhéa* (The Great Idea), the redemption – by force if necessary – of all territories that had historically been home to Greek Orthodox populations. To this end, Greece carried out successive annexations (the Ionian Islands in 1864; Thessaly in 1881) or provoked and fought a series of wars with Turkey between 1897 and 1919, some successful, others ending in ignominious defeat and near-bankruptcy for the Greeks. The country's largest growth occurred under the tenure of Eleftherios Venizelos, who emerged from a Crete still nominally Ottoman in 1910 to become prime minister. He engineered Greek participation in the First and Second Balkan Wars of 1912–13, which saw Crete, the east Aegean Islands, Epirus, Macedonia (with its vital city of Thessaloníki) and Thrace added to national territory, and out-manoeuvred a pro-German royal family to enter the First World War on the side of the Allies – and join in the spoils of battle allotted thereafter.

When Greece was given permission in 1919 to occupy the hinterland of Smyrna, a largely Christian port city on the west coast of defeated Turkey (who had sided with Germany during the recent war), ultra nationalists and not-so-nationalists alike openly fantasised about this leading to the imminent re-taking of Constantinople and the re-establishment of the Byzantine empire. Unfortunately, in this post-Versailles age, theirs was not the only ambition in the way of nation-building; the defeated Turks themselves had found a champion in Kemal Atatürk who, in a three-year-plus campaign, succeeded in driving not only the Greeks but the French and Italian armies from Anatolia. This culminated in the September 1922 sacking and burning of Smyrna and the flight of over a million Greek Orthodox refugees from Turkey – the so-called catastrophe (*katastrofí*). By the terms of the 1923 Treaty of Lausanne, Greece's borders were set in a fashion essentially unchanged to this day; the only updating of this situation occurred in 1947, when the Greek military assumed control of the Dodecanese archipelago, taken from a defeated Italy essentially as war reparations – and in deference to a long irredentist movement in those islands. Equally significantly, the treaty sanctioned a form of ethnic cleansing *avant la lettre*: nearly 1.4 million Greek Orthodox domiciled in Asia Minor, whether still there or already fled, were to take up residence in Greece, while nearly 400,000

Muslims were compelled to leave Greek territory for newly proclaimed republican Turkey. Overnight, aside from its other small remaining ethnic and religious minorities, Greece became a largely homogenous and increasingly urban country; the refugees were settled primarily on the outskirts of Athens, Thessaloníki and the largest towns of Crete and the east Aegean Islands.

All these demographic and territorial fluxes had strong political implications. Greek statecraft through much of the 19th century had been largely a matter of personality-based factions serving alternating terms of office under the ostensibly disinterested eye of King George I, often doing little other than reversing the accomplishments of previous, rival administrations. By his aggressive programme of domestic reform and his confrontation with German sympathiser King Constantine I, Venizelos injected for the first time a strong ideological component into Greek politics and briefly plunged the country into civil war (1916–17). 'New Greece' – those territories that had been added since 1912, plus the Ionian Islands – lined up behind Venizelos' republicans, while 'Old Greece' – essentially as it was in 1832 – declared for the king. Even in contemporary elections, traces of this *Dhihasmós* or National Schism are still clearly discernible in the regional share of votes taken by modern political parties.

But Greece, which (as Greeks never tire of reminding you) had anciently coined the concept of democracy (*dhimokratía*), had precious little of this commodity from 1922 onwards. To the basic polarity of Royalist versus Republican was added a third, more ominous faction: the military, which deposed King Constantine in that year and held power directly or indirectly for much of the 1920s as Greece struggled to digest the recent débâcle. Indeed, factions in the armed forces were to be instrumental in Greek politics for the next six decades. Although Venizelos returned to govern briefly during the 1920s and early 1930s, relying in great part on Asia Minor refugees who were in the main a fanatically republican constituency, the Great Depression and general European interwar turmoil rendered him ineffectual. These factors also gave rise to a fourth element on the Greek scene: a revolutionary Communist Party, whose ranks were again greatly swollen by disaffected refugees. The Communists were forced underground in 1936 by the recently reinstated new king, George II, and a military dictator, General John Metaxas, whose regime resembled many quasi-Fascist ones in central Europe until defying an Italian ultimatum in October 1940 and besting Mussolini's legions in the Albanian winter war before being swept aside by the invading Germans in April 1941.

The Second World War experience of Greece was among the most bitter on the continent: under a tripartite German-Italian-Bulgarian occupation, nearly half a million civilians starved to death during the winter of 1941–42 and 200,000 more were slaughtered in reprisal for resistance activities in Nazi death camps by the time the occupation ended in October 1944. Because of their familiarity with clandestine status and organisation, the Communist Party was in a natural position to lead the resistance to the occupation – which it did as a front group EAM, and its armed wing ELAS – and, with an eye to assuming postwar power, also to absorb or crush rival groups. By autumn 1944, ELAS controlled something like three-quarters of Greece, which posed considerable problems for the British expeditionary forces landing in Greece, one of whose remits was to escort the vastly unpopular King George II back from exile in Egypt. An abortive attempt by ELAS to seize power in December 1944 was thwarted by the British. Two unsatisfactory years of manoeuvrings among all the various factions and rigged elections followed until full-scale civil war broke out in spring 1947. This pitted the so-called 'Democratic Army' of the Communists, including many republicans in its ranks with nowhere else to go, against the Royalist 'National Army', which provided shelter for a number of collaborators with the occupation regime. The Communists initially had the upper hand but, ultimately, were no match for a National Army trained and supplied by the Americans, who had taken over from the British in their first post-war exercise in 'better dead than Red'. The insurrection was also doomed to failure – though the Communists could not know it at the time – by Stalin agreeing at Yalta to non-intervention in post-war Greece in exchange for being given a free hand in the rest of central Europe.

Though not as sanguinary as the Spanish Civil War, the Greek conflict lasted nearly as long (two-and-a-half years) and cast nearly as dark a shadow on the subsequent politics of the country. Greece entered the 1950s as an American protégé (if not to say satellite), with a system of 'guided democracy' where a first-past-the-post system guaranteed that minority parties were marginalised, the royal palace and military officers intervened shamelessly in parliamentary affairs and the Left could be represented only by a front party (the UDL), its members subject to constant monitoring by an ever-active secret police. To their credit, the American sponsors did see to it that Greece recovered materially from the dire state in which it found itself in 1949 and wiped out the age-old scourges of malaria, malnutrition and tuberculosis.

With rising prosperity and increased urbanisation came rising expectations, and the rule of Constantine Karamanlis' American-backed Greek Rally Party was successfully challenged in November 1963 elections by George Panandreou's Centre Union, direct heirs of the anti-Communist, anti-Royalist Venezelist tradition. Conflict with the palace and the far right was inevitable, especially given the lightning-rod personality of George's son Andreas, and the Centre Union government lasted barely 18 months, having accomplished just a smattering of promised reforms in civil liberties, education and relations with the rest of the Balkans. An even more discredited subsequent caretaker government, set to preside over fresh elections in May 1967, was elbowed aside in April by a group of unknown colonels who imposed the first military dictatorship in western Europe since the interwar period. Indeed, their ideology (such as it was) harked back to the Metaxas era, a rancid cocktail of anti-

Communism, Slav- and Turk-baiting, selective Orthodoxy and prophylactic Royalism (until young King Constantine II himself proved inconvenient by attempting to organise a rather clumsy counter-coup). The seven years of the colonels' rule were a major embarrassment to all except, perhaps, their American sponsors. The junta lost Greece valuable time in the development sweepstakes and – through the manner of its collapse – cost Cyprus its territorial integrity. Archbishop Makarios of Cyprus did not fit into the colonels' notion of 'selective Orthodoxy' and endured various junta-engendered attempts to overthrow him. They finally succeeded in July 1974, which merely provoked the Turkish invasion and partition of that unhappy island, a situation that has defied solution to this day.

Faced with this humiliation, the army finally mutinied and recalled Karamanlis from self-imposed exile in Paris to sort out the mess left by the colonels. The political landscape of Greece as it is now effectively dates from the first post-junta elections of November and December 1974. The first poll saw Karamanlis swept back into power at the head of New Democracy, successor to his governing National Radical Union Party of the late 1950s and early 1960s. George Papandreou had died during the junta and the Centre Union fared badly, but his son Andreas' newly constituted PASOK or 'Panhellenic Socialist Movement' logged a respectable 14 per cent at very short notice, a promise of things to come. The Communist Party contested the elections openly for the first time since 1936; or rather, the two communist parties, as the Far Left had split after the 1968 invasion of Czechoslovakia into Moscow loyalists (the KKE) and the Euro-communists, today the Synaspismós. The December 1974 vote was a referendum on the return of the king from exile; it went three to one against and, ever since, Greece has been a republic. 1975 saw the worst figures of the junta tried for high treason and jailed for life (with death sentences commuted). In the 1977 polls, PASOK almost doubled its tally, the Centre Union vanished for good, and the KKE and Synaspismós took the shares (nine and three per cent respectively) that they have done, with minor variations, in almost every subsequent election. Support for the Communists, who have since attempted to reinvent themselves as an anti-EU, anti-globalisation party, is strongest in Thessaly and Lésvos – places with a history of a local landed gentry and muddled land reform – Ikaría and working-class suburbs of Athens such as Peristéri and Kessarianí.

Finally, in October 1981, Papandreou the Younger steered PASOK to electoral victory, forming the first government from outside the Venezelist centre or Royalist right in Greek history. For better or worse, PASOK was to rule over 19 of the next 23 years: under Andreas until 1996, then through the premiership of the less flamboyant but ultimately more capable Kostas Simitis from 1996 until 2004. Their track record was decidedly mixed and Greece seemed to spend much of that time as the EU's designated problem child, but, with hindsight, PASOK's signal accomplishments have been promoting national reconciliation in the aftermath of the civil war, effecting a *rapprochement* with Turkey, improving the status of women, successfully integrating Greece into the EU and the single currency, and ejecting the military from politics once and for all.

Political normality could be said to have definitively arrived in the summer of 1989 with two signal, interrelated events both closely involving the Greek Communist Party: the formation, in June, of a four-month '*kathársis*' coalition, with their nominal arch-enemies Néa Dhimokratía, for the express purpose of excluding scandal-ridden PASOK from power; and, in late August – at a huge blast furnace outside Athens – the incineration of 16.5 million dossiers compiled by the security apparatus on individuals of all political persuasions since 1945.

In the run-up to the elections of March 2004, Premier Simitis stepped down from the helm of PASOK in favour of Foreign Minister George Papandreou – son of Andreas. He squared off with Kostas Karamanlis the Younger, nephew of the late elder Karamanlis, who had ended his career serving three terms as president of Greece (the official head of state, with the king now deposed). Karamanlis scored a five-percentage-point victory, and any lingering doubt that politics in Greece had essentially become dynastic was dispelled.

Greek politics is strongly regional as well. Whichever major party gains overall power, some local trends seem eternal. Crete, ever loyal to the memory of native son Venizelos, reliably returns 'green' (PASOK) deputies, as do the Dodecanese, Ionian Islands and (usually) the Cyclades, all outlying archipelagos that stand to gain from PASOK's typical largesse. The Peloponnese, except for the area around Pátra, generally stays true to its staunchly Royalist heritage and plumps for ND. Partly because of its experiences during the Civil War, central-west Greece is always in the 'blue' (ND) column, while Macedonia and Thrace – rather curiously in light of a strong Venezelist past – are also strongly ND with the frequent exception of Thessaloníki. As in many places, elections are, in fact, decided not by such 'safe' seats, but by the more populous swing constituencies in the main cities and by a complicated system of reinforced proportional representation that rewards the overall front runner with top-up seats.

Foreigners' Voting Rights

As an EU citizen with permanent residence status in Greece, you are barred from participating in the parliamentary fun but can – in accordance with reciprocal privileges across the EU – vote in the Euro elections (every five years in June, next in 2009) and municipal/provincial elections (held every four years, over two successive Sundays, next in October 2006). You may sign on to the voter rolls at your closest town hall at any time with the proper identification and you should then receive balloting information well in advance of whatever elections are pending. In the past, some municipalities have been more than a little reticent about publicising the necessary procedures for registration, presumably to spare themselves the embarrassment of a close local election decided by a number of foreigners – something not inconceivable on islands like Rhodes or Corfu, each with nearly 10,000 expats.

The Greek Orthodox Church

The Greek Orthodox Church was established as a national, state-controlled one in 1834, autonomous from the Ecumenical Orthodox Patriarchate in Istanbul (which does, however, still appoint bishops to Crete, the Dodecanese, and two regions of northern Greece confirmed as incorporated into the Greek state after 1923). It has always relished its self-appointed role as guardian of the Greek nation, especially during the years of the Ottoman occupation when supposedly only its ministrations kept Greek language and culture alive. While it is true that many priests – as the only (semi)-literate people in the land – doubled as teachers during this time, the 'secret schools' of nationalist myth are exactly that: mythical. Imperial Turkey had no particular interest in suppressing education among her subject peoples, illiteracy was the rule for much of Europe from the 15th to the 18th century, and after that period, higher academies of Greek learning flourished quite openly in what is now Greece.

The Athens-based Church's absolute power over social life has been broken only in increments since Greek independence: first by the new kingdom's appropriation of the assets of monasteries and convents to fund public education; then Venizelos' confiscation of extensive monastic lands for redistribution to refugees in the 1920s; and, most recently, by the legalisation of civil marriage and divorce during the 1980s. Problems arise from the fact that times have moved on, but, like other recipients of supposedly immutable, revealed truth, much of the Orthodox Church has not. Under its reactionary, publicity-seeking archbishop Khristodhoulos of Athens, lately in open dispute with Ecumenical Patriarch Vartholomeos, the national Church has become something of a national embarrassment. Rather than devote pastoral energy to the pressing social problems and hidden poverty among Greece's huge number of immigrants, its version of moral leadership has been to organise (unsuccessful) demonstrations against EU-mandated, new-style ID cards which omitted the bearer's religion; to oppose the building of mosques to service the large number of Muslim settlers; and (more understandably) to extract an apology for the 1204 Catholic sacking of Constantinople from Pope John Paul II during his May 2001 visit.

But the Church's medieval mindset has been most apparent it its continuing ban on cremation and near-hysteria on the subject of barcodes. Greece is the only EU country where cremation is forbidden; every summer, there's a malodorous backlog of corpses to be interred at the overcrowded urban cemeteries, while other families surreptitiously cart their relatives' remains to be burnt in more accommodating Bulgaria or Romania, under threat of excommunication. Greek Orthodox doctrine is adamant that immolation would compromise the Resurrection and that the bones of a saint (still revered as relics) might inadvertently be destroyed. Barcodes on ID cards and hand- or forehead-stamping for casino patrons and bank employees have really exercised the monks of Mount Athos in particular. They, and a considerable number of the lay faithful, see this as a Jewish-Masonic conspiracy, fulfilling *Revelations* 13:16–17 and 14:9, verses that relate to the Mark of the Beast.

On a day-to-day level, you're unlikely to encounter most of the above but might be at the receiving end of some petty bigotry – like the German woman who, living alone in Pylés, Kárpathos, was approached by the local parish priest and asked to end her allegedly scandalous existence by getting baptised into the True Faith and heading off to a nunnery on the mainland that had a vacancy; he was told rather sharply that her baptism in the Protestant Church of her birth was sufficient. Other priests, who have lived abroad, are multilingual, relatively progressive and clued-up about the world, and serve (as in centuries past) as valued teachers in small villages.

Despite often being a laughing stock among the chattering classes, the Church is still a powerful force for social cohesion. Even the most jaded, worldly urbanites, who attend liturgy only once a year for Easter, wouldn't think of not baptising their children or following up a civil registry marriage with a church wedding. Blasphemy is still considered bad form among all classes and there are laws on the book against it, so you should never imitate any irate labourer who vocally violates the Christ, Virgin, Holy Cross or a cartload of saints sacred to someone who has annoyed him. Men should wear long trousers, women skirts or dresses and both sexes should have their upper arms covered when entering a church; the non-Orthodox should keep unobtrusively to the rear of any ongoing service, unless it's a wedding or baptism to which you've specifically been invited.

Regionalism

Regional stereotypes and regional jealousies are well developed in Greece, something that goes back to the city-states of ancient times. These breakaway tendencies are greatly abetted by the many natural barriers to intra-Greek cooperation, be they formidable mountain ranges or habitually stormy seas. The concept of one's 'fatherland' (*patrídha*) is rather like Spain's *patria chica*, or *campanilismo* in Italy: not Greece as a whole, or even a particular province or island, but in all likelihood, a specific village. True pastoral transhumance is nearly extinct in Greece now, but a strong echo of it survives insomuch as city dwellers will, when possible, return to this village for extended periods during

July and August, when Greek urban conditions are frankly hellish. Such loyalties are quasi-tribal, and in some places (like northern Kárpathos), if you have even one grandparent who was an off-islander, you'll be regarded as an 'outsider' until the end of your days. The numerous descendants of the Asia Minor refugees are reckoned to have their true *patrídhes* in the lost territories of Anatolia, even though they've been resettled in Athens, Thessaloníki and select island or mainland villages for three generations now.

A nearly infallible rule has it that contiguous islanders always loathe each other, though islands separated by two or three intervening ones are at least neutral about each other if not actively cordial. The reasons can be current, as in small islands resenting an overbearing, large provincial neighbour, or historical, as in bad blood arising from competition or exploitation in the course of fishing and sponge-gathering, an abduction and forced marriage a few generations back, or participation in some long-ago rebellion against the Ottomans, at the neighbour's behest, with disastrous consequences. You will be assured that 'those people' are untrustworthy, inhospitable or worse, and that the climate is unhealthy, the houses all but uninhabitable, the water undrinkable, the beaches uncomfortable.

Stereotypes apply across a broader canvas as well. Athenians of however many years' establishment there are disliked in the provinces as arrogant, complaining and generally awkward. Between Athens and Thessaloníki, the country's second city, exists a state of permanent undeclared war, most visible on the football pitch when Panathinaïkos meets PAOK. Athenians disparage their northern rival as 'Bulgaria', but it would be more accurate to dub it 'Anatolia', given the Thessalonians' outrageously Turkified surnames and love of spicy foods, found only among descendants of the post-1923 refugees. *Ftohomána* (Mother of the Poor) and *Iy Protévoussa ton Prosfygón* (The Refugee Capital) were long the standard names for Thessaloníki, owing to the ring of refugee settlements all around it and the city's almost complete demographic transformation since 1923. Macedonians in general have been disproportionately prominent in the Greek arts scene in recent years. Like the Thracians, they have a reputation as foodies (*kalofagádhes*) and people who know how to have good time (*kaloglentzédhes*), and are valued as holiday season customers on the islands. Epirots are alleged to be stubborn and stingy, while Thessaly is famous as a stronghold of *tsípouro*, good grilled meat and Communism, not necessarily in that order. Peloponnesians are taxed with being strictly business, while everybody seems to like the native Cyclades islanders – supposedly the 'aborigines' of the region least tainted by foreign influence and invasion. The Ionian islanders, looking west to former colonial power Italy, are considered the most Latinate, and the least 'Third World-y'; frivolous but undeniably musical – the conservatories and popular orchestras of Zákynthos and Corfu are famous. Kefallonians are, as every other Greek knows, notoriously eccentric when not completely certifiable. By contrast, the islands of the east Aegean and Dodecanese are seen as suspiciously Anatolian in their way of life and heritage and not coincidentally does the central government lavish a great deal of attention on these frontier islands (*akrítika nisiá*) in terms of special grants and pilot infrastructure programmes to more securely clasp them to the bosom of the mother country. Crete is, of course, the original home of *levendiá*, an all-but-untranslatable word encompassing panache, heroism, generosity and a host of other favourable qualities. The Cretans, in turn, regard the rest of Greece with scarcely concealed contempt and would probably secede given the chance; periodically weapons pilfered from army depots, up to and including a tank or two, have been discovered squirrelled away in the countryside, presumably for seditious purposes.

Letting Your Greek Property

Around 70 per cent of British people who buy houses in Greece also let them at some time or another. They divide roughly into two groups. The first is people who see the property very significantly, or even exclusively, as an investment proposition, and want to rent out on a serious basis – that is, they want to make money by letting their property and will try to find the maximum number of tenants each year. The second group consists of people who are primarily buying a holiday home and are not so much looking to make a profit from renting as hoping to cover some or all of the costs of their new purchase through rental income, sometimes just by letting casually to family and friends.

There are fundamental differences in the way these two groups should approach the house-buying process. For the first group, this is a business. Just as in any business, the decisions they take about where and what to buy, whether and how to restore the property and what facilities to provide will be governed by the wish to maximise profit. They should put themselves in the position of the person whom they want to rent their property, and consider which part of the market they expect to appeal to. They should choose an area, buy a property, convert it and equip it solely with their prospective tenants in mind. The second group will have to bear in mind some or most of the same considerations, but overall, can make far fewer concessions to their tenants. Theirs is first and foremost a holiday home for their own use, and they will be ready to compromise on the more 'business-like' aspects of house buying (and so reduce potential income) in order to maximise their own enjoyment of it.

The section that follows relates mainly to the first group. If you identify more with the second category, you can pick and choose from the ideas within it, and there are also some points that are more directly relevant to your situation. And, whichever group that you feel you fall into, there is a very important point to remember: in either case, you are unlikely to cover all of your expenses and both capital and interest repayments on a large mortgage from letting your property, however efficiently you do so.

Location, Choice of Property and Rental Potential

The choice of the area in which to buy your rental property is by far the most important decision that you will make. There are many parts of Greece in which it is fairly easy to let a property regularly. On the other hand, there are thousands of properties around the country that are, commercially speaking, almost impossible to let. A rustic house in a rural backwater or island may find a few tenants each year, but they will not be anywhere near enough to generate a real commercial return on your investment. If you advertise any property well, you will always get some tenants. You will only begin to get repeat customers and a spreading circle of recommendations from previous tenants – one of the best ways of building up your customer base, since it saves on repeat advertising – if the house or flat itself, the area around it and the things there are to do there really satisfy or, better still, exceed people's expectations of an enjoyable time.

Climate and Attractions

Climate is a major factor. Anywhere around the Greek Mediterranean coast and the islands can usually be relied on to have hot, sunny weather during the prime summer holiday season from July to September but, for renting purposes, you will have much greater flexibility if you are in an area where you can also expect blue skies in April–June and October, and mild weather through the winter, except when the north winds blow. For one thing, you may want to use the house yourself in summer, and so will need to let it out at other times of the year (alternatively, if you want to maximise your rents, you will rent it out in summer, and use it yourselves in December–February). The regions with the greatest potential for summer, spring and winter lets are those that are prime holiday destinations: the Cyclades Islands, home to some of the most popular islands – Santoríni, Mýkonos, Náxos and Amorgós; the Ionian Islands, such as Corfu, Zákynthos and Kefalloniá; and Crete, Rhodes and Sými. On the other hand, in more rural and mountain areas, where the beach is not the primary centre of activity, the weather may be a little less important.

Of equal importance are the attractions of the area, both natural features such as spectacular landscape and 'tourist attractions'. The most obvious of them on the islands is, of course, access to a good beach, but it helps if there are other things there such as sailing, diving and other watersports facilities. For some clients, proximity to a charming, historic town would be a major asset, while for others, it might be being only a walk away from a nightlife scene. For families, it can be a big bonus to be within a short driving distance from major amusement parks, such as Aqualand in Corfu and Watermania water park in Mýkonos, or, failing that, to be near another of the child-orientated attractions found around the coast. Proximity to good golf courses and, to a much lesser extent, other sports facilities are major selling points (if not essentials) for a growing number of potential clients. A local attraction might be a craft centre.

Added to these 'activities' are the more everyday attractions of an area which, for most people, loom as large as the more spectacular features in their enjoyment of a holiday let. Most people who rent self-catering accommodation will want to be able to stock up on food, drink and other necessities without too much trouble, and, since they won't want to cook all the time, will also want to be able to eat out. They will appreciate it greatly – and your property will be much easier to let – if your villa is within easy distance (preferably walking distance) of at least a few shops, and a choice of bars and restaurants.

Access

As important as climate and the charms of the locality is the ability of tenants to get to your property. The area where your flat or villa is located must be reasonably accessible from the places where your prospective tenants live, and the property itself must be easy to find.

For most British visitors, convenient access means how easy it is to get there from a local airport with direct flights from a UK airport reasonably close to where they live. It is worth repeating here the travel industry figures that show that 25 per cent of all potential visitors will not come if it involves travelling for more than one hour from a local airport at either end of their journey, and that if the travelling time rises to 1V hours, this will deter around 50 per cent. Of course, this does not mean that if your home is over an hour's drive from an airport you will never let it – with characterful rural houses, for example, a different set of rules applies, and their very remoteness can be an attraction. For more conventional apartments and coastal villas, though, there is no doubt that finding interested tenants will be simpler if you are within the magic hour's distance of an airport.

Owners should not underestimate, either, the importance of being able to find the property easily. Navigation in the depths of rural Greece can be trying: there are few people to ask for directions (especially if you don't speak Greek) and few signposts of much help in locating a single villa or farm. Giving tenants decent maps and guidance notes on getting there is essential.

Letting Agencies

Strange as it may seem, the decision as to how you are going to let your property is one of the first that you are going to have to take, before you actually buy it. This is because if you decide to use a professional management or letting agency, it will alter your target market and therefore the area in which you ought to be buying. If you are going to let your property through a professional agency then it is worth contacting a few before you make a final choice of a location, to see what they believe they can offer in the way of rental returns. They will also be able to advise you on what type of property is likely to be most successful as rented property in that area.

If, on the other hand, you expect to find tenants yourself then you need to decide upon your primary market. Most British people who let their property themselves in Greece do so mainly to other British people or other foreigners, chiefly because of a lack of language skills.

The Right Property

Picking the right property is just behind choosing the right area in terms of letting potential. Not all properties let to the same extent – villas and flats that most potential clients find attractive let up to five times more frequently than others that do not stand out for any reason. New properties are generally cheaper to maintain than older ones; however, they are not likely to be as attractive to potential tenants. Most people going on holiday to rural Greece are looking for a character property, while most going to coastal Greece are looking for proximity to facilities and a pool. Even in beachfront villas, people usually like to see 'traditional' features – balconies, terraces, window boxes – rather than purely plain modern styles.

It's very useful, therefore, to pick a home that's pretty (if it isn't one of those big enough to count as spectacular) if you intend to rent it out. Most people will decide whether to rent a holiday home after they have seen only a brief description and a photograph, and of these two, the photo is by far the more important. The number of bedrooms is also important. In cities, you will generally get a better return on your investment in properties with fewer (one or two) bedrooms – a good deal cheaper to buy – than on bigger apartments. On the coast or in the countryside, where the majority of your guests may well be families, a three-bedroom property is probably the most popular.

The Right Price

When buying a property as a business you will be concerned to pay as little as possible for the property consistent with getting the right level of rental return. Whichever way you look at it, paying the minimum necessary for the property is the key to maximising investment performance.

If you are going to use the property not just as a rental property but also as a holiday home there is an additional factor to take into account: the amount of time that you will be able to use the property yourself consistent with getting a certain level of rental return.

Legal Restrictions

If you intend to let a property, you must also make sure, before you buy it, that there are no legal snarls that could inhibit your ability to do so. Check the following: is there tax on rental income; are there any restrictions on letting the property in your absence? Your lawyer should always check for this. In order to let property legally, you should also be registered with the tourist authorities, although many people ignore this. Restrictions for foreign property buyers, for example, apply to the border areas close to Turkey.

Equipping the Property

After the selection of an area and a property comes the fitting-out of the villa or flat with all the features that tenants expect. It should be well-maintained at all times, and the external decoration and garden and/or pool area should be kept in good condition as these are the parts that create the first impression as your guests arrive. Other than that, the facilities required will depend to some extent upon the target audience that you are trying to attract – if, for example, you are trying to attract mountain walkers, sailors or scuba divers, they will appreciate somewhere to dry their clothes quickly so that they can be ready to get wet again the following day.

This is a quick checklist of the main points to be taken care of when preparing any property for holiday tenants.

• **Documents:** Make sure that all guests are sent a pre-visit pack, including notes about and a map of the area, local attractions, how to get to the house, a map of the immediate area, emergency contact numbers and instructions as to what to do if they are for any reason delayed. Inside the property there should also be a house book. This should give much more information and recommendations about local attractions, restaurants and so on – collect as many local leaflets as you can – and a comprehensive list of contact numbers for use in the case of any conceivable emergency. The more personal recommendations you can give (best bakery, best taverna, etc.), the more people will appreciate it. Provide some space in it, too, or in a separate book, to be used as a visitors' book. As well as being a useful vehicle for obtaining feedback, this builds up positive feelings about your home, and can also be a means of making future direct contact with visitors who might have been supplied by an agency.

• **Welcome:** It is best if someone is present, either at the property or at a nearby house, to welcome your guests when they arrive. They can sort out any minor problems or any particular requirements. You should also provide a welcome pack: make sure that basic groceries, such as bread, milk, teabags, coffee, sugar and a bowl of fruit are left in the house to welcome your guests on arrival. A bottle of wine always goes down well, too!

• **Cleanliness:** The property must be spotlessly clean, above all in the kitchen and bathroom. You will probably employ a local cleaner, to whom you may well need to give some training and/or a detailed schedule, as people's expectations when going into rented accommodation are often higher than at home.

• **Kitchen:** This must be modern in facilities, even if traditional in style, and everything should work. The fridge should be as large as you can manage, since in hot weather your tenants will need to keep a wide range of things chilled. The kitchen should have a microwave and you should check regularly that there is sufficient cutlery and cooking equipment and that it is all in good condition. A cookbook giving local recipes is a nice extra touch.

• **Bathroom:** Or, these days, more usually bathrooms – en-suite bathrooms for each bedroom are the ideal. Make sure there is soap in the bathrooms and guests will also much prefer it if you provide towels as part of the service.

• **Laundry facilities:** A washing machine and drier are now fairly standard.

- **Bedrooms:** These should have adequate storage space. Most importantly, they should also have clean and comfortable beds, as nothing except dirtiness produces more complaints than uncomfortable beds. If you can afford it, bring good-quality, high-strength mattresses from Britain, where they are much easier to find, rather than buy locally and get the more expensive mattresses available in Greece, which, as anyone who has stayed regularly in Greek hotels below four-star level knows, tend to be uncomfortably soft. Your tenants will appreciate it and the mattresses will need replacing much less frequently. Beds should be protected from obvious soiling by the use of removable mattress covers, which should be changed with each change of tenant. All clients will much prefer it if you supply bedding as part of your service rather than expecting them to bring their own.

- **Living areas:** Furniture and upholstery should be comfortable and in good condition; a 'local' style is often attractive. There should be adequate means of cleaning, including a vacuum cleaner.

- **Heating:** An effective heating system, covering the whole house, is essential even in warmer regions.

- **Air-conditioning:** While a substantial asset, air-conditioning is not yet considered obligatory except in the most expensive lettings and can be expensive to run and maintain. In more basic lets, it's best avoided.

- **Swimming pool:** A pool is always highly desirable and will significantly increase your letting potential in almost any area. It need not be heated.

Marketing the Property

Properties do not let themselves, and anyone wishing to let out their Greek home at all regularly will have to do some marketing. In the early years, you will have to do more than later on because you will have no existing client base. As in any other business, the cheapest type of marketing is catching repeat clients, so a bit of money spent on making sure the property lives up to, or exceeds, their expectations (and so brings them or their friends back next year) is probably the best spend that you will make. Otherwise, there seems to be no correlation between the amount spent on marketing and the results achieved, and this is a field in which much money spent is often wasted. Something to remember is that any form of marketing of a holiday property is only as good as the quality of the response you give to people making enquiries.

Key points to remember in relation to marketing short-term lets are:

- **Choose the method of marketing most appropriate to your property and your circumstances.**

- **Follow up all enquiries and leads at once. Contact the people involved after a couple of weeks to see whether they have made up their minds.**

• Send any contacts your details next year at about the same time, even if they did not stay with you, as they may well be planning another holiday.

If you have decided to let your property yourselves, there are well-tried means of publicising your property in the the UK and Irish market. You can advertise in the full-colour *Athens News*, one of the few locally produced English language newspapers available in most resorts, or on select websites. However, your Greek must be good enough for you to handle all enquiries, and many people in this situation prefer to use a letting agency.

Directories and Web Directories

If your property is pretty then you are likely to get good results from the various directories and joint information and booking services that deal with self-catering properties to let in Greece. Most have moved over partly – or, increasingly, completely – from producing brochures and magazines to being website-based. Some provide a full booking service and take part in managing lettings while others, which are cheaper to use and give owners more freedom of manoeuvre, just give you space for photographs and a presentation of your property. The travel industry directory websites **www.uk-villasabroaddirectory. co.uk** and **www.travelgate.co.uk** have lists of the many such companies now operating. The most useful are monthly magazines that have joint 'noticeboard' services for independent owners looking for tenants.

Advertising in this way only really works if the services are inexpensive, because a private owner with only one property to let has only one opportunity of letting each week, and so a directory that produces, say, 50 enquiries for the first week in July is not particularly helpful.

Press Advertising

The problem with traditional advertising is its scattergun approach and, usually, its cost. As mentioned above, if you have just one property, you only need a very small number of responses and you cannot afford to pay a large amount in advertising fees for each week's let. Except for very upscale properties, advertising in magazines that specialise in Greek properties is too expensive, and is mainly used by property companies and agencies. For individual owners, better places to advertise are, in the UK, the small ad pages in newspaper travel sections such as the *Sunday Times* , the classifieds of *Greece* magazine, and, in Greece itself, the small adverts of *Athens News*. According to your target market, apparently unconnected special interest magazines – literary, historical, *Private Eye* – can be a good idea, because your ad doesn't get swamped by 20 others. On the other hand, you can also get very good results very cheaply by putting a card on your local supermarket noticeboard.

Personal Website and E-mail

The Internet offers tremendous opportunities for bringing a specialist niche product – such as an isolated villa – to the attention of a vast audience at very little cost. For no extra effort, it can allow people to find out about your Greek home not just in the UK and Greece but in Scandinavia, Germany, the US and other places that will surprise you. For independent owners offering property for holiday lets, it is recommended that they set up their own website. For many, it quickly becomes their primary means of finding new tenants.

Your website will be your principal brochure, with space to show lots of pictures and other information about the house and the area around it. It is much cheaper to have someone print off a copy of this brochure from their own computer than it is for you to have it printed and sent by post. If you don't know enough about the web to design a site yourself, it is now possible to find web-designers in the largest cities around Greece, who will create the site for you at low cost. It should also be listed on some of the many Greek property websites that can be found around the Internet, links to which are either free or quite cheap. You will soon find out which ones work for you, and which ones don't; some of the best are those that are regionally based.

As well as a publicity medium, the website can also be a means of taking book-ings. You will have to decide how sophisticated an electronic booking system you want, or whether you are happy just to use the Internet to make contacts. Actually taking money through the web by credit card is far too expensive an option for most independent property owners, so you will have to receive payments by more traditional means. Your website will, of course, have your e-mail address on it. Even if you do not set up a website, anyone letting out property with any consistency really should have e-mail, which is more and more people's favourite means of making such bookings. And remember to check it at least once a day.

Doing Deals

There are two kinds of 'mutual aid' deals that can be helpful to independent owners, both of which work best in slightly out-of-the-way areas. If your property, for example, is in a rural area where there is somebody offering a very local tourist service, it can be a good idea to make contact with them and to try to arrange for the people starting their hikes or attending their courses to stay over in your property. This can significantly increase your lettings, particularly off-peak. If you agree to pay the tour organisers a commission of around 20 per cent you will still be well ahead. The second type of 'deal' involves co-operating with other people in the area who let properties, assuming there are any. One of the frustrations of marketing your property is when you have four lots of people who all want to rent it for the same week. Getting together with others in a mutual assistance group will allow you to pass excess lettings to each other.

Your Own Contacts

All these methods aside, personal, direct contacts are still among the best means you have of marketing a property in Greece. If you want to use a second home for a fair amount of time yourself, you will perhaps only want to rent it out for, say, 25 weeks each year. Given that many people will take it for two weeks or more, you will probably therefore only be looking for around 10 to 15 lettings, and if you put the word out, these should not be hard to put together from friends and from friends of friends. Among the people who have an advantage in 'marketing' a holiday home in this way are those who work for large organisations and can publicise it internally. With most of your lettings, you will also have the additional advantage of knowing the people who are going to rent the property, which reduces the risk that they will damage it or fail to pay you. When renting to family and friends, or indeed work colleagues, you will have to learn how to raise the delicate issue of payment. You should be able to offer them a bargain price and still generate as much income as you would have done by letting through an agency. Make sure that you address this issue when you accept the booking, as doing so later can be very embarrassing.

Management Agencies

On the whole, the people who are most successful over time in letting their second homes are those who find their tenants themselves. This, however, requires a level of commitment that many people simply cannot afford. For non-resident owners, who cannot dedicate much time to keeping track of their property, it is far simpler to use a local letting agency. Agencies – or at least good ones – will be able to attract local Greek clients as well as foreigners of different nationalities. You will have to pay them a sizeable commission but they will argue that this will be recovered by the extra lettings that they make during the holiday season. This may or may not be true. Larger agencies, who publish glossy brochures, are best contacted well in advance, such as early autumn in the previous year, if you want a property to be advertised for the summer season; smaller agencies will take on properties at any time.

In all the resort areas, there are agencies that manage and let holiday properties, many of them local estate agencies, and there are also many that operate from Britain. If you decide to use one of them, the choice of agency is critical. Some are excellent, and some are crooks, and between the two, there are some that are just bumbling and inefficient. Agencies may hold on to rents for long periods of time, or let your house while telling you it is empty; others may just charge a 'signing on fee' to agree to put your property on your books and then do nothing to let it. In the past, many have assumed that foreign owners 1,000 miles away will never find out about anything they do. This is a field where it is important for owners to be demanding.

Selecting an Agency

When selecting a letting agency there are various checks to make.

- If it is a Greek agency, check whether they are professionally qualified and experienced. Many such services are offered as an adjunct to estate agencies, who should have qualified staff.

- Check their premises and make an initial judgement on whether they seem welcoming and efficient, and if there's evidence of letting activity.

- Check how capable they seem to be, especially if you're making contact before actually buying your property. Ask what type of property they think would be best for letting purposes in this area, how many weeks' rental they think you will be able to obtain, and how much they think they would generate for you after deduction of expenses and their own fees.

- Ask for references, preferably from other overseas clients, and follow them up. Phone other owners if you can, and ask whether there are happy with the overall performance of the agency and whether the financial projections given to them have been met.

- Look at what marketing they do. If they are reliant only on passing trade then, except in the most exceptional areas, they will not get good results.

- Ask to see a sample information pack sent to a potential client. You will be able to judge a lot from this.

- Ask to inspect two or three properties that they are already managing. If they are dirty or badly cared-for, then so will yours be, and it will not let.

- Check carefully what kind of contract they offer you; unless you are familiar with Greek law, it is sensible also to get it checked by your lawyer before you sign, as some give you far more rights than others (many also include restrictive conditions, such as insisting that you let the property in July and August, which you may not wish to accept). Make sure that the contract entitles you to full reports showing when the property was let and for what money; these must give a breakdown week by week, not by quarter- or half-year. You should also insist on a full breakdown of all expenses incurred in connection with the property, and ensure the contract gives you the right to dismiss the agency on fairly short notice.

Controlling the Agency

After you have appointed a letting agency, you need to keep a check on what they are doing.

- Check the reports you receive from the agency and check that the money you receive corresponds to the amounts shown in them.

- Let the agency know, in the nicest possible way, that you and all of your friends in the area check each other's properties every time you are there, and compare notes about which are occupied and the performance of your letting agencies.

• Phone the property every week. If someone answers the phone, make a note and ensure there is income shown for the week of the phone call.

• From time to time, have a friend pose as a prospective customer and send for an enquiry pack.

• If you can, call to see the property without warning to check its condition.

Formalising the Letting

If you let through an agency, they will draw up fairly standardised rental contracts for you and your tenants to sign. If you handle all lettings yourself, unless you rent only to family and close friends, it is advisable to give tenants a written contract in line with Greek law, the 'model' for which should preferably be drawn up with the advice of your lawyer when you first begin letting.

For the basics of rental agreements in Greece, see 'Renting before Buying', pp.95–6. From the point of view of landlords, the safest type of letting is a short holiday let of furnished property. To be classified as furnished, the property must have all the basic items required to live in a home (a bed, a cooker, a table, a refrigerator, some chairs, etc.), otherwise it could be treated as an unfurnished property, in which case, from the legal point of view, the tenant could claim that there was a permanent rental contract, potentially giving them the right to an extension after the contract's first term. Otherwise, a holiday letting is one that takes place in a recognised holiday season, which obviously means something different in a ski resort than in Corfu.

A properly drafted **tenancy agreement** will take into account all these factors and protect you in the event of a dispute with your tenants and, in particular, if any of them wish to stay on at the end of the tenancy. Tenants should be supplied with a copy. The rental contract should also stipulate what things are going to be covered by your insurance and what are not – typically, for example, tenants' personal possessions would not be covered under your policy. For information on taxation of rental income, see 'Taxation', pp.142–5.

References

Dictionary of Useful and Technical Terms

adherfomeriá	two adjacent properties originally built for siblings
ádhia episkevís	permit to carry out minor repairs to an existing property
ádhia ikodhomíseos	permit to carry out from ground-up construction
ádhia kykloforías	circulation papers for an automobile
ádhia paramonís	residence permit
adhiovrohopiitikó	waterproofing formula for marble or stone surfaces
afrós	(polyurethane) foam used for setting door/window frames
afthérato	literally, 'arbitrary, high-handed': a house built without permits
agorá	a town's commercial district; also purpose-built market hall
agriosykiá	wild fig, a common pest in ruined houses; its fruit is generally inedible
ah-fi-mi	abbreviation for *arithmós foroloyikó mitróön* or tax identification number
akhladhiá	pear tree
akrítika nisiá	frontier islands, where property purchase is subject to certain conditions
akrokerámata	stylised Medusa or acanthus ornaments placed at the corners of tile roofs
alexikéravno	lightning rod
alfádhi	spirit level
alkyonídhes méres	the 'halcyon days' of late January/early February
aller retour (sic)	pair of two-way electrical switches
ambazouár	lampshade, lampglobe
ámmos betoú	grey-blue sand for mixing concrete
ámmos thalássis	fine river sand for use in mortar and pointing
amorgá	roof ridge; also the longitudinal beam just underneath
andiprosopía	the practice of a property being bought on behalf of someone without the legal right to do so, by an *andiprósopos* (proxy)
anthopolío	florist
arhitéktonas	architect
armolóyima	pointing of stonework
arithmós foroloyikó mitróön	tax registration number
arvanítes	people, especially in the Argo-Saronic area and Attica, descended from medieval Albanian Orthodox settlers; *arvanítika* is their language
asfália	internal security police
asfalistírio	insurance policy document
ásprisma	whitewashing with lime
astári	primer specifically for metal
asvésti	lime
atsálines	steel objects (screws, hinges, etc.)
atsalómalo	steel wool
bakáliko	a traditional general store
bayoné	bayonet (base of lamp bulb)
betón	concrete: the national medium of modern Greek expression
bidhóni	plastic jerry can, useful for collecting spring water

bómba	pressure chamber of a water heater, convertible to a durable barbecue
bourí	stovepipe section
boutíli	butane gas bottle
bouzoúki	three- or four-stringed fretted lute, essentially the national instrument
boyiá	paint (the substance)
broúntzines	bronze objects (screws, hinges, etc.)
broútsa	brush (for cleaning, stripping)
dhasarhío	forestry administration
dhelfínia	'flying dolphins' (hydrofoils)
dhepósito	water storage tank
dhiamérisma	apartment
dhiavrotikó	'corrosive', as in paint-stripping compound
dhífyllo	double-leaved (shutter or door)
dhiglossía	the uneasy coexistence between *katharévoussa* and *dhimotikí* forms of Greece, until the early 1980s
dhikastikí apófasi	a court verdict or decision
dhikigóros	lawyer, solicitor
dhimarhío	town hall
dhímarhos	mayor
dhímos	municipality
Dhimósia Epihírisi Ilektrismoú (DEI)	national electric-power company
Dhimósia Epihírisi Ydhrévseos ke Apohétevsis	local water and sewage corporation
dhimósio skhédhio	municipal grid boundary of a 'built-up' area
dhimotikó tamío	municipal cashier's office
dhimotikí	vernacular 'street' Greek as spoken by the vast majority of Greeks since late medieval times
dhokári	a bearing beam, either squared off or left round as a tree-trunk
dhyári	two-room apartment
ektelonistís	customs agent
élato	fir
eleá	olive tree
eleónas	olive grove
Ellinikó Tahydhromío	the Greek post
ELTA	Greek post acronym
enikiazómena epiplómena dhomátia	furnished rented rooms; official designation for type of pension foreigners are most likely to manage
eniskhiiméni	'reinforced', as in high-load power points
eparhía	administrative unit between a *dhímos* and a *nomós*, roughly equivalent to an American county
ethnikó ktimatolóyio	national property registry, more or less complete only for the Dodecanese
epitropí	tribunal or board that meets periodically
ergolávos	general building contractor
etería periorisménis efthýnis (EPE)	limited-liability company
étisi	written petition

farmakío	pharmacy
fi-pi-ah	abbreviation for *fóros prostithémenis axías* or VAT
filodhórima	tip, employee bonus
filótimo	literally, 'love of honour', akin to the samurai code of *bushido* – covers a wide range of behaviours, from not eating the last piece of *baklavá* that you've promised to save for someone else, to committing suicide when your shipping company's boat sinks through your staff's negligence
fóros	tax
fóros isodhímatos	income tax
fóros megális akinitís perousías	large property tax (FMAP)
fóros metavívasis akiníton	transfer tax (FMA)
foúrnos	bakery (literally, 'oven')
fýlla	shutter leaves
galázia ámmos	same as *ámmos betoú*
galazópetro	blue-black slate
garbíli	fine-grade gravel for walkways, etc.
garsoniéra	studio apartment
glavaní	trap door
Grafío Synkinoníon	Greek equivalent of the UK's DVLA; where you go to get driving licences and car plates
grafiokratía	bureaucracy
grammatéas	secretary, clerk
gréypfrut	grapefruit; both the tree and the fruit
hartopolío	stationer's
hartósima (plural)	revenue stamps
halíki	construction-grade gravel
hasápis	butcher
hayiátis	overhanging second storey, often in lath and plaster
heroúlia	handles, knobs
homaterí	the municipal rubbish tip; also the kind of brown used sand for plastering
hóra	the main town of any island; usually the harbour and often bearing the same name as the island
hýma	in bulk, unpackaged; applies equally to wine, dry foodstuffs and jumbled, uncleaned antiques
iatrío	state-run outpatient medical practice
ídhi iyenís	store specialising in bathroom fixtures
ídhi kangelarías	hardware store; ironmonger's
ídhi khromáton	store selling paint, varnish, etc.
Ídhryma Kinotikón Asfalíon	The Greek social insurance foundation for waged employees, universally abbreviated IKA
ikópedho	plot of land
iróko	iroko; tropical hardwood used for balustrades, steps, etc.
kafenío	coffee house; traditionally the hub of Greek village life
kaïki	caïque; a small-to-medium-sized, short-haul, traditionally wood-built craft, designed more for cargo than passengers
kalémi	long mason's chisel
kalloúpia	wooden moulds

kalokeráki tou Ayíou Dhimitríou	warm, still October days
kámbos	a fertile agricultural plain, either inland or (less commonly) near the mouth of a stream
kángelo	banister or railing, wood or wrought-iron
kantári	tin measuring cup for bulk wine; also a steelyard-type scale
kapáki	narrow, tightly curved tiles used as top layer on traditional roofs
kapéllo thyéllas	rotating, 'chef's hat' ventilator for use atop chimneys
kariótiko	Ikarian paving stone
karótsi	wheelbarrow
karta kavsaeríon	exhaust emissions compliance card
kárvouna	charcoal
karýstou	paving stone from southern Évvia
karydhiá	walnut, the tree and the wood
kássa	wooden frame for doors or windows
kassétta	phone exchange box
kástano	chestnut (wood)
kástro	in the Cyclades, a semi-fortified precinct, designed by the Venetian overlords during the three-century tenure to guarantee security against pirates
katapaktí	trapdoor
katharévoussa	purified, artificial form of Greek imposed on the country after independence
kathetó	vertical, standing
kat(h)ikía	in many of the Cyclades, an isolated farmstead
katráni	cedar of Lebanon; heirloom wood found only in east Aegean/Dodecanesian houses
káva	bottle shop
Kéndro Tekhnikó Élengho Ohimáton (KTEO)	Greek equivalent of an MOT centre, state-run
keramídhia massalías	flat, 'Marseille-style' pan-tiles
keramídhia vyzantiná	curved, 'Byzantine' canal tiles
kinotárhis	more or less synonymous with *próedhros*
kinótiko grafío	village records office
kinótita	commune, village administration
klimatariá	grape vine trained as an abour
klironómi	heirs to a property
kodhikós	payment code, for paying a utility bill on-line
kollitó	literally, 'stuck on': a house with walls in common with neighbours
kopáni	mallet, mason's
koukouváyies	'owls': see *akrokerámata*
krános	helmet, required by law for motorcyclists
kratikó nosokomío	public hospital
Kratikó Tamío	national syndicate that runs bus services
kyparíssi	cypress; very hard wood suitable for interiors only
laïkí agorá	street market
lamptíra	any light bulb
lamptíres hamilís katanálosis	low-consumption bulbs
láspi	mortar (literally, 'mud')
latákia	crossbeams, slats

lemoniá	lemon tree
liakotó	sun veranda or conservatory
limenarhío	port police office, in large harbours
limenikós stathmós	marine station, in small ports
lío	smooth; the usual finish for rendering
líxi párondos logariasmoú	final date to pay a bill
lotiá	persimmon/sharon fruit tree
loyistís	accountant
lýkio	high school
máïstros	northwesterly summer wind of the Ionian Islands
manáviko	greengrocer's
mandhaláki	clasp for shutter or window leaf
mandhariniá	mandarin/tangerine tree
mándhra	literally, a 'pen'; a building supplies yard
mangáli	barbecue, grill
manganós	water wheel, found only on Híos
maóni	mahogany
marangós	woodworker, joiner
mármaro	marble
marmaroskóni	marble dust, a binding agent
mastihohoriá	the fortified 'mastic villages' of southern Híos
mástoras	traditional appellation for a skilled craftsman
meltémi	Aegean etesian north wind, often reaching Force 8 on the Beaufort Scale
mentesédhes	hinges
mesitikó grafío	estate agency
méson	literally, 'means': applying influence to get things done
mezedhákia	small portions of delicacies, like Spanish *tapas*
mihanáki	a small, usually geared, motorbike
mínio	lead oxide primer
minioné	'dainty-fied': mini-threaded base on a novelty lamp bulb
monofasikó	single-phase (electric current)
monokómmato	any one-piece construction
mónosi	dry insulating material for walls, attics, etc.
monotikó	insulation or waterproofing reagent for walls, etc.
mouriá	mulberry; messy but handsome shade tree
mýkitas	fungus, mildew
mykoniátiko	rough, *faux rustique* finish popular as a final, plastering coat
mystrí	mortar trowel
néfti	pine turpentine
neoclassical	building style, promoted especially by the retinue of the 19th-century King Otho, essentially an idealised version of received notions in Classical archictecture: façades with pilasters, fanlights with wrought-iron grilles over doors, windows proportioned to the 'golden mean', canal tile roofs with *akrokerámata* or corner ornaments, etc.
neróstohos xýlou	wood putty
nipagoyío	crêche, nursery school, kindergarten
nisiótika	island folk music

nomarhío	provincial government offices
nomárhis	provincial governor
nomós	province, prefecture
OAED	Greek equivalent of a UK Job Centre
odhigí	'guides'; in this sense the ridges in plasterwork indicated where electric wiring channels are to go
omoyéni	overseas nationals of demonstrably Greek descent
Organismós Tilepikinoníon Elládhos (OTE)	Greek telecom entity
Organismós Sidherodhrómon Elládhos (OSE)	national railway entity
origón	Oregon (spruce) wood
orizóndio	horizontal
oúzo	national anise-flavoured aperitif, distilled from grape pressings; like French *pastis*
oxiá	beech, the tree and the wood
pandófles	'slippers'; the Greek nickname for ro-ro ferries
papáki	a small, usually automatic transmission, motor scooter
paramethória periohí	border zone where property purchase by foreigners is restricted
patrídha	the fatherland; in Greece restricted to one's rural village or island
paximádhi	'biscuit'; the nut on a bolt
páyia endolí	standing order (bank)
péfko	pine, usually thus means native Greek pine
pérgoula, pergoúli	pergola, arbour for climbing plants
períptero	a street-corner kiosk
peristereónes	dovecotes or pigeon towers, a Venetian introduction found only on Ándhros and Tínos
perváza, pervázi	flange, especially over the join between plaster and wood window frame
petakhtó	literally, 'flying, airborne': the first rough coat of plastering
petréleo thérmansis	fuel oil
petrovámvakas	yellow-fibre insulation sheets
piestikó	pressure pump for water systems
piliorítiko	paving stone from Mount Pílio
pínakas	circuit-breaker panel (among other meanings)
pinéllo	paintbrush
pissóharto	tarpaper
pistopiitikó	certificate of any kind
pistopiitikó foroloyikís enimerótitas	tax clearance certificate
pítspyn	pitch pine, hard wood suitable for exterior use
plakákia	wall tiles
plákes	broad, flat fieldstones
plirexousía	power of attorney
poleodhomía	urban planning department
politikós mihanikós	civil engineer
portokaliá	orange tree
póthen éskhes	means test (government measure for charging tax on amounts that have not been declared)
posó pliromís	amount payable (on a bill)

príza	power point with three narrow holes for three pins, including ground; now superseded by *soúko*
próedhros	headman of a commune or village
prokatavolí	deposit paid in advance
prosarmostés	adaptors (for appliance plugs)
prosopikós tilefonitís	network message leaving/answering service, on fixed or mobile phone line, similar to BT's 1571
próto dhimotikó	primary school
pyrótouvles	fireplace bricks
rambouté	tongue-and-groove woodwork
rodhélla	washer, rubber or metal
rythmistís	regulator (as for gas flow)
sanídhoma	wood planking
saráki	wood-worm, boring beetles
sidherás	(wrought) iron worker
sklívoma	pointing of stonework
skoupidhótopos	municipal rubbish tip
skýla	long crowbar used for demolition
sóba	wood-burning stove
souidhikó	Swedish (pine); cheap, low-durability wood for interior use
soúko	'socket'; power point with two holes for thick pins
soúma	smoother version of *oúzo*, like French *marc* or Italian *grappa*
souvátisma	rendering or plastering
stegnokatharistírio	dry cleaner's
strémma (plural *strémmata*)	1,000 square metres, the standard unit of land in Greece
strósi	broad, open-curved tile set upside down as bottom layer
sykiá	fruiting fig tree
sýstima andikimenikís axías	objective value system for evaluating property
sýstima sinkritiká stihía	comparative criteria system for evaluating land
tahydhromikí thyrídha	post office box
tamievtírio	savings account
Tamío Paraktathikón ke Dhaníon	Legacies and Loans Fund; where you deposit rent in the event of a dispute with a landlord
Tamío Epangelmatiónke Viotekhnón Elládhos (TEBE)	the pension-and-benefits fund for the self-employed, analogous to Class 2 contributions in the UK
tavládhes	incised panels in wooden doors or shutters
tekhnítis	building trade specialist (mason, etc.)
tekmíria	indicators of tax liability
téli kykoforías	yearly road tax payable for cars and motorbikes
télos akinitís periousías	a form of local rates collected through your electricity bill
thermosífono	electric water heater
títlos ktíseos	official title deed
Tmíma Allodhapón	Aliens' Department
Tmíma Asfalías	Security Division (of the police)
traváka	wood framework supporting a tile or slate roof
triári	three-room apartment
trifasikó	three-phase (electric current)
tríkyklo	motorised tricycle with payload space
tsikoudhiá	Cretan grape-distillate firewater, often flavoured with terebinth seed
tsiménta	Portland cement

tsípouro	north-mainland firewater, rather stronger than *oúzo* or *soúma*
topografikó	site plan for a piece of real estate
tzakás	specialist builder of fireplaces and chimneys
tzamilíki	a matrix of window panes
tzíngo	zinc; also non-rusting zinc awnings for sheltering doors and windows from the rain
vasiká téli	basic two-monthly charges for a phone line
velatoúra	paint undercoat
vérga	rod attached to a shutter clasp
verykokkiá	apricot tree
vídha	screw, bolt
vidhotó	threaded (base for lamp bulb)
vítio	plastic cylindrical tank for water storage
vivliário	small booklet, especially an account passbook
vivliopolío	bookshop/stationer's
vóthros	cesspit
tríti thési	'third' or deck class on a conventional ferry
vevéosi	confirmation or verification
xirolithiés	dry-stone walling
xylapothíki	lumber yard
xýstra	scraper, especially for wood
yeótrisi	deep well-bore
yialóharto	sandpaper
yimnásio	middle school
yípsos	gypsum
ypéfthyni dhílosi	a petition or declaration made on officially stamped paper
ypothikofylakío	local land registry office
zýgi	plumb line

Directory of Contacts

Greek Embassies Overseas

Australia
9 Turrana Street, Yarralumla, Canberra, ACT 2600
t (02) 6273 3011

Canada
80 Maclaren St, Ottawa, ON K2P OK6
t (613) 238 6271

Republic of Ireland
1 Upper Pembroke St, Dublin 2
t (01) 676 7254

New Zealand
5–7 Willeston Street, Wellington
t (04) 473 7775

UK
1A Holland Park, London W11 3TP
basic information: **t** (020) 7221 6467
Appointments line: **t** 09065 540 744. You must pre-book an appointment for a visa on this number; walk-ins will *not* be seen
www.greekembassy.org.uk

USA
2221 Massachusetts Ave NW, Washington, DC 20008
Main switchboard **t** (202) 939-5800
www.greekembassy.org

Foreign Embassies and Consulates in Greece

Australia
Anastasíou Tsohá 24, corner D Soútsou, 115 21 Athens
t 210 64 50 404

Canada
Yennadhíou 4, 115 21 Athens
t 210 72 73 400

Tsimiskí 17, Thessaloníki (consulate)
t 2310 256 350

Republic of Ireland
Vassiléos Konstandínou 5–7
t 210 72 32 405

Kapodhistríou 20A, Kérkyra Town, Corfu (consulate)
t 26610 32469

New Zealand
Xenías 24, 115 28 Athens, **t** 210 77 10 112

UK
Ploutárou 1, corner Ypsilándou
t 210 7272 600

Aristotélous 21, Thessaloníki (consulate)
t 2310 278 006

Menekrátous 1, Kérkyra Town, Corfu (consulate)
t 26610 30055

Pávlou Melá 3, Neohóri, Rhodes Town, Rhodes (consulate)
t 22410 27247

USA
Vassilís Sofías 91
t 210 72 12 951

Níkis 59, Thessaloníki (consulate)
t 2310 242 905

Estate Agents

See pp.94–5 for general information on estate agents in Greece.

General/Across Greece

• **Hellenic Realty**, Route de la Vigne au Chat, 01220 Sauverny, France, **t** 00 33 (0)4 50 42 71 98; **www.hellenic-realty.com**. Principally old stone houses but also some upscale villas in the Cyclades, Dodecanese and eastern Peloponnese; not many listings but well-chosen.

• **Kthma Net**, Mavromhiháli 1, Kalamáta, Peloponnese; **www.realestate-greece.com**. Strong not only on the entire Peloponnese, but also Mount Pílio and a random selection of islands.

• **Ploumis Sotiropoulos**, Panepistimíou 6, 106 71 Athens, **t** 210 36 43 112, **f** 210 36 38 005, **ploumsot@otenet.gr**. They're the local affiliate of Sotheby's in Greece, so not surprisingly, they pitch top-end villas and restored palatial mansions across Greece.

Skópelos

• **Skopelos Net**, Skópelos Town, **t** 24240 22900/**t** 697 2554069, **www.skopelos.net/ forsale/index.htm**. An excellent roundup of restored traditional Skópelos properties, both in the main town and the countryside, from this award-winning website devoted to the island.

Messinía/Máni

• **Anemos Real Estate**, Kolokotróni 7, 1st Floor, 241 00 Kalamáta, **t** 27210 62408/**t** 693 6707917; **www.greekhouses.com**. Broad selection of new and old stone-built houses in villages and countryside, their specialty – no ugly cement villas here!

• **Mani Properties**, Dhimosthénous 12, Kalamáta, **www.maniprops.com**, **t** 27210 22031, **f** 27210 89543. Covers not just the Máni but much of the southern Peloponnese, including the entire Messenian Peninsula up to Kyparissía. Tends to be more houses and apartments than land.

• **Messiniaki Properties**, c/o Sara McKellen, **t** 27210 29228; **www.mckellen-messiniaki properties.gr**. Neoclassical buildings, apartments, plots in the Kalamata/Inner Mani area; few properties on view on the website.

Mýkonos (Cyclades)

• **Kypraios**, **t** 210 86 11 691, **f** 210 86 55 837; **www.kyraios.gr**. Principally quality, purpose-built villas on this island.

Tínos (Cyclades)

• **Yiorgos Sitaras**, Dhrósou 10, Tínos Town, **t** 22830 25668, **gsitar@thn.forthnet.gr**. Rural properties on Tinos; modern and traditional.

Mount Pílio

• **Pelion Property Consultants**, c/o Faris Nejad, Aspróyia, Néa Pagaséai, **t** 24210 87610/ **t** 697 2898828; **www.pelionproperties.com**. Villas, medieval mansions, stone cottages and apartments across the entire peninsula.

Halkidhikí

• **Halkidiki Homes**, Haniótis, Kassándhra, Halkidhikí, **t** 694 5312058/UK **t** 07816 654 376; **www.halkidikihomes.co.uk**. Apartments and villas in purpose-built developments.

Argo-Saronic Islands

• **Saronic Net**, c/o Kelsey Edwards, Ídhra, **www.saronic.net** – the portal for a trio of websites (**www.HydraDirect.com**, **www.PorosDirect.com** and **www.Spetses.Direct.com**), each with extensive property listings, mostly old houses in various states of repair (the main market here). The linked, semi-independent site **www.GreekIslandsReal Estate.com** is less useful but still worth a look.

Páros-Andíparos

• **Kastro Real Estate Agency**, c/o Kristel Henauer, Parikía, **t** 22840 24964, **f** 22840 28229; **www.realestate-greek-islands.com**. Range of properties, from old houses to coastal villa projects. Browsers are discouraged by having to log in to use the website. FIABCI.

• **Anael**, Andíparos, c/o Helen Faroupou or Anastasios Faroupos, **t** 22840 61431/**t** 22840 61508. Mostly new-built houses on Andíparos.

Náxos

• **Nikos Lagoyiannis**, Hóra, **t** 22850 29111, **f** 22850 29112; **lago@nax.forthnet.gr**.

• **To Neon**, c/o M. Kofantidou, Platía Protodhikíou, **t** 22850 26644; **www.naxosrealty. com**. A mix of older village houses and new, detached villas, mostly on Náxos but occasionally on surrounding islands.

Pátmos

• **Manidis**, Skála, **t** 22470 31407/**t** 22470 31607.

• **Konstantinos Kostaras**, Skála, **t** 22470 33222.

Both offer an assortment of houses and land.

Léros

• **Habit**, **t** 22470 28180/**t** 693 2435983.

• **Maria Tahliambouri**, Plátanos, **t** 694 368920.

Both have a good mix of old houses and land for building across the island.

Níssyros

• **Michael Andriotis**, **t** 22420 31003, **f** 22420 31103. Village ruins for restoration, land for building.

Sými

• **Doma Real Estate**, Yialós, **t** 22460 72619.

• **Sými Visitor Real Estate**, Yialós, **t** 22460 72755; **www.symivisitor.com**.

Both local agencies offer a variety of finished houses, ruins for renovation and building plots. Sými Visitor publishes its own eponymous, monthly island newspaper with extensive profiles of local property offered by both agencies.

Rhodes

• **New Millennium Properties**, c/o P.M. Mitton, **t** 22410 22142/**t** 694 566 8060. Mostly purpose-built villas, houses and apartments.

• **Savvaidis and Associates**, Ethelóndon Dhodhekanisíon 29, Neohóri, **t** 22410 70017/ **t** 22410 26281, **f** 22410 34663; **www.rre.gr/property**, **savvaidis@rho.forthnet.gr**. Village houses for restoration, purpose-built developments on the east coast, town apartments, land. FIABCI member.

• **Evstathiou Euroktimatiki**, Ethnikís Andístasis 83, **t** 22410 73819/**t** 22410 74917/**t** 694 437 4546. Especially active in Rhodes Old Town; also on Sými, Kárpathos, Kastellórizo, Tílos.

Sámos

• **Amphibious Activities**, c/o Alex Stravrinidist 22730 62055 (7–9pm only)/**t** 6937143949, **alexstav@otenet.gr**. Mostly village and free-standing contemporary houses. FIABCI member.

• **Samos Properties**, shopping mall behind National Bank, Vathý, **t** 80321, **f** 22083; **www.samosproperties.com**. Tends towards newer houses, available hotels (careful – Sámos has excess bed capacity) and building plots. FIABCI member.

Híos

• **Trapeza Akiniton**, c/o Nikos Valambous, Polykhronopoúlou 1, Híos Town, **t** 22710 81385, **f** 22710 81317, **akinita@otenet.gr**. Mostly houses and in-town apartments, some land.

Límnos

• **Lemnos Real Estate**, Límnos Harbour Quay; c/o Nikos Psarianos, **t** 22540 25650/ **t** 69444 20024; **www.limnosestate.com**. Mostly purpose-built and for-restoration houses in Káspakas and Kondiás, the main venues for outsiders buying here.

Lésvos

• **Mariana Kaldelli**, Plomári, **m-estate@otenet.gr**, **t** 22520 31711, **f** 22520 31740.

• **Petros Pitsiladis**, Kavétsou 14, Mytilíni Town, **t** 22510 44245.

• **Nirvana Travel**, Pétra; c/o Rebecca Michaelides, **t** 22530 41991, **f** 22530 41992; **nirvanat@otenet.gr**. Houses and land, mostly in the north of Lésvos around Pétra.

Crete

• **Cretan Traditional Homes**, **www.cretantraditionalhomes.com**, **t** (UK) (01763) 849309. Despite the name, a variety of new-built villas and apartments, as well as a few renovated village houses in Réthymno and Haniá provinces.

• **Crete Home Finders**, M. Sfakianáki 13, Áyios Nikólaos, **t** 28410 89494; **www.crete-home-finders.com**. Villas with pool, building plots, a few village houses, businesses changing hands; eastern Crete specialists.

• **Crete Homes**, K Tavlá 11, Áyios Nikólaos, **t** 28410 22534, **f** 28410 2623s; **www.crete-homes.com**. Somewhat limited listings of modern villas or apartments, new-built, high-standard stone houses and rather forlorn village houses; emphasis on eastern Crete and the Haniá area.

• **Kissamos Property**, Omoyenón Amerikís, off Platía Venizélou, Kíssamos (Kastélli), **t** 28220 24598/**t** 693 6912656; **www.kissamos.property.com**. Western Crete specialists, mostly old houses to fix and plots to build on, but also some new-built properties and full construction and management services for buy-to-let.

• **Ktimatoemboriki Kritis**, c/o George Kriaras, Sfakíon 10–12, Haniá, **t** 28210 56600, **f** 28210 58881; **www.real-estate-crete.gr**. A large portfolio of varied properties, strong on western Crete, which even includes the remote offshore islet of Gávdhos. FIABCI.

• **Real Crete Properties**, **info@discovercrete.co.uk**, **t** (UK) 01865 351056. Offshoot of an established travel agency; stone houses, both new-built and restored, in villages of western Crete.

Corfu

• **Corfu Estate Agents**, Aharávi, **t** 26630 64494; **www.corfurealestate.com**. Extensive listings, mostly old houses either finished or needing work, but also new-builds, apartments and land.

• **Corfu Property Agency**, Kapodhistríou 19, Kérkyra Town, **t** 26610 28141, **f** 26610 46663; **www.cpacorfu.com**. More of a slant towards contemporary apartments, villas and land.

Paxí

• **JM Property**, Lákka, c/o Jerry Mitsialis, **t/f** 26620 31175/**t** 697 7000348; **jm@jmproperty.com**, **www.paxos-greece.com** or **www.paxospropertyagency.co.uk**.

• **Paxos Property Co**, Gáïos, c/o Tassos Zenembisis, **t** 26620 32626/**t** 693 2201116, **f** 22620 32688; **www.paxos-greece.com**.

• **Paxos Property Agency**, c/o Chris Griffiths, Malpas, Cheshire, UK and seasonally on the island, **www.paxospropertyagency.co.uk**.

All of the Paxí agencies co-operate to some extent, sharing websites, etc. Be sure to consult all the sites to view a small selection of interesting properties on offer at any time.

Lefkádha

• **Pandev**, Nydhrí, **t** 693 7236 7777, **f** 26450 93258; **www.pandev.net**. A fair selection of properties on the island.

Kefaloniá

• **Kefalonia Estate Agents and Property Services**, Lixoúri, **t** 694 2628322, **f** 26710 93556; **www.keps.gr**. Full-service agency specialising in timber-framed quake-resistant houses, as well as (principally) sales of building plots in Kefalloniá's westernmost peninsula.

• **Erisos Real Estate**, **www.kefaloniaerisos.com**, **t** 26740 41431. Specialists in northern Kefallonia, from Ássos to Fiskárdho; it's an area with an upmarket reputation and the prices (mostly for land) are pitched accordingly.

• **Kefalos Real Estate**, Mánganos village, **t** 26740 41451. Specialists in the more upscale market of northern Kefalloniá; father-daughter team Takis and Anna Thomas also offer architectural and engineering services.

• **Vallianos**, K. Vergóti 9, Argostóli, **www.vallianoshomes.com**, **t** 26701 23888 (Chris Vallianos) and in Travliáta, **t** 26710 69800 (Tim Vallianos). Two returned Greek-American brothers offer both sales and construction services.

• **Vinieris**, Andóni Trítsi 99, Argostóli; **www.kefalonianproperty.com**. A variety of existing houses and building plots.

Climate

Average Daily Temperatures in °C/°F

	Athens	Crete	Mýkonos	Rhodes	Corfu	Mytilíni	Thess'íki	Vólos
Jan	11/48	12/54	12/54	12/54	10/50	10/50	6/43	10/51
April	16/60	17/62	17/60	17/60	15/60	16/60	13/55	15/58
July	28/82	26/78	25/76	27/78	27/78	27/80	24/75	25/77
Aug	28/82	26/78	25/76	27/79	27/78	27/80	24/75	25/77
Sept	25/76	25/76	23/74	25/78	23/74	23/74	21/70	22/71
Nov	15/58	18/64	17/62	17/66	15/ 58	15/58	12/54	15/58

Greek Holidays and Festivals

The following dates are national holidays, when the entire country grinds to a halt:

1 January
6 January
25 March
First Monday of Lent (movable date Feb/March)
Good Friday (movable date April/May)
Easter Sunday (movable date April/May)
Easter Monday (movable date April/May)
1 May
Pentecost/Whit Monday (variable May/June)
15 August
28 October
25 and 26 December

In addition, there a large number of saint's day festivals (*paniyíria*), including a few of the above legal holidays, which are celebrated with varying degrees of brio depending on the locale. Remember that any given saint's-day is also the name-day of anybody bearing that name and celebrated in lieu of birthdays.

Festivals

1 January　*Protokhroniá*. Also the feast day of Áyios Vassílios (Saint Basil of Caesarea). The appropriate greeting is '*Kalí Khroniá*'.

6 January　*Áyia Theofánia* or *Ta Fóta* for short. The *kalikántzari* (goblins) who run amok during the 12 days of Christmas are re-banished to the underworld by assorted rites of the Church. Chief of these is the blessing of baptismal fonts and the nearest natural body of water. At lakeside, seashore or riverbank locations, the local priest casts a crucifix into the deep, with local youths competing for the privilege of recovering it.

Feb/March　The pre-Lenten carnival season spans three weeks, climaxing the 7th weekend before Easter. Pátra is generally conceded to be the best venue, with fancy dress balls and a grand parade with floats, though Náoussa in Macedonia, Xánthi in Thrace, Ayiássos on Lésvos and the island of Skýros with its 'Goat Dance' rite all get honourable mentions.

25 March　*Evangelismós*. Conveniently for those who like to stress the identity of the Greek Orthodox Church and the Greek nation, the feast of the Annunciation and the nominal beginning of the Greek War of Independence in 1821 just happen to coincide. Accordingly, there is a conspicuous military presence in the various religious processions, not least that on the island of Tínos, where a miraculous icon is carried over a line of the unwell to effect cures.

April/May　*Páskha*. From the Thursday of Holy Week to the following Monday, Greece effectively shuts down to observe Easter. On Holy Thursday, eggs are painted red (they reappear in the *tsourékia* or braided Easter breads). Good Friday sees the womenfolk of adjoining parishes vying to produce the most elaborate *Epitáfios* or funeral bier of Christ, which is then solemnly paraded through the streets. In some places, Judas Iscariot is burnt in effigy. On Saturday, in the hour or so up to midnight, the *Anástasis* or Resurrection Mass is celebrated, with the flame of eternal life being passed from candle to candle amongst worshippers; it's considered lucky to get the candle home without being extinguished and to leave a cruciform smudge-mark on the lintel. The proper greeting, if you can hear anything above the high-decibel din of dynamite and rockets (none more extreme than on Kálymnos and Híos), is *'Khristós Anésti'* (Christ is risen), to which the response is *'Alithós Anésti'* (Truly He is risen). In the week up to Easter Sunday, you wish people *'Kaló Páskha'* (Happy Easter); on or after the day, you say *'Hrónia Pollá'* (Many happy returns). The 40-day Lenten fast is traditionally broken early Sunday morning with a bowl of *mayerítsa*, a soup made from lamb tripe, rice, dill and lemon. The rest of the lamb will be roasted on a spit for Sunday lunch. The best places to be for Easter – assuming you've secured accommodation well in advance – are Ídhra, Córfu, and Ólymbos on Kárpathos.

23 April   *Áyios Yeóryios.* Saint George is the patron of shepherds; traditionally, the best venue was the former pastoral village of Aráhova (now a prominent ski resort). If 23 April falls before Easter (during Lent), the festivities are postponed until the Monday after Easter.

1 May   *Protomayiá.* May Day is when town-dwellers traditionally head for the countryside to picnic, returning with bunches of wild flowers. Wreaths of these are hung on their doorways or balconies until they are burnt in bonfires on St John's Eve (23–24 June). There are also Communist demonstrations, claiming the *Ergatikí Protomayiá* (Working-Class First of May) as their own.

21 May   *Áyios Konstandínos* and *Ayía Eléni.* Constantine and his mother, Helen, were the first Byzantine rulers to promote Christianity, so this is also the name-day for two of the more common given names in Greece. More exotically, there are fire walking ceremonies in Langadhás and two other Macedonian villages.

May/June   *Áyio Pnévma.* Pentecost or Whit Monday marks the descent of the Holy Spirit to the assembled disciples, 50 days after Easter. At Pagóndas village on Sámos, there's a musical *paniyíri.*

29–30 June   *Áyios Pétros* and *Áyios Pávlos.* The joint festival of saints Peter and Paul, two of the more widely observed name days, is on the 29th, followed the next day by celebrations for the Gathering of (all) the Holy Apostles (*Áyii Apóstoli*).

20 July   *Profítis Ilías.* The feast of the Prophet Elijah is marked at his countless hill- or mountaintop shrines. The most famous is on Mount Taïyettos, near Spárti, with an overnight vigil.

26 July   *Ayía Paraskeví.* A very prominent female saint, the patroness of curing eye conditions, with numerous parish churches dedicated to her.

6 August   *Metamórfosis toú Sotíros.* The Transfiguration of the Saviour offers another pretext for festivities, particularly at Khristós Ráhon village on Ikaría, and on Hálki, where the date is marked by messy food fights with flour, eggs and squid ink.

15 August	*Apokímisis tís Panayías.* On the feast of the Assumption, or Dormition as it's styled in Orthodoxy, the entire country is in their ancestral village, or on holiday, or both; no casual accommodation will be available for love or money. There's another great pilgrimage to Tínos, plus major festivities at Páros, at Ayiássos on Lésvos, and at Ólymbos on Kárpathos.
August 29	*Apokefálisis toú Prodhrómou.* The Beheading of John the Baptist sees a popular pilgrimage to Vrykoúnda on Kárpathos. When malaria was the scourge of Greece, this was the aspect of the saint who gave relief from the fever – thus the epithet *Thermastís* (Heater) for churches celebrating this day.
8 September	*Yénnisis tís Panayías.* This day celebrates the unexpected birth of the Virgin Mary to elderly Ioakim and hitherto barren Anna, and accordingly, there's a pilgrimage of childless women to the monastery at Tsambíka, Rhodes. On Spétses, the anniversary of an 1822 revolutionary war naval battle in the nearby straits is marked by a re-enactment of the battle in the harbour.
14 September	*Ýpsosis toú Stavroú.* The last major summer festival, the Exaltation of the Cross, marks the recovery of the True Cross in Jerusalem by Constantine's mother Helen.
24 September	*Áyios Ioánnis Theológos.* The feast of St John the Divine (the 'Theologian' in Orthodoxy), observed most keenly on Níssyros and Pátmos, where at the eponymous monastery there are solemn, beautiful liturgies the night before and early on the morning.
26 October	*Áyios Dhimítrios.* Another popular name day, but Demetrius is also the patron saint of Thessaloníki, which shuts down for the duration.
28 October	*Óhi* Day. The major patriotic outbreak on the calendar: parades, folk-dancing and speeches to commemorate dictator Metaxas's apocryphal one-word reply to Mussolini's 1940 ultimatum: '*Ohi!*' (No!).
8 November	*Tón Taxiarhón.* The feast of the archangels Michael and Gabriel; major rites at the rural monasteries dedicated to them, particularly on Sými and Lésvos.
6 December	*Áyios Nikólaos.* St Nicholas is the patron of seafarers, with many chapels dedicated to him (and seemingly a fifth of the male population celebrating their name-days).
25 December	*Hristoúyenna.* Though much less prominent occasion than Easter, **Christmas** is still important, and in recent years, it has started to take on more of western trappings, with decorations, Christmas trees and gifts.
26 December	*Sýnaxis tis Panayías.* Today marks the Gathering of the Virgin's Entourage, not Boxing Day as in England.
31 December	*Paramoní Protokhroniá.* On New Year's Eve, as on the other 12 days of Christmas, a few children still go door-to-door singing the traditional carols (*kálanda*), receiving money in return. Adults sit around playing cards, often for money. The *vassilópitta*, a sweet loaf baked with a coin inside, is cut at midnight; the finder of the coin will have a lucky year.

Further Reading

Publishers are omitted from the list as they change frequently – current imprints are available through Amazon or other online retailers. Anything marked as o/p (out of print) can usually be found on specialist websites; try **www.abe.co.uk** or **www.bookfinder.com**.

Travel and Memoirs
Andrews, Kevin: *The Flight of Ikaros* (o/p)
Bouras, Gillian: *Aphrodite and the Others* (o/p)
Byron, Robert: *The Station: Athos, Treasures and Men*
Kanneli, Sheelagh: *Earth and Water: A Marriage in Kalamata*
Kark, Austen: *Attic in Greece*
Leigh Fermor, Sir Patrick: *Roumeli* and *Mani*
Levi, Peter: *The Hill of Kronos* (o/p)
Manus, Willard: *This Way to Paradise: Dancing on the Tables*
Miller, Henry: *The Colossus of Maroussi*
Pettifer, James: *The Greeks: The Land and People since the War*
Powell, Dilys: *The Villa Ariadne*
Salmon, Tim: *The Unwritten Places*
Simonsen, Thordis: *Dancing Girl: Themes and Improvisations in a Greek Village Setting*
Stone, Tom: *The Summer of my Greek Taverna*
Storace, Patricia: *Dinner with Persephone*
Zinoviev, Sofka: *Eurydice Street*

Food and Drink
Barron, Rosemary: *Flavours of Greece*
Dalby, Andrew: *Siren Feasts: A History of Food and Gastronomy in Greece*
Davidson, Alan: *Mediterranean Seafood*
Manessis, Nico: *The Illustrated Greek Wine Book*

Gardening
Tyrwhitt, Mary Jaqueline: *Making a Garden on a Greek Hillside*

Illustrated 'Coffee-Table' Books
Hellier, Chris: *Monasteries of Greece* (o/p)
Manos, Constantine: *A Greek Portfolio*
Ottaway, Mark: *The Most Beautiful Villgages of Greece*
Perry, Clay: *Vanishing Greece*
Slesin, Suzanne, et al: *Greek Style*

Ancient History and Classics
Beard, Mary and John Henderson: *The Classics: A Very Short Introduction*
Cartlege, Paul The Spartans: *The World of the Warrior-Heroes of Ancient Greece*
Davidson, James: *Courtesans and Fishcakes*
Finley, M. I.: *The World of Odysse*us
Hornblower, Simon: *The Greek World 479–323 BC*

Medieval History and Religion
Norwich, John Julius: *A Short History of Byzantium*
Runciman, Steven: *The Fall of Constantinople, 1453*
Ware, Archbishop Kallistos: *The Orthodox Church*

Modern Greek History
Clogg, Richard: *A Concise History of Greece*
Close, David H.: *The Origins of the Greek Civil War* (o/p)
Lidderdale, H. A., ed: *The Memoirs of General Makriyannis, 1797–1864* (o/p)
Llewellyn Smith, Michael: *Ionian Vision: Greece in Asia Minor, 1919–22*
Koliopoulos, John S. and Thanos M. Veremis: *Greece: The Modern Sequel, from 1831 to the Present*
Mazower, Mark: *Inside Hitler's Greece: The Experience of Occupation 1941–44*
Pentzopoulos, Dimitri: *The Balkan Exchange of Minorities and its Impact on Greece*
Woodhouse, C. M.: *The Struggle for Greece, 1941–49*

Anthropology and Ethnology
Boulay, Juliet du: *Portrait of a Greek Mountain Village*
Campbell, John K.: *Honour, Family and Patronage*
Danforth, Loring and Alexander Tsiaras: *The Death Rituals of Rural Greece*
Hirschon Renée: *Heirs of the Greek Catastrophe: The Social Life of Asia Minor Refugees in Piraeus*
Holst-Warhaft, Gail: *Road to Rembetika: Songs of Love, Sorrow and Hashish*
Karakasidou, Anastasia: *Fields of Wheat, Hills of Blood*

Greek Fiction in Translation
Doxiades, Apostolos: *Uncle Petros and the Goldbach Conjecture*
Kazantzakis: *Zorba the Greek, The Last Temptation of Christ, Christ Recrucified*
Mourselas, Kostas: *Red Dyed Hair*
Myrivilis, Stratis: *Life in the Tomb*
Papadiamantis Alexandros: *The Murderess* (o/p)
Sotiriou, Dido: *Farewell Anatolia*
Tsirkas, Stratis: *Drifting Cities*
Zei, Alki: *Achilles' Fiancée*

Greek Poetry in Translation
Cavafy, C. P.: *The Complete Poems of Cavafy*, translated by Rae Dalven
Elytis, Odysseus: *Collected Poems*
Ritsos, Yiannis: *Exile and Return: Selected Poems, 1967–1974* (o/p)
Seferis, George: *Complete Poems*

Guidebooks, General and Regional
Dorling Kindersley Eyewitness Travel Guide to Greece: Athens and the Mainland
Dorling Kindersley Eyewitness Travel Guide to the Greek Islands
Dubin, Marc: *Rough Guide to the Dodecanese and the East Aegean*
Edwards, Nick: *Rough Guide to the Ionian Islands*
Facaros, Dana and Michael Pauls *Cadogan Guide to the Greek Islands; Cadogan Guide to Crete; Cadogan Guide to Athens and the Peloponnese*
Fisher, John and Geoff Garvey: *Rough Guide to Crete*
Insight Guide to Greece
Insight Guide to the Greek Islands
Rackham, Oliver and Jennifer Moody: *The Making of the Cretan Landscape*
Various authors, *The Rough Guide to Greece*
Various authors: *Lonely Planet: Greece*
Wilson, Loraine: *The White Mountains of Crete*

Checklist: DIY Inspection of Property

Task   ✓

Title – check that the property corresponds with its description in the title:
   Number of rooms
   Plot size

Plot
   Identify the physical boundaries of the plot
   Is there any dispute with anyone over these boundaries?
   Are there any obvious foreign elements on your plot such as pipes,
      cables, drainage ditches, water tanks, etc.?
   Are there any signs of anyone else having rights over the
      property – footpaths, access ways, cartridges from hunting, etc.?
   Are any parts of what you are buying physically separated from the
      rest of the property – e.g. a storage area or parking area in a
      basement several floors below an apartment or a garage on a
      plot on the other side of the road from the house which it serves?

Garden/Terrace
   Are any plants, ornaments, etc. on site not being sold with the property?

Pool – is there a pool? If so:
   What size is it?
   Is it clean and algae-free?
   Do the pumps work?
   How old is the machinery?
   Who maintains it?
   What is the annual cost of maintenance?
   Does it appear to be in good condition?

Walls – stand back from property and inspect from outside:
   Any signs of subsidence?
   Walls vertical?
   Any obvious cracks in the walls?
   Are the walls well pointed?
   Any obvious damp patches?
   Any new repairs to walls or signs of re-pointing?

Roof – inspect from outside property:
   Does the roof sag?
   Are there any missing/slipped tiles?
   Do all faces of the roof join squarely?
   If there is lead flashing, is the lead present and in good order?

Task ✓

Guttering and Downpipes – inspect from outside property:
    All present?
    Do they seem to be in good order?
    Securely attached?
    Fall of the guttering constant?
    Any obvious leaks?
    Any signs of recent repairs?

Enter Property
    Does it smell of damp?
    Does it smell 'musty'?
    Does it smell of dry rot?
    Any other strange smells?

Doors
    Any signs of rot?
    Close properly – without catching?
    Provide a proper seal?
    All locks work?

Windows
    Any signs of rot?
    Open and close properly – without catching?
    Provide a proper seal?
    Window catches work?
    Any security locks? Do they work?
    Any sign of excessive condensation?

Floor
    Can you see it all?
    Does it appear in good condition?
    Is there any sign of cracked or rotten boards, tiles or concrete?

Under Floor
    Can you get access under the floor?
    If so, is it ventilated?
    Any sign of rot?
    What are the joists made of?
    What is the size (section) of the joists?
    How close are the joists?
    Are joist ends in good condition where they go into walls?
    What is maximum unsupported length of joist run?
    Any sign of damp or standing water?

Task ✓

Roof Void

Is it accessible?
Is there sign of water entry?
Can you see daylight through the roof?
Is there an underlining between the tiles and the void?
Any sign of rot in timbers?
Horizontal distance between roof timbers?
Size of roof timbers (section)?
Maximum unsupported length of roof timbers?
Is roof insulated – if so, what is the depth and type of insulation?

General Woodwork

Any signs of rot?
Any signs of wood-boring insects?
Is it dry?

Interior Walls

Any significant cracks?
Any obvious damp problems?
Any signs of recent repair/redecoration?

Electricity

Is the property connected to mains electricity?
If not, how far away is the nearest mains electricity?
Check electricity meter:
    How old is it?
    What is its rated capacity?
Check all visible wiring:
    What type is it?
    Does it appear to be in good physical condition?
Check all plugs:
    Is there power to the plug?
    Does a plug tester show good earth and show 'OK'?
    Are there enough plugs?
Lighting:
    Do all lights work?
    Which light fittings are included in sale?

Water

Is the property connected to mains water?
If not, what is the size of the storage tank?
If not connected to the water supply, how near is the nearest
    mains water supply?
Do all hot and cold taps work?

Task ✓

Water (*cont.*)

Is flow adequate?

Do taps drip?

Is there a security cut-off on all taps between the mains and tap?

Do they seem in good condition?

Are pipes insulated?

Hot Water

Is hot water 'on'? If so, does it work at all taps, showers, etc?

What type of hot water system is fitted?

Age?

Gas – is the property fitted with city (piped) gas? If so:

Age of meter?

Does installation appear in good order?

Is there any smell of gas?

If the property is not fitted with city gas, is it in an area covered by city gas?

If it is in an area covered by city gas, how far away is the nearest gas supply?

Is the property fitted with bottled gas? If so:

Who is the supplier?

If there is a safety certificate, when does it expire?

Where are bottles stored?

Is the storage area ventilated to outside of premises?

Central Heating – is the property fitted with central heating? If so:

Is it 'on'?

Will it turn on?

What type is it?

Is there heat at all radiators/outlets?

Do any thermostats appear to work?

Are there any signs of leaks?

How old is the system?

When was it last serviced?

If it is oil-fired, what capacity is the storage tank?

Fireplaces

Is property fitted with any solid fuel heaters? If so:

Is there any sign of blow-back from the chimneys?

Do the chimneys (outside) show stains from leakage?

Do the chimneys seem in good order?

Task ✓

Air-conditioning

Which rooms are air-conditioned?
Are the units included in the sale?
Do the units work (deliver cold air)?
If the units are intended also to deliver heat, do they?
What type of air-conditioning is it?
How old is it?
When was it last serviced?

Phone

Is there a phone?
What type of line is it?
How many lines are there?
Is there an ADSL line?
Does it all work?
Number?

Satellite TV

Is there satellite TV?
If not, is the property within the footprint of satellite TV?
Who is the local supplier?
Does it work?
Is it included in the sale?

Drainage

What type of drainage does the property have?
If septic tank, how old is it?
Who maintains it?
When was it last maintained?
Is there any smell of drainage problems in bathrooms and toilets?
Does water drain away rapidly from all sinks, showers and toilets?
Is there any inspection access through which you can see
    drainage taking place?
Is there any sign of plant ingress to drains?
Do drains appear to be in good condition and well pointed?

Kitchen

Do all cupboards open/close properly?
Any sign of rot?
Tiling secure and in good order?
Enough plugs?
What appliances are included in sale?
Do they work?
Age of appliances included?

Task   ✓

Bathroom

Security and condition of tiling?
Is there a bath?
Is there a shower?
Is there a bidet?
Age and condition of fittings?
Adequate ventilation?

Appliances

What appliances generally are included in sale?
What is not included in the sale?

Furniture

What furniture is included in sale?
What is not included in the sale?

Repairs/Improvements/Additions

What repairs have been carried out in the last two years?
What improvements have been carried out in last two/10 years?
What additions have been made to the property in last two/10 years?
Do they have builders' receipts/guarantees?
Do they have building consent/planning permission for any
    additions or alterations?
Are any repairs needed? If so, what, and at what projected cost?

Lifts

Are there any lifts forming part of your own property?
How old are they?
When were they last maintained?
Do they appear to be in good condition?

Common Areas

What are the common areas belonging jointly to you and other
    people on the complex?
Are any repairs needed to those areas?
Have any repairs already been approved by the community?
If so, what and at what cost?

Disputes and Defects

Is the seller aware of any disputes in relation to the property?
Is the seller aware of any defects in the property?

Index

Greece touring atlas

FORMER YUGOSLAV
REPUBLIC OF
MACEDONIA

BULGARIA

①

②

③

ALBANIA

Kastoria

KASTORIA

PELLA

KILKIS

Kilkis

Serres

SERRES

DRAMA

Drama

Xanthi

XANTHI

KAVALA

Kavala

RODOPI

EVROS

Alexandroupolis

TURKEY

Kozani

KOZANI

Katerini

PIERIA

Mt Olympus

Thermaic
Gulf

THESSALONIKI

Thessaloniki

IMATHIA

CHALKIDIKI

Mt Athos

Kassandra

Thassos

Samothraki

Limnos

TURKEY

IOANNINA

GREVENA

LARISSA

Aegean

Corfu

THESPROTIA

Ioannina

TRIKALA

Trikala Larissa

Igoumenitsa

ARTA

KARDITSA

Karditsa

Volos

MAGNESIA

Skiathos

Alonissos

Sea

Parga

PREVEZA

Arta

Paxi

EVRITANIA

Skopelos

Lesbos

Preveza

Lefkada

Karpenisi

Lamia

Skyros

Ionian

AETOLOAKARNANIA

FTHIOTIDA

Evia

Ithaca

FOKIDA

Nafpaktos

Delphi

Chalkis

Chios

Sea

Kefalonia

Gulf of Patras

BOEOTIA

Thebes

Patras

ACHAIA

Gulf of Corinth

Corinth

Athens

ATTICA

④

Andros

Kyllini

ELIS

CORINTHIA

Mycenae

Aegina

Tinos

Ikaria

Patmos

⑤

Zakynthos

Pyrgos

Olympia

ARCADIA

ARGOLIS

Nauplio

Epidauros

Kea

Kythnos

Syros

Mykonos

Naxos

Koufonissi

Amorgos

Astypalaia

MESSENIA

Tripolis

Megalopolis

Hydra

Spetses

Serifos

⑦

Sifnos

Paros

Ios

Kalamata

LACONIA

Sparta

Myrtoan Sea

Kimolos

Antiparos

Sikinos

Anafi

Gythio

Monemvasia

Milos

Folegandros

Santorini

⑥

Kythera

Chania

Kastelli
Kissamou

Rethymnon

Heraklion

C r e t e

Ag. Nikolaos

Sitia

Paleochora

Chora
Sfakion

Gavdos

⑧

N

80 kms

4 0 miles

Mediterranean Sea

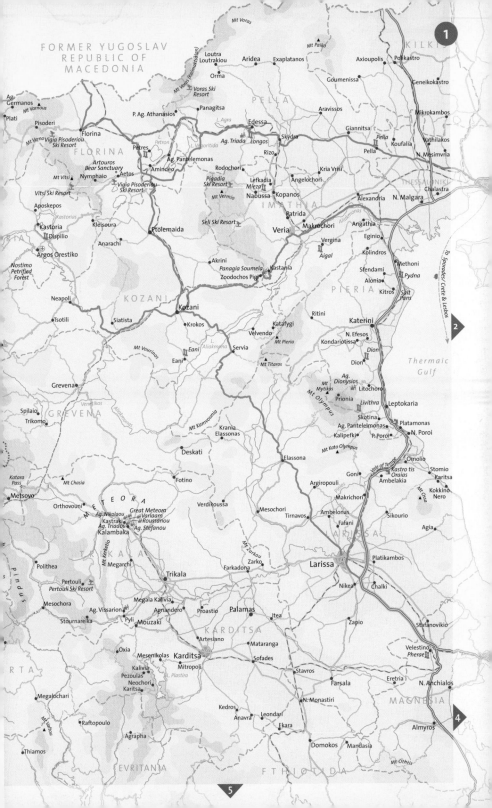

FORMER YUGOSLAV
REPUBLIC OF
MACEDONIA

N

20 kms
10 miles

A. Poroia
Mt Kerkini
Vironia
L. Doirani
Rodopoli
Kerkini
L. Kerkini
Palatiano
Lithotopos
Efkarpia
Mt Mavrovouni
KILKIS
Ag. Georgios
Axioupolis
Polikastro
Kilkis
Lachanas
Goumenissa
Geneikokastro
Mt Voras
Mt Paiko
Mikrokambos
Asiros
Loutra
Loutrakiou
Aridea
Exaplatanos
Orma
Aravissos
Giannitsa
Vathilakos
THESSALONIKI
PELLA
Pella
Koufalia
Liti
Langadas
Edessa
Skydra
N. Mesimvria
L. Koronia
P. Ag.
Athanasios
Panagitsa
L. Agra
Ag. Triada
Longos
Rizo
Pella
Diavata
Pefka
FLORINA
L. Petron
L. Vegoritida
Petres
Ag. Pantelemonas
Rodochori
Kria Vrisi
Angelochori
Chalastra
Thessaloniki
Amindeo
Pigadia
Ski Resort
Lefkadia
Mieza
Kopanos
Alexandria
N. Malgara
Panorama
Mt Chortiatis
Mt Vermio
Naoussa
IMATHIA
Patrida
Angathia
Thermi
Seli Ski Resort
Veria
Makrochori
Aliakmonas
Gulf of
Thessaloniki
Ptolemaida
Vergina
Eginio
Ag. Triada
Vasilika
Akrini
Aigai
Kolindros
Methoni
Epanomi
Petralona
Cave
Panagia Soumela
Kastania
Sfendami
Pydna
Ormos
Zoodochos Pigi
Alonia
Epanomis
Petralona
KOZANI
Kitros
Salt
Pans
PIERIA
Kozani
Ritini
Katerini
N. Kalikratia
Krokos
Katafygi
N. Efesos
Velvendo
Mt Pieria
Kondariotissa
Dion
Thermaic Gulf
N. Moudania
Servia
Dion
Eani
Mt Titaros
Ag.
Dionysios
Litochoro
Mt Vourinos
Eani
Mt Mytikas
Prionia
Livithra
Leptokaria
Sani
GREVENA
Mt Olympos
Skotina
Platamonas
Mt Kamvounia
Ag. Pantelelmonas
P. Poroi
N. Poroi
Krania
Elassonas
Kalipefki
Deskati
Mt Kato Olympus
Omolio
To North Sporades
Fotino
Flassona
Vale of Tempe
Kastro tis
Oraias
Stomio
Verdikoussa
Goni
Ambelakia
Karitsa
Argiropouli
Mt Ossa
Kokkino Nero
Mesochori
Makrichori
Sikourio
Tirnavos
Ambelonas
Fafani
Agia
Agiokambos
TRIKALA
LARISSA
Mt Zarkou
Zarko
Larissa
Platikambos
Farkadona

To Sporades/ Crete & Lesbos

Pilios

Aliakmona

1

4

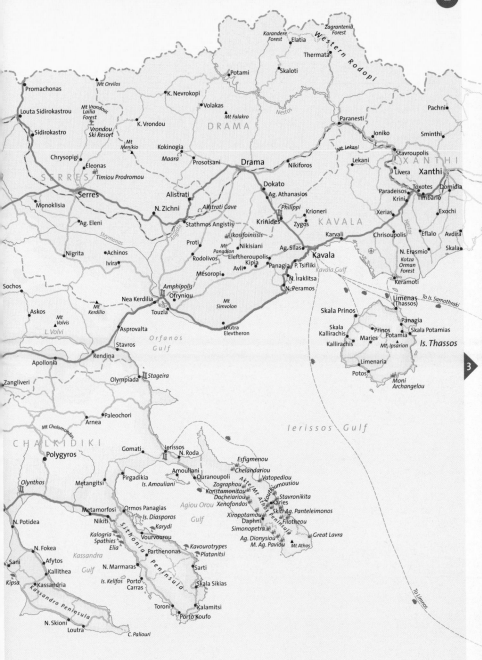

BULGARIA

Karandere Forest
Zagrantenia Forest
Elatia
Western Rodopi
Thermata
Skaloti
Potami

Promachonas
Mt Orvilos
K. Nevrokopi
Volakas
Pachni

Louta Sidirokastrou
Mt Vrondous Lailia Forest
K. Vrondou
Mt Falakro
DRAMA
Paranesti
Ioniko
Sminthi

Sidirokastro
Vrondou Ski Resort
Mt Menikio
Kokinogia
Mt. Lekani
Lekani
Stavroupolis

Chrysopigi
Eleonas
Maara
Prosotsani
Drama
Nikiforos
Livera
Xanthi

SERRES
Timiou Prodromou
Dokato
Ag. Athanasios
Paradeisos
Toxotes
Domidia

Serres
Alistrati
Philippi
Krioneri
Krini
Timbario

Monoklisia
N. Zichni
Alistrati Cave
Krinides
Zygos
KAVALA
Xerias
Exochi

Ag. Eleni
Stathmos Angistis
Ikosifoinissis
Ag. Silas
Karvali
Chrisoupolis
Eflalo
Avdira

Nigrita
Proti
Mt Pangaion
Nikisiani
Eleftheroupolis
Kavala
N. Erasmio
Skala

Achinos
Rodolivos
Kipia
Panagia
P. Tsifliki
Kotza Orman Forest

Ivira
Avli
N. Iraklitsa
Keramoti

Sochos
Mesoropi
N. Peramos
Kavala Gulf
Limenas (Thassos)
To Is. Samothraki

Amphipolis
Ofryniou
Skala Prinos
Panagia

Askos
Nea Kerdilia
Mt Simvolon
Skala Kallirachis
Prinos
Skala Potamias

Mt Kerdilio
Touzla
Loutra Elevtheron
Maries
Potamia
Is. Thassos

Mt Volvis
Asprovalta
Kallirachis
Mt. Ipsarion

L. Volvi
Stavros
Orfanos Gulf
Limenaria

Apollonia
Rendina
Potos
Moni Archangelou

Zangliveri
Olympiada
Stageira
Ierissos Gulf

Paleochori
Arnea
Gomati
Ierissos
N. Roda
Roda

Mt Cholomondas
Esfigmenou
Chelandariou

CHALKIDIKI
Polygyros
Pirgadikia
Amouliani
Ouranoupoli
Vatopediou
Koutloumousiou

Olynthos
Metangitsi
Is. Amouliani
Zographou
Stavronikita

Metamorfosi
Ormos Panagias
Konstamonitou
Docheiariou
Karies
Skiti Ag. Panteleimonos

N. Potidea
Nikiti
Is. Diasporos
Xenofondos
Filotheou

N. Fokea
Kalogria Spathies Elia
Karydi
Xiropotamou
Daphni
Ag. Dionysiou

Sani
Vourvourou
Simonopetra
M. Ag. Paviou
Great Lavra

Afytos
Parthenonas
Kavourotrypes
Platanitsi
Mt Athos

Kipsa
Kallithea
N. Marmaras
Sarti

Kassandria
Is. Kelifos
Porto Carras
Skala Sikias

N. Skioni
Toroni
Kalamitsi

Loutra
Porto Koufo
C. Paliouri

To Limnos

20 kms
10 miles

N

B U L G A R I A

Zagrantenia Forest
Karandere Forest
Elatia
Western Rodopi
Thermata
Potami
Skaloti
Mt Orvilos
Promachonas
K. Nevrokopi
Volakas
Pachni
Louta Sidirokastrou
Mt Vrondous Lailia Forest
Vrondou Ski Resort
K. Vrondou
Mt Falakro
Nestos
Paranesti
Joniko
Sminthi
Sidirokastro
Mt Menikio
Kokinogia
D R A M A
Lekani
Mt Lekani
Stavroupolis
X A N T H
Chrysopigi
Eleonas
Maara
Prosotsani
Drama
Nikiforos
Livera
Xanthi
S E R R E S
Timiou Prodromou
Dokato
Paradeisos
Toxotes
Domidi
Serres
Alistrati
Ag. Athanasios
Krini
Timbario
Monoklisia
N. Zichni
Alistrati Cave
Philippi
Krioneri
Xerias
Exochi
Ag. Eleni
Stathmos Angistis
Krinides
Zygos
K A V A L A
Chrisoupolis
Eflalo
Avdira
Strymonas
Proti
Ikosifoinissis
Nikisiani
Karvali
Skala
Angitis
Nigrita
Achinos
Mt Pangaion
Eleftheroupolis
Ag. Silas
N. Erasmio
Ivira
Rodolivos
Kipia
Panagia
Kavala
Kotza Orman Forest
Sochos
Mesoropi
Avli
P. Tsifliki
Keramoti
THESSALONIKI
Amphipolis
Ofryniou
N. Iraklitsa
Mt Simvolon
N. Peramos
Kavala Gulf
Limenas (Thassos)
Askos
Mt Kerdilio
Nea Kerdilia
Skala Prinos
Panagia
Mt Volvis
Touzla
Loutra Elevtheron
Skala
Kallirachis
Prinos
Potamia
Skala Potamias
L. Volvi
Asprovalta
Orfanos Gulf
Maries
Mt Ipsarion
Is. Thassos
Stavros
Kallirachis
Apollonia
Rendina
Limenaria
Olympiada
Stageira
Potos
Paleochori
Moni Archangelou
Arnea
Ierissos Gulf
Mt Cholomondas
Gomati
Ierissos
N. Roda
CHALKIDIKI
Polygyros
Esfigmenou
Chelandariou
Vatopediou
Olynthos
Metangitsi
Pirgadikia
Amouliani
Ouranoupoli
Zographou
Koutloumousiou
Is. Amouliani
Konstamonitou
Docheiariou
Metamorfosi
Ormos Panagias
Xenofondos
Stavronikita
Skiti Ag. Panteleimonos
Nikiti
Is. Diasporos
Agiou Orou
Xiropotamou
Karies
N. Potidea
Karydi
Daphni
Filotheou
Kalogria
Spathies
Elia
Vourvourou
Gulf
Simonopetra
N. Fokea
Parthenonas
Ag. Dionysiou
Great Lavra
Kassandra Gulf
Kavourotrypes
Platanitsi
M. Ag. Paviou
Mt Athos
Sani
Afytos
Sithonia Peninsula
Kipsa
Kallithea
N. Marmaras
Sarti
Kassandra
Is. Kelifos
Porto Carras
Skala Sikias
Kassandra Peninsula
Toroni
Kalamitsi
N. Skioni
Loutra
Porto Koufo
C. Paliouri

2

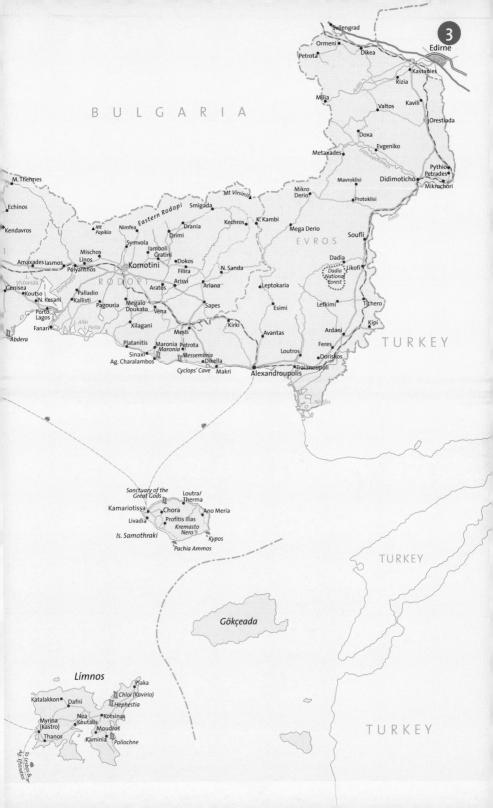

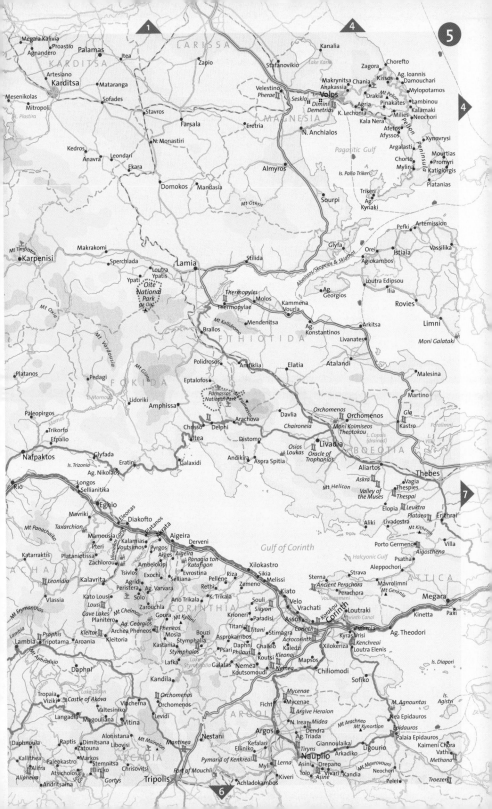

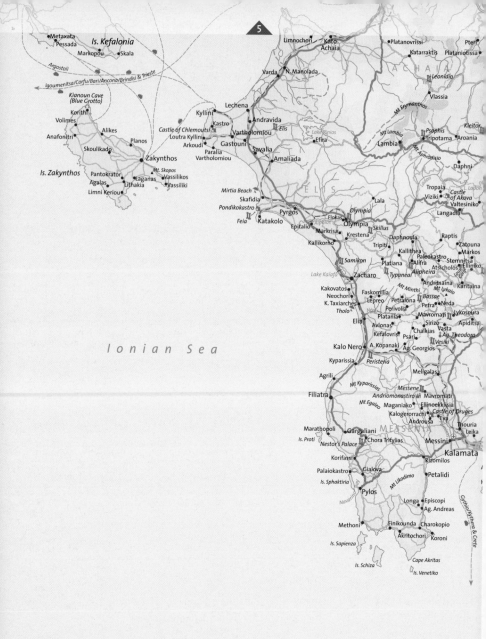

Metaxata
Pessada
Is. Kefalonia
Markopou •Skala
Argostoli

Igoumenitsa/Corfu/Bari/Ancona/Brindisi & Trieste

Kianoun Cave
(Blue Grotto)
Korithi
Volimes
Anafonitri
Alikes
Planos
Skoulikado
Is. Zakynthos
Zakynthos
Pantokrator
Mt. Skopos
Agalas
Lithakia
Laganas•Vassilikos
Limni Keriou
Vassiliki

Limnochori •Kato
Achaia

•Platanovrissi
Katarraktis •Platan̄iotissa
Pter
•Varda •N. Manolada
ACHAIA
•Leonidia
Kyllini
•Lechena
•Andravida
•Vlassia
Kastro
Castle of Chlemoutsi
Loutra Kyllini•Vartholomiou
Arkoudi
Gastouni
Paralia
Vartholomiou
Elis
Savalia
Amaliada
Mt Erymanthos
Mt Lambia
Lambia
Psophis •Kleitor
Tripotama•Aroania
Mt Aphrodisio
•Daphni

Lake Pinios
Efira
ELIS
Mirtia Beach
Skafidia
Pondikokastro
Feia
•Katakolo
Pyrgos
Olympia
Flokas
Epitalio•Markrisa
Olympia
Skillus
Krestena
Daphnoula
Kallikorno
Tripiti
Kallithea
Samikon
Platiana
Paleokastro
Alifra
Atsicholos
Elliniko
Lake Kaiafa
Zacharo
Typaneai•Aliphera
Andritsaina
Mt Minthi
Kakovatos
Faskomilia
Mt Lykaio
Kantaina
Neochori
Lepreo•Petralona
Bassae
K. Taxiarches
Petrona•Petra•Neda
Tholo
Perivolia
Petra
Lykosoura
Platania
Mavromati
Apiditsa
Elia
Avlonas
Sirizo•Vasta
Kefalovrisi
Psari•Chalkias•Ag. Theodora
Kalo Nero
A. Kopanaki
Ag. Georgios
Vesiki
Kyparissia
Peristeria
Meligalas
Agrili

*Lala
Tropaia
Viziki*
Castle of Akova
Valtesiniko
Langadia
Raptis
Zatouna
Markos
Stemnitsa

Lala
Daphnoula

Mt Kyparissias
Andriomonastiro
Filiatra
Mt Egaleo
Messene•Mavromati
Maganiako
Ellinoekklisia
Kalogerorrachi
Castle of Druges
Androusa
Eva
Thouria•Leika
Marathopoli•Gargaliani
Is. Proti
Chora Trifylias
MESSINIA
Messini
Kalamata
Nestor's Palace
Korifassi
Rizomilos
Palaiokastro
Gialova
Petalidi
Is. Sphaktiria
Pylos
Mt Likodimo
Longa•Episcopi
Navarino
Ag. Andreas
Methoni
Finikounda•Charokopio
Is. Sapienza
Akritochori•Koroni
Is. Schiza
Cape Akritas
Is. Venetiko

Gythio/Kythera & Crete

I o n i a n   S e a

N

20 kms
10 miles

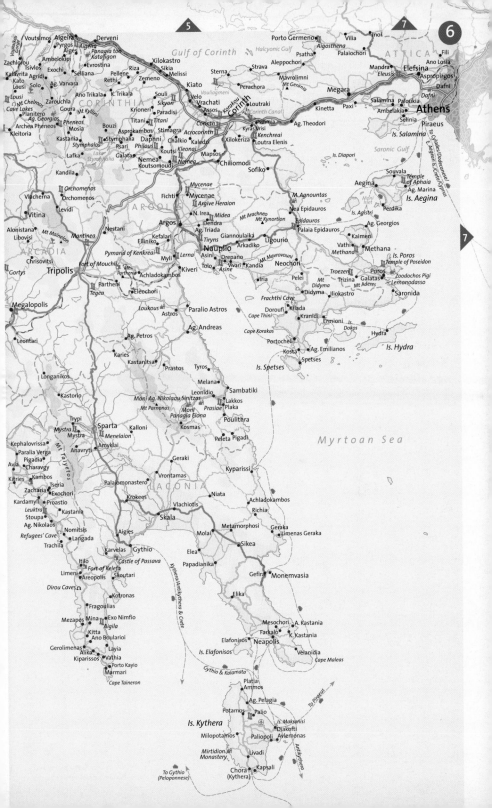

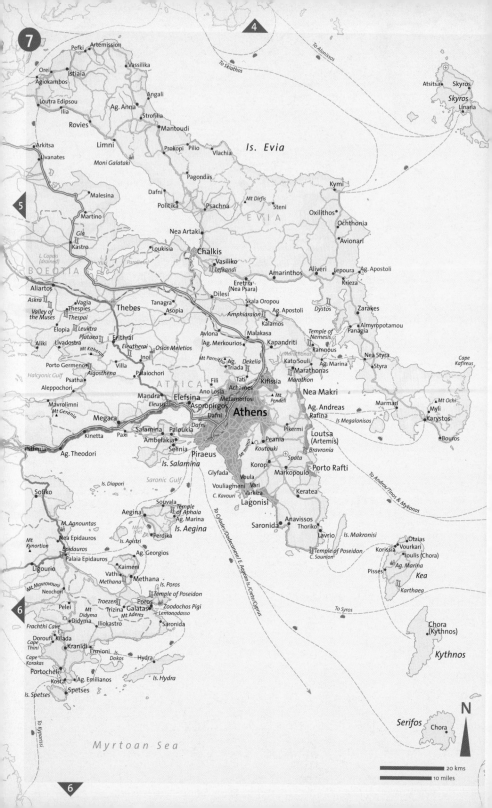

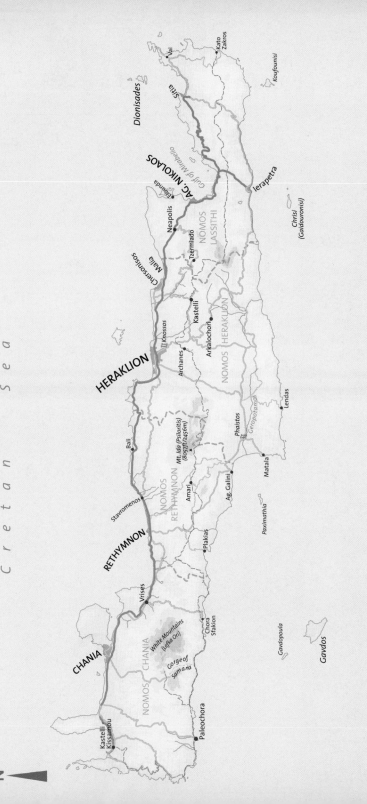

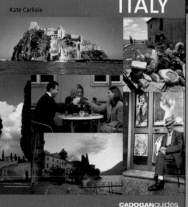

THE SUNDAY TIMES
WORKING AND LIVING
ITALY

Kate Carlisle

CADOGANguides

THE SUNDAY TIMES
WORKING AND LIVING
SPAIN

Harvey Holtom

CADOGANguides

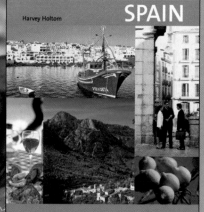

THE SUNDAY TIMES
WORKING AND LIVING
FRANCE

Monica Larner

CADOGANguides

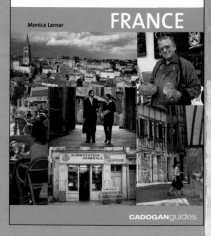

Also available:

WORKING AND LIVING
PORTUGAL

CADOGANguides